Challenges to Deterrence

Challenges to Deterrence

Resources, Technology, and Policy

Edited by
Stephen J. Cimbala

PRAEGER

New York
Westport, Connecticut
London

Library of Congress Cataloging-in-Publication Data

Challenges to deterrence.

1. Deterrence (Strategy). 2. Nuclear warfare.
I. Cimbala, Stephen J.
U162.6.C47   1987   355'.0217   87-2227
ISBN 0-275-92350-9 (alk. paper)

Copyright © 1987 by Praeger Publishers

Library of Congress Catalog Card Number: 87-2227
ISBN: 0-275-92350-9

First published in 1987

Praeger Publishers, One Madison Avenue, New York, NY 10010
A division of Greenwood Press, Inc.

Printed in the United States of America

∞
The paper used in this book complies with the
Permanent Paper Standard issued by the National
Information Standards Organization (Z39.48-1984).

10 9 8 7 6 5 4 3 2 1

This work is dedicated to the memory of Dr. S. F. (Red) Nicol, from whom I learned much, and to whom I owe much, along with generations of Penn State students, faculty, and administrators.

Contents

Acknowledgments

The editor gratefully acknowledges the suggestions and encouragement of Catherine Woods, Noreen Norton, and Mia Crowley at Praeger Publishers. I also want to acknowledge the support of Pennsylvania State University/Delaware Campus administrative and clerical staff, including Lynn M. Haskin, Edward Tomezsko, and Diane Wolf.

Introduction

Stephen J. Cimbala

Both the concept and the practice of nuclear deterrence are under siege. Although nuclear war between the superpowers has not occurred, scholars and policy makers express progressively less assurance that deterrence cannot fail or, if it does, that the consequences will be other than national and societal disaster. If the findings of nuclear winter studies can be believed, even planetary disaster is a plausible consequence of U.S.-Soviet nuclear exchanges beyond a certain threshold.

In this collection, we have sought to avoid theological disputes about what deterrence is. Professional disputation is mainly concerned not with these issues of theology and taxonomy but with the political viability of deterrence under varying conditions of stress. Each section of the collection attempts to place under a microscope some components of the deterrence dilemmas facing U.S. and allied policy makers.

Notwithstanding this disclaimer, it should not be assumed that theological issues are without significance. There is an abstract, as well as a policy-relevant, distinction between, for example, a defense-dominant superpower strategic relationship and one that rests primarily upon offensive forces. Although not assumed unimportant, these issues are presumably treated in other studies and will be included in the chapters below as means to other ends, to the extent that they are brought up at all.

Carnes Lord considers the probable evolution of U.S.-Soviet strategic competition and judges that the political uncertainties will be more significant than the technical ones. The idea of mutual deterrence based upon a threat of mutual societal vulnerability has become increasingly suspect because of increased awareness of the Soviet threat, fear of war, increased visibility for arms control, and Soviet exploitation of Western public opinion. At the same time, the U.S. president and the executive branch of government in general, relative to the Congress, have suffered a decline in power and authority over foreign and defense policy issues. Modernization of U.S. strategic forces will be held hostage to the whims of the American policy-making process. The issue of strategic defenses has been made important by President Ronald Reagan's Strategic Defense Initiative (SDI), but a variety of scenarios for SDI deployment or delay are conceivable.

Four clusters of technology will have special importance and perhaps revolutionary implications for the U.S. and Soviet strategic forces of the future, according to Lord: directed energy, computers and microelectronics, stealth, and superhardening. A fifth technology—nonacoustical antisubmarine warfare (ASW) sensing—could influence significantly the strategic balance, were it proved effective. Of particular importance in the near term will be stealth technology and its incorporation into the next generation of tactical and strategic aircraft, perhaps negating large Soviet investments in theater and strategic air defenses. Stealth technology will also improve the penetrativity of cruise missiles and contribute to U.S. and North Atlantic Treaty Organization (NATO) efforts to establish air superiority over the theater battlefield.

According to Lord, improvements in technologies for gathering and processing information will have great consequences for the evolution of superpower strategic force structures and capabilities. Strategic command, control, and communications for offensive and defensive forces will require improved systems for sensing, mapping, tracking, and assessing the results of combat. Even technologies now considered improbable by mainstream assessments may find their places in future deterrent relationships, including newer generations of chemical and biological agents mated to intercontinental delivery vehicles.

Kevin Lewis emphasizes the difficulties in projecting the strategic future and then proceeds to accomplish that very task, within acknowledged constraints. The present strategic planning context, according to Lewis, should be assumed to have a "memory." The future is an extension of the past, in an other than obvious sense. There are dominant forces and trends that are not reversed simply by our declaring an intention to do so. What we are facing, according to Lewis, are new perturbations within a context of underlying stability.

Deficiencies in strategic reasoning are most commonly the result of partial instead of holistic focus aggravated by misperception of the relationship between stability and change. According to Lewis, too much strategic reasoning emphasizes idiosyncratic departure from precedent and insufficient consideration of management issues. Many proposals for rapid change also ignore the dynamic interrelation of strategic activities. Very little of importance happens in a fortnight. As an example, the penetrativity of the U.S. B-52 strategic bomber force has been pronounced dead by numerous analysts, although in fact incremental improvements have extended its lifetime well beyond the scenarios of pessimists.

Most important, Lewis notes that real war planners confront a dilemma. Although no one can guarantee that superpower nuclear exchanges could be controlled short of Armageddon, it is important to plan for the possibility that control might be exercised. This anomaly is not necessarily a contradiction between theory and practice, provided the effort to create additional, and more limited, options is not confused with an expectation that the control of escalation can be taken for granted.

Underneath the nuclear umbrella, U.S. conventional forces may have to fight. Understanding the motivations and expectations of military personnel thus becomes extremely important. David Segal, Jesse Harris, Joseph Rothberg, and David Marlowe consider the relationship between deterrence, combat orientation, and peacekeeping missions in the U.S. Army. In the post-World War II period, the United States witnessed important changes in manpower policy and in the definition of military missions. The primary objective of armed forces became the negative one of preventing the opponent from using his maximum military credibility, instead of the traditional and positive objective of using maximum force to defeat the opponent. Military missions emphasized deterrence and peacekeeping along with war fighting. Concerns were raised that the personnel recruited and trained for a constabulary force might not consider going to war as part of their normal mission.

Morris Janowitz's formulation of the constabulary concept recognized the limitations of deterrence to the upper end of the conflict spectrum (The Professional Soldier, New York: The Free Press, 1971). The constabulary concept complements deterrence but is not equivalent to it. It refers primarily to low-intensity operations designed to maintain peace or to contain conflicts from expansion. Segal and his coauthors draw quantitative data from the study of U.S. soldiers assigned to the Multinational Force and Observers (MFO) in the Sinai under the Camp David Accords. Among the more interesting findings are those related to perceptions of the Sinai and Grenada missions by soldiers who had been in both places. The data demonstrate a preference for higher-intensity operations among soldiers who had also been exposed to the lower-intensity duties of peacekeeping. More generally across the entire sample, exposure to low-intensity operations sensitizes military personnel to the gradation of combat intensity, compared with the relative insensitivity of those without that exposure.

One of the more important reasons for the nontraditional tasking of combat forces, according to Dagobert Brito and Michael Intriligator, is the requirement for mixed strategies imposed by the destructiveness of strategic nuclear weapons. Pre-World War II theories of strategic bombardment saw airpower as a means to destroy the war-making capacity or morale of the enemy without conquering his armed forces. The atomic bomb was the presumed extension of conventional strategic bombardment theories. Moreover, the effects of nuclear weapons were hard to miniaturize and control. Nuclear wars between major powers would be difficult to contain, and collateral damage would be extensive.

Models developed by Brito and Intriligator contrast two generic strategies for investment in weapons: a war arms-investment strategy and a deterrence arms-investment strategy. If two countries adopt deterrence arms-investment strategies while assuming that the opponent is using a war arms-investment strategy, the result is unstable. Only a mixed strategy of war arms investment and deterrence arms investment provides equilibrium. Although these results hold for arms races based on nuclear weapons, they do not for conventional arms races. In the case of conventional arms races, the war investment strategy is always optimal, according to the authors, leading to an equilibrium in weapons levels and avoidance of an upward spiral in armaments.

The next four contributors consider some of the ways by which nuclear war might break out. Charles Hermann focuses on the problem of crisis instability that can coexist within a system that is apparently stable. The configuration of the international system might suggest a structural inhibition against superpower nuclear aggression, but this does not preclude the development of crises as apparently normal concomitants of bipolarity. In crises, circumstances may disrupt situation assessment, decision controllability, and force survivability.

Actually crises can, as Hermann notes, have both positive and negative effects upon the quality of decision making. They can circumvent some of the bureaucratic and organizational factors that inhibit effective day-to-day policy making. But the negatives are equally apparent. Crises can create stress for individuals, increases in uncertainty, unfamiliar conditions, and unnecessary secrecy. Important for crisis stability are changes in the characteristics of strategic weapons, changes in strategic alerts, changes in the command and control of nuclear forces, and changes in strategic plans. Future U.S.-Soviet crises might involve mutually reinforcing rather than unilateral alerts. One might note also that the risks of both inadvertent and accidental escalation (frequently confused) are increased during crises. Strategic war plans are also pertinent to crisis stability. Two problematical examples are launch under attack and preemptive decapitation options.

Patrick Morgan notes that cases of surprise attack are neither overwhelming nor negligible in number. A surprise attack is strategic in two senses: the scale of the attacker's objective and the defender's perception of the consequences. In nearly all cases that have been studied, the attacker is successful in achieving surprise per se, but not necessarily victory. Since states are normally suspicious of one another's intentions in an anarchical international order, vulnerability to surprise requires some explanation.

One reason for successful surprise is that initiative rests with the attacker. Limited, irrelevant, or distorted information available to the defender is another. These are contributory factors but insufficient explanations for surprise. Cognitive influences on decision making are of more general explanatory power: how individuals and groups think about policy problems.

Morgan notes the importance of perception, or the categorizing and evaluating of stimuli by means of cognitive structures already present in the mind. These cognitive structures are abstractions and simplifications: they include assumptions and beliefs, values, images, theories, strategies, and plans. Cognitive structures resist change and become part of personal and group identities. Thus there is a strong tendency to overlook information or points of view that are discrepant from previously established cognitions. As applied to international politics, these hypotheses would suggest that victims of surprise either did not expect attack or underestimated the consequences of defeat because of cognitive limits in decision making.

The cognitive and other decision variables emphasized by Hermann and Morgan will be important in determining NATO and Warsaw Pact expectations about deterrence on the central front in Europe. George Quester considers the relationship between U.S. and Soviet doctrine, limited war, and nuclear weapons. The Warsaw Pact has frequently found it advantageous to emphasize the possibility of limited conventional war in Europe and disadvantageous to discuss limited nuclear war; NATO has the reverse emphasis. These and other formulations of adversary perceptions are confused by the difference between what either side really sees and what it might pretend to see. Self-confirming prophecies can evolve from declaratory improvisations.

According to Quester, the truth about limiting nuclear war involving the superpowers is that limitations are neither guaranteed nor precluded. Leaders in the United States recognize our advantage in allowing for gradual escalation, and Soviet leaders know the benefits for them of declaratory emphasis upon limited conventional war. Whereas the consequences of nuclear war in Europe are obviously going to involve immense and unprecedented societal destruction, the consequences of conventional war are more open-ended. Increased reliance upon conventional forces by NATO might decouple U.S. nuclear weapons from European deterrence and create conventional strength that would threaten the Soviet position in Eastern Europe.

Like past conventional wars in the Middle East, conventional war in Europe might follow none of the expected patterns. Uncertainties extend to the level of basic personnel competencies. Scenarios of the past may be less controlling for the future. In the future, NATO may endorse no-first-use doctrines and denounce limited nuclear use; the Soviet Union may reject no-first-use doctrines and accept scenarios for limited nuclear war.

A final process by which superpower nuclear conflict might be initiated or expanded is by proliferation of nuclear weapons. Louis René Beres argues that various states in the volatile Middle East may aspire to acquire nuclear weapons under two mistaken assumptions. The first mistake is the assumption that they will provide security. The second is that a regional balance of terror can be stable.

A regional mélange of nuclear-armed Middle Eastern states would be faced with several dangers. First, an expanded number of nuclear powers would undermine deterrence stability. Second, divergent strategic doctrines within the region would also be detrimental to stability. Third, aggressors in a nuclear multipolar region might feel that they could attack their opponents while obscuring the identity of the attacker. Fourth, the microproliferation of nuclear weapons into the hands of terrorists would be encouraged. Other factors also lead to the expectation of regional multipolar nuclear instability in the Middle East should proliferation take root.

As related to the Hermann discussion, Beres notes that vulnerable nuclear forces, which the forces of Middle Eastern states are likely to be, tempt authorities to rely upon imprudent command and control measures (such as preemption or launch on warning). Precautions against the accidental use of nuclear weapons on the part of Third World states might not be as extensive as they are for the United States and the Soviet Union. New nuclear states would also probably increase the number of national decision makers who have fingers on the trigger relative to the command systems of established nuclear powers. For these and other reasons, preventing nuclear proliferation in the Middle East is imperative, but it is also improbable, unless the United States and the Soviet Union concur on approaches to limitation of their own nuclear arsenals.

The geopolitical context within which nuclear deterrence must take place is frequently omitted from scholarly and policy discussion. Robert Harkavy is the first of four authors who put contemporary and previous strategic policies into that context. Harkavy notes that new political and technological developments may be creating more interest in the politics of access for U.S. strategic and other forces. Development of strategic defenses and of additional mobile and dispersed launchers also suggests more heterogeneous basing requirements.

Historical evidence for the importance of strategic basing in

superpower deterrence relationships is considerable. Despite the
Cuban missile crisis of 1962, Cuba remained a Soviet strategic asset
for intelligence, surveillance, and maritime replenishment. During
the 1950s and 1960s, the balance of overseas assets was in favor of
the United States and against the Soviet Union. Although it might seem
that both sides are now less dependent than they formerly were upon
overseas launching platforms, the infrastructure that supports superpower strategic force structures, including their eyes and ears, requires overseas and overhead basing. In addition to Harkavy's very
complete list of examples, one might also note the recent U.S.-Soviet
agreement to allow resident monitoring of nuclear tests by nationals
of the other country.

Both superpowers rely heavily upon combat support and technical
facilities abroad. These include navigation aids, satellite tracking and
control, intelligence gathering, and seismology. Antisubmarine warfare imposes special and significant external basing requirements.
Both sides have globally deployed ASW aircraft, and attack submarines
assigned ASW missions require forward bases for repair and maintenance. Networks of underwater sound surveillance systems (SOSUS)
provide information on submarine movements across coastlines,
straits, chokepoints, and critical sea lines of communication (SLOC).
As for the availability of overseas bases as such, the trend seems to
be for these facilities to be less intrusive on Third World sovereignty
if they are to survive as components of U.S. policy. And the importance
of strategic bases during crises might differ from their roles under
normal conditions; during a crisis, overseas facilities could become
hostages to nuclear escalation or symbols of alliance commitment or
both.

As noted by John Allen Williams, the United States depends for its
power projection upon its preeminent maritime power, and U.S. policy
emphasizes the priority of defending Europe. Maritime strategy must
reconcile both sets of obligations.

According to Williams, the U.S. Maritime Strategy originated as
a strategy to deter and, if necessary, fight global and protracted conventional war against the Soviet Union. It has since expanded to include
other aspects of naval power, including responses to Third World
crises. The Maritime Strategy is a global strategy that is applicable
to the defense of Europe, not a European strategy applied globally.

Williams examines the importance of Third World locations in
strategic perspective and indicates the roles for U.S. maritime power
in the relevant theaters of operation. Inside and outside the Western
hemisphere, Soviet and surrogate forces pose potential threats to U.S.
interests. With Harkavy, Williams notes the evanescent character of
overseas bases and the importance of deploying forces capable of independent operations.

Threats to U.S. security include the prospects of increased challenges within the spectrum of low-intensity conflict. These conflicts are difficult to deal with because of their ambiguous character; the threat they present is incremental and indirect. Thus domestic support for U.S. military action is often weak or nonexistent. Another inhibiting factor is the Eurocentrism in U.S. policy that dominated policy making until the crisis in Iran and the Soviet invasion of Afghanistan during the Carter administration. Many Americans share policy makers' lack of familiarity with other than European cultures. Although Williams does not argue that U.S. European commitments should be reduced, he does suggest that attention to Third World issues be increased. The Maritime Strategy accommodates both kinds of challenges in Williams' view, although one might well ask whether the post-Gramm-Rudman fiscal climate will prevail over the requirements of deterrence.

Jeffrey Record takes off from the platforms established by Harkavy and Williams by noting that geography denies an identity of interests between Americans and Europeans. It is of necessity the case that U.S. interests lie in confining any war to Europe while Europeans' priorities must emphasize threatening the Soviets with early escalation beyond Europe. The absence of identical interests is compounded by deficient NATO military preparedness. The conventional forces of NATO might be inadequate to withstand Soviet conventional attack, and resort to nuclear escalation given existing theater and strategic balances would be self-defeating.

According to Record, NATO's conventional defenses amount to little more than a nuclear tripwire. Its principal weaknesses are the absence of adequate operational reserves and barriers or other fortifications necessary to implement its "forward defense" concept. Soviet attackers might not need large numerical superiority against NATO defenders without barriers and adequate reserves. Modern technology and doctrine have also increased the benefits of surprise attack against a defender who does not anticipate the tactics and operations of the attacker, a point made by Morgan and applied by Record with special implications for Europe. Related to this is the lack of assurance that NATO political leaders will take prompt and effective action in response to warning.

Record acknowledges that the Soviet Union would be handicapped by deficiencies in its own political and military preparedness for war. He argues, however, that some Soviet weaknesses have been overstated and others would prove irrelevant. The Soviet Union does lack unconstrained access to the high seas; geography that works to its advantage in land warfare conspires against Soviet maritime successes. However, the outcome of the war at sea might not be decisive for Europe's political or military fate. The NATO countries could lose the war on land before the influence of seapower proved decisive or even meaningful. Nor can Soviet technological inferiority compared with NATO be assumed now, even if it were justifiable earlier. Thus the prospect of conventional war in Europe poses for NATO a war fought amid serious disadvantages, although not hopeless ones provided certain deficiencies are remedied.

In global conventional warfare, Soviet concerns would include their European and Asian flanks. Stephen Gibert evaluates Japan's role in deterrence within the context of Western allied interests and the requirements that are particular to Japanese politics.

The Soviet Union has in recent years strengthened its military position in the Far East. Its aspirations are held in check by the U.S. military presence in the western Pacific and in northeast Asia and by the hostility of the People's Republic of China (PRC). These constraints may not hold in the future without modification of U.S. and other policies. The Japanese need to assume a more assertive military posture and to improve significantly their capabilities in order to rest deterrence in East Asia on a firm pedestal.

Gibert considers the subject of an enhanced deterrent role for Japan by reviewing the potential Japanese contribution to a restored Eurasian balance of power, by an appraisal of Japan's military posture and the character of the U.S.-Japanese "alliance," and by noting the policy implications for the United States should it insist upon a change in the status quo, described (without mincing words) by Gibert as unacceptable.

In the geopolitical context, according to Gibert, it is one of the great ironies of the century that Soviet power seems so menacing, despite the potential combined opposition of Western Europe, the United States, China, and Japan. Part of the reason is the substandard defense commitment of Japan. Military efforts by Japan comparable to those made by Western Europeans would face Soviet planners with insoluble dilemmas. Significant domestic obstacles stand in the way of any redefined Japanese security posture, however. The United States-imposed Japanese constitution following World War II was cast in a framework of war renunciation. Postwar Soviet expansion suggested to U.S. planners the need to rebuild German and Japanese military power.

Measured by expenditures for defense or the quality and quantity of forces, Japanese efforts fall short of their own and allied U.S. needs. The Japanese Self-Defense Force (JSDF) is marked by serious deficiencies. According to experts, the JSDF has insufficient stocks of equipment, inadequate force levels, insufficiently modernized ground forces, and command and control weaknesses. Japanese air defenses are weak and their equipment obsolete. As for Japanese maritime forces, they are unable now and in the foreseeable future to control critical straits leading from the Sea of Japan into the Pacific or to extend SLOC protection to about one thousand miles south of Tokyo, as hoped by U.S. planners.

In the final section, strategic force structures and the retaliatory options based upon them are considered in terms of the challenges they present to deterrence stability. Jonathan Medalia discusses the development of the Midgetman small intercontinental ballistic missile (SICBM) program from a concept into a proposed strategic program for the 1990s. The Scowcroft Commission report in April 1983 and the resulting executive-legislative consensus transformed Midgetman into a high-priority development program. However, the program is very controversial. It has raised issues of cost, strategy, and arms control that are at the core of administration relations with Congress.

Midgetman is proposed as a single-warhead mobile missile in order to improve its survivability and to diminish its attractiveness as a target compared with Multiple Independently Targetable Reentry Vehicle (MIRV) missiles based in silos. Improved survivability reduces Soviet fears of a U.S. first strike for fear of losing its missiles to a Soviet preemption. Single warhead missiles are thought to offer less lucrative targets for each offensive reentry vehicle compared with multiple warhead missiles. Although these attributes seem attractive to Midgetman supporters, the political viability of Midgetman is also based upon its status within a package of small ICBM, MX, and arms control that congressional leaders and the Reagan administration, at least temporarily, agreed to.

Medalia considers whether Midgetman as envisioned at present is survivable, stabilizing, supportive of arms control, and cost-effective. The survivability of Midgetman against plausible Soviet threats seems to be its strongest point. Adaptive Soviet attack strategies could be offset by adjustments in options available to the defender, including increases in the deployment area, missile defense for mobile missiles, and increased launcher hardness. Arms control could limit the Soviet threat to Midgetman by constraining deployments of additional Soviet warheads or of systems capable of adaptive attack tactics.

Although it seems contributory to deterrence and crisis stability and compatible with arms control, Midgetman's weakest case, according to Medalia, appears when the criterion of cost-effectiveness is introduced. Midgetman is compared by the author in terms of life-cycle costs with proposed or notional MX, B-1B bomber, and Trident II deployments. In these terms, Midgetman is comparatively expensive. The MX compares favorably with Midgetman in cost per deployed warhead, but the reverse is the case in a comparison according to cost per surviving warhead. Building more Trident submarines and arming them with Trident II missiles is another alternative to Midgetman, and Trident compares favorably with Midgetman in terms of cost-effectiveness, survivability, and arms control verifiability.

D. Douglas Dalgleish and Larry Schweikart focus on the sea-based leg of the U.S. strategic deterrent. Trident II missiles deployed in Trident submarines will significantly improve U.S. survivable counterforce capabilities. This improvement has produced some controversy about the possible use of Trident/Trident II as a first-strike weapons system. The authors contend that whether improved submarine-launched ballistic missile (SLBM) systems are used in a first-strike strategy is a political decision and is not determined by technology. Trident/Trident II would allow the United States to retaliate against Soviet silos before they could be reloaded and used against counter-value targets.

According to the authors, Trident II (D-5) can perform the functions for which both MX and Midgetman are intended. Trident would provide the same strategic punch as MX, and Midgetman, as already noted in this volume, may not be cost-effective compared with alternatives. A principal concern about the U.S. nuclear-powered missile-firing submarine (SSBN) force has been the fidelity of strategic command, control, and communications (C^3) relative to the sea-based force. Although communications with the SSBN force are not as flexible as those with the ICBM force, there are alternative paths by which essential messages should get through. Although it was beyond the authors' charge to review, one might also note that plausible tasking for Trident/Trident II would make the C^3 problem more manageable. Employment of SSBN forces for limited nuclear options (LNO) and other sub-SIOP (Single Integrated Operational Plan) skirmishing would detract from their optimal assignments; cruise missiles based on submarines and other platforms would seem more appropriate for LNO missions. More important than the C^3 issue may be the continuing measure-countermeasure competition between efforts to make submarines undetectable and improved technologies for finding them.

According to Stephen Cimbala, political questions about causes and reasons have been subordinated to technical issues in many if not most deterrence discussions. He considers the rationale for promptly and massively responding to a Soviet attack on the U.S. homeland that would destroy many important counterforce targets but leave others, including forces and cities, surviving. In that instance, and contrary to canonical strategic analysis, it might be inadvisable to retaliate with massive and prompt counterforce attacks against the remaining Soviet counterforce and command target base.

As the U.S. strategic force structure shifts toward sea-based and bomber deployments and away from fixed-based ICBMs, a retaliatory strategy involving delayed rather than immediate large attacks becomes more feasible. It may also be more desirable. The disadvantages of prompt counterforce and counter-command attacks may outweigh the advantages. Moreover, the deployment by either or both superpowers of strategic defenses poses some of the same trade-offs between fast/automatic and slow/deliberate responses. Fast/automatic activation of defenses may improve postattack firepower ratios if deterrence fails, but the connection between strategy and policy may be weaker than it would be for more controlled and deliberate employment of defenses.

Part I

The Evolving Strategic Environment: Implications for Strategy and Armed Forces

On the Future Strategic Environment

Carnes Lord

Forecasting the general shape of the U.S.-Soviet strategic nuclear
competition is no more hazardous than predicting other developments
in the U.S.-Soviet relationship and, in some respects, is probably
less so. The lengthening life cycle for strategic weaponry is such that
only one wholly new generation of these systems is likely to intervene
between the present and the early years of the next century, and that
generation is likely to incorporate technologies that are extant or at
least foreseeable with some degree of assurance. This is not to suggest that there are not substantial uncertainties in any such forecasting.
But it seems fair to say that the chief uncertainties derive less from
the technical than from the political sphere. This is true above all in
the case of the United States, where the political future of the current
administration's commitment to strategic defense can by no means be
considered assured. But it is true in significant measure for the Soviet
Union as well. Here, a systemic economic crisis, coupled with the
military-scientific challenge posed by the U.S. Strategic Defense
Initiative (SDI), may force fundamental changes in the Soviet approach
to strategic conflict.

Accordingly, consideration will first be given here to the political
or political-military factors bearing on the future strategic environment. Then the technological developments with the greatest potential
for dramatically affecting the strategic nuclear situation will be briefly
reviewed. Finally, the various categories of strategic offensive and
defensive forces will be surveyed.

POLITICAL FACTORS

The strategic arsenal of the United States has been decisively—
and, in recent years, increasingly—shaped by political factors. As a
major item in the defense budget, strategic forces have always at-
tracted the attention of Congress. And public opinion has always been

3

of importance in defining the outer bounds of acceptability of particular strategic programs, in terms of their social impact (for example, civil defense or MX basing) as well as their fiscal burden. Over the last decade and a half, however, the emergence of arms control as a central political issue in the United States and the West generally has increasingly drawn strategic forces into the arena of political debate. Particularly in Western Europe, but to a significant degree also in the United States, popular antinuclear sentiment has become a factor to reckon with in strategic planning.

The reemergence of a vocal antinuclear movement in the 1980s and its sympathetic reception among substantial segments of the intellectual and policy elite throughout the West appear to reflect a fundamental weakening of the political consensus that supported the U.S. strategic force posture during the 1960s and 1970s. The causes of this development are not entirely clear but no doubt include a growing awareness of the increased Soviet military threat and a fear of war, a lessened understanding of the Soviet regime and its global ambitions, a greater diffusion of the complex of assumptions associated with the idea of arms control, and increasingly effective Soviet intervention in the Western debate by means of propaganda, political action, and so-called active measures.[1] At all events, the idea of nuclear deterrence resting on the threat of mutual annihilation—which formed the public rationale for U.S. strategic forces, if not the actual basis of U.S. nuclear strategy, for twenty years—seems to have lost fundamental legitimacy in the eyes of Western publics.

At the same time, structural changes in governmental processes in the United States—the relative decline in the power and authority of the executive branch since Watergate and the concomitant rise of Congress, the media, and various independent centers of national security expertise—have led to a situation where the president and his national security advisers have at best an uncertain control over the formulation of strategic nuclear policy. (Consider in this connection the role played over the last several years by the Scowcroft Commission and other bipartisan presidentially appointed bodies in the development of U.S. national security policy in critical areas.) As a result of all this, the modernization of U.S. strategic forces will almost certainly continue to be held hostage, in more or less unpredictable fashion, by the American political process.

The Strategic Defense Initiative announced by President Reagan on March 23, 1983, has, as now seems clear, fundamentally altered the terms of the political debate over strategic forces in the United States. By offering a plausible alternative to the notion of mutual assured destruction, the SDI has provided a potential cure for the nuclear anxieties of the public, while at the same time throwing out a technical challenge well calculated to capture the popular imagination and galva-

nize the energies of the scientific and defense industrial communities.
In fact, public opinion polls have consistently shown levels of support
for strategic defense of upwards of 70 percent, whereas only 10 to 15
percent of those polled tend to favor new offensive nuclear systems
such as MX. [2] This suggests that a shift toward a defense-dominant
strategic posture will be very sustainable politically over the long
term. In the short term, however, hostility to SDI among influential
segments of the scientific and policy elite could well succeed in terminating or greatly circumscribing the program following a change of
administration.

Assuming the SDI survives beyond 1988, it will probably survive
in some form into the twenty-first century. But the shape of a U.S.
strategic defense program will certainly depend to a large extent on
a continuing debate on the merits of population defense and arms control, a debate whose outcome cannot now be foreseen. It is altogether
possible that efforts will be made in Congress to resolve current uncertainties about strategic defense policy. There appears to be growing congressional interest today in the possibilities of active defense
of the U.S. intercontinental ballistic missile (ICBM) force as well as
in antitactical ballistic missile (ATBM) systems for the defense of
U.S. allies. Over the next several years, congressional pressure
may increase to deploy terminal BMD as a partial solution to the survivability problems of the MX and Midgetman ICBMs, particularly if
budget stringencies appear to force a choice between offensive force
modernization (Midgetman and strategic command, control, and communications enhancements) and strategic defenses. Alternatively, congressional and other opponents of SDI could attempt a variety of tactical
approaches to delaying or derailing any near- or medium-term BMD
deployments.

Of course, Soviet behavior over the next decade will also be of
considerable importance to the eventual outcome of such a debate.
Continuing Soviet intransigence over arms control may eventually
dampen enthusiasm in the West for new agreements on strategic
offense or defense. By the same token, a combination of Soviet negotiating flexibility and anti-SDI propaganda could contribute importantly
to limiting the scope or slowing the momentum of the SDI, whether
or not a new, comprehensive agreement limiting strategic arms is
actually reached.

It is also important to keep in mind allied attitudes concerning
strategic forces and particularly strategic defense. Allied support
for the SDI has so far been grudging at best. All NATO governments
have officially or unofficially voiced concerns that SDI destabilizes
the strategic balance by undermining deterrence based on a mutual
offensive threat, by decoupling the United States from Europe, and
by calling into question the Anti-Ballistic Missile (ABM) Treaty and

opening up a new arms race in strategic offensive systems. Depending
on the precise military and political implications for Europe, a U.S.
decision to cease or reduce compliance with the ABM Treaty and consideration of near-term deployment of any sort of ballistic missile
defense system will almost certainly generate strong allied opposition,
which in turn will have repercussions for the U.S. domestic debate.
On the other hand, if current interest on the part of some of the allies
in the development of ATBM capabilities against shorter-range Soviet
ballistic missiles continues and grows over the next decade,[3] it could
well happen that NATO and the United States will move toward a consensus on the desirability of near-term BMD for point and area defense
of military targets both in Europe and in the continental United States.

With respect to offensive forces, the safest assumption is that all
new U.S. systems will remain politically at risk to some extent, particularly ICBMs. The prolonged agonizing over deployment of the MX
seems increasingly likely to recur with Midgetman in the 1990s, if not
indeed sooner. The submarine and bomber legs of the strategic triad
have been relatively immune to political scrutiny, but there are signs
that this situation is changing. Congress appears increasingly restive
over cost and performance characteristics of the stealth advanced
technology bomber (ATB). And it cannot be assumed that the ATB and
indeed the D-5 equipped Trident nuclear-powered ballistic missile-
firing submarine (SSBN) will remain untouched indefinitely by criticisms based on considerations of strategic stability and arms control.

Soviet strategic forces seem virtually immune to internal political
challenge, but even in the Soviet case it is necessary to take wider
political factors into account. The new Gorbachev regime has tied
its political fortunes to effecting fundamental improvements in the
performance of the Soviet economy. While it is too soon to assess
with any confidence the implications of the Gorbachev economic program for the Soviet military, overall priority in the near term has
clearly been given to modernizing Soviet industry in high-technology
areas such as computers and electronics, and it is not unreasonable
to expect this priority to continue even beyond the current five-year
plan. This could lead in the late 1980s to difficult choices affecting
modernization of the defense industrial base, which will be necessary
to prepare for building the next generation of major weapon systems.[4]
Depending on the success of the Gorbachev reforms, it could also lead
to absolute constraints on the ability or willingness of the party leadership to sustain high levels of procurement of strategic offensive systems. It is important in this connection not to confuse Soviet defense
industrial capabilities with Soviet intentions. Recent intelligence community projections have credited the Soviets with the capacity for production of up to 16,000 to 21,000 strategic nuclear warheads by the
mid-1990s at current or moderately accelerated rates of procurement.

Yet there is little reason to suppose that the Soviets recognize a military requirement for a strategic arsenal of this size or are likely to be able to afford a buildup of this magnitude in the light of other pressing economic and military needs.[5]

The interesting question is whether the challenge of the SDI, together with the economic constraints just discussed, could bring the Soviets to rethink in a fundamental way their current strategic doctrine, with its heavy emphasis on strategic offensive forces in a damage-limiting role. Such a rethinking could lead the Soviets to transfer the damage-limiting mission of their ballistic missile forces to greatly expanded strategic defenses, while perhaps placing greater emphasis on the role of air-breathing systems and conventional forces capable of very protracted conflict. It could conceivably lead to a comprehensive strategic arms control agreement involving real reductions in ballistic missiles and the legitimization of a greater role for strategic defenses. Soviet options in this regard will be explored in greater detail below.

TECHNOLOGICAL DEVELOPMENTS

The future of strategic forces, and the strategic and operational doctrines governing their employment, will be decisively affected by technological developments currently foreseeable or in process. Four technologies (or clusters of technologies) may be singled out as virtually certain to have far-reaching if not revolutionary implications for strategic warfare over the coming decades: directed energy, computers and microelectronics, stealth, and superhardening. A fifth type of technology—nonacoustic sensing for antisubmarine warfare—could, if it proves effective, radically alter the strategic role of ballistic missile submarines. A sixth—genetic engineering—could give rise to a new dimension of strategic weapons and strategic conflict. All of the technologies mentioned have potential significance not only for strategic conflict but for warfare at virtually every level.

Directed energy technology, comprising various types of lasers and particle beams, is in some of its forms a relatively mature technology well on its way to weaponization. It has important applications for surveillance and target acquisition, as well as for antisatellite (ASAT) warfare and air and ballistic missile defense. It is one of the core technologies envisioned by proponents of the SDI for eventual territorial BMD, operating in a ground- or space-based mode against Soviet ballistic missiles in their boost phase. Particular progress appears to have been made recently in research on ground-based lasers utilizing pop-up relay mirrors in space, which are likely to have substantial advantages over comparable space-based systems in terms of cost and survivability.[6] Ground-based lasers for ASAT and air defense are under active development by the Soviet Union as well as the United States, and operational systems may be available by the end of this decade. Soviet laser research is in general well advanced, and it has been estimated that the Soviets could have prototypes for ground-based lasers for BMD by 1990, though an operational system could probably not be ready for deployment until at least the late 1990s, and a full-scale space-based laser system would not be available until the next century. Other strong Soviet efforts are under way in the area of particle beam technology.[7]

The effect of directed energy technology on the relationship between strategic offense and strategic defense is a complex question. It is not clear how lasers will be able to cope with passive defense measures used to protect satellites and ballistic missiles, or with the various technologies or tactics (such as fast-burn ICBM boosters) potentially available to circumvent or defeat the defense; and the extent to which strategic defenses will themselves be vulnerable to suppression by the offense remains a central concern. A better understanding of the operational characteristics of directed energy weapons is necessary before useful answers can be given to most of these questions. But what can certainly be said is that directed energy weapons will provide a dimension of defensive capability in strategic (as well as theater and naval) warfare for which there is no simple offensive response, and at the very least they can be expected to impose substantial cost and performance penalties on offensive systems and severely complicate operational planning for a potential attacker.

Remarkably little thought seems to have been devoted to date to the implications of stealth technologies for the military environment of the future. Yet those implications are certain to be far-reaching. In fact, the United States has made rapid strides in recent years in translating into operational systems a variety of technologies for minimizing the radar signatures of aircraft, and efforts are currently underway to incorporate these technologies into the next generation of cruise missiles and satellites. The penetrativity of the B-1 strategic bomber now beginning to be deployed will be enhanced substantially by the addition of stealth features; a revolutionary stealth fighter-bomber (the F-19) appears to be essentially operational today; and the Advanced Technology Bomber currently under development will become the penetrating element of the strategic bomber force in the 1990s.[8] These aircraft (together with the next generation of air force and navy tactical aircraft, which should enter the inventory in the mid-1990s) will increase enormously the offensive capabilities of U.S. strategic and theater forces and will essentially neutralize the vast Soviet investment in theater and homeland air defenses of the past several decades. It seems highly unlikely that the Soviets will be able to develop effective counters to these capabilities until well into the next

century, if then. In addition, stealth technology has great potential
for improving the penetrativity of U.S. cruise missiles of all kinds
in the face of increasingly effective Soviet defenses, not to speak of
its contribution to ensuring air superiority over the theater and tactical battlefield. It also has important defensive applications, particularly with respect to passive defense of satellites and air defense
(strategic as well as theater and tactical).

Of course, stealth systems will be only as survivable as their
platforms and bases and will be dependent on adequate strategic and
tactical warning. An increasing reliance by the United States on stealth
systems would arguably give the Soviets increased incentives to launch
preemptive strikes on their bases and command and control networks.
Providing prelaunch survivability for strategic stealth aircraft, maintaining adequate connectivity with them, and ensuring their refueling
and recovery will most likely be the critical problems facing the United
States in this area.

The possibility that the Soviets will acquire or develop comparable
stealth technologies must be kept in mind. Barring a catastrophic
compromise of U.S. programs, however, it seems likely that the
Soviets will remain a decade or more behind the United States in deployed stealth systems for the foreseeable future. It is probable that
by the turn of the century the Soviets will manage to field some stealth-
modified aircraft and missiles and possibly an array of first-generation
systems comparable to those currently under development in the United
States. However, U.S. advances in sensing technologies will probably
be able to contain this threat within reasonable bounds. It should be
kept in mind that the effectiveness of stealth countermeasures will
depend to a considerable extent on technical progress in computing
and data processing, areas in which the United States is likely to retain a commanding advantage. There is every reason to suppose that
the U.S. lead in stealth technologies will provide strategic benefits
of incalculable importance at every level of conflict.

There are a number of technologies that may affect the future of
the ICBM and its relationship to other strategic forces in important
ways, but superhardening is the one with the clearest revolutionary
potential.[9] It now appears that ICBM silos can be hardened far beyond
what was thought possible until very recently—on the order of 25 to 50
times beyond current nominal values for U.S. silos. This relatively
inexpensive process would make ICBMs essentially invulnerable to
anything but a direct hit by existing warheads where cratering effects
would disturb the silo's orientation. (Recent studies have also shown
that craters produced by nuclear explosions are much smaller than
was previously believed.) It therefore makes considerably more attractive a fixed basing mode both for MX and for a new small ICBM.
At the same time, it could substantially improve the technical and cost

effectiveness of a limited active defense of fixed ICBMs. Superhardening technologies also could have important applications for protecting critical command and control functions. There are countermeasures to superhardened silos—multimegaton warheads or warheads designed for earth penetration, but the weight of such warheads would exact a severe performance penalty from current Soviet ICBMs.

Dramatic improvements in technologies for gathering and processing information are likely to have great consequences for the future of strategic forces by revolutionizing command, control, communications, and intelligence (C^3I) and by improving the accuracy, responsiveness, and flexibility of strategic systems. Strategic Defense Initiative will depend decisively on such technologies to meet the stressing requirements for surveillance, acquisition, tracking, and kill assessment of attacking missiles or reentry vehicles.[10] But the future military environment as a whole will be reshaped by these technologies. Advances in digital mapping techniques will revolutionize targeting for all U.S. military systems over the next decade.[11] The development of "smart" conventional munitions and the achievement of real-time battlefield intelligence is in the process of revolutionizing theater and tactical combat, with important implications for the strategic level of conflict. Here too, it should be noted, it is virtually certain that the United States will maintain a significant technological advantage over the Soviet Union for the foreseeable future.

Development of a variety of nonacoustic sensors for antisubmarine warfare (ASW) is a technology area with the potential to affect dramatically the U.S.-Soviet strategic relationship, although insufficient evidence is publicly available to judge or even guess intelligently at the likelihood of technological breakthroughs or the time frame in which they might occur.[12] The combination of the promise of stealth technologies with the threat of a Soviet breakthrough in ASW could encourage a fundamental reorientation of U.S. strategic doctrine, with the eventual superseding of SSBNs by bombers as the element of the strategic triad best combining invulnerability with offensive reliability and effectiveness. It should be noted, however, that the Soviet nonacoustic ASW threat is likely to depend primarily on satellite-based surveillance systems, as well as on improved real-time targeting capabilities and command and control. It would thus be vulnerable to counteraction by U.S. ground-, space- or possibly sea-based ASAT weapons and eventually by a comprehensive U.S. BMD deployment.

Finally, it is important to pay some attention to the area of biotechnology, if only to highlight a dimension of strategic military power in the broad sense that is too often completely neglected in assessments of the nuclear balance and the strategic level of conflict. It is now clear that the Soviets have proceeded with an extensive effort in the general area of chemical and biological warfare (CBW) since at least the late 1960s, in direct contravention of existing international arms control agreements (in itself an important measure of the seriousness of their interest).[13] In particular, they are in the process of developing an entirely new generation of biological agents that are more varied and flexible, easier to manufacture and handle, and harder to counter than existing agents.[14]

Chemical-biological warfare has been generally viewed as an adjunct to the tactical/operational battlefield. Soviet biological weaponry, however, particularly the new generation of agents, seems largely, if not exclusively, intended for strategic missions. There is reason to believe that the Soviets have at least considered the use of ICBMs for delivery of biological agents.[15] Perhaps more worrisome yet, however, is the potential of biological weapons for special operations and sabotage in periods immediately preceding and following the outbreak of general war. Specially targeted biological warfare attacks within the United States would be ideal precursors to a Soviet nuclear strike, eliminating key military and political authorities and disrupting U.S. strategic C^3 while making difficult or impossible an immediate U.S. decision to resort to nuclear weapons.[16] To the extent that SDI and improved air defense of the continental United States threaten to deny the Soviets the option of a damage-limiting nuclear strike against the United States, biological weapons may well become an increasingly integral and important component of the Soviet strategic arsenal.

SOVIET DOCTRINE

Before reviewing possible developments within the various categories of strategic forces, it may be useful to raise the more general question of the nature and extent of foreseeable evolutions in U.S. and Soviet strategic doctrine. For the Soviets, doctrine has always played an extremely important role in paving the way for changes in the Soviet strategic force posture. This has been less true for the United States, where doctrine has generally had a post hoc character and served largely bureaucratic and political functions. Strategic Defense Initiative, however, represents perhaps even more a doctrinal than a technological revolution in U.S. strategic nuclear policy, in spite of the fact that its doctrinal implications have been spelled out by the current administration only belatedly, if at all.[17]

There is little reason to expect any fundamental changes in Soviet doctrine for nuclear war. In spite of substantial moderation of their public language on these matters since the 1970s, the Soviets will continue to view their strategic forces as an instrument geared primarily to the requirements of military victory in a general war.[18] Accordingly, they will continue to pursue superiority at the nuclear level, with the aim of deterring resort to nuclear weapons by a NATO

faced with defeat at the conventional level or, if necessary, initiating
a preemptive nuclear strike against nuclear forces and other military
targets in Western Europe and the United States. At the same time,
recognizing that the size and characteristics of present-day nuclear
arsenals make it unlikely that either side could inflict a disarming
initial blow, the Soviets will continue to plan for the possibility of a
protracted general war. In this connection, they will continue to
place high priority on large and survivable strategic reserve forces
and enduring command and control, as well as on continuity of political
leadership and critical economic functions. All of this implies that the
Soviets will continue to place a premium on the protection of Soviet
national territory by active as well as passive measures, especially
active defense against ballistic missiles. To suppose that the Soviets
have in any way doctrinally renounced their long-standing interest in
BMD is, in any event, to make a fundamental error. In spite of their
eagerness to press any argument into the service of their current
propaganda campaign against the SDI, the Soviets have been careful
not to call into question the legitimacy or feasibility of strategic defenses as such. [19]

     At the same time, as noted earlier, it is conceivable that signifi-
cant changes could occur over the next ten to twenty years in certain
aspects of Soviet nuclear strategy. As the Soviets analyze the challenges potentially facing them should the United States successfully
capitalize on its prospective technological advantages, particularly
in the area of strategic defense, they might well consider a reorientation of their strategic doctrine away from its current dependence on
land-based ICBMs and a strategy of nuclear preemption. Such a reorientation might involve the transfer to expanded strategic defenses
of the damage-limiting mission of ICBMs, with the latter relegated to
the role of a secure reserve force, coupled with greater reliance on
air-breathing systems for strategic offensive missions and on strengthened conventional forces for theater attack. Implicit in such a move
would probably be a downgrading of Soviet assessments of the likelihood of a nuclear war developing out of conventional conflict and a
shifting of research and development and procurement priorities from
nuclear weapons toward advanced conventional systems and technologies. There are already indications that the Soviets are taking increasingly seriously the scenario of a protracted war fought with conventional weapons. [20]

     With regard to the United States, it is unclear as yet to what
degree the SDI will assume the character of a general doctrinal revolution in U.S. national security policy in the direction of a defense-
dominant strategic posture. To date, the administration has been
reticent concerning the implications of SDI for aspects of strategic
defense other than ballistic missile defense, and it has been reluctant

to address the issue of requirements for limited BMD for point or area defense of military targets in the near to mid term. It has also been reluctant to draw out the implications of SDI for the current program of modernization of strategic offensive forces or to indicate whether or how the current commitment to SDI has altered the basis of current U.S. nuclear strategy and planning. As a result, and in the absence of technologies capable of providing full protection of the continental United States or its allies, the extent to which SDI represents a fundamental rethinking of the requirements of deterrence remains somewhat ambiguous. There appears to be an increasing recognition of the virtues of even very imperfect defenses both as an enhancement of deterrence and as a hedge in the event deterrence fails. But the military as well as the civilian leadership of the nation seems deeply reluctant to make the case for strategic defense in terms of a warfighting posture or of political objectives that might be achieved through prevailing in a nuclear war.

What is true of American leaders is true to a much greater degree of the leaders of NATO Europe. It can be anticipated that the fiercest resistance to a doctrinal revision of U.S. nuclear strategy will come not from domestic critics but from Europeans accustomed to regarding an offense-dominated world as the key to strategic stability and cheap deterrence of a Soviet invasion of Western Europe. In view of the failure of the Western Europeans to adjust their strategic outlook in response to the dramatic improvement of Soviet military capabilities throughout the 1970s, there is little reason to expect any near-term change in their tendency to think of East-West security questions in political rather than military terms. Western Europeans will no doubt continue to support an inflexible version of NATO's flexible response doctrine—that is, a conventional and theater nuclear defense of Europe coupled to U.S. strategic nuclear use at the lowest possible threshold. From this perspective, strategic defenses only threaten to undermine the deterrent effect of the strategic offensive forces of the United States (and of Britain and France). That strategic defenses might in fact enhance the credibility of the U.S. guarantee of Western Europe by preserving those military and societal assets necessary to wage a protracted war does not figure in the Western Europeans' calculations. Evidently, this reflects their fundamental inability or unwillingness to contemplate a protracted war—nuclear or otherwise—in which Europe would unavoidably serve as the central theater of conflict. On the other hand, as noted earlier, growing Western European concern at the threat posed by Soviet short-range conventionally armed ballistic missiles to alliance nuclear assets may create a common doctrinal basis for pursuit of limited ballistic missile defense of military targets in Europe and in the United States (as well as for general improvement in NATO's air defense posture) in the relatively near term.

Lengthy speculation about the role of arms control in the evolving strategic relationship between the United States and the Soviet Union would be out of place here. In any event, it seems increasingly unlikely that arms control will have a fundamental or even important effect on the strategic environment of the coming decades. Both sides will probably see it as in their interest to maintain the framework of the ABM Treaty until at least the early 1990s, although erosion of the treaty regime through legal amendment, overt or covert violation, or circumvention (for example, through extensive ATBM or ASAT deployments) seems probable as well. As for strategic offensive forces, the growing intractability of the verification problem,[21] the difficulty of negotiating equitable trade-offs among increasingly diversifying strategic arsenals, and the diminishing of the perceived political benefits of arms control on both sides leave little room for optimism concerning the prospects for agreed limitations on strategic offensive systems in the foreseeable future.

Let us now look more specifically at strategic offensive and defensive force structures and interactions.

There is, as discussed above, a strong likelihood that political factors will continue to constrain the modernization of the U.S. ICBM force. It can be confidently predicted that the political troubles of MX will be revisited with Midgetman, especially in view of the problematic strategic rationale and very high costs associated with the program to date. A variety of options will be available to solve the problem of the vulnerability of the current ICBM force—hard mobile basing, deep underground basing, superhard silos, and various forms of active defense. Many questions remain concerning the operational merits of the first two possibilities, and political objections to both of them can be imagined. Superhardening seems very promising, but costs remain uncertain. And, as indicated earlier, the relationship of ICBM modernization to the SDI is at present almost wholly opaque.

Yet other questions will remain concerning the positive rationale for the Midgetman small ICBM and its cost-effectiveness, particularly in an environment of expanding Soviet defenses and an increasingly hard Soviet target base. It will be plausibly argued that the prompt counterforce requirement can be assumed by the D-5 SLBM, while other counterforce missions can be taken over by stealth bombers and by air- and sea-launched cruise missiles. Depending on the anticipated performance of air-breathing stealth systems and on the solution of current problems involving target acquisition and C^3 for sea-based systems, such an argument may prove to be not only plausible but compelling. On the other hand, it is perhaps not altogether fanciful to wonder whether decreasing concerns about ICBM vulnerability and increasing perceptions of ICBM cost-effectiveness, penetrativity, and lethality might not lead to a revival of interest in MX in the 1990s.

   With regard to sea-based strategic forces, it is likely that the
political consensus supporting the sea-based leg of the triad and its
modernization with the Trident SSBN, the D-5 missile and a Trident
successor will sustain itself for the foreseeable future. The counterforce capability of the D-5 will remain a potential source of political
trouble, but it will be difficult for opponents to come up with an attractive alternative. It also seems certain that over the next decade
nuclear-armed SLCMs for land attack will become widely dispersed
throughout the U.S. fleet, thus substantially expanding the role of the
navy (surface as well as subsurface) in supporting strategic missions.
By the turn of the century, the navy will also deploy new stealthy
carrier-based fighters and strike aircraft that will further increase
its capabilities for power projection against the Soviet homeland as
well as for general theater missions in a global conflict.

   As for the bomber leg of the triad, it seems well within the realm
of possibility that a strategic stealth bomber force could become the
premier U.S. strategic service in the next century. This could occur
if the future of the ICBM is clouded by lengthy debate over the merits
of Midgetman, while Soviet advances in ASW raise questions about the
survivability of the SSBN force (which will be reduced to about twenty
boats by the late 1990s in any event). On the other hand, the possibility
should not be excluded that the ATB will come under political fire once
its performance characteristics have become more widely known, either
on technical and cost-effectiveness grounds or because it could be
argued to provide the United States with a destabilizing first-strike
capability in an environment of increasingly effective defenses against
ballistic missiles. From a military point of view, the dual-use potential of stealth theater and strategic strike aircraft may come to seem
an increasingly attractive feature (in spite of their reported limitations
in bomb loading capacity), as new conventional munitions with pinpoint
accuracy will make possible not only theaterwide nonnuclear air attacks
but even limited nonnuclear strategic engagements. Dual-use ALCMs
could also support such operations. In the very long run, this prospect
could lead to a fundamental shift in U.S. strategy for general war.
Conceivably, U.S. nuclear targeting of the Soviet Union could eventually be restricted to the relatively limited number of superhard command and control facilities.

   As stated earlier, it is unclear to what extent SDI will effect a
doctrinal revolution in the direction of a defense-dominant posture for
the United States. To the extent that SDI begins to provide an effective
defense against ballistic missiles from the 1990s on, however, it will
greatly increase Soviet incentives to improve their offensive capabilities
in other areas. Even moderate Soviet success in developing stealth-
modified air-breathing systems by the turn of the century could have
serious consequences for the strategic balance, if the United States

continues to neglect its continental air defenses. The same is true of
Soviet development of new biological warfare agents for possible strategic use. However, a U.S. commitment to development and deployment of the full range of strategic defenses—BMD, air defense, ASW,
ASAT, "land defense" (that is, defense of key civilian and military
facilities against sabotage and special operations), and civil defense—
is likely to encounter formidable political difficulties because of the
societal impact in the United States of many of these forces and capabilities. A serious revival of civil defense, to name just the most
obvious case, could become a particularly hard political bone of contention. Nonetheless, the logic of SDI is likely to exert an increasingly
strong pull in this direction.

With regard to BMD, it is premature to predict precisely how
political and technical factors will interact in the development of SDI.
Political factors (and a misplaced technological utopianism) may operate to delay deployment of any BMD system until well into the next
century, causing rejection of piecemeal deployments of first generation
systems (whether conventional or directed energy) as they mature in
favor of a comprehensive defense anchored by a highly effective boost-
phase directed energy component. On the other hand, concern over the
vulnerability of the U.S. ICBM force and other military targets in the
continental United States—notably, the C^3 network—could conceivably
give SDI a shorter-term, lower-tech focus on point and area defense.
In the latter case, it is possible that a limited defense of critical targets (especially the National Command Authority (NCA), Strategic Air
Command (SAC), and NORAD (North American Air Defense) headquarters and at least some ICBM fields) could be available by the mid-
1990s. A minimal system, designed to remain within current ABM
Treaty constraints, might be deployed for protection of the NCA in
Washington. Again, however, political factors are liable to complicate
any such effort.

As for air defense, the United States is currently engaged in a
program of extensive modernization and upgrading of its capabilities
in this long dormant area, and studies are being undertaken of the
future of continental air defense and its relationship to the SDI. Eventually, the United States should be able to exploit the potential of
stealth technology to procure new generations of air defense interceptor aircraft and associated missiles that could, together with improved warning and battle management systems, greatly improve U.S.
capabilities against the Soviet air-breathing threat. At the same time,
the United States should be able to minimize the need for a costly and
vulnerable air defense infrastructure comparable to that possessed by
the Soviets, with warning and battle management functions being performed increasingly by air- and space-based sensors and command
elements. The United States will also most likely place higher priority

on the development and acquisition of an advanced strategic air defense missile system, possibly in conjunction with the NATO allies.

Passive measures for civil and land defense are likely to attract increasing attention to the degree that active air and ballistic missile defenses are seen to promise a relatively high level of effectiveness in limiting damage to the United States. But it remains unclear whether or to what extent political support will be forthcoming for civil defense measures to protect key industrial facilities, important communications nodes and other infrastructural targets (such as electric power installations and oil refineries), and the general population.

Perhaps even more than in the case of offensive forces, the future of SDI and of strategic defense generally is likely to be decisively influenced by political and cultural intangibles such as national leadership and the fortunes of doctrinal and propaganda battle. That arms control will offer an alternate route to national security that would permit blocking off the technology and policy avenues explored above is a possibility that will continue to fascinate Western elites in spite of its increasing implausibility. At the same time, it would be wrong to discount unduly the imperatives of technology. Certainly, the Soviets do not do so. It is well to remember that, twenty years before a U.S. president spoke of the coming obsolescence of the ballistic missile, a Soviet general could write:

> There are no limits to creative human thinking, and the possibilities offered by modern science and technology are tremendous. And I think that it is theoretically and technically quite possible to counterbalance the absolute weapons of attack with equally absolute weapons of defense, thereby objectively eliminating war regardless of the desires of resisting governments.[22]

NOTES

1. See, for example, Alex R. Alexiev, "The Soviet Campaign Against INF: Strategy, Tactics, and Means," Orbis, Summer 1985, 319-50; and more generally, Richard H. Shultz and Roy Godson, Dezinformatsia: Active Measures in Soviet Strategy (Washington: Pergamon-Brassey's, 1985).

2. Recent polling results are assembled in Keith B. Payne, Why SDI? (Fairfax, Va.: National Institute for Public Policy, 1985), 33-44.

3. See the recent discussion of this question by West German Defense Minister Manfred Wörner, "A Missile Defense for NATO Europe," Strategic Review 14 (Winter 1986): 13-20.

4. See Central Intelligence Agency and Defense Intelligence Agency, "The Soviet Economy Under a New Leader," in 99th Cong., 2nd Sess.,

<u>Application of Resources in the Soviet Union and China–1985</u>, hearing before Subcommittee on Economic Resources, Competitiveness, and Security Economics of the Joint Economic Committee of the U.S. Congress (Washington: U.S. GPO, 1986), 57–61.

5. Statement of Lawrence K. Gershwin, National Intelligence Officer for Strategic Programs, in 99th Cong., 1st Sess., <u>Soviet Strategic Force Developments</u>, joint hearing of Subcommittee on Strategic and Theater Nuclear Forces of the Senate Armed Services Committee, and the Defense Subcommittee of the Senate Committees on Appropriations (Washington: U.S. GPO, 1986), 14–15.

6. Brendan M. Greeley, Jr., "SDIO Reduces Research Efforts, Marks Gains in Ground Defense," <u>Aviation Week and Space Technology</u>, March 10, 1986, 29–42; and Lt. Gen. James A. Abrahamson, "Report to the Congress on the Strategic Defense Initiative," in 99th Cong., 1st Sess., Senate Armed Services Committee Hearings, <u>Department of Defense Authorization for Appropriations for Fiscal Year 1986</u>, pt. 7 (Washington, D.C.: GPO, 1985), 4093–4104.

7. Department of Defense, <u>Soviet Military Power</u> (Washington, D.C.: GPO, 1986), 45–47.

8. See Bill Sweetman, "The Vanishing Air Force—Stealth Technology Goes Operational," <u>International Defense Review</u> 17 (August 1985): 1257–59.

9. See Edgar Ulsamer, "The Prospect for Superhard Silos," <u>Air Force Magazine</u>, January 1984, 74–77.

10. See Abrahamson, "Report to the Congress on the Strategic Defense Initiative," 4083–92.

11. See Edgar Ulsamer, "DMA Digitizes the World," <u>Air Force Magazine</u>, March 1986, 17–18.

12. See, for example, Edgar Ulsamer, "Penetrating the Sea Sanctuary," <u>Air Force Magazine</u>, September 1984, 29, and "Disquiet for the Silent Service," <u>Air Force Magazine</u>, October 1984, 25–28.

13. An excellent overview is available in Manfred R. Hamm, "Deterrence, Chemical Warfare, and Arms Control," <u>Orbis</u> 29 (Spring 1985): 119–63.

14. William Kusewicz, "Beyond 'Yellow Rain,'" <u>Wall Street Journal</u>, April 25 through May 18, 1984; and Jonathan B. Tucker, "Gene Wars," <u>Foreign Policy</u> 57 (Winter 1984/85): 58–79.

15. Bill Geertz, "Soviets Fill Craters, Dig New Ones to Fool U.S. in Missile Accuracy," <u>Washington Times</u>, August 7, 1985.

16. See particularly Joseph D. Douglass, Jr., and H. Richard Lukens, "The Expanding Arena of Chemical-Biological Warfare," <u>Strategic Review</u> 12 (Fall 1984): 71–80. Also worth noting is the emphasis given by the Soviets to protection of their own population from the effects of strategic CBW attack by the United States. See Leon Gouré, <u>War Survival in Soviet Strategy: USSR Civil Defense</u> (Coral

Gables, Fla.: University of Miami Center for Advanced International Studies, 1976), 62-63, 78-79.

17. The most thorough and satisfying account of administration policy on SDI to date is The President's Strategic Defense Initiative, a pamphlet issued by the White House in January 1985. See also Department of State, The Strategic Defense Initiative, Special Report no. 129, June 1985.

18. That the changes in recent years in Soviet declaratory policy concerning nuclear war have reflected real disagreements between party and military leaders seems probable, but these disagreements would appear to revolve around the question of the relative emphasis to be given to foreign policy considerations in the formulation of nuclear doctrine rather than military-technical questions concerning Soviet strategy for nuclear war. See Dan L. Strode and Rebecca V. Strode, "Deterrence and Defense in Soviet National Security Policy," International Security 8 (Fall 1983): 91-116.

19. In a 1982 pamphlet, then Chief of the General Staff Marshal Nikolay Ogarkov stated in no uncertain terms that "the experience of past wars convincingly demonstrates that the appearance of new means of attack has always invariably led to the creation of corresponding means of defense. . . . This applies fully even to the nuclear-missile weapons." Vsegda v gotovnosti k zashchite Otechestva (Always Ready to Defend the Homeland) (Moscow: Voyenizdat, 1982), 36. For Soviet doctrinal and programmatic interest in strategic defense through the 1970s, see particularly Michael J. Deane, Strategic Defense in Soviet Strategy (Coral Gables, Fla.: University of Miami Advanced International Studies Institute, 1980); and Sayre Stevens, "The Soviet BMD Program," in Ashton B. Carter and David N. Schwartz, eds., Ballistic Missile Defense (Washington, DC: Brookings Institution, 1984), 189-209.

20. That the Soviets are engaged in a revision of basic doctrine on this and related matters is apparent above all from the recent study of Col. Gen. M. A. Gareyev, Deputy Chief of the General Staff, M. V. Frunze—Voyennyy teoretik (M. V. Frunze—Military theoretician) (Moscow: Voyenizdat, 1985); see the translated excerpts in Strategic Review 13 (Fall 1985): 102-4.

21. See Carnes Lord, "Verification—Reforming a Theology," The National Interest, no. 3 (Spring 1986): 50-60.

22. Gen. Maj. Nikolay A. Talenskiy, "Antimissile Systems and the Problem of Disarmament," International Affairs (October 1964), reprinted in Bulletin of the Atomic Scientists 21 (February 1965): 27.

Revolution or Resolution in Strategic Nuclear Affairs?

Kevin N. Lewis

INTRODUCTION

In explaining four decades of nuclear force developments, commentators select either of two conceptual formats for characterizing the events that have led to the present situation and its associated dilemmas. In the first, the "slide show" portrayal, the evolution of strategy, forces, war plans, budgets, and so forth, appear to be the results of a series of discrete choices, crises, and the like. At its roots, this method is rather journalistic: in retrospect—just as with current affairs—there always appear to be certain particularly pressing points on which we can go one way or the other: to war or peace, to weapon X or weapon Y, to arms control or arms race, to a refined strategy or an indiscriminating one. The present world, in this view, is the result of a long list of individual branch points followed over time, all concatenated together—and thus yielding a unique terminal result. Much of the tendency toward this approach can be attributed to the unremittingly spectacular nature of nuclear forces and issues and the great emotionalism and political salience that accompany such grave matters. Another force pulling some observers in this direction is that style of history that has been denigrated as placing too much emphasis on Great Men, Great Battles, and so forth.

Another approach, for want of a better expression, might be termed a "motion picture" perspective on strategic history. Here a number of factors, many of them only tangentially related to any refined domain of strategy and strategic choices (or unrelated altogether) blend together and influence each other over a historical continuum. Here, it is hard to single out critical or pivotal turning points or their initiators or to assign credible weight to any individual force, cause, or factor. Recently, many scholars have come to the conclusion that, like other historical topics, the evolution of nuclear strategy in all its parts is best analyzed in this fashion. Contributing to the adoption of this more complex and sophisticated perspective has been the appearance of many historians of strategy trained in the subtle business of nuclear posture planning and the steady emergence of ever more primary data on the manifold determinants of historical force and strategy developments.

Following upon the lead of historians, those concerned not with the past but with the future have sought to express future possibilities of great interest by viewing alternative future worlds, not as terminal nodes resulting from our selection of a single route through some flow chart of future history, but rather as the outcome of a continuing evolutionary process (the outcomes of which are not always predictable in light of the countable, definable, and otherwise identifiable developments that occur from day to day). As in many other academic undertakings, needless to say, in considering the predicates of strategic choice, historians enjoy a great advantage over those who would seek to predict the nature of future strategic environments and say how some present issues and choices might be managed in order to improve our relative position in the "outyears."

While the historical record can be carefully analyzed to reveal the reasons behind previous choices about force structure, employment strategy, declaratory policy, and so on,[1] those who would attempt to evaluate current issues—or, for that matter, indulge in crystal ball gazing—confront at least two serious hurdles. First, even with all available data and the soundest assessment techniques, projection of the forms the strategic future may take is risky because not all important events are under our control and because summing separate choices is not always a matter of adding up the constituent parts: as the Chinese put it, "prediction is always hard—especially when it comes to the future." The wisdom of that statement is immediately endorsed by even the most cursory survey of our previous nuclear prognostications. For one—albeit extreme—example, in 1921, following some early breakthroughs in nuclear physics, a thoughtful commentator wrote:

> When we have discovered the secret of the atom and can
> control its force, it is likely all nations will be ready and
> willing to lay down their arms and abolish their armies
> and navies. Statesmen will be glad to sit around a table
> and compromise their differences without any talk of
> force, for a power will be available in the world so mighty
> in its potentialities that no person would dare consider its
> use except for some constructive purpose.[2]

To impugn neither meteorologists or strategists, then, strategic forecasting sometimes makes weather prediction look like a precise science.

The second handicap impeding reliable assessment and prediction results from the confusion, chaos, and general turbulence that surround the emotional and tendentious issues raised in the course of nuclear strategy development and other planning. No strategic question is ever so straightforward that one cannot find a vast array of divergent (often extremely so) opinions on the matter. How, for instance, can at least two parties agreeing on the basic principle of nuclear winter, and in possession of roughly the same facts, formulate diametrically opposed policy recommendations? Even if nuclear forces cost nothing, even if there were no alliance issues to manage, and even if bewildering technological uncertainties vanished, there would probably be no diminution in the volume or acrimony of the ongoing strategic debate. Naturally, over time, the emotional quality of the debate, like the pain experienced in a trip to the dentist, is forgotten, and the cool facts of the matter seem more apparent. Generally speaking, then, what seems confused and contentious today may be far more easily interpreted by more detached observers enjoying the benefit of twenty-twenty hindsight.

Today, of course, we are confronted with a staggering array of current choices and issues that promise to make some previous debates look trivial by comparison. Among the leading issues are these:

● Should we move toward a so-called defense-dominated world or retain the basic retaliatory premises on which both sides have planned for so long?
● Should we adhere to the form and substance of arms control results and techniques that have been hammered out over a considerable period of time or abandon these in favor of such new notions as deep cuts, build-downs, no first use, and pledges?
● Confronting some trying problems in modernizing the B-52/Minuteman/Polaris Triad which has served us so well, should we build a new generation of forces more or less in the same style or should we opt for some more radical departure from past trends?
● Are our various assumptions about Soviet behavior in need of major revision?
● Are we nearing the end of the conceptual road in terms of developments of employment concepts or should we push on to explore new issues associated with such problems as the targeting of mobile forces, protracted nuclear operations, highly specific targeting options, and conflict in space?
● How, with so little data in hand, should we account for such postulations as nuclear winter in our overall planning?

In short, we are left with a basic question: can these and related matters be simply cast as evolutionary developments, like many others? If not, how should the trends and patterns we have come to identify over time be adjusted—or, for that matter, are entirely new approaches needed? And if so, how can some quite different kinds of issues be integrated into what has come by now to be a traditional approach to the larger nuclear question?

To resolve this question, I will presume to steal a page from the historians and begin with two assumptions. I will first assume that the same kinds of factors and processes that have shaped the history of strategic developments to date will continue to influence events for at least the near future. In other words, the present strategic planning context has a memory, and a good one at that. Second, I will assume that confusion, chaos, and eccentricity are to history what pain is to the body: sensations often hard to remember much after the fact. Thus, as we survey the current strategic debate—as it concerns basic policy, weapon system acquisition issues, budget options, and any number of related matters—it is worthwhile to view the future before us as an extension of the past.

Starting from these assumptions, we can then begin to approach the question of whether we should attempt to depart from the historical patterns of the past two decades. One point of view has already come to its conclusion: that major patterns reflect "good reasons:" forces, plans, and strategies have not grown like Topsy. But there is a dissenting view, as well, as one encounters discontent with the direction, pace, and character of many evolutionary patterns; many advocates would have us reject our strategic legacy in favor of some substantially new approach to nuclear deterrence.

This paper seeks to lay down some basic propositions that might serve as a framework of sorts in what is bound to be a heated and enduring debate over the nature of deterrence and its means through the rest of the century. These propositions are as follows. First, the strategic planning environment as a whole is now in the early stages of a transition of major proportions. This is by no means a new or unique phenomenon: the most cursory review of the strategic past reveals a kind of historical periodicity in the unrest associated with strategic matters as a whole.[3] The changes perceived as decisive events sometimes unfold in a way that is certainly not discrete, spontaneous, or very distinguishable at the time.[4]

Nonetheless, it is possible to look back and identify certain trends and themes that make it possible to designate different strategic epochs as specific entities. One interesting aspect of these epochs is that their pace of change seems, like the Earth's rotation, to be steadily slowing down over time. It took about five years to move from our vague post-World War II concepts of atomic war to the so-called massive retaliation strategy. The massive retaliation notion was ten years later superseded by a strategy emphasizing flexible response. And, two decades after that, we currently seem to reside at another crossroad of sorts. If this pattern persists, it would take yet another doubling before we come upon the next epoch—in about 2020 A. D.

This deceleration in the pace of strategic change seems to fly distinctly in the face of recent statements and allegations that we are now on the brink of fateful strategic choices. Indeed, a quick glance at the headlines suggests that we are approaching a kind of "white water" phase after a relatively more leisurely trip down a more sedate strategic stream. While it may be possible to embark upon some radical transformations in the short run, I will suggest that attempts to adjust the strategic planning context abruptly in the near term will probably meet with failure. Such attempts could as well lead to significant jeopardy.

That being the case, I will consider, as a second point, some of the potential pitfalls we may encounter were we to attempt a more modest departure from the relatively restrained pace of change from the strategic environment of recent years. It is probably best to manage any coming strategic transition of this type in kind: by gradual, not radical, steps, unless it can be shown that some of the new concepts being considered probably do take into account certain important realities influencing strategic nuclear planning.

NEW PERTURBATIONS TO AN
EXISTING CONDITION OF STABILITY

The fact that we may over time have reached something approximating a state of relative equilibrium in our ongoing strategic evolution has not, obviously, ruled out the potential for major shifts. In fact, we are now confronting more new developments that could require adjustment of recent patterns of strategic planning than we have at any point in the recent past. The question of interest is how much of a basic compensation in our planning and strategy will ultimately come of them.

Many of these changes have been widely discussed recently, so I now present only a brief summary of the more important ones.

● Technological Changes. The strategic operational environment has been much transformed lately by advances in technology. Weapons and sensors have become much more effective, so even very hard fixed targets have become vulnerable over time. In response to this development, we will see more imprecisely locatable targets[5] (for just one instance, the Soviets are now in the process of beginning to deploy the mobile SS-X-24 and SS-25 intercontinental ballistic missiles [ICBMs]). But how to find and attack these assets on a timely basis is a new operational challenge of major proportions. Other technological possibilities of note may include the attack of strategic targets with nonnuclear munitions, new strategic defensive and space combat technologies, and steadily improving command, control, and communications capabilities.[6]

- Political Shifts. One doesn't need reminding that nuclear force planning has become extraordinarily politicized. The new political environment—as it regards the mobilization of domestic consensus, the generation of alliance support, and our dealings with the Soviets— will play an increasingly pivotal (some might say overwhelming) role in our strategic planning exercise as a whole.
- Changes in the Balance. The relative military advantages of the United States and the Soviet Union, and the significance of these, are also the subject of hot dispute. The steady improvement in Soviet capabilities over the past twenty years relative to our own, the existence of major asymmetries within the U.S. and Soviet (and their respective coalitional) postures, and the dissimilar security requirements of the two superpower blocs challenge some of the assumptions that have traditionally underpinned many strategic calculations. For just one example, differences apparent in Soviet and U.S. force design philosophies now seem to rule out a tradi- tional one-for-one "bean count" approach to arms control, while providing no new method for counting in its stead.
- Thinking about Policy and Strategy Issues. Changing theater con- ventional balances have influenced our strategic calculus, as has an increasingly vigorous competition among conventional and stra- tegic forces for defense resources. Moreover, there has been a steadily improving understanding of Soviet nuclear thinking, which must be—and increasingly is—taken into account in U.S. planning.

Such developments as these have been a catalyst behind a number of searching explorations of the theoretical and practical foundations on which U.S. nuclear planning enterprises of all sorts are based. How does nuclear power relate to other national means when it comes to the deterrence of Soviet attacks on crucial forward U.S. interests like Europe? What is the best way to deter the Soviet use of nuclear weapons in the first place? How can war goals be pursued with nuclear weapons should deterrence fail? How can war be ended short of all-out devastation? How much should we spend on nuclear, as opposed to other, forces? Yet these are the good old questions with which we have grappled for decades.

In the face of new developments in the broad strategic setting, we find ourselves in receipt of the proverbial good news and bad news. We are finally coping adaptively with the set of operational require- ments with which we have been struggling since the 1960s. Though we postponed for a decade a follow-on generation of weapons to the original B-52/Minuteman/Polaris Triad, we have finally generated the resources needed to modernize the total posture, and we are apparently continuing to bring our force structure planning and our employment planning more closely into line. That is the good news. The bad news is that these are not the 1960s any more; these are the 1980s. So, in addition to more internal consistency, changes of a broader scope may be required—but of what kind? Should these adjustments follow traditional patterns, and if so, to what degree should we meld new developments with traditional concepts? How, if at all, can we modify our forces, strategies, plans, and the like, at the margin? What, if any, radical solutions are called for?

Increasingly, one hears calls for the latter, albeit from many very different quarters. The list of radical options has, within the last five years, included the following:

- the Strategic Defense Initiative (SDI)
- the nuclear freeze movement
- no-first-nuclear-use proposals
- adjustment of strategy and doctrine in light of the nuclear winter proposition
- deep cuts as a means to meaningful arms control
- nonnuclear strategic options
- protracted nuclear war
- new nonnuclear theater defense concepts

Each of these would seem to call for a substantial overhaul of the way our nuclear planning establishment might go about its business. Compared with more gradual, cautious, evolutionary responses to the changing context, which, then, is a sounder approach? To begin to answer this question, consider in more detail some of the forces that may well continue to influence the strategic evolutionary process of the next two decades.

FACTORS INFLUENCING THE EVOLUTION OF STRATEGY

In short, we can currently discern a confluence of two powerful forces that could strongly shape our strategic planning process over the next decade or two. One of these derives from the historical pattern, noted above, that has for some time featured a condition of relative stability. Certainly the continuation of this phenomenon does not and would not imply any period of stagnation in the strategic posture: the posture as a whole would continue to evolve incrementally in any case under the influence of the same kinds of forces that have shaped

developments to the present time. Rather, if historical patterns continue to be valid, it is questionable whether the transition phase from
the early 1980s looking to the 1990s will be as dynamic as was the
view from the late 1950s and early 1960s looking toward the late 1960s.

History demonstrates, in fact, that strategic change will proceed
at a measured and fairly stable pace unless we radically amend the
way we do things. Proposals are currently circulating that do advocate
fairly dramatic shifts in the way we go about our strategic business.
While a number of these proposals speak to developments that could
be many, many years down the road, that should not obscure the fact
that present decisions and actions can have major implications for
even the long-term future.[7]

In my view—a pessimistic one, perhaps—we have an imperfect
grasp on the key variables that combine to shape the strategic future:

- We do not have a good feel for how we can translate abstract theories
  or concepts into practical results.
- We lack sufficient understanding of many key variables (notably
  Soviet and allied responses to our various options).
- Our historical experience and the nature of the probable domestic
  U.S. policy environment suggest that even the best laid plans stand
  a high probability of not working out as intended.

For these and other reasons, a cautious approach to transition
management is obviously indicated. At the same time that we evaluate
new possibilities, we should avoid great breaks with the past. The
current strategic situation may bespeak a chaotic picture, but it is
in the form it is today for good reasons, which we cannot and should
not try to strike from our memories. Though there may be enormous
dissatisfaction with various aspects of the current strategic context,
it is incumbent upon us to try to live with it for the time being. Rather
than depart radically from historical trends, it is probably safer and
cheaper to move forward fairly modestly. This will come as objectionable advice to many involved in the current strategic debate, but the
inherent stability of the strategic context up until now is too valuable
a legacy to jettison casually. In short, the present situation may be
complex, confusing, and frightening, but it is stable enough that we
should not abdicate it without sufficient cause.

It is useful to follow up on this argument for a balanced and gradual
strategic transition by demonstrating the pitfalls toward which radical
solutions have in the past, and probably would also in the future, tend
to lead us. The historical record discloses many lessons pertinent to
the present popularity of radical options. Yet, the same deficiencies
that overthrew prior proposals—or, worse, led to problems as attempts were undertaken to implement substantial reformations in short

order—would be at work today in virtually every case. This is not to
suggest that the following four major problems could not somehow be
gotten to grips with; rather, the point is that before embarking on
some major new initiative, its proponents should be able to articulate
and lay out responsible roadmaps that insure against the following
common oversights in arguments for radical change.

First, the various subcomponents of many strategic programming
and policy problems must not be considered independently of one another. Public policy issues, military and civilian alike, have an irresistible tendency to fragment into a number of highly compartmen-
talized subdebates. But once a major debate decomposes into its various and sundry elements, many aspects of an ongoing project will be
managed and promoted in ways that may have nothing to do with other
parts of the larger problem. In many cases, different parts of a program will drift apart in contradictory directions. When the time comes
to relink the components of a contemplated program or concept, the
resulting crazy quilt of decisions and capabilities may only by chance
resemble the coherent and unified whole anticipated at the outset.

But this outcome, which arises so many times that it would be
conspicuous should it be totally absent, often does not encourage many
participants to look beyond the alluring aspects of their corner of the
debate to consider the larger picture. This failing has, of course,
many historical antecedents. One of the most notable can be found in
the 1950s nuclear planning situation in which enormous disconnections
between planners at different nuclear commands, and between nuclear
and conventional capability planners, were rife.[8]

Consider some more current cases in point. It may be surprising
to consider the possibility that the MX ICM was at one time one of the
more favorable weapons acquisition successes in recent memory. It
is hard to imagine a more cost-effective weapon system on a per-
warhead-delivered basis. The program remained ahead of schedule,
under budget, and exceeded its performance goals. Unfortunately,
things were never so rosy with its basing mode. The MX was conceived at a time when there seemed no overwhelming disadvantages
to fixed silo basing, a planning assumption that was undermined during
subsequent years, leaving us with an ideal silo-based missile rather
less suited to alternative (for example, mobile) deployment modes.

Similarly, the more avid proponents of so-called Confidence
Building Measures (CBM) have fallen into a similar trap. If only better means of communicating and otherwise resolving crises were
available, they claim, potential military disasters might be averted.
But however sensible some of the proposed technologies and procedures for communicating with adversaries in crises might be, CBM
enthusiasts often neglect the far more important matter of why long-
term major power competitions go bad and lead to serious military

confrontations in the first place. It is all well and good to improve
techniques for communicating, but if a larger view of the root sources
of confrontation is not factored into the equation, good communications
may only illustrate the extent to which the basic issues at stake were
irresolvable without some drastic kind of action.[9]

The Strategic Defense Initiative holds out perhaps the greatest
promise of disassociating into an archipelago of independently handled
issues. We have technologists, strategists, budget experts, political
analysts, polemicists, and others vigorously debating some side issue
or other, but few bother to cast their cases in terms of larger strategic issues. This fission of the debate into various fragments is, admittedly, a natural consequence of the enormous uncertainty, novelty,
and complexity of nuclear force issues, but the fact that few people
are asking big questions—for example, if SDI works, can the enemy
counter it? If they can't counter it, can we afford it? If we can afford
it, is it good for our coalitions?—is not necessarily a good sign.

For instance, some would-be strategic defenders eagerly anticipate the day when we can neutralize those very dangerous Soviet heavy
ICBMs (now represented chiefly by the SS-18).[10] But although this
capability might be highly valuable in some scenarios (for example,
major counterforce exchanges), the mutual possession of such defenses might be highly unproductive in other scenarios. Even if Soviet
missile defenses were inferior to ours, they might be adequate to
frustrate U.S. attempts to execute limited nuclear options in support
of a failing regional defense effort, say in Europe. Since it has been
NATO, not the Soviets, who have sought to counterbalance an apparently unsatisfactory conventional defense situation with threats to use
nuclear weapons on a limited basis, deployment of even modest antimissile defenses could drastically undercut our basic theater defense
strategies. In other words, concentration on only the value of boost-
phase intercept capabilities in selected major attack scenarios blinds
us to the implications of SDI for other kinds of issues. Exactly the
same criticism can be leveled on any of the recent no-first-use proposals.

A second deficiency in much strategic reasoning that tends to
encourage excessively ambitious thinking about strategic alternatives
is the widespread disinclination toward consideration of what one
might, for want of a better expression, call management issues. It
is hard to concentrate on the day-to-day problems of implementing
war and program planning guidelines, managing force operations, and
paying for the posture when there are grand issues of policy and strategy to be resolved. Although it is impossible to take on directly many
components of the strategic management problem for reasons of sheer
complexity, security classification, technical difficulty, and the like,
many an apparently good strategic idea has nonetheless withered on

the vine because conceptual appeal ends up counting for little if it is not based upon a sound foundation.

Several examples will convey a sense of how neglecting mundane matters can undermine the loftiest strategic cerebrations. One concerns the preparation of the so-called Single Integrated Operational Plan (SIOP), which is the central strategic war plan that contains the various options we might elect to unleash against our adversaries. Some options may be very refined. Given a certain objective, planners would translate attack goals into tremendous operational detail: what aircraft should deliver what weapon at which target at what time to inflict a specified level of damage, and so on. Coordinating among perhaps thousands of warheads atop thousands of launchers across intercontinental distances and in the face of determined enemy defenses is a demanding task, and the more flexibility we build into plans, the harder flexible planning seems to get. But the task must be done, and to do so it is necessary to boil high-level national capabilities and aims—for example, seek to deter the Soviet Union by maintaining the ability to inflict a presumed degree of unacceptable damage on it—down to a myriad of times, coordinates, countermeasures frequencies, and so forth.

Thus, a few years ago, a new idea was briefly in vogue. It was suggested that the SIOP be modified to threaten those in the Soviet Union who were really the bad guys. After all, the average Soviet citizen didn't vote for, and probably didn't like his or her leadership. So why hold them hostage to U.S. retaliatory threats? Why not threaten Soviet decision makers where it hurt by aiming U.S. attacks at them personally and at their means of controlling their possibly unwilling subjects (for example, at the military or the KGB)? At first glance this idea seems fairly insightful, but such discriminating targeting is usually not technically feasible. For instance, just how does one continuously target Kremlin officials fleeing Moscow by car or plane? How does one knock down the local KGB headquarters with a nuclear weapon without doing horrible damage to local citizens who might loathe that particular instrument of repression? In short, for want of an appreciation of some basic technical realities, a new conceptual notion came to absorb much criticism.

A second example can be extracted from the recent annals of arms control: specifically, the nuclear freeze. Again, like the countercontrol targeting case, the freeze notion has a certain gut appeal. But no one even bothered to explain just what would be frozen. There are a number of reasons for defining exactly the basis of a freeze, and they are more than simple technicalities. Should we prohibit the replacement of old warheads on a one-for-one basis with new warheads that may be safer as well as more effective (that is, do we want to freeze a given level of mechanical safety to prevent a possible growth

in effectiveness)? Should we freeze levels on important nonnuclear
adjuncts to offensive delivery forces, such as aerial tankers (which
can refuel, and extend the range of, cargo and tactical airplanes, as
well as bombers) and air defense fighters (which can defend friendly
airspace in Europe in a conventional war, as well as our homeland in
a nuclear exchange)? Do we freeze reconnaissance capabilities that
are equally adept at verifying the freeze and finding new targets to
support warfighting ambitions? We may all despise excessive legalism,
but somewhere, someday, somehow, we have to apply legal methods
to all treaty arrangements. If we are not specific in our treaty language and rules, we are at best wasting our time, and we are at worst
laying the foundation for subsequent differences of opinion that might
arise when both sides perceive that the other has violated the spirit
of excessively vague treaties.[11]

A third failing is that many proposals for rapid change ignore the
dynamic character of nearly all strategic activities. Basically, many
people seem to discount the fact that in the strategic world very little
of true substance happens overnight—at least in peacetime.[12] It takes
years to overhaul forces and war plans. It takes years to persuade
domestic, allied, and adversary observers to concur with new policy
initiatives. During these intervals, there are many opportunities for
adjustments in other aspects of one's posture, in the balance, in technological bases, and so on. But such potentially significant developments tend to be washed out when we view strategic evolution as a
series of snapshots and not as a moving picture.

Take the history of the competition between U.S. manned bombers
and Soviet air defenses as a classic case in point. For a quarter of a
century, reports of the imminent demise of at least the B-52, and
perhaps of the manned bomber concept as a whole, have circulated.
Yet two decades after the downing of Francis Gary Power's U-2, the
Soviets still had trouble dealing with two quite tame Korean Airliners.
Even against a fully alerted Soviet air defense system, there is good
reason to believe that our current force of B-52s—which were considered by some to be so vulnerable in the early 1960s that a new aircraft
(the B-70) was essential—would perform their missions extremely well
today.

Strategic Air Command's (SAC) continuing ability to penetrate
heavily defended Soviet airspace over the past twenty years has, in
the absence of a new, follow-on bomber, been assured by the constant
modification of this force at the margin to anticipate new defensive
threats. For every highly touted—and expensive—Soviet interceptor,
radar, or missile to appear for two decades or more, SAC conceived
a more inexpensive countermeasure to maintain force effectiveness.
When high-altitude penetration became too risky, bombers were
ordered to penetrate at low altitudes. As key radars and control cen-

ters became too menacing, plans were made to suppress them with missiles prior to bomber arrival. As terminal and barrier defenses became too dangerous, we equipped bombers with decoys, counter-measures, and standoff missiles so that defenses could be jammed, overwhelmed, or simply bypassed. No estimate has appeared in public, but the cost exchange ratios in the bomber-air defense competition probably have run consistently in our favor. That is, for every dollar the Soviets have spent to foil SAC, we have neutralized the effort with pennies or maybe dimes. In the end, then, it will be the sheer effects of age—the physical wear and tear on aircraft and the growing costs of maintenance that begin to afflict elderly weapons systems—that signal the demise of the B-52, not threat developments. To overlook such dynamic issues, in short, can lead one to quite a biased view of the real strategic problems before us.

A fourth and final failing is in effect a philosophical one: the inability of many radical change doctrines to tolerate a certain irresolvable dilemma that will always haunt nuclear planners. The dilemma is basically this. On the one hand, no one can ever guarantee the end of a nuclear conflict on acceptable terms. Thus, any nuclear confrontation might escalate to a point where the damage done would eclipse any national objectives that might have been at stake in the first place.

On the other hand, unless we relegate nuclear forces to a doomsday device role—one in which they would only deter a like Soviet threat—we must behave as though it were possible to conduct some kind of meaningful limited nuclear operation. Why? Because we would never want to unleash an all-out attack (because of the mutual results) if some kind of alternative course were available to us. Moreover, we can never know what the Soviets might themselves attempt. As little as we may like to anticipate a flexible nuclear employment contingency, we must for the sake of prudence prepare for some kind of response options other than those that ensure mutual suicide. A flexible employment capability also has certain side benefits. For one, we can use some limited nuclear threats to avoid having to raise the very expensive armies, air forces, and navies that might in some cases be needed to deal with Soviet conventional power on a one-to-one basis.

Given the unbelievable destructive power of world nuclear forces and the enormous resources invested in these arsenals (more than a trillion dollars by the United States alone since 1945, in $FY85), it is unsatisfying to have to acknowledge that many, if not most, of our decisions must necessarily be subject to this dilemma, which cannot, in my view, ever be resolved or evaded. To some people the dilemma is downright intolerable, and through history many different approaches, all of them chimeras so far, have been explored in efforts to escape this awful quandary. In the 1950s, some thought that air defenses or a first strike might eliminate the Soviet retaliatory threat,

allowing us to prevail in nuclear conflict, but the proliferation of
Soviet forces and the advent of the ballistic missile (not to mention
their option of going first) pulled the rug out from under those proponents. For a while, it was also supposed that a nuclear war might
be confined to some kind of purely tactical nuclear engagement. However, the residents of future nuclear battlefields objected, and, moreover, even tactical nuclear victory would do nothing to rule out Soviet
strategic reprisals. Others have identified arms control as yet another way out of the dilemma, and now Star Wars is seen by some to
be beckoning us toward a viable exit from the terrible business of
mutual deterrence.

But, barring some change in the basic laws of physics or of human
nature, some magic solution to the dilemma should not reasonably be
expected in the near term. We must for the time being face some
awful risks and contradictions, no matter what. Radical solutions
with all-purpose objectives are likely to be no-purpose solutions.
Therefore, the case can be made that we might pursue more modest
solutions, unless satisfactory radical results can be assured ahead
of time.

The preceding is not intended as a decisive case against radical
as opposed to incremental solutions, but it should be sufficient grounds
for recognizing the need for great caution in any attempt to deviate
substantially from the evolving strategic context as we have known it
for two decades. One might also add that, even should some of the
usual pitfalls be avoided, there are a few additional cases to be made
against radical initiatives. These potential problems must also be
satisfactorily hedged against before we launch major new initiatives:

- Radical changes tend to be inefficient and overly costly. The hasty
  U.S. effort to build up its ground commitment in Vietnam in the
  spring of 1965 is a classic case in point.
- Radical changes tend to generate alliance turmoil and popular anxiety. In the early 1950s, NATO adopted a doctrine (MC-14/1) and
  a plan (the Lisbon plan) calling for a major rearmament program
  to meet the Soviet conventional threat to Western Europe. However,
  the plan was too ambitious and was doomed to failure from the start.
  Subsequent feelings of frustration and confusion led to the subsequent
  adoption of the diametrically opposed massive retaliation strategy.
- Radical changes tend to inspire occasionally excessive adversary
  behavior. From a Soviet point of view, their implied threats of missile superiority in the late 1950s must seem to have backfired. For
  a missile gap did emerge as a result of Western fears of Soviet missile superiority, but the gap was stacked in the wrong direction from
  the Soviet vantage point.
- Radical changes tend to promote disconnections in leaders' minds

between the ideal and the real that could lead to dangerous misunderstandings in crises. Feelings of security in the atomic bomb shortly
after World War II were dashed when President Truman learned to
his great shock and regret how little atomic firepower was actually
in hand.
- Radical changes come at the expense of other established priorities.
Every dollar spent on some new undertaking will—barring an enormous readjustment in our defense concepts and in the willingness of
democratic peoples to spend money on defense in peacetime—come
out of the hide of some other military capability.

THE STRATEGIC PLANNING CONTEXT
IN TRANSFORMATION

Academic investigators, official analysts, the general public,
and those who may fall into various hybrid categories frequently find
themselves in wide-ranging debates on any number of issues relating
to nuclear deterrence and, should it come to it, the use of nuclear
weapons to defend national security interests. Based not only on inspection of popular media, then, but on the declarations of the official
or professional community as well, it would be hard to avoid the conclusion that the strategic planning environment founders in perpetual
turmoil and upheaval. New technological possibilities seem to present
themselves daily. Strategies for the conduct of nuclear operations
seem to be revised annually. We seem to land regularly on our allies'
doorsteps with new concepts for theater defense that sometimes call
for the enhancement of selected nuclear capabilities and sometimes
for the abandonment of others. Recently, the very political and philosophical bases underlying nuclear deterrence have been challenged
from several directions, whether the case made has been for Star
Wars, a no-first-use strategy, deep cuts in offensive arms, an offensive posture capable of fighting and prevailing in protracted nuclear
war, or what have you. And throughout, the mad juggernaut of the
arms race allegedly careens unchecked, as new and more terrifying
weapons are apparently added to national arsenals at nothing less than
a feverish pace.

Such atmospherics belie, in my view, the actual state of play in
the broad field of strategic affairs. Reports of abrupt shifts in strategy,
plans, and so forth, would come as startling news to those charged
with the actual design and implementation of posture, employment
options, and related initiatives. Viewed in terms other than declaratory ones, in fact, the U. S. strategic planning and policy context as
a whole has for nearly two decades been reasonably stable (although
there are certainly exhilarating episodes from time to time).

There has been a steady convergence in our thinking about operational employment strategy. Concepts of strategic flexibility, first articulated officially in the early 1960s, have been steadily if not swiftly fleshed out over time. The present employment concept, the "countervailing strategy" (actually a late Carter administration notion, although Reagan administration recapitulations do not, apparently, diverge substantially), is intended to be sensitive to such factors as known Soviet doctrinal inclinations, the practical difficulties attendant upon any strategy incorporating employment flexibility, and the necessary corollaries of a flexible operational strategy (for example, survivable command and control and adequate connectivity). Most people now agree on two key facts: that employment flexibility is an essential basis for strategy, but that there are significant limitations on the degree to which the principles called for by a flexible employment strategy can be translated into operational reality.

Substantial consensus has emerged on both sides of the Atlantic that U.S. nuclear forces can play only a limited role in the deterrence of potential adversary aggression that is less than all-out. In other words, the domain of possible challenges to which threatened nuclear use might be relevant has steadily contracted over time. We are moving away from the all-purpose deterrent employment strategy of the 1950s to one that is increasingly specialized. At the same time, there is widespread agreement on the need to backstop a vanishing margin of nuclear superiority with a more effective and credible conventional deterrent capability.

Strategic budgets have stabilized as a share of the DOD budget as a whole. Between fiscal years (FY) 1968 and 1983, spending on strategic nuclear forces (that is, Program I) averaged a highly consistent 8.6 percent of DOD TOA (Total Obligational Authority). Absolute strategic spending has increased somewhat, however, inasmuch as defense budgets have grown steadily in real terms over the past decade. But even though we are now undertaking a comprehensive modernization program, strategic spending still falls short of the levels experienced historically. For instance, over the sixteen-year period FY68-FY83, cumulative Program I TOA amounted to $282 billion (in $FY85), compared with a total of nearly twice as much ($547 billion) spent during the 16 fiscal years before that.

The strategic force structure has, in many ways, stabilized as well. Although it seems inconsistent with much recent rhetoric, the current new Triad of offensive delivery vehicles—MX, Trident, and B-1—were originally intended to replace their predecessors on a one-for-one basis.[13] This replacement process, simultaneously involving all three legs of the Triad, is now necessarily so vigorous, costly, and controversial, of course, because more orderly, one-at-a-time modernization initiatives were deferred frequently in the 1970s. Recent developments have combined so that the new-generation Triad will not be fully procured, but new systems (like Midgetman and the advanced technology bomber) should compensate for some of the difference. True, new weapons programmed are more capable than the ones they replace, but then again, the environment within which they would operate is a more demanding one, too.

These instances are cited to illuminate the fact that the evolution of forces, plans, budgets, and strategic concepts is not really so turbulent as much popular rhetoric might lead one to believe. Certainly U.S. strategic initiatives have sought to keep pace with, at the very least, significant changes in the external operational environment. For instance, U.S. force attributes reflect changes in pertinent Soviet target arrays. United States nuclear efforts have, moreover, been influenced by domestic and foreign political phenomena: the inability of Secretary Schlesinger to pursue a limited civil defense program (one consistent with his other flexible employment efforts) is a case in point. But in relative terms, stability obtains.

It is useful to ask why such stability has, in fact existed. Consider the following incomplete list of explanations.

- Force structure changes take increasingly long to implement. Even if we did resolve to proceed at full speed with some new weapon concept, the fielding of an effective military capability may be realized only after a decade or more of effort. If anything, this phenomenon becomes more and more striking over time. For instance, when the decision to deploy Polaris was made in the 1950s, it took roughly five years to move an entirely new kind of complex program (the submarine, as well as associated missile systems) from the drawing board into the field. By contrast, SAC documented an official requirement for a new ICBM (MX)—a weapon concept that they understood quite well—in 1972! And once on line, new weapons— even ones that meet their design specifications—can take quite some time to shake down so that they operate smoothly on a day-to-day basis in the hands of regular forces (as opposed to factory teams).
- War plans take years to modify substantially. As suggested above, strategic employment plans are intricate entities. Recent estimates have suggested that if some new slant to targeting plans were to be introduced today, it would take on the order of two years to find its way into the hands of operational units.
- Other security problems occupy our attention more and more. In the 1950s and early 1960s, nuclear forces may have occupied center stage. But in the wake of the Vietnam War, other problems—such as responding to improved Soviet conventional capabilities in Europe (put on line while our attention was diverted to Southeast Asia) and dealing with the collapse of what once passed for our security ar-

rangements for Southwest Asia—have imposed a redoubled call on
our energies and resources. We face the so-called modernization
inflation problem in our force structure planning. We must endure
a growing operations and manpower burden, and our allies' contribution to defense on a worldwide level has declined compared with
previous decades. In short, there is a tremendous competition for
resources among the enterprises represented in the Defense Department budget, and it is hard to imagine that we would ever see the
rates of real defense budget growth that would make it possible to
underwrite painlessly all priority defense programs. It is widely
believed (and in my view, correctly so) that the probability of nuclear war occurring is more a function of the failure of Western
conventional deterrence in key regional theaters than a function of
some minor perturbation of the superpower nuclear balance. For
this reason, if no other, nuclear forces have declined in relative
overall importance.

- More people are involved, and are better able to participate, in the
strategic debate. This is self-evident and self-explanatory. With
increasing public understanding of, and participation in, the strategic debate as a whole, the development of general political consensus
becomes more important. Issues that were considered only in the
most vague or aggregated terms a couple of decades ago are now
dissected in detail in many forums. For example, Congress would
never, twenty-five years ago, have intervened much in the determination of technical issues pertinent to the then new ICBM program.
By contrast, today Congress is deeply involved, to the point where
there are statutory limits on no less than the weight of a future Midgetman small ICBM! Some think that this process has gone too far,
while others welcome it: for our purposes, the point simply is that
there are more, and often better-informed, players in the strategic
debate than ever before.

For these and other reasons, the nuclear planning problem in the
1970s may not have been the main attraction to many defense planners.
As the total defense planning problem became larger and more complex, it was inevitable that strategic issues should wane in relative
importance. Now, none of this should be taken to suggest that the ongoing development of strategy, weapons, and so on, is simply running
out of steam and slowing to a glacial pace, nor that we have become
casual and sloppy about nuclear issues now that our posture and strategy are well into middle age. Rather, substantial change is possible
and, in my view, beginning to transpire, but, unless we change the
way we approach business, not at any breakneck speed. Barring unusual developments, we should witness no dramatic changes in force
levels, employment concepts, posture planning principles (such as

maintaining a Triad), alliance doctrinal principles, or arms control concepts (for instance, the need for some perceptible state of parity).

CONCLUSIONS

I have based the foregoing on the assumptions that historical patterns in the evolution of the strategic context can be discerned and that these patterns are, if you will, there for good reasons. Barring the repudiation of these assumptions, the following conclusions can be suggested:

Looking back from the 21st century, we will see the period of the late 1970s to mid-1980s as the dawn of a period of significant transition in the strategic scene. The major new influences that will determine the nature of any new strategic environment are now nascent but will represent nonetheless the product of a process of gradual evolution.

Attempted radical changes from historical patterns tend to pose serious problems. Abrupt attempts to change long-term trends in the short run can not only lead to a host of troublesome minor effects (such as inefficiencies or breakdowns of popular consensus) but under some circumstances can also have more catastrophic consequences. This is not to say that there is not some possible schema for a pattern of an ultimately radical transformation. However, at least at the present time there is no candidate change of this type that is sufficiently well conceived that we can be confident that troubles can be avoided in its straightforward pursuit.

In any case—and even if we have an adequate roadmap to identify the many potential pitfalls before us—implementing any particular set of radical changes will involve difficult transition management problems. Tenacity and consistency will be essential. Finally, there will be limitations on the results that even the best plan and management techniques can bring about. Not all key events are under our own control.

My conclusion, then, is that we must accordingly be rather patient. We should follow Euripides' warning that "a man pursuing great things might not gain the things present."

NOTES

1. Even when a particular choice may not have been optimum, or even very sensible, historians can usually develop plausible explanations for the failure to perform better.

2. World's Work, May 1921, cited in New Yorker, March 25, 1985, 130.

3. One can distinguish between various degrees of agitation in the strategic debate. There are, at one end of the spectrum, controversies over fairly specific matters, such as the need for intermediate-range nuclear force (INF) weapons or the acquisition of stopgap deterrent forces (B-1B, MX) pending the arrival of an entirely new generation of forces, now represented by the advanced technology bomber (ATB) and the small intercontinental ballistic missile (SICBM). At the other end of the spectrum are debates about policy, strategy, and forces, such as the one commonly associated with the arrival of the Kennedy administration.

4. At every stage of the game, moreover, there are significant mismatches and disconnections among our strategic posture, war plans, strategies, defense arrangements with allies, and the like.

5. Generally speaking, an ILT is the same as a mobile or movable target.

6. One additional change of a technical sort involves the nuclear winter hypothesis. But it remains unclear just what the total policy ramifications of nuclear winter would be if the hypothesis is proved.

7. For example, demonstrating uncertain SDI technologies in a manner that leads to ABM treaty abandonment may matter little in the present, but this eventually may come back to haunt us if we decide later that our original assumptions about strategy or technology were incorrect.

8. For example, different service and even branch targeting was not coordinated until the late 1950s, with the result that some targets were being "overkilled" while others went unstruck. Indeed, many times on-target conflicts were shown to be written into the various uncoordinated war plan.

9. See K. N. Lewis and M. A. Lorrell, "Confidence Building Measures in Historical Perspectives, Orbis, Summer 1984.

10. The chief advantage of a space-based Ballistic Missile Defense System in this regard is that ICBMs would be attacked during their boost phase, prior to the time at which a missile's post-boost vehicle dispenses its individual warheads. Thus, highly fractionated missiles, that is, launchers with many warheads, are relatively unattractive, and the Soviets would presumably channel their offensive initiatives into less menacing programs.

11. Existing U.S.-Soviet treaties are prepared in great detail, but even so, there is still much disagreement on the fine points, and this often leads to trouble. One need only survey the several recent controversies surrounding alleged Soviet violations of any number of arms control treaties to see that even the degree of specificity we have seen so far is no guarantee against misunderstandings down the road.

12. Some changes—for instance, modifications in operational

tactics, alert rates, and the like—can be implemented in quite short order, of course.

13. That is, 200 MX at 10 MIRVs each (for a total of 2000 RVs) replace 2100 RVs on Minuteman II and III; 240 B-1s were to replace a like number of B-52G and H bombers; and 25 Trident SSBNs, each with 24 SLBM tubes and an availability rate of on the order of 70 percent, put on station about as many missile tubes as did the full 41-boat Polaris/Poseidon force.

Deterrence, Peacekeeping, and Combat Orientation in the U.S. Army

David R. Segal, Jesse J. Harris,
Joseph M. Rothberg, and David H. Marlowe

INTRODUCTION

The advent of the age of nuclear military technology at the end of
World War II produced a major change in the military manpower policies of the United States, reflecting a new era of military strategy.
In pre-Napoleonic Europe, wars were limited in size, scope, and
objective, and they ended when they had served the political purposes
of sovereign states.[1] From the Napoleonic Wars and the French Revolution, however, the European states adopted a mobilization model,
raising much larger armies than previously through combinations of
militia call-ups, conscription, and voluntarism when they were at war;
fighting larger-scale wars with larger forces to achieve military objectives; and largely demobilizing the force when peace was restored.[2]
They did maintain small cadre forces in peacetime to allow them the
flexibility to respond to situations that called for military force, but
they did not require mobilization. The newborn American nation,
tracing its military traditions to European roots, emulated this pattern
from the outset, and a small standing federal force was frequently
engaged in relatively low-intensity military operations.

This chapter was written during David R. Segal's tenure as a
guest scientist in the Department of Military Psychiatry, Walter Reed
Army Institute of Research. The interpretations contained in the paper
are the views of the authors and are not to be construed as official or
as reflecting policies of the Walter Reed Army Institute of Research,
the Department of the Army, or the Department of Defense. The final
stages of this research were supported in part by a grant from the
General Research Board of the University of Maryland to David R.
Segal.

In the post-World War II world, the lethality and speed of delivery of new weapons available to potential enemies made full demobilization an untenable policy. Rather, the United States maintained a relatively large force in being during a period that, in earlier days, would have been regarded as peacetime.

This change in military manpower policy was accompanied by an expansion in the definition of the mission of the military. No longer would the primary goal of armies be simply to use the maximum capability at their disposal to engage and defeat an enemy. Rather, their primary goal became preventing an enemy from using his maximum military capability. The mission of military forces was transformed from one solely emphasizing war fighting to one emphasizing peace-keeping as well.[3] However, if peacekeeping failed, armies would have to revert to the goal of fighting and winning wars. The minimization of intensity became important again because of the availability of nuclear weapons, and warfare and politics became increasingly intertwined. At the same time, however, the ascendancy of air power and the doctrine of massive retaliation made the role of a land army in actual combat ambiguous. Rather than preparing for flexible responses to a range of scenarios, levels of intensity between deterrence and total war were largely disregarded from the late 1940s until the Vietnam era.

From the outset, this change of mission definition was postulated to be problematic for military forces. Morris Janowitz, who formulated the concept of constabulary forces, suggested that a large force in being during peacetime, constantly prepared to act, committed to the minimum use of force, but capable of engaging in large-scale combat operations if necessary, might have difficulty maintaining its essential combat readiness.[4] This theme was subsequently echoed by Jonathan Alford, who noted the "insolubility" of the problem of maintaining the combat effectiveness of a volunteer military force—particularly a ground combat force—that is indefinitely placed in a deterrence posture.[5] Similarly, Gregory Foster suggests that deterrence has an effect on "the fighting ethic," and that in the American case, the fighting ethic has suffered.[6] We regard the fighting ethic as part of the attitudinal/motivational component of combat readiness.

Most of the data that exist on the combat ethic fail to support the concerns of Janowitz, Alford, and Foster. David Gottlieb's interviews with junior enlisted personnel at Fort Sill suggested that even those in combat specialties did not really think about going to war as part of the job of a peacetime army.[7] His respondents, however, had not been fully socialized to the soldier role. By contrast, studies of personnel in combat units, who had undergone more complete organizational socialization, show that they regard going to war as part of the job and that they are prepared to do that job.[8] This fact has turned up consistently in our interviews with personnel in our most rapidly deployable infantry divisions and ranger battalions in the continental United States and with combat personnel fulfilling deterrence functions in West Germany and in South Korea, as well. The combat ethic in general seems not to be problematic among U.S. combat troops. The effect of constabulary duty on this ethic, however, has not been as thoroughly analyzed. This paper assesses the impact of constabulary duty on the combat ethic. It is our thesis that constabulary operations, although recognized as highly likely, are interpreted by U.S. soldiers as deviations from their primary mission: to be prepared to go to war.

Some conceptual clarification is in order and may shed light on the issue. Although the concepts of deterrence and constabulary operations have been used interchangeably in some of the literature, they are not equivalent. They refer to different ends of the combat-intensity spectrum. While nonnuclear forces fulfilling a deterrence function were in part a tripwire during the 1950s and early 1960s, they were expected to meet a first-echelon assault by opposing forces with their own force. Constabulary troops, by contrast, were to use minimal force—and to minimize the force used by others. As we shall show, while low-intensity constabulary operations might contribute to a dulling of the cutting edge of combat forces, particularly in the short run, they need not do so. More important, soldiers today who have finished a tour of constabulary duty are quickly returned to a regimen aimed at preparing them for combat operations that can rapidly resharpen the edge, because current doctrine and training recognize the flexibility of response required of modern armies.

The strategy of deterrence, as it has evolved in the post-World War II world, is concerned with the upper end of the combat-intensity spectrum: in the extreme, nuclear confrontation between the Soviet Union with the Warsaw Pact nations on the one hand and the United States with its NATO allies on the other. This is the war for which our forces are to be prepared. The deterrence posture basically asserts that each major power has sufficient military capability that even if it is attacked and a large portion of its military power and indeed its society are destroyed, it will nonetheless be able to retaliate and impose a level of destruction on the attacking nation that the attacker would find unacceptable. A society does not need weapons superiority to assume a deterrence posture. It merely needs sufficient retaliatory strength to impose destruction on an enemy after suffering a massive attack and the will to use that strength. The consequence of the process, to the extent that it is successful, is not the achievement of worldwide peace, but potential substitution of surrogate conflict for superpower conflict. Deterrence may prevent the nuclear powers from going to war against each other, but it does not preclude a major power from going to war against a nonnuclear power, for exam-

ple, the Soviet Union in Afghanistan or the United States in Grenada.
Nor does it preclude nations that are not members of the nuclear club
from going to war against each other, even if they have alliances with
one or the other nuclear power.[9]

Janowitz's formulation of the constabulary concept was derived
in part from a recognition of the limitations of the strategy of deterrence to the upper end of the intensity spectrum. The constabulary
concept complements, but is not equivalent to, deterrence. It refers
to operations, primarily at the lower end of the conflict-intensity
spectrum, that are aimed at maintaining peace or at resolving or containing conflict situations. Thus the question becomes not whether
deterrence undermines the fighting ethic and combat effectiveness of
soldiers, but whether low-intensity military operations, including
peacekeeping duty, do so. Since U.S. troops have deployed on low-
intensity military operations in the recent past, empirical data can
be brought to bear on this issue. Previous research has shown that
U.S. military personnel regard low-intensity warfare to be more
likely than high-intensity warfare during the next decade.[10] Our data
allow us to consider whether this has changed over time and, if so,
whether the change might be attributable, in part, to participation in
constabulary operations. We are also concerned with whether participation in low-intensity operations sensitizes soldiers to the fact that
combat intensity can be viewed as a continuum, rather than simply a
dichotomy of high versus low.

DATA

Our analysis draws quantitative data from an ongoing study of
U.S. soldiers assigned to the Multinational Force and Observers
(MFO) on peacekeeping duty in the Sinai in support of the Camp David
Accords. To date, personnel in five American infantry companies
have been surveyed at different points in time:

- Unit a, a company in the first U.S. battalion to go to the Sinai. Unit
  a was surveyed at three points in time: before the deployment, midway into the six-month deployment, and after its return.
- Units b and c, two additional companies that were surveyed as control groups at the same points in time as unit a. The results of these
  surveys are discussed by David Segal and his coauthors.[11]
- Unit d, a company from the third U.S. battalion to be rotated to the
  Sinai. Unit d was surveyed after returning to the United States.
- Unit e, a company assigned to the fifth American battalion to go to
  the Sinai. Predeployment data were collected from unit e at the
  same time that unit d was surveyed.

Unit d had participated in the October 1983 invasion of Grenada between the time of its return from the Sinai and the time it was surveyed. It thus had participated in two low-intensity operations within the year prior to being surveyed. Unit e was one of the few units in the Eighty-second Airborne Division that did not participate in the Grenada invasion. The surveys from these five units serve as our quantitative data base. We interpret these data in the context of scores of less structured interviews with soldiers conducted in the course of continuing field research on the army by members of our research team.

RESULTS

Expectations Regarding Conflict Scenarios

Figure 1 presents the percentage of soldiers in units a and b reporting each of a range of conflict scenarios to be very likely during the next decade. Unit a was surveyed prior to its deployment to the Sinai and after its return. Unit b underwent jungle warfare training during this period and was surveyed at the same time points. If con-

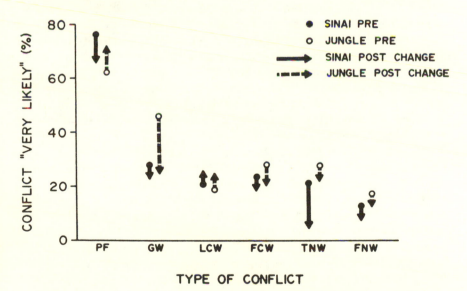

FIGURE 1   Change in Soldiers' Evaluations of the Likelihood of Combat Scenarios before and after the First Sinai Peacekeeping Deployment (PF = peacekeeping force; GW = guerrilla war; LCW = limited conventional war; FCW = full conventional war; TNW = tactical nuclear war; FNW = full nuclear war)

stabulary duty in particular were to contribute to complacency among
combat soldiers, we would expect estimates of the likelihood of high-
intensity combat to decrease among soldiers who had returned from
the Sinai. If this decrease were due specifically to the peacekeeping
experience, we would not expect to observe a similar pattern in the
unit that underwent jungle warfare training during the same period.

Prior to the Sinai deployment, soldiers in both units felt that low-
intensity operations (peacekeeping operations and guerrilla war) were
more likely than high-intensity conflict (tactical or strategic nuclear
war). In both units, there was a general tendency for estimates of the
likelihood of conflict to decrease, although toward the middle of the
continuum there was a slight increase in both units in the percentage
thinking that limited conventional war was very likely, and the unit
that had not gone to the Sinai increased its estimate of the likelihood
of peacekeeping operations. For all of the nonnuclear scenarios, the
postdeployment measurements were very similar for the two units.
For the two nuclear scenarios, however, the declines were much
more marked for the soldiers who had been in the Sinai, and the units
were proportionally further apart on these measures. Constabulary
duty thus may contribute to a decline in expectations of the likelihood
of high-intensity warfare. Note, however, that the general pattern is
one of anticipated declines across the range of combat-intensity scenarios, regardless of whether the unit had been on peacekeeping duty.

Figure 2 repeats the postdeployment estimates gathered from unit
a and compares them with postdeployment data gathered from unit d,
which deployed as part of the Sinai MFO and returned a year later.
Predeployment data were not gathered from this latter unit. These
data do include two additional scenarios—tactical use of chemical
weapons and tactical use of biological weapons—that were not included
in the earlier predeployment surveys.

It appeared from figure 1 that unit a assigned a high likelihood to
peacekeeping operations and low likelihood to nuclear conflict but did
not differentiate much among intermediate scenarios. This is more
obvious in figure 2, with the chemical and biological scenarios added,
both of which are placed in the intermediate range. A very different
pattern appears, however, with unit d, which reflects a much clearer
gradation of likelihood estimates between low-intensity conflict and
high-intensity war, with peacekeeping and strategic nuclear war defining the extremes.

A second set of indicators of conflict scenarios is derived from
a series of questions that asked our respondents about the importance,
to them, of invasions of the continental United States or of U.S. allies
in Western Europe, the Far East, the Middle East, or (in the most
recent data collection only) the Central America, South America, and
Caribbean area. They were asked to rate each scenario on an impor-

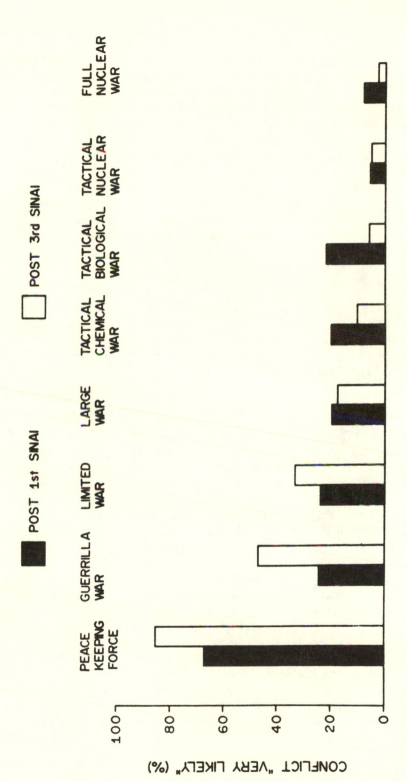

FIGURE 2 Percentage of Soldiers Reporting Each Conflict Situation as "Very Likely"

47

tance scale ranging from one (most important) to seven (least important). If being in a constabulary posture were to dull the sharp cutting
edge of our combat capability, we might expect the importance ratings
assigned to the continental U.S. and Western European scenarios to
decline over time or the Middle Eastern scenario to increase in importance. As table 1 shows, this was not the case with regard to
absolute importance ratings, although events clearly shaped relative
ratings.

TABLE 1   Mean Importance Rankings of Geographical Conflict
          Scenarios (by date of survey administration)

Date	CONUS	WESTEUR	MIDEAST	FAREAST	CARIB
March 1982	2.0	2.6	2.7	3.0	—
July 1982	2.0	2.4	2.8	2.9	—
January 1984	2.1	2.6	2.6	2.8	2.4

Source: Compiled by the authors.

Differences among units surveyed at the same point in time were
negligible. Therefore, we report only means for each survey administration. The March 1982 data were collected from units b and c midway
through the first Sinai deployment. The July 1982 data were collected
from these same units and from unit a after the latter returned from
the Sinai. The January 1984 data were collected from unit e and from
unit d after it had returned from the Sinai and from Grenada.
    At each of the three points in time, the continental United States
scenario was regarded as the most important and the Far Eastern
scenario the least important. Importance ratings did not differ significantly across time for either of these scenarios. Neither did the
absolute importance ratings differ significantly across time for the
Western European scenario, which had ranked as the second most
important in the first two survey administrations. In the third survey
administration, however, in the wake of the bombing of the headquarters of a marine amphibious unit on peacekeeping duty in Beirut
and following the invasion of Grenada, both the Caribbean and Middle
Eastern scenarios received higher relative importance rankings than
did the invasion of an ally in Western Europe. That is, events moved
these two scenarios up in their relative rankings but not at the cost
of decreasing the absolute importance ratings given to the European
scenarios.

The constant absolute importance assigned by combat soldiers in our survey to the NATO alliance is reflected in interviews with combat soldiers in Europe as well. In no other location are U.S. troops so well versed in what specific opposing units they will be facing in the event of a war, what the capabilities of those opposing units are, or what the responsibilities of their own units are. And while they are not anxious to go to war, they have no doubt of their ability to fulfill their responsibilities should the need arise. The deterrence posture has not dulled their combat ethic.

Evaluations of Military Operations

Another indicator of the potential effect of low-intensity operations on the combat orientation of soldiers is their evaluation of those operations. The literature on peacekeeping operations almost universally suggests that a major problem with such missions is boredom.[12] The postreturn study of the first U.S. infantrymen to serve in the Sinai MFO showed over 30 percent of them reporting it to be boring and over 40 percent suggesting that it was not an appropriate mission for their unit.[13] Observations of the troops while deployed showed the boredom contributing to "creeping Bedouin syndrome"—adaptation to the desert environment involving temporal disorientation and decreased energy and attention levels.[14] To the extent that such symptoms persist, they clearly may contribute to decreased combat effectiveness. Indeed, David Segal and Katharine Gravino have hypothesized that the low activity level of peacekeeping operations may have contributed to security lapses at the marine headquarters that were bombed in Beirut in October 1983.[15] When combat soldiers return from peacekeeping duty, however, they are returned to a regimen of realistic combat training. We feel that this return to preparation for the deterrence, as opposed to constabulary, function, quickly overcomes whatever residual lethargy remains from constabulary missions.

The questions about the excitement and appropriateness of the Sinai peacekeeping operation that had been asked of the first unit to serve there were asked as well of the third unit after its return. In addition, parallel questions were asked of the latter unit about Grenada. The Grenada operation was of higher intensity than the Sinai peacekeeping operation—there were opposing forces, fire was exchanged, and U.S. military personnel were killed and wounded. On the other hand, the Grenada operation lacked the intensity and magnitude of the Korean and Vietnam conflicts. If our respondents had substituted a constabulary ethic for the combat ethic, they would respond more favorably to the Sinai mission. If on the other hand, as we suggest, combat troops continue to view going to war as their primary job, then

even troops who have served constabulary duty will express a preference for Grenada-type operations.

Table 2 presents the attitudes regarding the level of excitement
and appropriateness of the Sinai mission expressed after return by
soldiers who participated in the first and third deployments—units a
and d—as well as responses regarding Grenada expressed by soldiers
from the latter unit, which had also served in Grenada. The third unit
to serve in the Sinai found it less boring than had the first. This is

TABLE 2   Evaluations of Sinai and Grenada Missions
           (in percent)

Mission Rated	Unit a	Unit d	
	Sinai Mission	Sinai Mission	Grenada Mission
Exciting	15.7	9.1	61.4
Interesting	43.1	73.9	38.6
Like garrison duty	9.8	4.5	0.0
Boring	31.4	12.5	0.0
Appropriate	54.9	48.3	98.9
Not appropriate	43.1	51.7	1.1

Source: Compiled by the authors.

perhaps because recreational facilities that had not been constructed
in time to serve the first unit were available a year later and because
troops on the third deployment were able to travel more widely in the
Middle East than soldiers in the first U.S. unit assigned to the Sinai
MFO had been. At the other extreme, the third unit also found the
Sinai assignment less exciting. The novelty of the mission had worn
off. However, 30 percent more of the soldiers in unit d than in unit a
found the Sinai peacekeeping mission interesting. On the other hand,
where a small majority of the first unit had reported that the Sinai
peacekeeping mission was appropriate for soldiers of the 82d Airborne Division, a small majority of the third unit reported that it was
not.

The most impressive differences in table 2 are between the evaluations of the Sinai and Grenada missions by the troops who had been
in both places. None of the soldiers found Grenada boring, and over
60 percent found it exciting, compared with fewer than 10 percent who
found the Sinai mission exciting. And almost all of the soldiers said
that the Grenada operation was appropriate for their unit. These data

demonstrate a preference for higher-intensity operations among soldiers who have participated in low-intensity operations. Participation
in a peacekeeping mission has apparently not diminished the action
orientation of these soldiers, at least in the short run.

SUMMARY

The establishment and maintenance of a large peacetime armed
force in being in a deterrence posture and the occasional assignment
of elements of that force to constabulary operations have raised questions about how the combat readiness of such a force can be maintained.
Since World War II, the force has been expected to be prepared for
high-intensity warfare on the European continent. Most soldiers today, however, believe that such a scenario is unlikely and assign
higher likelihood estimates to other combat theatres and to lower-
intensity engagements. At the same time, they recognize that the
lower-probability operations are potentially the most devastating.[16]

The lessons of history have borne out these expectations: we have
trained and prepared for another total war in Europe since the post-
World War II period. Our subsequent military engagements have been
elsewhere in the world than Europe and have been skewed toward the
lower end of the combat-intensity spectrum. Training for the deterrence function, however, has kept U.S. soldiers cognizant of their
role in high-intensity war. In addition, since the Vietnam War era,
national policy has called for a posture of more flexible military
response, and army doctrine and training have reflected this policy.

Recent low-intensity operations—participation in the Sinai MFO
and the 1983 invasion of Grenada—give us a basis for evaluating the
effect of participating in such operations on the combat orientations
of paratroopers. We do not argue that combat orientation is equivalent
to combat effectiveness, but rather that the former is a motivational
component of the latter, a necessary but not sufficient condition for
combat effectiveness.

During the period under study, we noted decreases in likelihood
estimates of most conflict scenarios, low- as well as high-intensity.
This was true of troops who had been on constabulary duty in the Sinai
as well as those who deployed for training. If there is a mission factor
operating here, it would seem to be the general posture of deterrence,
rather than assignment to a specific peacekeeping operation.

One effect that exposure to low-intensity operations does seem to
have is to sensitize soldiers to the gradation of combat intensity. When
the first U.S. troops to participate in the Sinai MFO returned to the
United States, they clearly differentiated the lowest-intensity operations (peacekeeping) from the highest-intensity (tactical and strategic

nuclear war). They reflected no differentiation in the broad intermediate range, from guerrilla warfare through conventional warfare to tactical chemical and biological warfare. Charles Moskos has noted this lack of discrimination as a general phenomenon.[17] By the middle of the second year of U.S. involvement in the Sinai MFO, however, soldiers were recognizing such distinctions.[18] Analysts have argued for the importance of maintaining the capability of a range of military responses short of the use of nuclear weapons in support of our posture in the international system.[19] Our data suggest that military doctrine and training in support of this objective is effective.

Participation in low-intensity operations did not appreciably alter the absolute importance ratings that soldiers assigned to the two highest-intensity military threats: invasion of the United States and invasion of a NATO ally. At the same time, events did increase the relative importance rankings of other scenarios, suggesting an increased level of political awareness among soldiers.

Perhaps most important for our considerations, soldiers who had served both in the Sinai and in Grenada—two low-intensity missions which nonetheless differed markedly in their level of intensity—showed a marked preference for the latter mission and a feeling that the higher-intensity mission (Grenada) was the more appropriate for their unit. At least for soldiers in elite combat units, the evidence from our research and from other studies of combat units should allay the fears of Janowitz, Alford, and Foster that participation in constabulary operations and a general deterrence posture might make it difficult to maintain a combat ethic and might lull soldiers into an attitude of complacency. In the aggregate, these data present a picture of soldiers in combat units who, even in an era of deterrence and constabulary operations, regard going to war if called upon as the job that they are to do and regard being prepared to do that job—as well as participating in low-intensity operations—as their peacetime mission.

NOTES

1. See Carl von Clausewitz, On War, ed. Anatol Rapoport (Baltimore: Penguin Books, 1968), 19-20.

2. See Morris Janowitz, Military Conflict (Beverly Hills, Calif.: Sage, 1975), 70-88; and Jacques Van Doorn, "The Decline of the Mass Army in the West," Armed Forces and Society 2 (1975): 147-57.

3. Morris Janowitz, The Professional Soldier (New York: Free Press, 1960), 418.

4. See Morris Janowitz, "Toward a Redefinition of Military Strategy in International Relations," World Politics 26 (1974): 499-500, and "Beyond Deterrence: Alternative Conceptual Dimensions," in The

Limits of Military Intervention, ed. Ellen P. Stern (Beverly Hills, Calif.: Sage, 1977), 384-85.

5. Jonathan Alford, "Deterrence and Disuse: Some Thoughts on the Problem of Maintaining Volunteer Forces," Armed Forces and Society 6 (Winter 1980): 247-56.

6. Gregory D. Foster, "The Effect of Deterrence on the Fighting Ethic," Armed Forces and Society 10 (Winter 1984): 276-92.

7. David Gottlieb, Babes in Arms (Beverly Hills, Calif.: Sage, 1980).

8. See Charles W. Brown and Charles C. Moskos, "The American Volunteer Soldier: Will He Fight?" Military Review 65 (1976): 8-17; William C. Cockerham and Lawrence C. Cohen, "Volunteering for Foreign Combat Missions," Pacific Sociological Review 24 (July 1981): 329-54; and David F. Burrelli and David R. Segal, "Definitions of Mission among Novice Marine Corps Officers," Journal of Political and Military Sociology 10 (Fall 1982): 299-306.

9. See David R. Segal and Katharine Swift Gravino, "Peacekeeping as a Military Mission," in The Hundred Percent Challenge, ed. Charles D. Smith (Cabin John: Seven Locks Press, 1985), 36-68.

10. See David R. Segal, "From Political to Industrial Citizenship," in The Political Education of Soldiers, ed. Morris Janowitz and Stephen D. Wesbrook (Beverly Hills, Calif.: Sage, 1983), 285-306.

11. David R. Segal, Jesse J. Harris, Joseph M. Rothberg, and David H. Marlowe, "Paratroopers as Peacekeepers," Armed Forces and Society 10 (Fall 1984): 487-506.

12. Charles C. Moskos, Peace Soldiers (Chicago: University of Chicago Press, 1976); and Segal and Gravino, "Peacekeeping as a Military Mission."

13. See Segal, Harris, Rothberg, and Marlowe, "Paratroopers as Peacekeepers."

14. Jesse J. Harris and David R. Segal, "Observations from the Sinai: the Boredom Factor," Armed Forces and Society 11 (Winter 1985): 235-48.

15. Segal and Gravino, "Peacekeeping as a Military Mission."

16. See James B. Motley, "A Perspective on Low-Intensity Conflict," Military Review 65 (January 1985): 2-11.

17. Charles C. Moskos, "The American Enlisted Man in the All-Volunteer Army," in Life in the Rank and File, ed. David R. Segal and H. Wallace Sinaiko (New York: Pergamon, 1986).

18. See Barbara Foley Meeker and David R. Segal, "The Effect of Low-Intensity Operations on Soldiers' Perceptions of Combat Intensity" (Paper prepared for the annual meeting of the American Sociological Association, New York, August 1986).

19. See Robert Jervis, The Illogic of American Nuclear Strategy (Ithaca, N.Y.: Cornell University Press, 1984).

Deterrence May Require Mixed Strategies

Dagobert L. Brito and Michael D. Intriligator

INTRODUCTION

In a recent paper, we developed a formal model of two countries acting as rational agents, countries in which conflict, war, and redistribution may all occur.[1] Each of the countries is concerned with economic rights to consumption in a two-period model in which force can be used to redistribute these rights. The first period of the model is one of a potential arms race in which countries choose between consumption and investment in arms. The second period of the model is one of a potential conflict as countries bargain and may use force or the threat of force to attempt to reallocate resources. We were able to show that there are both distributions of wealth and power that are stable and distributions of wealth and power for which conflict and war may occur. What surprised us was that in the case in which both countries have full information and the initial distribution is such that there are no transfers, there are no Nash equilibria (that is, equilibria in which no country can gain by changing its strategy unilaterally) in the space of pure strategies. Rather, equilibriums require mixed strategies, that is, probability mixtures over the pure strategies.[2] Thus, an arms race in which the goal is to deter the other side may be unstable. This was a different result from what we had obtained with other arms race models, although S. J. Brams and D. M. Kilgour, in their model of deterrence, have also found that the efficient solution can be obtained as an equilibrium if both parties adopt a mixed strategy.[3] This paper attempts to explain why mixed strategies may sometimes be necessary for deterrence and to develop the implications of this instability result for policy.

HISTORICAL BACKGROUND AND POLICY IMPLICATIONS

B. H. Liddell-Hart, in his history of World War II, argued that the doctrine of strategic bombing evolved simply to justify the existenc

of an independent Royal Air Force.[4] General Hugh Trenchard was a
leading advocate of the theory that airpower could be used "as a means
of direct attack on the enemy state with the object of depriving it of
the means or will to continue the war." In the United States General
Billy Mitchell was the primary advocate of this theory. Both felt that
airpower could be used to destroy the enemy's capacity to wage war.
Unfortunately, they were ahead of their time, and attempts to do so
in World War II were expensive and not very effective. In April 1941,
the theoretical error of drop was assumed to be 1,000 yards, but the
Butt report in 1941 stated that during raids on the Ruhr only one-tenth
of the bombs fell within five miles of their targets. In May 1942, 1,046
bombers were used to destroy 600 acres of the city of Cologne, but at
the cost of 40 bombers. In June 1942, 904 bombers attacked Bremen,
inflicting little damage and losing 5 percent of the bomber force. In
1943, 200,000 tons of bombs were dropped on Germany, yet German
production rose by 50 percent. It is not surprising, therefore, that in
the context of the times the goal of bombing evolved from destroying
the enemy's ability to fight to destroying the enemy's morale. The
result was Hamburg, Dresden, and Tokyo. The atomic bomb was a
logical extension of this theory of strategic bombing. It was an eco-
nomical and efficient means of destroying cities, industries, and the
enemy's will to fight. While it did not do anything that was not already
being done by both sides in the war, it also introduced a fundamental
discontinuity into the strategy space of the nuclear powers. It did so
both in the trival sense that there are no little nuclear weapons and
in the more fundamental sense that, given current limitations in command, control, communications, and intelligence, a small nuclear
war may not be feasible.

There were two developments, however, that have been largely
overlooked and that may lead to alternatives to nuclear weapons in the
future. The first was the effectiveness of the raids in 1944 against
German oil production. By September 1944, German fuel production
was reduced to 10,000 tons a month, while the Luftwaffe needed
160,000 tons a month to operate. Albert Speer, Hitler's minister of
armaments, was able to build fighter planes, but the Germans did not
have the fuel to fly them or to train pilots.[5] The second was the effectiveness of the V-1 and V-2 against British morale. Although the German rocket attacks on England did not cause as much actual damage
as the Blitz, the blow to British morale was devastating. The reason
was, we suggest, that while being attacked and being able to fight may
actually unite a people against an attacker, being attacked without
being able to respond is psychologically cataclysmic.

We would like to argue that recent technological developments
suggest that it is time to return to the ideas of Trenchard and Mitchell
in our use of nonnuclear warheads. We have in the past relied upon

nuclear warheads for deterrence, but since deterrence may require
mixed strategies, there can be fundamental discontinuities in their
use, implying instability. Fortunately, because of substantial improvements in accuracy we now have the technology to deliver nonnuclear warheads within a few hundred feet. It should be possible for
the United States and other major powers to develop in the near future
the capability of attacking and destroying the economic choke points
of a country, such as oil refineries, airports, waterworks, electrical
generation plants, military targets, and nuclear reactors with conventional explosives; doing so would eliminate the discontinuity of
mixed strategies and thus restore continuity to strategic warfare.

THE TWO-PERIOD MODEL

In our two-period model there are two countries in conflict for
the rights to a flow of a single homogeneous good.[6] For example, they
may be in contention for a territory that yields a fungible resource,
such as oil, or the right to a market that yields income. In the first
period, this good may be consumed or used to produce weapons, as
in the usual guns-versus-butter trade-off. This process is irreversible, so weapons cannot be converted back into goods during the second
period. In the second period, the distribution of the good can be altered
either by war or by negotiation. The outcome of war depends on the
amount of fighting engaged in by either country, and the amount of
fighting is in turn limited by the country's weapon stocks as determined by its choices during the first period. War produces an externality which is a public bad and which offsets the utility of consumption
in the second period. Countries are assumed to be rational and non-
altruistic, and they will choose to fight if the expected value of such
a strategy is greater than that of not fighting.[7] If they do not fight,
then they can negotiate a redistribution of resources in the second
period. Each country is informed as to all of the parameters of the
problem other than the degree to which the war externality enters into
the objective function of the other country. Thus, assuming utility is
separable and linear in the externality, it consists of the utility of
first-period consumption plus the utility of second-period consumption, but it is reduced by the disutility of the public bad that is produced by war, such as nuclear fallout or the loss of trade due to wartime disruption of commerce. The sensitivity of utility to the disutility
of war depends on a parameter that is known to the own country but is
not known to the other country.

The first period is one of a potential arms race, in which each
side decides on the amount it will consume (and thus add to utility) but
also the amount that it will use to buy arms (which could be used in the

second period). Each country faces a resource constraint stating that the total of consumption plus investment in weapons is fixed. Furthermore, total resources of the two sides are fixed, given the fact that they are in conflict over the rights to the flow of a single homogeneous good. Thus in the first period each country decides on the guns-versus-butter choice of consumption or acquisition of weapons.

The second period is one of a potential conflict, using the weapons both have chosen in the first period. There are, in fact, three possibilities for this period. First, both countries could choose to behave passively and preserve the status quo, that is, the initial rights to the good. Second, one country could propose a redistribution agreed to by the second country. Third, one or both countries could propose a redistribution not agreed to by the other side that could lead to conflict and possibly to the outbreak of war. In the conflict outcome, the externality that results from the war is given by the sum of the fighting pursued by both sides, as measured by the amount of weapons the countries commit to the war. This fighting results in a redistribution of the rights to the good, where committing more weapons shifts the distribution in favor of the country that commits more weapons to the fight. The amount of fighting either country is capable of is limited by its level of weapons, which was determined, in part, by the initial distribution of resources in the first period.

Thus, in the first period, each country chooses between goods and investment in weapons. This investment has two implications: first, it provides each of the countries with the ability to fight in the second period; and, second, it may reveal information to the other country about the sensitivity of its utility function to the disutility of war.

Each of the countries can choose one of two possible strategies for investing in weapons. First, it can adopt a war arms-investment strategy in which it invests in weapons as if it planned to engage in fighting in the second period. Second, it can adopt a deterrence arms-investment strategy in which it invests in a sufficient level of weapons so as to deter the other country from initiating a war in the second period.

THE FULLY INFORMED CASE

In the fully informed case each country maximizes utility in full knowledge of the sensitivity of the other side to the disutility of war. The result will be a pair of reaction functions that give the weapons purchased by each as a function of the weapons purchased by the other and that can be interpreted as the discrete time analogues of the Richardson equations of the arms race.[8] In this case the countries are both using a war arms-investment strategy, buying weapons in the first period for possible use in the second. The resource constraint is then always binding, implying that it is possible to solve for the reaction functions of both countries. These reaction functions show the weapons purchased by each country as functions of the weapons purchased by the other, and together they describe the dynamics of the arms race. In this fully informed case an equilibrium exists, and it depends on the initial economic resources of the countries involved. In fact, for any given initial allocation of the good there exists an equilibrium weapons allocation that is consistent with the reaction functions. Furthermore, because weapons acquisition is at the expense of consumption and because fighting causes a reduction in utility, there exists a set of initial allocations that are strictly preferred to the war allocation by both countries. Certain of these preferred initial allocations might, however, require an initial transfer of resources from one country to the other. If voluntary transfers are possible, then the war arms-investment strategy is not consistent with rationality in this certainty model. This is a major logical difficulty with the arms-investment strategy in the fully informed case.

An alternative to the war arms-investment strategy is the deterrence arms-investment strategy. Allowing for a voluntary transfer from one country to the other in the second period, the problem for the country adopting a deterrence arms-investment strategy and making the transfer is to maximize total utility of consumption over both periods, subject to the incentive constraint that the other country (which is employing a war arms-investment strategy) be no worse off after the transfer than the utility level it could have achieved by war.[9]

The solution to this problem represents the maximum consumption the country can achieve while guaranteeing that it would not be optimal for the other country to engage in war. The solution of this optimization defines a reaction function for one country that, together with that of the other country, defines the arms race for the case where the first country adopts a deterrence arms-investment strategy and the other country adopts a war arms-investment strategy. If there are voluntary transfers, then an implication of this pair of reaction functions is that an equilibrium level of weapons exists, and the allocation that results from the first country adopting a deterrence arms-investment strategy and the other adopting a war arms-investment strategy is a Nash equilibrium.

MIXED STRATEGIES

Consider now the fully informed case, as before, but one in which there are no voluntary transfers and both countries adopt a deterrence arms-investment strategy. In this case, remarkably, there is no equi-

librium in pure strategies. In this case the process of both countries
reducing weapons could lead to war. For example, if one side reduces
weapons because the other side is adopting a deterrence strategy, the
first side could do better by adopting a war arms-investment strategy.
The allocation that results if both countries adopt the deterrence arms-
investment strategy, while each assumes that the other is using a war
arms-investment strategy, is not a Nash equilibrium. At this point,
each country would prefer to reduce its level of weapons.[10] If both
countries were to adopt a deterrence arms-investment strategy, the
resulting allocation would be unstable, since if either country observed
that it was at such a point it would find it advantageous to switch to a
war arms-investment strategy. In fact, there is a Nash equilibrium
in the space of mixed strategies.

A graph of the reaction function can be used to illustrate why a
Nash equilibrium requires mixed strategies in this case of full information and no transfers between countries. The reaction functions in
this case are shown in figure 3. To motivate the figure the countries
are identified as U, the United States, and S, the Soviet Union. The
axes show the weapons held by each of the countries, so each point in
the figure represents a particular pair of weapons (w_U, w_S). The reaction functions for each of the countries consists of two parts, one
at low levels of weapons held by the opponent and the other at high
levels of weapons held by the opponent.[11] Consider, for example, the

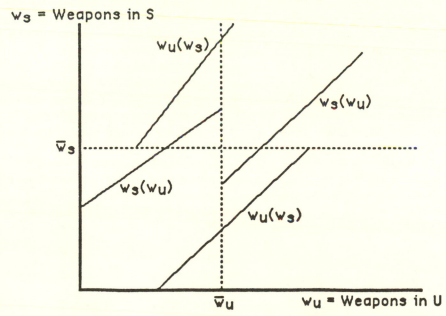

FIGURE 3   Reaction Functions in the Case of Full Information with No
            Voluntary Transfers (U = United States; S = Soviet Union)

U reaction function. At low levels of S weapons, in particular, for w_S less than $\overline{w}_S$ the war arms-investment strategy is best, as U can obtain the redistribution of resources in the second period from investing in weapons and fighting. At high levels of w_S, however, in particular above $\overline{w}_S$, the deterrence arms-investment strategy is best, as U can avoid a costly investment in weapons in the first period. Thus there is a switch at $\overline{w}_S$. The reaction function $w_U(w_S)$, rises with w_S, showing that U will buy more weapons than S does, using a war arms-investment strategy. At $\overline{w}_S$, however, the reaction function shifts to the upper segment $w_U(w_S)$, again increasing with w_S, but starting from a lower base, using a deterrence arms-investment strategy. Similarly $w_S(w_U)$, the reaction function for S, rises with w_U, but makes a discontinous jump down at the critical value $\overline{w}_U$ for which S switches from a war arms-investment strategy to a deterrence arms-investment strategy.

The discontinuity of each reaction function implies that to achieve an equilibrium it is necessary for both countries to use a mixed strategy. With appropriate probabilities assigned to the use of a war arms-investment strategy (consistent with the other side having low levels of weapons) and remaining probabilities assigned to the use of a deterrence arms-investment strategy (consistent with the other side having high levels of weapons), an equilibrium exists in figure 3. Without such mixed strategies there is no equilibrium. For example, if each side believes that the other has a high level of weapons, then each will adopt a deterrence arms-investment strategy. The result will be an endless upward spiral in armament—an arms race without end.[12]

There are two possible ways to avoid the instability implied by figure 3. One is to allow for voluntary transfers. This approach avoids the discontinuity in the reaction functions, but it is clearly politically unacceptable, involving one country voluntarily giving part of its endowment to the other side. The other way is to avoid the discontinuity by relying on weapons that do not have extreme effects on utility, in particular, on nonnuclear rather than nuclear weapons. With such weapons the war investment strategy is always optimal, leading to continuous reaction functions, an equilibrium in weapons levels, the avoidance of the use of mixed strategies, and the avoidance of an endless upward spiral in armaments, a never-ending arms race.

CONCLUSION

The theoretical two-period model of a potential arms race followed by a potential conflict yields a dilemma. The outcome is either a necessary transfer payment of resources from one country to the other or a

mixed strategies equilibrium, which implies, once weapons levels
are high enough, an endless arms race. Both of these outcomes are,
for different reasons, unacceptable. The former is unacceptable
politically, while the latter is unacceptable in terms of the economic
costs of the arms race. A way out may be through restricting weapons
to those that do not have extreme effects, in particular use of nonnuclear rather than nuclear weapons. This policy conclusion, which
stems from a theoretical analysis, is consistent with the implications
of a historical analysis of the use of nonnuclear strategic weapons in
World War II.

NOTES

1. See D. L. Brito and M. D. Intriligator, "Conflict, War, and
Redistribution," American Political Science Review 79 (1985): 943-57.
2. For a discussion of mixed strategies, see J. von Neumann and
O. Morgenstern, Theory of Games and Economic Behavior, 2d ed.
(Princeton, N.J.: Princeton University Press, 1947). To use mixed
strategies the players in a game each choose not a particular strategy
but a set of probabilities over the set of all possible strategies, leaving
to a chance device keyed with these probabilities the selection of a
particular strategy. Certain two-person zero-sum games that do not
have an equilibrium in pure strategies have such an equilibrium in
mixed strategies. Thus by allowing probability mixtures over the set
of strategies it is possible to have an equilibrium that otherwise doesn't
exist. On the concept of a Nash equilibrium, see J. F. Nash, "Equilibrium Points in N-Person Games," Proceedings of the National
Academy of Sciences, USA, 36: 48-49. 1950. For discussions of the
concepts of mixed strategy and Nash equilibrium see M. D. Intriligator,
Mathematical Optimization and Economic Theory (Englewood Cliffs,
N.J.: Prentice Hall, 1971).
3. See S. J. Brams and D. M. Kilgour, "Optimal Deterrence,"
Social Philosophy and Policy 3 (1985): 118-35.
4. See B. H. Liddell-Hart, History of the Second World War (New
York: Putnam, 1970).
5. See A. Speer, Inside the Reich (New York: Macmillan, 1970).
6. See Brito and Intriligator, "Conflict, War, and Redistribution."
7. See B. Bueno de Mesquita, The War Trap, 2nd ed. (New Haven,
Conn.: Yale University Press, 1971).
8. See L. F. Richardson, Arms and Insecurity (Pittsburgh: Boxwood Press, 1960); and M. D. Intriligator, "Strategic Considerations
in the Richardson Model of Arms Races," Journal of Political Economy
83 (1975): 339-53.
9. The incentive constraint here is similar to the "self-selection

constraint" in the optimal tax literature. See J. Mirrlees, "An Exploration in the Theory of Optimal Income Taxation," Review of Economic Studies 38 (1971): 175–208.

10. The allocation is not a Nash equilibrium, but it is a saddle point for this non-zero-sum game.

11. The discontinuous nature of each reaction function can be understood in terms of the utility of one country, say U, as a function of the weapons held by the other, w_S. The utility function decreases with w_S and it depends on whether U adopts a war arms-investment strategy or a deterrence arms-investment strategy. For low levels of w_S the former will dominate, while for high levels of w_S the latter will dominate. The switch point w_S is where the utility curves intersect: for w_S below $\bar{w}_S$ the war arms-investment strategy dominates, while for w_S above $\bar{w}_S$ the deterrence arms-investment strategy dominates, yielding the reaction curve $w_U(w_S)$ in figure 3. The discontinuity depends fundamentally on the absence of voluntary transfers as, in the case of such transfers, the war arms-investment strategy always dominates where the amount of the transfer depends on its investment in weapons.

12. To show this, start from, say, a w_S well above $\bar{w}_S$. The reaction of U is shown on $w_U(w_S)$, and the process continues. This process will lead to continued growth in weapons acquisitions, up to the resource constraint. For a related model generating a similar upward movement in weapons on both sides see M. D. Intriligator and D. L. Brito, "Heuristic Decision Rules, the Dynamics of the Arms Race, and War Initiation," in Dynamic Models of International Conflict (Boulder, Colo.: Lynne Reiner, 1985).

Part II
Unhinging Deterrence: Imminent Risks and Challenges to Stability

Trends toward Crisis Instability: Increasing the Danger of Nuclear War

Charles F. Hermann

INTRODUCTION

The mind resists accepting nuclear war as remotely possible in any way except as the product of a monstrous accident or a demented leadership. Under what imaginable conditions might thoughtful policy makers in the United States or the Soviet Union reason that they have no real choice but to order the use of their strategic arsenal against the other side? Leaders in each country have stated repeatedly that both sides would experience enormous, unacceptable destruction in such an event. Time and again they have said no objective of national policy could be realized through nuclear war.

Yet we must not dismiss the possibility that under some circumstances—perhaps most likely in a crisis in Europe or the Third World in which either the Soviet Union or the United States believes the other has violated its vital interests—the fear arises that this time the problem will not be resolved without war. Then the policy makers must ask themselves, if major war is inevitable, would we be vastly better off by being the first to use strategic nuclear weapons rather than by allowing our enemy to do so? Suppose their conclusion is yes, that the side that strikes first could have a decided advantage and that its people just possibly might suffer significantly less.

Thoughtful policy makers could be expected to reject that conclusion initially. (What does it mean to "suffer less" in a nuclear war?

An earlier version of this chapter was presented at the Thirteenth International Political Science Association meeting in Paris, France, July 15-20, 1985. The author wishes to express appreciation to the following individuals for their comments on the earlier draft: Lt. Col. Ronald E. Blum (USAF), Dr. A. J. R. Groom, Dr. Margaret Karns, Dr. John Sigler, and Dr. David Sorenson.

65

What if the assumptions of an advantage in going first are mistaken? Suppose the parties can yet get out of the situation honorably without war?) If the crisis intensifies, any hope of avoiding war may sharply decline. Under such circumstances, high-level policy makers may find themselves reasoning as follows: Surely the other side has made the same calculations about the possible advantages of a first strike. Our trusted advisers report that our intelligence warns of preparations on the other side enabling them to launch a massive nuclear attack very quickly. The advisers repeat that all the calculations indicate a definite advantage to the side first using nuclear weapons against key targets. They urge that the enemy not be given this chance. The decision must be made at once.

Policy makers in such a situation have become immersed in the ultimate crisis of the nuclear era. International politico-military crises involving the United States or its allies confronting the Soviet Union or its allies have been a recurring characteristic of the forty some years since World War II. Perhaps, as Kenneth Waltz has suggested, such crises result partially from the bipolar structure of the international system.[1] Although in some respects, such as in economic relations, the world today is more pluralistic, the military alignment in international politics substantially continues the bipolarity that Waltz speculated might result in more crises and fewer wars among the major powers than a balance-of-power configuration. Nuclear weapons or the nature of the antagonists may also contribute to the caution that has resulted in frequent crises, but relatively fewer overt hostilities, between the superpowers. For whatever reason, crises, not superpower wars, have characterized Soviet-U.S. competition.

Embedded in every superpower confrontation exists the possibility that somehow things might escalate or get out of control, thereby resulting in the ultimate crisis. The conventional wisdom, at least among most Western analysts, is that the likelihood of policy makers either in the United States or in the Soviet Union actually using nuclear weapons is exceedingly remote. Many observers believe that the use of nuclear weapons is more likely to result from their proliferation to other countries or their acquisition by terrorist groups. Such subjective estimates often cite the cautious and conservative decision making about nuclear weapons among the leaders in both Washington and Moscow and their accumulated experience in both crisis and weapons management. Nevertheless there is reason for concern about crisis stability as it affects the use of nuclear weapons by the Soviet Union and the United States.

Crisis stability can be understood as a special subset of the more general phenomena of deterrence stability.[2] When both sides know that each has a sufficient second-strike capability to threaten unacceptable damage to the other, even after suffering the most potent attack of which the adversary is capable, then deterrence stability exists. Essentially, assurance of sufficient second-strike capability means that under prevailing conditions no adversary can hope to realize any objective through resort to nuclear war.

Crisis stability refers to the ability of a deterrent force to preserve its necessary requirements for effective retaliation under the adverse conditions that frequently arise in an international political crisis. In crises, more frequently than in normal situations, circumstances can arise that disrupt such essential features as the valid assessment of the current situation, force survivability, and decision controllability. Fear of the disruption or loss of such features may increase the perceived advantages of a preemptive strike. Any aspect of a crisis that increases the temptation to use nuclear weapons, beyond that existing in a normal deterrent condition, contributes to crisis instability.

It should be apparent that crisis stability concerns the relationship between weapons, strategy, and the policy makers who must decide on their use and who must activate the weapons and associated personnel according to a plan. Crises normally do not alter strategic weapons systems directly. They can, however, affect the conditions under which political and military leaders assess those systems, their performance, and the plans for their use. In short, crisis stability primarily concerns momentary situational changes that affect the calculations of the human component of deterrence stability.

Although the debate over exactly what constitutes an international crisis continues, sufficient consensus exists to identify a class of international activities as crises. From the point of view of the policy makers in a country, we can say that an international politico-military crisis exists when they perceive a severe threat to the basic values of the political system from sources at least partially outside their polity; when they believe there is relatively short time before the situation, if unaltered, will evolve in a way unfavorable to them; and when they have an increased expectation of military hostilities or a sharp escalation if some hostilities already exist.[3]

For some time, analysts have discussed whether crises typically reduce the quality of decision making and, therefore, necessarily reduce deterrence stability.[4] Although no one can offer a definitive response to this issue, a strong argument can be made that as a class of situations, crises can simultaneously generate both positive and negative features with respect to decision making quality. On the one hand, crises can focus and hold the attention of authoritative policy makers who otherwise cannot afford to concentrate on a single issue for long; they can establish circumstances under which stultifying

bureaucratic procedures are overcome and domestic obstacles eliminated so that resources can more readily be mobilized; and some individuals—particularly in the early stages—may find their energy increased and their imagination stimulated by the challenge. On the
other hand, crises may trigger disruptive psychological and physiological stress in individuals. They may produce such unfamiliar conditions and increases in uncertainty about information and the actions
of others that a severe imbalance arises between the actors' capabilities and the requirements for coping with the problem, with a resulting
substantial increase in perceived task complexity; at times secrecy
and the need for swift action may shunt off from policy makers available sources of information or analysis. Pressures of group dynamics,
distorted by an "us-them" orientation, may cause policy makers to
miss or forgo careful examination of dissenting perspectives, double
checks on information and analysis reliability, or complicated and
time-consuming analyses and proposals. In sum, whether the overall
effects of crises are positive or negative may depend on a number of
factors, such as the personal qualities of the individuals involved,
how they are organized, and the resources available to them.

But to say that the decision-making effects of crises as a general
class are ambiguous or conditional must not permit us to overlook the
possibility that with respect to strategic deterrence the context for
decision making in crises may be changing. In fact, it is precisely
that point that is the thesis of this chapter: the superpowers continue
to engage in a variety of activities that reduce crisis stability. This
changing context makes it increasingly more difficult to maintain deterrence stability in future crises and thus increases the likelihood
of war.

CONDITIONS FOR CRISIS STABILITY

Earlier we alluded to three conditions for maintaining deterrence
stability in a crisis—valid assessment, force survivability, and decision controllability. The first of these conditions, valid assessment,
concerns the ability of those who operate the deterrence system to
determine accurately whether or not the defended polity and its forces
are under attack or face momentary attack—and if so from what source.
Accidental nuclear war haunts policy makers in the nuclear age. Failure of warning systems or incorrect attribution of nuclear detonations
to a particular adversary could lead to the incalculable tragedy of
launching strategic forces when no appropriate provocation occurred.
Equally critical for the maintenance of a credible deterrence is the
necessity that a warning system will promptly identify any true assault.
For crisis stability the question must be posed: Have the superpowers

introduced features that make it less likely in a crisis that policy makers will retain confidence in their ability to obtain valid assessment?

Force survivability entails the well-understood requirement of any second-strike capability to be able to withstand an adversary's initial attack undertaken in circumstances most favorable to the aggressor. A sufficient portion of the deterrent force must be expected by both sides to have a high probability of surviving and then to be capable of inflicting a retaliatory strike or strikes producing on the aggressor unacceptable damage—at whatever that level of damage is understood to be. The general question to be asked is whether changes have been introduced such that in a crisis the policy makers have reduced confidence in the survivability of a significant portion of their strategic systems.

It is tempting to characterize the requirements of controllability in terms of the frequently used concept of command and control (about which more will be said later). Certainly command and control constitute a significant part of what must be examined, but there is more. Control must entail the human process of decision making—of engaging in analytical choice processes—that produces the commands and results in the exercise of control. The growing attention to command and control introduces numerous critical issues about the physical properties and operation of strategic systems.[5] These concerns must be complemented, however, by attention to the environment for human decision making under which command and control is to be exercised. Some may regard it as absurd to consider the quality of the decision-making environment in which policy makers engage in decisions about the use of strategic weapons. Yet no one would willingly want to create conditions that compounded the difficulty of engaging in decision making about nuclear weapons use. But have we done so? In a future crisis would policy makers have time to check the accuracy of information, to obtain multiple assessments of its meaning, to review options or invent new ones? Would they face indescribable pressure for action or delegation of authority? Would the intended organizational procedures compound their concerns about their future abilities for exercising control?

To answer these questions we must review recent and emerging developments and practices—many of them quite familiar—that affect the context in which any future crisis involving the Soviet Union and the United States would occur. At least four areas require review. They are changes in the characteristics of strategic weapons, changes in the strategic alerts, changes in command and control of nuclear weapons, and changes in strategic plans. Clearly there are connections between these developments, but with respect to crisis stability, each can be viewed as producing some separate effects.

WEAPONS SYSTEMS CHARACTERISTICS

It is hardly a new idea to suggest that characteristics of weapons systems have an impact on the process by which policy makers decide on their use or nonuse. Thus, the shift from liquid fuel rockets, which may take hours to prepare, to solid fuel rockets, which are ready for almost immediate launch, may force a different set of decision requirements on policy makers. Both the superpowers have engaged in a more or less continuous upgrading and modernization of their strategic forces. The changes in the inventory of strategic weapons of greatest salience to crisis stability might reasonably be said to have begun with the U. S. deployment in the early 1970s of Multiple Independently Targetable Reentry Vehicles (MIRVs), which are now deployed by both sides in sufficient numbers and are combined with substantial improvements in warhead accuracy to pose a threat to the survivability of fixed-base intercontinental ballistic missiles (ICBMs). The resulting hard-target kill capability, or ability to destroy with substantial probability hardened missile silos, has put a major portion of each side's strategic force at risk from the other side's possible first strike. This problem has been widely discussed and can be presumed to be well understood by responsible authorities on both sides. In fact, the most troubling consequences for crisis decision making of the assumed increased risk to ICBMs as well as bomber bases may be the steps taken in both countries to remedy the difficulty. (This will be discussed below.)

Even without these second-order effects, MIRVed accurate systems such as the Minuteman IIIs, MX, SS-18s, and SS-19s will produce a pressure, greater than in early post-World War II crises, for preemptive attack if the likelihood of nuclear war seems pronounced. Because both sides have ICBMs at risk, each will be attempting to calculate whether the other side may be planning to preempt. As a result, there will be an increased tendency to interpret any ambiguous military activities as indications of preemption, which in turn could trigger decisions to use one's own weapons before they are destroyed.

Both sides have become highly dependent upon a variety of satellite systems for command, control, communications, and intelligence (C^3I) for their strategic systems. Among other purposes, satellites provide warnings of immediate preparations for the use of large numbers of strategic weapons and the earliest indications of actual rocket launches (initially from the detection of the substantial infrared radiation emitted during a missile's boost phase). Satellites also are critical for navigation of the strategic forces. The Soviet Union has led the way in the development of antisatellite (ASAT) rockets designed to destroy satellites in space. Just as the Soviet Union followed the United States in MIRV development, so the United States has followed the Soviet Union's initiative in the pursuit of an ASAT system.

Antisatellite capability on both sides appears unperfected at present. Even if improved, the present generation of such weapons would appear to threaten only low-orbit satellites or those in highly elliptical orbits, called Molniya orbits. Most U.S. strategic satellites are stationed in very high orbit, although the Soviet Union is reported to have its early warning satellites in highly elliptical orbits. Both countries, however, maintain numerous low-orbit military satellites of great importance for intelligence purposes, and these systems could be vulnerable in the near future. According to Richard Garwin and his coauthors: "The ability to destroy low-orbit military satellites, coupled with the fear that the opponent may at any moment attack one's own satellites, could therefore create an irresistible temptation to remove the opponent's satellites. As a consequence the ability to destroy low-orbit satellites promptly could inflame a political crisis or minor conflict that might otherwise have been resolved by diplomacy if there were no antisatellite weapons."[6] More vulnerable to immediate disruption—particularly in the West—are the small number of down-link receiving stations for key satellites and the lines by which their signals are relayed to policy makers. Sabotage, rather than high-technology ASAT, pose an increasingly recognized risk.

Clearly, the destruction of satellites at any time, and particularly during a crisis, would be regarded as a violation of existing treaties and an act of extreme provocation. Even without actual attacks, the knowledge of the existence of antisatellite weapons on both sides will compound tensions in a future crisis. The launch by the other side of new intelligence satellites during a crisis—a common practice—could be construed as masking the orbiting of antisatellite capability. Should one side experience the malfunction of one or more satellites during a crisis, its leaders might conclude that they have been victims of deliberate interference with their necessary capability for valid assessment of the current situation. The existence of a substantial antisatellite capability would be perceived as reducing stability in a crisis regardless of whether such weapons were used. Like land-based ICBMs in silos, satellites have become vulnerable, particularly those in low earth orbit. At the moment this particular destabilizing feature may be a greater threat to the Soviet Union than to the United States, although both face the problem.[7]

Optimally the momentous decision about the use of nuclear weapons should be taken under circumstances that promote thoughtful reflection and analysis. The magnitude of the consequences certainly separate this potential decision from all others. Yet both the United States and the Soviet Union push the development and deployment of weapons systems that continuously erode the available decision time. Current ICBMs take 25 to 30 minutes to reach most targets in the other country from their present sites. The time for dealing with the ultimate crisis—whether and how to respond to information that such an attack is in progress—would, under the best of circumstances, be several minutes less, assuming the first evidence comes moments after the actual launch of such weapons. Both sides have available missile systems that reduce warning time to well under ten minutes by the use of submarine-launched ballistic missiles (SLBMs) that traverse much shorter distances from their location in offshore subs. Pershing IIs and, for European members of NATO, the SS-20s pose the equivalent decision-time-reducing systems.

The ultimate decision-time-reducer will be weapons designed to attack ICBMs or SLBMs in their boost phase. For the present generation of ICBMs, the boost phase begins when the main rocket engines start firing just before lift-off and ends when the final stage rocket engines shut off—an elasped time of three to five minutes. Both sides are currently working on systems designed to attack missiles in their boost phase. To destroy missiles (perhaps up to 1400 in a full-scale attack) in the boost phase, the defensive systems must identify rocket launches, track their flight paths, launch interceptor beams or projectiles, and assess what damage was done for possible second efforts— all within five minutes. Clearly no human decision making can be introduced into such a highly restricted time frame. In such circumstances, computers must determine whether a missile launch is only a test, a manned space mission, or a defective sensor. Its malfunction could not only precipitate a crisis but could also plunge opponents in an existing crisis into vastly greater escalation. Severe consequences could flow from the perception by policy makers that the other side intends to relinquish to an automated system control over the initiation of strategic defense—possibly involving the detonation of nuclear devices. If the adversary believed the system would work and believed during a crisis that war seemed increasingly inevitable, he would know that his first strategic move would have to be massively overwhelming. Furthermore, both sides would regard any evidence during a crisis of the defense system's malfunction as a period of acute opportunity or vulnerability.

In summary, the characteristics of recent and planned weapons systems adversely affect all three of the factors that are conditions for deterrence stability in a crisis—valid assessment, system survivability, and decision controllability. Both the United States and the Soviet Union have introduced weapons with these adverse implications. Although there are some discernible direct effects on crisis stability from these new weapons systems, the most significant consequences are the second- and third-order effects. To deal with these weapons, policy makers take other steps or form new mental images that, in turn, seriously reduce stability in a future crisis. It is important to recognize that every new strategic weapons system does not necessarily erode crisis stability. A mobile, single warhead missile or strategic bomber, for example, would not appear to have such grave effects as those systems described above.

STRATEGIC ALERTS IN AN ERA
OF ESSENTIAL EQUIVALENCE

On three occasions since 1960, the United States has put its global military forces on an increased alert status during a crisis with the Soviet Union. These include the collapse of the summit conference in May 1960, the Cuban Missile crisis in October and November 1962, and the final days of the Middle East War in October 1973.[8] Not much comparable information appears to be publicly available regarding the Soviet Union. To date, however, it does seem that the United States and the USSR have not put their worldwide strategic forces on a high state of alert at the same time. The question is whether conditions now exist so that in a future crisis, simultaneous strategic alerts might be more likely. The basic military purpose of an increase in strategic-alert status is to heighten the preparedness for war by taking steps to reduce the time between a subsequent order to use force and the actual initiation of coordinated military action. At least, the United States has demonstrated its willingness to use a heightened alert status as a means of signaling to the other side quickly and dramatically its resolve to protect threatened vital interests. Clearly that was the intent of the U.S. alert during the Yom Kippur War: to signal rapidly that the United States would regard the introduction of Soviet troops into Egypt as contrary to U.S. vital interests.[9]

Whether the Soviet Union's leadership will elect to follow the U.S. precedent and use an increase in strategic-alert status as a means of signaling in a future crisis is unknowable, but the mutual preception of the increased size and relative capabilities of Soviet strategic forces, as compared with their size and capabilities in 1973, might invite such action. At a minimum, Soviet leaders may feel they can no longer allow the Americans to engage in such actions without a comparable response to curb bluffs and to communicate that they are equally prepared to defend their vital interests.

Beyond the use of strategic alerts as a signaling device, there is another reason for expecting mutual high strategic alerts in future crises. If both sides perceive the growing vulnerability of a significant portion of their strategic systems to the other's preemptive attack, then prudence compels one to move such forces to a higher state of preparedness when the likelihood of a major war seems to have suddenly increased.

If heightened strategic-alert status in some superpower crises

are expected, and perhaps necessary, that does not alter their implications for crisis stability, particularly if the escalated levels of
strategic readiness are mutual. It is reasonable to assume that higher
alert levels involve some weakening of centralized control over nuclear
forces. The unavoidable dilemma between negative controls ("don't
launch without confirmed authorization") and positive controls ("be certain to launch when orders are given") must inevitably shift in favor
of positive controls under high-alert conditions. How might the shift
in balance toward positive control happen in a crisis? After all, simply putting more bombers at the ends of runways or on airborne alert
or sending more missile-carrying submarines to station at sea does
not necessarily reduce the negative checks against launching an attack.
The shift occurs in several ways. In an acute crisis the U.S. president
(and perhaps his Soviet counterpart) could be expected to delegate
authority to initiate use of nuclear weapons down the chain of command. This would be a necessary precaution against a possible enemy
attempt to immobilize the strategic system by instantly killing the
president, the secretary of defense, the chairman of the joint chiefs,
and those in the constitutional chain of command with a very small
number of nuclear weapons. In contrast to the normal peacetime disposition of managers of the strategic system to disbelieve and check
repeatedly any information indicating an incoming attack, in a crisis
such messages would be more credible. Because the nuclear use
authority would be dispersed, more individuals would be in a position
to make separate and independent judgments that this time the message
is real. The problem would be most sensitive with submarines placed
on a higher alert status, as submarines have no physical constraint
on launching nuclear weapons outside the boats' crews themselves and
outside communication while making maximum effort to avoid detection
is difficult. Finally, each side's alert preparations would almost certainly be quickly detected by the other side. (Quick detection by the
Soviets is precisely why the United States went to a higher level of
strategic alert in 1973 to signal its resolve.) The temptation to respond to the other side's alert with a still higher state of one's own
would feed not only the physical changes in the two systems but the
psychological state of the respective, enlarged group of policy makers,
each with a finger on the nuclear trigger.[10]

   At higher alert levels in a crisis a greater danger arises that
action will occur—either unauthorized action or actions with unanticipated effects—that will be misconstrued by the other side as moving
beyond preparation to a commitment to attack. In the Cuban missile
crisis, many such actions occurred. With mutual high alerts, the
number and reduced tolerance of such events could be extremely
troubling. Finally, simultaneous high levels of alert may complicate
the task of orchestrating de-escalations back to lower alert conditions

when such action by one side would appear to give the other decided advantages. In sum, mutual high alert status in a crisis affects decision controllability and, ironically, system vulnerability (which is what increased alert is designed to reduce).[11]

COMMAND AND CONTROL OF NUCLEAR WEAPONS

The command and control of nuclear weapons, or C^3I, have become the subject of increased attention in recent years for both policy makers and analysts. Among those who have addressed the issue, few have been more unequivocal about the danger to crisis stability of the highly vulnerable strategic command and control systems than Bruce Blair. He contends that while a great deal of discussion has been addressed to the increased vulnerability of land-based ballistic missiles, their current vulnerability is quite limited when compared with that of the command and control of nuclear forces:

> Crisis instability is more likely to stem from command
> system vulnerability. The condition of the U.S. command
> structure creates a potentially severe penalty for delay in
> releasing weapons and thus encourages early release by U.S.
> authorities. By the same token the creaky state of our command
> system offers Soviet leaders potentially great rewards
> for prompt action; the situation discourages indecision and
> late release by Soviet authorities. Command vulnerability
> not force vulnerability, then, is the main potential source
> of crisis instability.[12]

With respect to crisis stability, two command and control issues seem paramount:

- Elements of command and control remain one of the most vulnerable elements of the strategic system susceptible to a first strike.
- Highly centralized control of nuclear weapons by the highest national authority poses an exceptionally vulnerable target.

Command and Control Vulnerability

The general vulnerability of command and control results from numerous factors, ranging from the "softness" of many elements of the system (for example, satellite receiver stations, radars, and telephone lines) to the uncertain effects of nuclear detonations on the performance of electronic equipment and certain radio frequencies (for

example, the ability of the electromagnetic pulse, or EMP, from a
high-altitude nuclear explosion to create harmful voltage surges over
a wide area), and from the increased operational requirements as a
result of adopting more complicated strategic plans to increased complexity resulting from the tighter integration of more components.

John Steinbruner relates results of a computer simulation performed by two colleagues on the hypothetical communication network
for a squadron of fifty Minuteman II missiles and the implications when
various links in the system are destroyed.[13] Despite the redundancy
of communications built into the system, the simulation reveals substantial failures of both positive and negative controls, even under
moderate damage when initial orders are changed. Of course, the
model concerns only a small part of the system as it might perform
under a limited set of hypothetical conditions. It suggests, however,
the difficulty of sustaining control after some elements of the command and control system have been damaged and the potential problem of modifying plans after an attack.

As with so many of the consequences for crisis stability, the main
effects appear to flow from the policy makers' awareness of the vulnerability and their efforts to cope with it. Because each side knows
that key elements of the other side's command and control system can
readily be disrupted by a modest force and that such an attack could
offer a chance of prohibiting a substantial, effective counterattack,
there is a temptation to consider a preemptive strike. This is particularly so knowing that one's own side might be made similarly inoperative by an equivalent assault. If war seems likely (which is what a
crisis is about), the command and control system may become a factor, not for controlling the situation and promoting a resolution of the
crisis, but a pressure for a preemptive nuclear attack.

> If war should ever appear unavoidable, military commanders
> on both sides charged with executing their assigned missions
> would inevitably seek authority to initiate an attack, what-
> ever prior national security policy may have been. They
> would do so with a forcefulness that would depend directly
> on the intensity of the crisis. The pressures on political
> leaders at that point would be severe. Although there is no
> reason to doubt their continued desire to avoid war, there
> are strong reasons to doubt their ability to contain their
> respective strategic organizations.[14]

National Authority Vulnerability

Control of nuclear weapons by the highest national authorities has
been a widely accepted principle since the beginning of the nuclear age.

With the proliferation of strategic systems in geographically diverse locations, the problem of maintaining control has become more complex. In characterizing the evolution of the American system, Paul Bracken uses the analogy of a rifle trigger and safety catch combination in which the trigger is inoperative so long as the safety catch is on. "The primary command centers were to serve as triggers, but their ability to fire would be refrained by the viable functioning, and the survival, of the presidential command center. If the safety catch of the system were destroyed, direct operational control would devolve to the primary command centers."[15] Obviously, many steps have been taken to insure the accessibility of the president (or his successor) to the primary command centers; the constant proximity of the military aide with the authorizing codes and the standby maintenance of the National Emergency Airborne Command Post are examples of such precautions.

As with other parts of the command and control system, the centralized control—both the safety catch and the primary triggers—represent a fairly small number of targets. The Soviet Yankee class submarines off the Atlantic coast of the United States, the American Pershing II missiles in Europe, and nearby American Poseidon and Trident submarines all have missiles with flight times of under twelve minutes capable of destroying the high command centers. The time from the moment of detection of their launch to impact on their targets could in many circumstances be insufficient to remove the designated authorities to safety. In fact, the key subordinate commands also could be subject to similar prompt attacks, creating the specter of a society abruptly deprived of its top political and military leadership from a decapitation strike. (The evolution of such a possible strategy as a threat to crisis stability is discussed below.)

Once again the crisis stability problem is created by the increasing danger of the steps taken to cope with the command and control susceptibility to attack and the resulting perceptions. Bracken describes the U.S. system designed to meet this problem as one of "cascading authority," whereby through a practice of predelegated authority, the ability to authorize an attack is passed to consecutive lower levels of military command before an attack. Assuming higher levels of authority are lost, then by prearrangement these officers decide on the use of the weapons under their command. It is the knowledge that the higher authority may disappear suddenly that poses the direct danger of predelegated command to crisis stability.

The reason that the Soviet Yankee submarines off the Atlantic coast or the Pershing 2 missiles in Europe are such intrinsically dangerous weapons is not the physical damage that they can do to the White House or the Kremlin. Rather,

it is that each of these weapons injects ambiguity into the
enemy command. The existence, not the use, of these
weapons compels commanders to anticipate that their political high commands are not likely to survive more than
five minutes in a nuclear war. . . . In a war, or even in
an intense alert, the command will then see the smallest
disruption or unusual action in this context.[16]

Once authority over the use of nuclear weapons has been predelegated in a crisis, how does one continuously and confidently insure
designated commanders that higher authorities are still safe and re-
taining authority? After the crisis is over, how is authority firmly
recovered? These are the kinds of problems posed for crisis stability
by eroding decision control.

STRATEGIC PLANS

Not only the weapons, the means for their control, and the occasions on which readiness is suddenly accelerated, but also the pre-
arranged plans for their use can affect crisis stability. Indeed, actual
changes or perceived changes in these other factors often motivate
changes in strategic war plans. The two current proposals with powerful implications for crisis stability appear to stem from analyses of
changing characteristics in weapons and the increasingly recognized
problems of command and control vulnerability. The two proposed
plans are launch under attack and a preemptive decapitation strategy.

Launch under Attack

Launch under attack represents a possible response to the perceived growing vulnerability of land-based, fixed-site intercontinental
ballistic missiles (ICBMs), whose protection through hardening appears to some to be overwhelmed by sufficient numbers of accurate,
MIRVed warheads possessed by the other superpower. Such a strategy
also offers greater assurance that retaliation can be implemented with
an intact command and control system and thus represents a better
chance for a coordinated and effective counterstrike. In addition, it
recognizes that at the beginning of a nuclear exchange an opponent
would act to disperse and otherwise protect moveable strategic systems such as bombers and submarines that were at their bases. These
are time-urgent targets that one has the best chance of destroying by
attacking quickly before they are moved. (An aggressor might be reluctant to move all these assets prior to his initial attack because it
could reveal his intention.)[17]

One would hope to acquire some advanced (or strategic) warning of an adversary's intention to use a substantial number of strategic weapons prior to their actual launch. Preparations necessary for a large-scale initiative should be evident from various monitoring systems, although efforts to mask such activity can be assumed. We have already seen that moving to a high-alert status in a crisis may be compelling as a precautionary step against being the victim of a surprise attack. Such mobilization could mask intentions to actually initiate a strike.

Thus, in a crisis, the possibility of strategic warning is uncertain, and such warning almost certainly would be ambiguous. It is only after information processing centers had interpreted signals from intelligence sensors of an attack under way that a tactical warning could be flashed to command centers. It might be the first seemingly clear indication in a crisis of the adversary's intent to use nuclear weapons. If one's own ICBM sites appear to be the probable targets of such an attack, the policy makers would face the much discussed problem of losing a substantial portion of their hard-target, quick-response strategic force in less than thirty minutes. The so-called use-'em-or-lose-'em decision would be posed. Ordering a launch of the targeted systems before they are destroyed by incoming warheads is the proposed plan for launch from under attack.

It should be obvious that if a coordinated and directed use of missiles is to succeed under such extreme conditions, a careful, detailed strategy for this contingency must be established in advance. Knowledge by an adversary that such a strategy is contemplated must have implications for its behavior in a severe crisis. If a launch-from-under-attack plan were to have any reasonable hope of success, it would require putting strategic forces on a high state of alert once an international crisis occurs. To minimize delay, launch procedures must be linked very closely to warning sensors. To insure that an enemy cannot prevent quick response by initially attacking the command and control system, other steps are required. It would probably be necessary to implement a predelegation of authority to use nuclear weapons, perhaps on some kind of fail-deadly plan. [18]

Such a hair-trigger strategy requires the tight integration of all parts of the strategic system. As Bracken has noted, "Tightly coupled systems are notorious for producing overcompensation effects."[19] Information in any part of the system gets repeated and amplified, and the costs of any verifications or checks that take more than a moment may insure the defeat of the time-urgent plan. The tendency in any launch-from-under-attack plan would be to switch off, under high conditions of alert, certain normal negative controls that might fatally delay its implementation.

Information processing under such conditions would likely appear much different than it would in the same strategic command and control system under normal conditions or even in a crisis without a commitment to a launch-from-under-attack plan. Crisis stability would be sharply degraded as any real or false signals surged through the system. Not only the authorities in the country using such a plan but also their counterparts on the other side would be severely affected if they suspected that in a crisis their adversaries were committed to a launch-from-under-attack plan.

Preemptive Decapitation

Under the prevailing conditions of mutual deterrence, policy makers in both the Soviet Union and the United States both now and in the future are expected to conclude that no objectives or goals are remotely worth the horrors of nuclear war. Thus the balance of terror, no matter how despicable, enables us to avoid nuclear war. But in a crisis, would these same calculations prevail under the conditions in which, for example, one side believed the other had adopted a launch-from-under-attack policy? Or suppose the policy makers fully recognized and accepted the implications of the other circumstances described in this chapter. Might they still believe that nuclear war was not worth any of their goals but conclude that such a war now seemed extremely likely or perhaps inevitable? On such an occasion might leaders be tempted to implement a preemptive first strike against the most vulnerable element of the other side's strategic forces—the command and control system—in the belief that it offered a better chance of survival? It would be imperative to attack first with a preemptive strike that would be targeted not exclusively or even primarily against the strategic forces themselves, but against the political and military command centers, the strategic communication nodes, and the information processing centers that constitute the brain of the highly integrated force. Such targets appear to be well identified by both sides, and their numbers are small. According to Blair, "Half the 400 primary and secondary U.S. strategic C^3I targets could be struck by Soviet missile submarines on routine patrol."[20] Steinbruner makes a similar point:

> Fewer than 100 judiciously targeted nuclear weapons could so severely damage U.S. communications facilities and command centers that form the military chain of command that actions of individual weapons commanders could no longer be controlled or coordinated. . . . The loss of central coordination would . . . probably have even greater consequences for the operation of Soviet forces than it would for the United States.[21]

Steinbruner suggests that a decapitation strike against the political and military nuclear command and control system offers several advantages. First, it is likely to reduce the damage of any retaliatory response because the response would lack controlled coordination. (Should retaliation be undertaken? When? Against what targets?) "Second, it offers some small chance that complete decapitation will occur and no retaliation will follow."[22] Thus such a plan identifies the opponent's most vulnerable link and could be perceived to offer one possible chance, if war cannot be avoided, of victory.

The consequences for crisis stability of a decapitation strategy are staggering. It imposes powerful incentives on both sides for a preemptive nuclear strike if, in a crisis, war is perceived to be nearly inescapable. It also greatly increases the likelihood of war by loss of control or miscalculated escalation.[23]

SUMMARY AND CONCLUSIONS

The thesis of this chapter is that both the United States and the Soviet Union have gradually engaged in a variety of activities that have seriously eroded the stability of their deterrence systems to withstand the effects of a direct international crisis without ending in war. Characteristics of certain weapons systems, configurations of command and control, practices of increasing the alert status of strategic forces, and potential strategic plans to deal with these developments will in times of crisis reduce the likelihood of valid assessment, increase system vulnerability, and decrease the ability of the policy makers to exercise control. It is not that a politico-military crisis must inevitably result in nuclear war, but that these developments have made that outcome more, rather than less, likely. Some observations with implications for improving crisis stability can be drawn from this analysis.

- Both the Soviet Union and the United States have contributed to the erosion of crisis stability and both would experience the increased pressures that would result in a future crisis; therefore, there is a symmetry to the problem. This condition should provide both sides with motivation to improve crisis stability.
- Proposals for improving crisis stability should be evaluated in terms of their impact on the factors contributing to reduced stability and their effects. In other words, we should ask how proposed improvements address the sources of the problem or the difficulties they create or both.
- The gradual reduction in crisis stability results from human activities that appear to have been initiated for various purposes unrelated

to maintaining crisis stability. Although it should be possible to reverse some of these effects in a gradual process, attention must be given to the other needs that both sides felt required the actions leading to the current situation.

- Assuming that political and military authorities in both countries eroded crisis stability inadvertently, there needs to be more explicit consideration of the effects on crisis management when considering future modifications in strategic forces and their planned operation.
- Under present circumstances it would appear critical that policy makers on both sides immediately become aware that the dynamics of a future crisis in which they might become involved would be different from and more volatile than some in the past—even recognizing that major power crises always have been extremely dangerous situations.

NOTES

1. Kenneth N. Waltz, "The Stability of a Bipolar World," Daedalus 93 (Summer 1964): 881-909.

2. On the relationship of deterrence or strategic stability and crisis stability, see Leon V. Sigal, "Warming to the Freeze," Foreign Policy 48 (Fall 1982): 54-65. Further discussion of crisis stability appears in Bruce G. Blair, Strategic Command and Control (Washington, D.C.: Brookings Institution, 1985).

3. For evidence in the movement toward consensus on a definition of crisis, at least from a decision-making perspective, compare Charles F. Hermann, ed., International Crises (New York: Free Press, 1972); Robert A. Young, ed., "A Special Issue on International Crisis," International Studies Quarterly 21 (March 1977): 3-248; and Michael Brecher, ed., Studies in Crises Behavior (New Brunswick, N.J.: Transaction Books, 1978). The definition of crisis used here is a variation on Brecher's modification of my own earlier efforts. I accept his introduction of the expectation of military hostilities as particularly appropriate for delimiting the class of problems to be examined in this chapter.

4. See Charles F. Hermann and Linda P. Brady, "Alternative Models of International Crisis Behavior," in International Crises, ed. Charles F. Hermann, 281-303, for an examination of the alternative models of crisis effects.

5. Paul Bracken, The Command and Control of Nuclear Weapons (New Haven, Conn.: Yale University Press, 1983); Blair, Strategic Command and Control; Ashton B. Carter, "The Command and Control of Nuclear War," Scientific American 252 (January 1985): 32-39; and Stephen J. Cimbala, "U.S.-Soviet Command Reciprocity: The Interde-

pendence of Survivable Leadership," Armed Forces and Society (forthcoming).

6. Richard L. Garwin, Kurt Gottfried, and Donald L. Hafner, "Anti-Satellite Weapons," Scientific American 250 (June 1984): 45-55.

7. Ashton B. Carter, in "Satellites and Anti-Satellites," International Security 10 (Spring 1986): 46-98, suggests that the ASAT threat to satellites may be exaggerated. The coordination and time required using ASATs to eliminate all active satellites of either country performing a certain function such as early warning, navigation, communication, or photoreconnaissance would be quite substantial. Some space missions may be more readily disrupted by means other than antisatellite missiles, such as attacking their ground communication stations, system-generated electromagnetic pulses from nuclear explosions in space, or ground-based directed energy weapons. Countermeasures against these and other attack modes may be possible and may still allow a satellite to perform some of its mission before being destroyed. Nevertheless, Carter concludes, "ASAT attack on some space missions is both tempting and relatively easy. Complex satellites in LEO [Low Earth Orbit] will probably remain fairly cheap to attack in relation to their cost, and if they are engaged in threatening military activities they will present an irresistible temptation for ASATs. . . . Covert ASATs and the possibility of breakout [from any future ban on ASATs] might be much less far-fetched in an ASAT treaty regime than in the ABM [antiballistic missile] treaty regime" (pp. 88-89). Thus, the problem for crisis stability would appear to be real.

8. See Scott D. Sagan, "Nuclear Alerts and Crisis Management," International Security 9 (Spring 1985): 99-139.

9. See Barry M. Blechman and Douglas M. Hart, "The Political Utility of Nuclear Weapons: The 1973 Middle East Crisis," International Security 7 (Summer 1982): 132-56; and Henry A. Kissinger, Years of Upheaval (Boston: Little, Brown, 1982), 579-87.

10. Richard N. Lebow, in Nuclear Crisis Management (Ithaca, N.Y.: Cornell University Press, forthcoming) envisions three broad ways in which a superpower crisis could result in war—preemption, miscalculated escalation, and loss of control. In his view, increased strategic alerts above normal levels represent a primary means by which the sides could lose control.

11. Several readers of an earlier version of this chapter correctly noted that there has been no trend toward increased use of strategic alerts; on the contrary, they have occurred less frequently: there have been none since 1973, despite incidents such as the invasion of Afghanistan or the Soviet shooting down of the Korean airliner. Perhaps there is increased sensitivity in the policy community to the implications of strategic alerts. The assumption of this chapter remains, however, that a higher level of strategic alert in the late 1980s would be far more

serious than in 1973 because of the changing nature of the force systems of the two sides and the greater likelihood that the expanded Soviet capability would make it more likely that they would respond with a higher alert level of their own.

    12. Blair, Strategic Command and Control, 209.

    13. John Steinbruner, "Launch under Attack," Scientific American 250 (January 1984): 37–47.

    14. Ibid., 47.

    15. Bracken, Command and Control, 196–97.

    16. Ibid., 231.

    17. A distinction should be made between launch under attack (LUA) and launch on warning (LOW). A launch-from-under-attack strategy would initiate retaliation only after evidence of the explosion of one or more nuclear weapons on or over U.S. territory. Launch-on-warning strategies involve beginning the retaliatory strike after receiving tactical warning of an incoming attack, that is, after sensors had detected the liftoff and flight trajectory of enemy missiles. Launch on warning presumably provides a few minutes more time but increase the risk that the information of an attack is in error. Lebow suggests that the distinction in practice might not be very great between the two strategies. Both, however, appear different from a preemptive strike, which could be initiated on the basis of strategic warning that an enemy is preparing to launch an attack and is generating its strategic forces (Lebow, Nuclear Crisis Management).

    18. Bracken contrasts a fail-deadly command system with the more common fail-safe. In fail-safe systems, strategic weapons are not permitted to go beyond reversible commitment to attack without final authorization from the highest command authority. In fail-deadly systems, unless a coded signal is received from the highest authority at regular intervals, weapons are to be launched (Bracken, Command and Control, 299–330).

    19. Bracken, Command and Control, 55.

    20. Blair, Strategic Command and Control, 189.

    21. John D. Steinbruner, "Nuclear Decapitation," Foreign Policy 45 (Winter 1981/82): 18–19.

    22. Ibid., 19.

    23. Lebow, Nuclear Crisis Management.

Nuclear Deterrence and
Strategic Surprise

Patrick M. Morgan

INTRODUCTION

Strategic surprise attack has been a serious problem for statesmen throughout this century, for great powers and lesser states alike.
Like most disasters, it doesn't happen often, just enough to be a major
concern. The number of cases is not overwhelming but not negligible
either, and such attacks have played a major role in international politics: "Of the major wars in Europe, Asia, and the Middle East that
have reshaped the international balance of power over the past several
decades, most began with sudden attacks."[1]

At the outset I should indicate that our subject is a strategic <u>mili-
tary</u> surprise. Nonmilitary surprises that could be considered strategic, for example, the Arab oil boycott in 1973, are not included. In
further defining the subject, the main difficulty arises with the term
"strategic." Surprise is easy enough to understand, as is a military
surprise attack, but what makes an attack strategic? There is no tidy
answer, but in general a surprise attack is strategic in two dimensions.
One is the scale of the objective. The goal is to markedly alter the
military situation so as to greatly enhance the attacker's ability to
achieve his national political objectives. In this sense the attack is a
central component of national strategy. The other dimension is the
defender's perception of the scale of the possible consequences: it is
seen to strike at his overall strategy for achieving his national objectives. Naturally, there is a gray area between strategic and tactical
surprise, leading to clashing judgments as to what constitutes a sufficient alteration, attempted or achieved, of the military relationship
between the states involved. Like many concepts in the social sciences
the essence is clear enough but there is some fuzziness at the margins.

Three other preliminary points must be made. The subject is strategic surprise via an attack. Strategic surprise via defense is quite
conceivable and has occasionally occurred—the United States at the
battle of Midway is a good example—but is not our concern here. Next,

strategic surprise can be employed not only at the outset of a war but in the middle or even at the end. (An example of the last was use of the atomic bomb to shock Japan into surrender.) Finally, a strategic military surprise for a state is not confined to a direct attack on its forces or territory. It may be badly surprised by an attack on a third party, and it may well be the ultimate target of that attack. The United States would find a Soviet surprise attack on Western Europe or Iran quite strategic in nature, and presumably the Soviet Union would have had the resulting damage to U.S. interests in mind in mounting it.

The reasons strategic surprise attacks have been employed in this century are easy to understand.[2] Some relevant factors are environmental in nature. Fundamental is the semianarchical character of international politics and the existence of severe political conflicts among states, leading periodically to wars. Thus war has continued to be an ultimate possibility because it is still an ultimate recourse. This is a necessary but far from sufficient condition for strategic surprise because it is nothing new; conflicts, anarchy, and war have always been a large part of international politics, while strategic surprise has appeared far more frequently in this century than earlier. Thus we need to emphasize another factor, the steep rise in the potential stakes of modern warfare due to a set of interlocking developments that began in the nineteenth century and have continued to unfold ever since. Technological changes that upgraded the destructiveness of weapons were married to political, economic, and organizational changes that made it possible to vastly expand the scale of warfare, both at any one time and in the length of time it could be sustained. The technological changes that occurred are obvious. The political developments included modern nationalism and methods of mobilizing mass support. Economic factors ranged from vast growth in the wealth of various societies to the increased ability of governments to tap it for wars. Organizational factors included civilian bureaucratic instruments to pull political, economic, and technological resources together for military activities and, on the military side, the emergence and refinement of general staffs.

All this made possible wars of terrible cost and devastation in the weapons involved; numbers of troops required, casualties incurred, portion of national economic output consumed, and in social, economic, political, and psychological consequences. A state, even a great power, had to confront the possibility not just of defeat but of utter defeat, of its dissolution as a territorial and political entity. Even in triumph a state could find the costs intolerable, the consequences exhausting, the victory Pyrrhic. As the potential stakes of modern warfare escalated sharply, there was a corresponding escalation of incentives to gain victory quickly and cheaply, such as by resorting to strategic surprise.

Strong incentives were not enough. These developments, until the emergence of nuclear weapons, could contribute at least as well if not better to the defense in a war as to the offense. The key was to find ways to exploit these developments in a surprise attack. This called for an appropriate strategy based on an intellectual appreciation of the need for a quick and decisive victory. Thus not all states chose to seek strategic surprise, indeed most did not, as they lacked either sufficiently strong incentives to think in decisive offensive terms or the requisite strategy. But given the overall incentives, it is not surprising that appropriate strategies have periodically emerged.

VULNERABILITY TO STRATEGIC SURPRISE

It is clear enough why states have sometimes sought a strategic surprise.[3] This is especially the case with great powers, facing as they have the most powerful opposing forces and the possibility of the largest and most costly wars.[4] It can also be true for smaller states, as the potential costs and the destructiveness of their wars have risen. A good example of the incentives is the present Iran-Iraq conflict, which has piled up casualties and which has been costing Iraq close to half of its gross national product.[5] But seeking a strategic surprise is not the same as attaining it. Explaining its occurrence requires going beyond the reasons why states attempt it to explore the reasons why governments fall victim; understanding those reasons turns out to be a complicated matter.

In nearly all cases that have been studied, the attacker is successful in achieving surprise.[6] (The military outcome of the attack is far less often a success.) In fact, only two cases of failure to achieve surprise when this was a central objective can be found—the Bay of Pigs and the Japanese failure at the Battle of Midway. (There are numerous failures to achieve tactical surprise in twentieth-century military history.) As successes we can count the Japanese attack at Port Arthur in 1904; the Schlieffen Plan; Hitler's seizure of Norway in 1940; his attack on the West in 1940; his attack on the Soviet Union in 1941 (and even the Battle of the Bulge); the Japanese attacks at Pearl Harbor, in Malaya, and in the Phillipines in 1941; the Soviet attack in Manchuria and U.S. atomic bombing of Japan in 1945; the North Korean invasion of the South, the Inchon landing, and the Chinese intervention, all in 1950; and the Israeli attacks in 1956 and 1967, topped off by the Arabs' venture in 1973. Surprises all. Evidently surprise is not all that difficult to achieve.

Yet apart from situations in which nuclear weapons and modern delivery systems would be used, where warning time could be only a few minutes, the vulnerability of states to surprise is not intuitively obvious. States are normally suspicious of each other's intentions. If anything, they seem hypersensitive to the possibility that they might be attacked. Often they maintain large forces to cope with this possibility, as well as significant intelligence resources. In addition, modern strategic surprises have occurred between states embroiled in very serious conflicts that made war a distinct possibility, or even between states already at war. Thus the habitual wariness of the states involved should have been reinforced. Why, then, have defenders so often been surprised?

It is in unraveling this puzzle that contemporary studies have made their most significant contribution. Since our subject is the relationship between strategic surprise and deterrence, not simply strategic surprise, we can settle for a brief overview of the findings. With that in hand we can turn to the heart of the subject.

The first reason surprise is difficult for states to avoid is that the initiative rests with the attacker. This applies to the time for the attack, its nature, the specific point of attack, and ultimately whether to go through with the attack or call it off. The defender's predicament is that he must prepare for a range of contingencies encompassing the possible combinations of who, whether, when, where, and how. Preparing for all possibilities is never feasible, so, in the absence of perfect information, the defender must select combinations that seem most probable (or most dangerous) to guide his preparations. Where the attack involves a combination different from the ones anticipated by the defender, a surprise results. Unfortunately for the defender, accurately anticipating several parts of the eventual combination is not enough to avoid a nasty shock. For instance, knowing you are going to be attacked, by whom, and roughly when may still leave you stunned by where and how, as the French and British learned in 1940.

Another factor is that a strategic surprise attack is far from normal or frequent. If a state concludes an attack will not occur it is going to be right many more times than it is wrong. The fundamental improbability of the thing, from the start, cripples efforts to predict it in advance.

Next come the limitations of information. Some information that would help probably doesn't exist, which foils trying to find it. An example would be the specific conditions under which the Soviet Union will launch a nuclear attack. No conclusive historical evidence exists, for the Soviet Union or other states. Even knowing what Soviet leaders think are appropriate conditions for an attack would be insufficient, for they may be incorrect as to what their behavior would really be under those conditions.

A different problem is that relevant information exists but isn't available. This may be owing to insufficient opportunities or capabilities for collecting it, or poor collection, or secrecy, or most likely some combination of these. As with information that doesn't exist, this means the defender must make do with an incomplete picture, filling in gaps by extrapolation and guesswork. Closely linked is the likelihood that information the defender does possess is ambiguous. These two are related because the ambiguity of available information is often due to the absence of other information. The meaning of a state's military buildup is unclear when hard information about its intentions is lacking. Hence anything that limits available information helps make what is available ambiguous. This is the major effect of the attacker's secrecy. Case studies indicate that attacker secrecy will usually be far from successful—a fair amount of information on what is coming ends up in the hands of the defender anyway. The contribution of secrecy is to limit the amount and nature of that information so that it remains ambiguous, open to multiple interpretations and permitting the defender to select the wrong one. Other things can contribute to this ambiguity as well, such as when information is obtained from a source of dubious reliability.

Added to this is the presence of information that appears relevant and is wrong but not plainly or obviously so. It may be incorrect due to a defective sensor system, an erroneous report from a trusted source, or distortion in transmission. Or it may be wrong because of attacker deception. Unlike secrecy that passively misleads by withholding information, deception actively misleads by disseminating incorrect information. Most disturbing to cope with is a bundle of information in which information not obviously erroneous is embedded in a good deal known to be true, and in fact this is one basis for successful efforts at deception.

Incorrect information adds to ambiguity by lending support, in many cases, to some of the alternative interpretations from which a choice must be made. It also complicates deriving the correct interpretation by cluttering up the analytical process, thereby drawing off time, attention, and other resources. This cluttering is further magnified by the presence of information that is irrelevant to the problem at hand but that draws attention anyway because it is important for other matters. If a government, its key officials, even its relevant analysts could simply drop everything else to give their undivided attention to information bearing on the possibility of an attack, chances of predicting it in advance might well improve.

Incorrect information and information that is irrelevant but hard to ignore give us the two components of information overload. This is something very likely to afflict great states that have numerous international responsibilities, a plethora of international relationships, and elaborate resources for gathering information. All contribute to the size and density of the sea of information in which they are immersed.

Cognitive Difficulties

One can go too far in emphasizing these problems. For instance, the attacker has the initiative, but conditions are likely to constrain his options. Only certain kinds of attacks, maybe only one, can inflict a strategic defeat, and there may be few windows of opportunity for such an attack. This gets the defender's task of ascertaining when, where, and how an attack could occur down to manageable proportions, drastically cutting the realistic contingencies for which detection must be attempted and preparations made. In addition, attempts at strategic surprise may be rare, but they have always been associated with conditions that are readily detected: intense political conflict, a crisis or confrontation, even an ongoing war. This makes the "who" and the "why" more readily apparent. Once those conditions exist, the defender's estimated probability of a surprise attack should rise significantly.

As for defects in available information, they would more fully account for failures in threat perception if it was not clear from case studies that in most instances a fair amount of information as to what was brewing was in the defender's hands and somebody in fact predicted the attack or regarded it as highly likely. Sometimes these predictions or strong suspicions were lodged at lower levels; in other cases they cropped up among high-level officials.

This makes it necessary to treat the factors discussed thus far as contributing to the difficulty of anticipating a strategic surprise but not sufficient to account for it. Thus, in the literature, cognitive factors bearing on the analysis of information are treated as the true source of the problem. Governments get caught unprepared primarily because of the ways people, individually and collectively, think.

Careful studies have established that perception involves categorizing and evaluating stimuli by means of cognitive structures already present in the mind.[7] The mind is not a passive receptor of data about reality. It is an energetic, active agent that vigorously employs what it already knows to guide its search for information, the selection of stimuli to be given attention, the sorting and labeling of information received, and the making of judgments as to meaning. These cognitive structures are of various sorts: assumptions and beliefs, values, images, theories and working hypotheses, and strategies and plans. This list applies to groups as well as to individuals.

These cognitive structures are abstractions and simplifications. To encompass all aspects of all stimuli would mean chaos and confusion, so perception is always selective. There is also a powerful tendency toward balance and consistency in cognitive structures to minimize confusion and uncertainty while supplying an orderly, efficient, and reliable treatment of stimuli. "Satisficing" is also employed

selection and interpretation of stimuli by trying out possibilities until a seemingly satisfactory fit emerges with cognitive structures, rather than until the best possible interpretation has been uncovered.[8]

How flexible are these cognitive structures and the perceptions they shape, particularly when confronted by contrary evidence? It seems they resist change, sometimes quite strongly, for the following reasons (among others). As they embody prior experiences and learning, they are comfortable and useful, often becoming part of an individual's or group's self-identity and thus hard to part with. And since perception involves selection from available information, selection will likely be biased in ways that conform to and reinforce these structures, a process facilitated when information is ambiguous. There is also a bias against seeing information that confirms one's views as also consistent with alternative interpretations. Individuals and groups are also prone to "bolstering," mental maneuvers that reinforce existing views in the face of contrary evidence.

Thus people come armed with a battery of preconceptions, with settled patterns of perception and analysis. Portions of this mental equipment can be challenged, revised, and discarded; under the right circumstances this can even occur quickly and smoothly. But the norm is that these things are relatively static, applied routinely and repetitively. Willingness to alter them varies with circumstances, with individuals and groups and with their training and experience. It probably varies over time and with health or age. Thus generalizing about the inertia behind preconceptions is difficult beyond stating that it is normally substantial.

It follows that there is a strong tendency to overlook information that clashes with existing views, to interpret it so that it sustains those views, or to reject it. It also follows that once cognitive structures and the perceptions they dictate are well established, it takes more and better information to lead to their being discarded rather than retained. Where change seems required, people will tend to shift their views to the minimum extent necessary, starting at the margins.

Another implication is that a cybernetic approach to perception is relevant.[9] The mind (or the group or organization) focuses on a fairly limited set of what are considered critical variables, and perception (plus behavior) is adjusted only to changes in those variables. This permits much information to be virtually ignored or handled in routine fashion and narrows the search for information. Discrepant information, if it does not pertain to dominant preoccupations or key variables normally monitored, is likely to get short shrift.

Application of the foregoing perspective to strategic surprise is relatively straightforward. Decision makers, agencies, and governments are rich in cognitive structures pertaining to international politics. Among their preconceptions are ones pertaining to opponents and the possibility that they might attack. Decision makers are vulnerable to a strategic surprise to the extent that their preconceptions are insensitive to that possibility, that they shape their perceptions and predictions accordingly, and that they resist change even as warning signs accumulate.

Case studies have found that in the target state views prevailed that either treated a surprise attack as highly unlikely, even impossible, or as not meaning a strategic defeat. The defender believed that the opponent would not attack, would not attack soon, would not be able to attack effectively, or would not attack in an unanticipated fashion. In most cases the defender was wrong on one or more counts, despite sufficient information—if interpreted correctly—to get it right. Defenders often had difficulty seeing things as they appeared to the attacker, such as the reasons or incentives for the attack or the risks and opportunities involved, and frequently underestimated the attacker's military capabilities. Often they misread the evidence as to when an attack would occur.

I should point out that these types of errors appear to be widespread in international politics. Studies of crises have found similar misperceptions, again in spite of available evidence, held by decision makers who initiated crises.[10] The same is true of governments that initiated wars, whether or not by strategic surprise. Thus the emphasis on cognitive factors in explaining vulnerability to strategic surprise is reinforced by a good deal of other research.

A final difficulty, one that has cognitive and politico-organizational aspects, is the cry-wolf syndrome. Most attacks have been inflicted on defenders who had experienced prior warnings that had proven incorrect. The impact of the cry-wolf syndrome is threefold. The credibility of future warnings is diminished. In addition the credibility of the source is undermined. Agencies and officials naturally take this into account, and the result is an unwillingness to initiate or pass along cries of alarm or a moderation of expressions of concern. Finally, when the attack comes the initial response is slowed, much like the reaction to a fire alarm of people who have been through too many fire drills.

Politico-Organizational Difficulties

Apart from the handicaps for the defender already reviewed, there are others having to do with the nature of government. One of the more obvious is that information is a political resource in domestic, bureaucratic, and intragovernmental politics, and as such it is hoarded, manipulated, leaked, and selectively received and interpreted. For instance, warning of a surprise attack is apt to carry with it the politically potent implication that certain officials and their policies have been misguided. In many instances that is one reason the warning is issued. When a warning can be seen as a political ploy it is easier to discount or dismiss. Warnings can be motivated by bureaucratic political objectives and rejected for the same reason.

A larger aspect of the relationship between politics and vulnerability to strategic surprise is that political power distorts the processing and analysis of information. In a fundamental sense, power is the freedom to not have to listen. To be able to have things one's own way can include preserving one's own way of looking at things. Hence the cognitive limitations referred to above can be heightened by the subtle corruptions of power. One way this occurs is that power affects the weight accorded to information and interpretations of it: if those who belittle the likelihood of a strategic surprise have more power than those who do not, the former can not only more readily act on their views and dismiss the alternatives but even inhibit expression of the alternatives.

However, there is another side to power. It is often less a matter of rule than of persuasion, of constructing a consensus to sustain one's position and get decisions made and implemented. This can make it difficult to attend to a warning properly when it means facing the need to do something where no consensus is apparent about what that something is. In particular, it can mean reopening a policy question that earlier was politically costly, even agonizing, to settle.[11] It can mean a shift in the subtle relationships among decision makers, even a reshuffling of the government, to forge a new consensus. As a result, warning can be politically disturbing, something the decision maker can't afford to hear.

This leads to a further point. For a government to know that its previous view is incorrect and it is facing the distinct possibility of a disastrous attack requires collective learning—a number of people, several major agencies, one or more groups of officials, must learn this together. For all practical purposes, a government often doesn't know something until, among relevant officials and agencies, a consensus to that effect has emerged. The result is apt to resemble the Hegelian dialectic: the accepted view that an attack is a remote possibility competes with the new view that it is coming, and the resulting synthesis heightens wariness and uncertainty but falls far short of full acceptance of warning and an energetic response.

An additional complication is that response to warning is never free. There are organizational and economic costs, most obviously in going on alert or mobilizing forces. Routines are disrupted, the economy and budget may be strained. What happens if the warning proves false? Then the costs will be criticized as unnecessary, with aspersions cast on the decision makers' competence and grasp of reality. Another cost is associated with the desire to avoid provoking an attack; many appropriate responses to warning may appear likely to have that effect. Sensitivity to these costs can inhibit not only response to warning but even perception of it. These are, after all, costs that can be readily anticipated. The costs of not responding to warning are less certain and obvious if there have been false warnings previously, if the available information is uneven and ambiguous, and if a surprise attack is statistically improbable.

SOLUTIONS—OF A SORT

An obvious way to try to deal with the problem of strategic surprise is to improve the gathering of information: seeking more, trying for better intelligence penetration of opponents, multiplying sources. It has been suggested that, at least for some states, information gathering capabilities are now so powerful and improving so steadily that vulnerability to being surprised has been or can be eliminated.[12]

Drawbacks to this solution are fairly obvious. Where states are burdened with information overload, this is likely to exacerbate it. If the ambiguity of the information gathered is not eliminated, then having more around may increase uncertainty. If the crux of the problem is not information but what is done with it, then simply gathering more won't help. This is an effective solution only if the additional information markedly clarifies the situation so as to break through cognitive barriers, and such clarification cannot be guaranteed.

Thus many proposed solutions have less to do with improved collection of information than with bettering the interpretation of it. A common suggestion is to multiply sources of interpretation to promote debate and offset bureaucratic and other manipulations of information. Under this heading fall the use of agencies with overlapping responsibilities, an institutionalized devil's advocate, the multiple advocacy approach proposed by Alexander George, and regular recourse to outside (nongovernmental) advisors and consultants.

These solutions are not without problems. As Irving Janis suggests, resolution of major issues where doubt or uncertainty is heightened by contending views can be an exhausting experience, and officials may seek emotional refuge in groupthink.[13] Thus, effective management of decisions within competing interpretations of the evidence is dependent on decision makers' tolerance of ambiguity. Alas, some leaders are averse to ambiguity.

The presence of conflicting analyses can produce other unfortunate results. Analysis by compromise, often at the lowest common denominator, is ubiquitous. Vis-à-vis an impending attack this would mean greater concern but not unqualified acceptance of the idea that it was

coming. If such compromises are normal, this invites inflated statements of contrasting views to gain leverage.[14] The natural reaction
is to treat all extreme assessments as inflated. This is not a good
prescription for refining a government's grasp of reality. Another
possibility is that, offered alternative interpretations, the policy
maker will simply select the one he finds most congenial, which will
do little good if he regards a surprise attack as implausible (not least
because of the wisdom of his policies).

Another result could be paralysis. Multiplying viewpoints may
raise the difficulty of deciding anything, as officials respond by avoiding a decision or by procrastination. A major split within the government over different viewpoints could mean hesitancy and indecision.
Another problem is particularly applicable to the United States. An
analysis that clashes with the view finally adopted is likely to be
leaked, arming opponents outside the government and bolstering
critics within. When this happens, an administration is often charged
with being weak, confused, and incoherent. One way to control these
political costs is to curtail analyses that differ from the view adopted,
something high officials have been known to attempt.

Another solution would be to reward success and punish failure,
favoring those who display imagination, intellectual flexibility, and
other qualities that seem appropriate, particularly when the individual
correctly departed from prevailing views. The idea is to uncover people who see things more clearly than others and to move them to positions where they could make a difference in detecting an attack in
advance.

To do this, it would help if we knew more about what makes for
success. Robert Jervis suggests that those correct when most others
are wrong are not necessarily more imaginative or open to new
ideas.[15] They may be right primarily because they happened to hold
suitable prejudices or preconceptions for the situation at hand. This
makes success a matter of luck. Rewarding success would therefore
do little or nothing to increase the chances of it in the future. Or it
may be that an accurate perception is a matter of having a fortuitous
relationship to the problem, being properly situated to see the one
facet of the situation or portion of evidence that provides the correct
perception. Again, rewarding success may not reduce vulnerability
to surprise, because the prior success did not arise from qualities
the individual possessed.

We must also remember that government is a matter of large
organizations staffed by myriads of people. They can't all be icono-
clasts. Running things calls for many more qualities than those we
have been considering. People must be advanced and rewarded for
lots of reasons—loyalty, administrative skills, ideological fervor,
and so on. With this in mind it would seem easier to try to get high

officials to be more open-minded or imaginative than to try to ensure that only such people get to be high officials.

A way to prevent incorrect preconceptions of high officials from corrupting the government's perceptions is to distance analytical agencies from the highest policy-making circles. But this won't help if it is the analysts who hold the incorrect views, a situation one can find in the case studies (for example, in the period before the Cuban missile crisis). There is also the problem of making the horse drink— leaders may not accept an agency's correct, and alarming, conclusion. This is likely if leaders, due to the gap between analysis and decision making, have little knowledge of how the conclusion was reached, no sense of the intellectual operations involved or the reliability of the sources used, and a strong desire to reject the conclusion because it is improbable and unwanted. Then there is the difficulty of separating intelligence (or other analytical resources) from the policy maker without having it become so unresponsive to the latter's needs and concerns that it becomes irrelevant.

Another option is to study past examples of success and failure. Does this help much? One reason it doesn't is that while this is an excellent way for scholars to learn something, they aren't the ones who need to absorb the lessons. The same can be true of retrospective studies within an agency (such as those conducted by the CIA). It is also worth considering that the cognitive defects discussed earlier are not, under normal circumstances, defects at all. If human mental equipment is unsatisfactory under very unusual circumstances because of how well it works normally, then lessons derived from rare occurrences can never be effectively absorbed and applied.

Also disturbing are the defects in retrospective analysis when the outcome of the event is known, a phenomenon identified by Steve Chan.[16] One does not have to be as skeptical as he is to feel uneasy about the explanation of strategic surprise vulnerability that descends from Roberta Wohlstetter's classic study[17] through the rest of the literature. Perhaps studies have imposed their own preconceptions on the historical data, so that what we think we know is what we were primed to find. Why should we expect governments to do better?

We might well conclude that trying to improve the treatment of information will never be helpful enough, just as trying to increase the amount of information turns out to be of limited use. If this is the starting point for analysis of the problem, what can be offered in the way of solutions?

Other Solutions

A solution virtually ignored in the literature but that has definitely occurred to governments is to attack first. It is clear that the defender is at a serious disadvantage in trying to detect a strategic surprise

attack in time to cope with it. And if it can't be coped with, because
a successful defense is physically impossible, the problem is even
worse. Attacking first cancels the disadvantage. The Israelis did this
in 1967; fearing a surprise attack, they went first. The Soviets talk
about getting in the first blow once it is clear war is going to break
out. This solution shades into another, which is technically a retaliatory measure, launch under attack. Here one goes not first but before
the enemy attack has arrived.

There are, of course, major difficulties. Unless a state's forces
are constantly primed for an attack—a rather provocative posture—
the solution may be precluded because enemy plans are not detected
in time. Also, if the defender has a great aversion to war, this solution can be used only as a last resort when war seems unavoidable,
but for the reasons cited earlier it may be impossible to know that
until it is too late. Attacking first may be politically unattractive because of concern about appearing provocative, a desire to avoid bearing the onus of going first (the Israelis' position just before the October
1973 war), or fear of contributing to crisis instability or an inadvertent stumble into war. Finally, this solution encourages excessive preoccupation with one's own plans at the cost of insufficient attention to
the opponent's, a defeat in French preparations for World War I and
in British plans to occupy Norway in 1940.

Another solution would be arms control to strip states of their
capacity to launch a meaningful strategic surprise. Efforts along these
lines appeared in the peace settlements after World War I, with the
victors imposing restrictions on the losers' ability to rapidly constitute large armies by barring military conscription. In the 1930s the
French emphasized defensive weapons and postures as the proper goal
of international disarmament agreements, restricting offensive forces.
Another example would be the idea behind the MDFR (Mutual and Balanced Force Reductions) negotiations (to the West). Related is arms
control that, while not eliminating military capabilities for attack,
tries to erase the capacity to achieve surprise. One thinks of the
Eisenhower Open Skies proposal or the U.S.-operated electronic
monitoring stations set up in the Sinai as part of the Israeli-Egyptian
agreement on Israel's withdrawal.

The examples illustrate a major difficulty—most proposals of this
sort have not been sufficiently acceptable to the parties involved to be
adopted or, for the Germans after 1918, permanently adhered to. The
crux of the matter has usually been that for one or more of the parties,
never being able to attack and have the advantage of surprise is to be
confined to a kind of war, should one occur, that is unacceptable. If
they have to fight, the Soviets want to preempt, to go on the offensive
and fight on the enemy's territory. The Israelis do, too, After this
come the other standard difficulties—fear that the arms control is

really spying in disguise, fear that one side's military advantages will be frozen in place, difficulty in getting the proper political climate for agreement, and so forth.

Still another solution is to establish a buffer zone, either outside the state's territory or at its edges, and to have some military capability at the border to slow an initial attack until a proper response can be prepared. The Soviets have used Eastern Europe for this purpose, as have the Israelis with the Sinai, for a time, and the Golan Heights. Israeli border settlements are designed to offer initial military resistance to an attack, while the KGB has its own small army of border troops for the same purpose. For NATO, various analysts have suggested that border fortifications and lightly armed forces (such as German reserve units) be used to slow an initial Soviet thrust and to allow more substantial forces to be brought to bear a bit further back, with more time to get ready.[18]

Unfortunately buffer zones aren't always possible and often they aren't cheap. NATO has been unable to dispense with forward defense because of the political necessity of keeping the Germans satisfied. Of course, border defenses are useless if the enemy can use nuclear weapons and delivery systems of sufficient range. Against modern conventional forces it can be difficult for border units or semimilitary settlements to provide much of an initial defense.

The Supreme Solution

The previous discussion is a theme and variations on how strategic surprise vulnerability is a fact of life in international politics. The problem is basic, the solutions of limited utility. The last type of solution we reviewed at least has the virtue of recognizing this. If you cannot eliminate the possibility of being surprised, at least you can make preparations accordingly. The final solution also accepts the possibility of surprise.

The dominant solution in our time, dominant in the sense that it is the one on which major states rely most heavily, is nuclear deterrence via a second-strike retaliatory capability. Deterrence penetrates to the heart of the problem in two ways. By promising retaliation via forces that can survive an attack, no matter how surprising and severe, deterrence seeks to cancel the strategic objective of the attack—the attack is unable to alter the military relationship between the two parties sufficiently to permit the attacker to achieve his national objective. Then deterrence promises such a severe retaliation that any other incentive for the attack is stripped away. If the attack cannot achieve its strategic objective and will provoke unacceptable damage, then the point of it is cancelled. The enemy's physical capacity to launch an attack by surprise is not blocked or dominated. Vulnerability to a strategic surprise remains; only the incentive to inflict it is removed.

Hence, one way to think about nuclear deterrence is that it is not just for preventing war, but for coping with a particular version of it—a version that has played a prominent role in the military history of this century. In fact, preventing strategic surprise had much more to do with the development of deterrence than preventing war per se. Bernard Brodie declared at the dawn of the nuclear age that the point of nuclear forces would be to prevent wars, not to fight them, but the idea took some time to sink in. We can now see why. True nuclear deterrence theory and policies did not emerge until the 1950s in the United States and, eventually, in the Soviet Union. This was so because it was not until then that these two countries faced a real possibility of a (nuclear) strategic surprise attack; it was this that provoked deterrence theory. Prior to this, U.S. plans for war with the Soviet Union treated Western Europe more or less as a buffer zone: it was assumed that the Soviets would overrun much of the continent and even parts of the Middle East, using blitzkrieg tactics, and would enjoy the benefits of surprise. Nuclear weapons would be used in conjunction with a World War II style mobilization of the United States to win the war.[19] Deterrence theory really grew out of wanting to avoid another surprise attack like Korea (hence the massive retaliation doctrine) and then from fear of a direct surprise attack on the United States (Robert Wohlstetter's "delicate" balance of terror).

The essence of Western deterrence theory came to be preservation of a second-strike capability, accepting vulnerability to surprise attack as unavoidable. This also shaped the U.S. approach to strategic arms control. The objective became stable deterrence via mutual vulnerability to attack or retaliation under mutual second-strike capabilities.

Under the flexible-response variant of deterrence theory, the problem of strategic surprise was also highlighted. In mutual nuclear deterrence, if neither superpower can readily use its strategic forces, then strategic surprise might be employed at the conventional level by an attacker confident that escalation is forestalled. That is, solving the strategic surprise problem at the highest level does not necessarily solve it at lower levels and might even exacerbate it by inviting a clever or daring opponent to exploit the nuclear stalemate. Just the possibility of this could supply important political leverage, especially in a confrontation. Hence, in the classic flexible-response view, forces must be maintained to cope with military contingencies at all levels, especially to guard against surprise attacks.

Strategic surprise is important in Soviet military thinking as well. We have already noted Soviet attachment to the buffer zone and border defenses solution, which does little to cope with a strategic nuclear attack. We should also recall the Soviet emphasis on bomber defenses and a persistent interest in a modest form of missile defense, another way to try to handle strategic surprise but not really very satisfactory. The Soviets stockpile so much military equipment at least partly as a hedge against being caught by surprise, as they were in 1941, but that may not be of much help in the event of a nuclear attack. Thus the Soviets also have turned to nuclear deterrence.

The Soviets seem, from the start, to have counted on detecting Western preparations for a surprise attack in advance. If much Western thinking about the need for a second-strike capability has been conditioned by the difficulty of penetrating Soviet secrecy, Soviet thinking has been shaped by the openness of its opponents. The Soviets were less sensitive to the vulnerability of bomber bases and missile sites to surprise attack in the Khrushchev era than Americans were. To this day the Soviets keep a smaller portion of their strategic forces on alert and a lesser share of their submarine-launched ballistic missiles (SLBMs) on station than does the United States. There is also a steady refrain, in Soviet literature on nuclear war, to the effect that the political leadership will judge when war has become unavoidable or, in a war, when Western nuclear weapons are about to be used, and then the armed forces will deliver preemptive strikes, in Europe or in the United States.

The Soviets have also stressed the utility of surprise, including strategic surprise, in the fighting of wars and have designed their forces with this in mind. The NATO countries have been concerned about the offensive readiness of Soviet forces in Central Europe, and one objection to the SS-20 has been the additional capability it gives the Soviet Union in this regard. Soviet strategic forces are similarly designed for time-urgent, hard-target-kill capability. Finally, the Soviets stress the capability to achieve victory as the essence of deterrence. The prospect of losing is what deters an attacker, not just the prospect of serious damage. Such a strategic doctrine makes little sense, when confronting over ten thousand strategic nuclear weapons, unless one plans damage-limiting strikes at the outset coupled to defensive and civil-defense capabilities. This has meant rigid Soviet unwillingness in arms control negotiations to trade away their preemptive capabilities.

Having described deterrence as the supreme solution to the problem of strategic surprise, we need to consider its limitations or drawbacks. One persistent difficulty has to do with vulnerability. In effect, mutual nuclear deterrence requires that just the right amount of vulnerability be maintained amidst weapons the effects of which, if used, cannot be calculated with precision. This permits recurrent fears that the right sort of vulnerability hasn't been achieved, that the United

States is too vulnerable to a Soviet attack: the bomber gap, missile gap, hard-target-kill gap, and current command, control, communications, and intelligence (C^3I) gap controversies fuel these fears. The resulting uneasiness has tended to push up the size of nuclear stockpiles and complicate arms control efforts, while leaving lingering doubts about the stability of nuclear deterrence.

Another difficulty has to do with the troublesome matter of credibility, which is in turn linked to vulnerability. It turns out, fortunately, that it is very difficult for a government to bring itself to use nuclear weapons, even when its opponent could not reply in kind and when not doing so means greater casualties or even defeat in a war. States have chosen to accept the costs, casualties, and losses: in Korea, Vietnam (for both the United States and China), the Falklands, Afghanistan, and the Middle East (if reports of Israel's nuclear stockpile are correct). Opponents of nuclear powers have therefore been able to attack, in several instances by surprise, as if nuclear weapons did not exist.

Such reluctance to use nuclear weapons can only be greater when the opponent can respond in kind. It has long been suggested that extended deterrence under such conditions is of uncertain, some would say minimal, credibility. It has also been asserted that a direct attack on a nuclear power by another nuclear power, even with nuclear weapons, might go unanswered if nuclear retaliation would only bring greater destruction of the defender's society (the scenario for a Soviet attack on U.S. missile silos, for example).

Earlier we noted the preoccupation with this in the classic version of flexible response. Unfortunately, flexible response is of dubious value in this regard.[20] For one thing, adoption of a true flexible response posture tends to be taken as evidence that one's nuclear deterrence threats should not be believed, the customary U.S. problem in dealing with its Western European allies. The United States has persistently pressured its allies to strengthen their conventional forces while insisting that U.S. nuclear guarantee is quite credible, a contradiction readily apparent in Europe.

The trouble is that building up of conventional forces does not eliminate states' traditional vulnerability to strategic surprise. While it is relatively easy to figure out how to defend Western Europe when one can see the attack coming well in advance, guarding against a strategic surprise is much more difficult for all the reasons cited earlier. This applies in other parts of the world where U.S. commitments are involved—the Persian Gulf and the Far East, for example. The present solution in Europe is the NATO version of flexible response, which is also advocated by analysts at the MAD, or mutual assured destruction, end of the deterrence theory spectrum. Here the problem of strategic surprise is to be managed by strategic nuclear deterrence via the risk of escalation—an opponent must see that any major attack carries with it the possibility of escalation, some uncontrollable risk of disaster, and therefore any such attack will be rejected. The obvious difficulty with this is that we are once again left relying on a supreme solution, strategic nuclear deterrence, that is of uncertain credibility.

A third difficulty with nuclear deterrence is that, by the nature of the weapons involved, it contributes a good deal to the dimensions of the strategic surprise problem in that forces for retaliation can also be excellent for a surprise attack. Thus it is not a solution most of us would like to see more widely adopted by states via horizontal nuclear proliferation. It is also a uniquely dangerous solution in terms of the possible consequences if it ever fails. Then there is the risk that quick-reaction or launch-on-warning postures will be adopted to ease vulnerability to attack, thereby increasing chances of war by accident or by the defender's provocative behavior in a crisis. To ensure retaliation, nuclear deterrence also invites decentralization of decision making on use of nuclear weapons in a crisis or in the initial stage of a war, which is not very attractive.

Finally, nuclear deterrence is expensive. Development of nuclear forces in Britain and France has eaten into funds for conventional forces. When the burden of conventional forces for a true flexible response posture is added on, peacetime defense budgets are hard to sustain in democratic societies. Even where the government is relatively free to spend what it wishes, in the Soviet Union, the burden of the armed forces on the economy is obvious.

CHALLENGES IN THE FUTURE

The first challenge we face is to reexamine the entire matter of strategic arms control. One of the striking features of the nuclear era is that, in and through strategic surprise, the difficulties in achieving arms control are multiplied. Consider how the classic U.S. conception of strategic arms control has worked out in practice. As a solution to the problem of strategic surprise, nuclear deterrence involves piling up forces for retaliation. The U.S. view was that if both superpowers had a strong interest in stable deterrence, then they ought to be able to agree on limiting their strategic forces to preserve each other's second-strike capability. What this view neglects to consider is that if deterrence fails, or appears on the verge of breaking down, the ideal way to fight the war that follows is to be able to deliver a devastating damage-limitation attack, the more surprising the better. After all, the existence of the nation depends on it. Those who would do the fighting plan accordingly. Critics rail against the warfighting scenarios and plans that result, but unless deterrence is

absolutely guaranteed to work, governments, especially military
forces, will develop them anyway.

Thus, strategic arms control has been an exercise, largely
futile, in attempting to prevent the lure of a strategic surprise capability to limit damage (should deterrence fail) from overwhelming the
utility of deterrence in preventing strategic surprise attacks. We have
accumulated enough experience to know that this probably cannot be
done. The Pentagon has consistently striven for a war-fighting posture
with considerable damage-limitation capabilities. In the 1950s, whatever the official strategic doctrine, the war plans called for an initial
massive, paralyzing blow. [21] In the 1960s, the doctrine of counterforce
targeting was strongly pushed by the air force in the direction of a
first-strike capability. The later official emphasis on MAD was
countered by service pressure for an antiballistic missile (ABM)
system that would have tended to erode MAD. The Strategic Arms
Limitations Talks (SALT I) agreements supposedly to institutionalize
MAD did not cover multiple independent reentry vehicles (MIRVs), at
Pentagon insistence, guaranteeing a growing damage-limitation capability, particularly when the Pentagon insisted, as one price for supporting the agreements, on funding for the MX. In recent years the
Minuteman III has been made considerably more effective against hard
targets, the Pentagon has insisted on deployment of the Pershing II
(for war-fighting purposes), and development of the hard-target D-5
continues.

American attention has naturally been drawn to similar Soviet
responses to the inner logic of nuclear deterrence—an interest in defensive systems and a commitment to damage-limitation offensive
forces. The Soviets have therefore been unwilling to budge on first
the SS-9 and later the SS-18 and SS-19 numbers in negotiations. Their
entire orientation in the European theater is likewise toward nuclear
(and where possible conventional) forces that can take out Western-
theater nuclear weapons in a preemptive attack. [22]

This search for strategic surprise capabilities is almost universally ascribed to flawed doctrines, archaic ways of thinking, bureaucratic pressures, or expansionist aims (Soviet or American). We
must get beyond this and understand that, ultimately, it is inherent
in mutual nuclear deterrence. It can only result in eroding the deterrence regime and its associated arms control arrangements and negotiations. This is the plain lesson of the proliferation of capacities for
destroying hard targets and the renewed U.S. interest in ballistic
missile defense.

What are we to make of this? One possibility is that nuclear deterrence can be stable only at very high levels of nuclear forces so
that enough would survive any possible attack. Dagobert Brito and
Michael Intriligator (among others) have elaborated on this (see their

chapter in this book), concluding that below a certain point each side's arsenal would become too vulnerable to preemption. Hence arms-control efforts must be redesigned, with less attention to reducing those arsenals in favor of more concern for avoiding crises, preventing accidents, and curbing horizontal proliferation. [23] Unfortunately this does nothing about the credibility problem, with its attendant risks that deterrence might fail.

Another possibility is that a solution is at hand to the vulnerability problem at lower levels of strategic forces. Bruce Berkowitz has argued that we are on the verge of having strategic nuclear weapons become much more difficult to find:

> As strategic weapons become smaller and more mobile, the targets of a [counterforce] attack will disappear into the countryside. As the targets of a counterforce strike vanish, so does the probability of such an attack. [24]

Coupled with more hardening of C^3I assets, the result would be a more stable deterrence. If a smaller portion of each side's strategic force is at risk, then deterrence could be maintained with smaller arsenals. Whether we would see any reductions is another matter, because (as Berkowitz notes) arms control would need to be revamped. The technological changes making missiles harder to attack would simultaneously cripple the capacity of national technical means of verification to count each side's forces. It is also clear that nothing in this makes any inroads on the credibility problem, the Achilles' heel of nuclear deterrence.

A third possibility would require that we begin by reworking our conception of just what it is that nuclear deterrence does to prevent great power wars. Such a war can be deterred if there is a reasonable probability, to near certainty, that it will be awful. No government in its right mind would want a replay of World War II; the prospect of a war that bad ought to be enough for deterrence. Such wars were awful enough by 1914. If so, why did two of them occur? The answer, suggested earlier, is that leaders could be convinced that a way had been found—usually via a strategic surprise—to conduct the war so that it wouldn't be awful. Instead it would be short and lead to an overwhelming victory. What this means is that nuclear deterrence has added little or nothing to war prevention by enlarging the level of destruction involved; that level was high enough already. Its key contribution has been as a solution to the strategic surprise problem, by erasing the credibility of short-victorious-war schemes.

Analysts of deterrence against criminals in domestic affairs have concluded that it mainly works when punishment is certain; the scale of the punishment has less to do with successful deterrence than a high probability of lawbreakers being caught and punished. What if this is also true in deterrence in international politics? For one thing, this would accord with the preceding point. For another, it would follow that if nuclear deterrence is not particularly credible, as we pointed out earlier, it will sooner or later be challenged. Putting the two together, we could get more mutual deterrence at lower levels of potential destruction—war has to be seen as inevitably awful, not catastrophic, to be deterred—with weapons we would be less reluctant to use, so that a major response to an attack would be more certain.

Deep cuts in nuclear forces on both sides would not, therefore, necessarily mean a serious loss in deterrence capabilities. The same degree of mutual deterrence might be achieved by being able to make war inevitably awful for an attacker just on the conventional level. Hence a reduction, or elimination, of nuclear weapons—stepping away from nuclear deterrence—would not mean making the world "safe" for conventional war unless it were still possible either to achieve strategic surprise or to conceive of achieving it. In short, if great powers could devise an alternative way of coping with the strategic surprise problem, they might well be able to do without nuclear deterrence with no true loss in security. This would seem to be a very suitable subject for arms control, not with a MAD framework but under a deterrence sustained by less than MAD levels of strategic forces.

But this brings us back to the discussion in the first half of this chapter, which emphasized how difficult it is to eliminate vulnerability to strategic surprise. If there is no real substitute for nuclear deterrence as a solution, then we are stuck with it—warts and all. The elimination of nuclear deterrence would indeed make the world "safe" for a conventional World War III or for lesser conventional conflicts of great severity. Whether this is correct is the question arms controllers should be asking and investigating.

Thus the ideal agenda for arms control would emerge from the answers to the following questions. First, can mutually acceptable ways be found to limit or cancel the great powers' vulnerability to strategic surprise on the conventional level? If so, then these states could put themselves in a position to credibly threaten to fight on such a large scale conventionally to keep deterrence just as effective as it is now, even more so because their threats would be more believable, without any nuclear weapons. If not, then we need at least some nuclear weapons as a hedge against a conventional strategic surprise attack. Thus the next question: what would be the lowest number of nuclear weapons necessary if the right sort, that is, those least vulnerable to surprise attack, were deployed? Assuming agreement to this point, how can we then design arms control to monitor the necessary changes in existing nuclear arsenals and verify adherence to the agreed limits?

This would mean putting an end to considering strategic arms control in isolation from conventional capabilities, which has always been unfortunate because nuclear deterrence first emerged in part as an answer to the strategic surprise problem at the conventional level. However, it would also mean trying to revive the intellectual basis of the U.S. approach to SALT—mutual avoidance of strategic surprise capabilities—but in the larger sense of forgoing those capabilities at the conventional as well as the nuclear level. The earlier analysis on why arms control hasn't been of much use in resolving the strategic surprise problem suggests how difficult this could be.

Without an agenda of this sort arms control is unlikely to be any more relevant than it turned out to be in the 1970s. We will see the retention of very large strategic arsenals, growing difficulty in accurately monitoring them, and thus, in Berkowitz's words, reliance within deterrence on "stability without arms control."[25] This brings us to the final possibility with respect to arms control, the current administration view.

The relationship between deterrence and strategic surprise is perhaps the best vantage point from which to consider the implications of ballistic missile defense, particularly the Reagan Strategic Defense Initiative (SDI). The president's ultimate objective of putting nuclear deterrence aside, while laudable, must be considered in light of the strategic surprise problem. If nuclear deterrence is an essential solution to that problem, dispensing with deterrence would reopen it. But if we have alternative ways of coping with it, then doing away with our reliance on nuclear deterrence would make a good deal of sense. (The same analysis applies to any proposal for nuclear disarmament.)

It is generally agreed that the complete elimination of nuclear deterrence via ballistic missile defense alone is technically unrealistic, and thus it is not really necessary to evaluate SDI on those terms. Instead, we need to consider how a partially effective ballistic missile defense system could affect nuclear deterrence as our preeminent solution to the strategic surprise problem. A simple, to the point of simplistic, response is that a modest SDI will reduce the effectiveness of any strategic surprise attack, thereby reinforcing deterrence. This is a possibility that has been seized upon by SDI supporters. (The most suitable form of SDI for this would be a hidden, preferential defense of retaliatory forces so the opponent cannot tell which forces are to be defended.)

However, this ignores the dynamic relationship between defense and surprise attack. Planning a strategic surprise involves creatively putting arms, training, strategy, and tactics together in new, unusual ways.[26] A fixed defensive system becomes an obstacle to be designed around in strategic surprise planning. The Strategic Defense Initiative will evoke intense efforts to get around it; the greater the perceived likelihood of war the more intense those efforts. We have already seen demonstrations of this in the Soviet and U.S. military programs to design around deterrence, discussed earlier, and in the ingenious U.S. programs now under way to cope with a possible Soviet ballistic missile defense system.

The administration's answer, in part, is a refocusing of strategic arms-control efforts. The SALT emphasis on sharply restricting strategic defensive systems has been abandoned, and the new objective is to explore the utility of such defenses and, should they prove feasible, to arrange their deployment in nonprovocative ways so as to retain stable deterrence until it can be eliminated. Attempts to design around strategic defenses would be curbed by much greater restrictions on offensive forces.

The most immediate hurdle to overcome here is to convince the Soviets to go along, even if they are convinced the result is likely to be a replay of SALT. The Soviet definition of what constitutes stable deterrence for the interim and how to proceed will be conceptually at variance with the U.S. perspective. This will complicate negotiations and make each side uneasy about what the other is up to. The resulting delay in reaching agreement, alongside bureaucratic pressures behind various weapons systems, will once again mean that technological change outruns negotiations and drives much that is eventually created. We should operate under the assumption that this is about the best we can expect.

More likely is a schizophrenic arms-control process, elements of which have already begun to emerge. To propose installing a defensive system is to threaten to degrade the opponent's deterrent, particularly if a partial defensive system is coupled to damage-limitation offensive capabilities. If we continue to want a damage-limitation capability should deterrence fail, so do the Soviets. This requires continued efforts to frustrate strategic defenses. Thus to propose cuts in offensive forces in concert with installation of strategic defenses is to pull in opposite directions. So is trying to retain the old SALT objective, stable deterrence, while seeking to eliminate one of its basic features, the ban on effective ABM systems. This is a recipe for arms-control failure.

Putting aside strategic arms control, another challenge pertains to the scenario widely considered the most likely route to a deterrence failure, the outbreak of war between superpower clients in a sensitive area that leads to a superpower confrontation that eventually escalates. One way the superpowers have sought to contain this possibility is by arms transfers, both to maintain regional military balances that may prevent such wars and to enable clients to defend themselves so intervention on their behalf will not be necessary. The trouble is that modern conventional arms make excellent resources for strategic surprise, while their destructiveness and expense increase the incentives to seek a strategic surprise (to avoid a grinding slaughter like the Iran-Iraq war).

We can see the result in past cases. Israel has had every reason to seek to make any war with the Arabs short and decisive by resorting to strategic surprise. By 1973 the Arabs had much the same incentive—war could mean huge losses and severe economic strain. Strategic surprise is a good strategy for a client seeking a fait accompli because it fears superpower intervention, and a superpower whose client is being defeated is likely to see the victor as having just this in mind. In any event, if either combatant achieves a strategic surprise, it could leave the superpowers with very little time for crisis management and a near panic at the thought that without intervention the situation will soon be irretrievable; this appears to have happened in Moscow during the October 1973 war. The American reaction to the North Korean invasion in 1950 is a good example of the superpower intervention that can result from a strategic surprise, in that situation one that provoked intervention from the other side. Suppose the second intervention had been by Soviet troops rather than Chinese?

Strategic surprise capabilities are spreading with the proliferation of modern weapons. This makes a dangerous war that invites superpower confrontation a good deal more plausible, putting us closer to the modern-day equivalent of August 1914. For too long we have ignored this particular implication of conventional arms transfers, seeing regional military buildups as a danger or (in the Reagan administration) as a benefit, without grasping the strategic surprise dimension.

CONCLUSION

We have considered the ways in which the history of nuclear deterrence in theory and practice is deeply intertwined with the problem of strategic surprise. We have noted the difficulties in either relying on nuclear deterrence to solve the problem or in finding alternative solutions. We have concluded by reviewing some challenges for the future that should be better understood for coping with the complications of deterrence.

Left unsaid was that the pressures to design around nuclear deterrence, via strategic surprise capabilities, or to exploit the credibility problem via strategic surprise at lower levels, could be most directly eased by the emergence of a broad political rapprochement among the great powers. Why we do not devote more energy and attention to this is the major mystery of our time. We prefer to attach ourselves to unreliable solutions to strategic surprise, solutions that by their very nature compel us to live with the problem in its most extreme and dangerous form.

NOTES

1. Richard K. Betts, Surprise Attack (Washington, D.C.: Brookings Institution, 1982), 3.

2. See Klaus Knorr and Patrick Morgan, Strategic Military Surprise: Incentives and Opportunities (New Brunswick, N.J.: Transaction, 1983).

3. A more extended discussion can be found in Patrick Morgan, "The Opportunity for a Strategic Surprise," in Knorr and Morgan, Strategic Military Surprise, 195-245.

4. That war is most burdensome for great powers is demonstrated in Melvin Small and J. David Singer, Resort to Arms: International and Civil Wars, 1916-1980 (Beverly Hills, Calif.: Sage, 1982), 167-73, 176-77.

5. U.S. Arms Control and Disarmament Agency, World Military Expenditures and Arms Transfers 1985 (Washington, D.C.: ACDA, 1985), 67.

6. See Knorr and Morgan, Strategic Military Surprise.

7. The discussion here draws heavily on Robert Jervis, Perception and Misperception in International Politics (Princeton, N.J.: Princeton University Press, 1976); Joseph de Rivera, The Psychological Dimension of Foreign Policy (Columbus, Ohio: Merrill, 1968); Richards J. Heuer, Jr., "Cognitive Factors in Deception and Counterdeception," in Multidisciplinary Perspectives on Military Deception, eds. Donald Daniel and Catherine Herbig, et al., (Monterey, Calif.: Naval Postgraduate School, 1980); and Morgan, "Opportunity for Strategic Surprise."

8. James G. March and Herbert A. Simon, Organizations (New York: Wiley, 1958).

9. See John Steinbruner, The Cybernetic Theory of Decision (Princeton, N.J.: Princeton University Press, 1974).

10. See Richard Ned Lebow, Between Peace and War (Baltimore: Johns Hopkins University Press, 1981); and Glenn Snyder and Paul Deising, Conflict Among Nations (Princeton, N.J.: Princeton University Press, 1977). On misperceptions among governments that initiated surprise attacks, see various chapters in Knorr and Morgan, Strategic Military Surprise. A major analysis of barriers to perception and learning by governments is Lloyd Etheredge, Can Governments Learn? (Elmsford, N.Y.: Pergamon Press, 1985).

11. Examples can be found in Alexander George and Richard Smoke, Deterrence in American Foreign Policy: Theory and Practice (New York: Columbia University Press, 1974), 170-72.

12. See the discussion on this point in Betts, Surprise Attack.

13. Irving Janis, Groupthink (Boston: Houghton Mifflin, 1982).

14. See Henry Kissinger, "Domestic Structure and Foreign Policy," in Kissinger, American Foreign Policy, 3rd ed. (New York: Norton, 1977), 33.

15. Jervis, Perception and Misperception in International Politics, 175-81.

16. Steve Chan, "The Intelligence of Stupidity: Understanding Failures in Strategic Warning," American Political Science Review 73 (March 1979): 171-80.

17. Robert A. Wohlstetter, Pearl Harbor, Warning and Decision (Stanford, Calif.: Stanford University Press, 1962).

18. See William Kaufmann, "Nonnuclear Deterrence," in Alliance Security: NATO and the No-First-Use Question, ed. John Steinbruner and Leon Sigal (Washington: Brookings Institution, 1983); and Betts, Surprise Attack, 224-27.

19. One can trace the development of early U.S. strategic thinking on war with the Soviet Union in Thomas Etzold and John Louis Gaddis, eds., Containment: Documents on American Policy and Strategy, 1945-1950 (New York: Columbia University Press, 1978).

20. See Patrick Morgan, Deterrence, A Conceptual Analysis, 2nd ed. (Beverly Hills, Calif.: Sage, 1983), especially the last chapter; and Robert Jervis, The Illogic of American Strategy (Ithaca, N.Y.: Cornell University Press, 1984).

21. See David Alan Rosenberg, "The Origins of Overkill: Nuclear Weapons and American Strategy, 1945-1960," International Security 7 (Spring 1983): 3-71.

22. Stephen Meyer, Soviet Theater Nuclear Forces, Adelphi Papers nos. 187-88 (London: International Institute for Strategic Studies, Winter 1983/84.

23. Dagobert Brito and Michael Intriligator, Non-Armageddon Solutions to the Arms Race, Center for International and Strategic Affairs reprint no. 1 (Los Angeles: University of California, 1984).

24. Bruce Berkowitz, "Technological Progress, Strategic Weapons, and American Nuclear Policy," Orbis 29 (Summer 1985): 254.

25. Ibid., 257.

26. Relevant discussion can be found in Knorr and Morgan, Strategic Military Surprise, and in John Mearsheimer, Conventional Deterrence (Ithaca, N.Y.: Cornell University Press, 1983).

Limited War and Nuclear Weapons: Will Washington and Moscow Have to Swap Doctrine?

George H. Quester

INTRODUCTION

The purpose of this chapter is to attempt to sort out one of the more persistent risks of confusion about Soviet and Western military strategy as applied to the possibilities of conventional or nuclear war in Central Europe and to speculate about how such statements of strategy (along with the basic political and military situations that determine such strategy) might undergo a dramatic reversal in the next two decades.

NUCLEAR ESCALATION, LIMITED WAR

We again and again hear statements like the following: "The Russians do not believe in limited nuclear war." While such a statement quite often produces nods of knowing agreement, it unfortunately can mean two very different things.

First, the statement could mean that the Soviets objectively do not believe that a war could be kept limited once nuclear weapons had been introduced, that is, that they feel they cannot count on any new firebreaks or barriers to escalation, once the conventional-nuclear line had been crossed. (On this factual point, of course, they might find many Western analysts reaching similar conclusions, while other Western analysts might, however, find such pessimism to be too closed minded.)

Alternatively, the statement could mean that the Soviets do not want the limited nuclear war possibility to be maintained, that they "do not believe in it" in the same way that most of us "do not believe" in drug use, that is, that the Soviets might well act so as to keep a war from being limited once it had become nuclear.

The second is not so much a statement about Soviet beliefs as about Soviet preferences, preferences that might well derive from the objective situation. The objective situation would presumably be what has worried Western planners for three decades: the Soviets might have the capability and the intention of invading and conquering Western Europe by the use only of conventional forces, and thus they would want to confront the United States and NATO with the prospect that any attempt to blunt and reverse such a conventional aggression by the introduction of battlefield nuclear weapons would surely induce an all-out escalation to a thermonuclear World War III.[1]

It makes strategic sense, from this perspective, for the Soviets to pretend that they see no possibility of limited nuclear war, for this then tends to wipe out much of what might insure NATO against Soviet military aggressions of a World War II variety. It makes sense for the Soviets to radiate signals that they do not believe in limited nuclear war, even when this mostly means that the Soviets will be committing themselves to plans and procedures that make such a prediction self-confirming, plans and procedures that work to guarantee that the first use of nuclear weapons will lead to all-out use.

Have there been any such confusions and obtuseness about strategic policies and declarations on the Western side? Indeed there have, in ways where exactly the same kind of double-edged wording might have been used, producing some of the same confusions, but simply transposed down one rung of the ladder of escalation.

What might someone have said about the Eisenhower Administration's comprehension of the new theories of limited war, as put forward by William Kaufmann and Bernard Brodie and others in the middle 1950's?[2] The statement might well have been as follows, again with listeners nodding in knowing agreement: "The Eisenhower people do not believe in limited war." But again the statement would have carried two significantly different meanings.

First, it could have meant that Eisenhower and Dulles really did not understand the possibility that a war of the future, particularly a war in Europe, could be fought only with nonnuclear weapons. Or this could have meant that the U.S. administration did not believe in limited war in the sense that this administration did not approve of it, did not want to encourage the prospect, and thus would configure U.S. plans and procedures, in a self-confirming way, so that any war could be expected to become a nuclear war.

While we have had waves of clarification in the West, interspersed with waves of nostalgia for Eisenhower's approach, much of the strategic confusion on the Western side persists, amid conclusions that "NATO does not believe in a purely conventional war."

These Western statements again are more statements of preference than of belief, again determined by the objective situation. If the Warsaw Pact is assumed to have an advantage in conventional capabilities and to be uniquely tempted by the prospects of a conventional mili-

tary conquest, NATO will want to confront the Soviet leadership with
a greater likelihood that any such war cannot remain conventional but
will inexorably become nuclear.

The two postures are remarkably parallel in the confusions and
debates they cause among analysts, analysts who always must wrestle
with whether they are discussing the analytical acumen of the two sides
or the strategic needs. The two postures are a full step out of synchronization, straightforwardly because of the opposite political and military positions of NATO and the Warsaw Pact.

The Warsaw Pact has normally needed to stress the possibility
of conventional limited war and the impossibility of nuclear limited
war. NATO has conversely needed to stress the impossibility of limited conventional war and the possibility of nuclear limited war.

This author is convinced that it has always been a mistake to take
Soviet or Western strategic pronouncements at face value as analytical efforts and then to become distressed that one side or the other
side may be failing to be perceptive about reality. What we may rather
be encountering here is each side's attempt to pretend to see reality
and thus to impose some self-confirming shape on reality; the ploys
are remarkably similar, even while the two sides have opposite games
to play for two very different rungs of possible escalation.

This is basically a view that assumes that each side <u>sees</u> reality
more or less as any bright analyst would see it, while each side <u>pre-
tends to see</u> such reality in a strategically self-serving way.

CONFLICTING INTERPRETATIONS OF SOVIET DOCTRINE

Before moving ahead to discuss the real possibilities for the
present and for the future, we will have to digress to sort out one
other possible confusion. It is often stated that the Soviets had written
off any possibilities of nonnuclear war in Europe in the 1960s and
1970s and have only more recently begun considering and planning
for the possibility of a limited conventional war between NATO and
the Warsaw Pact. Such statements are based on observations of Soviet
manuevers and dissections of Soviet military manuals, often skipping
over the official Soviet premise that the NATO side will have been the
first to escalate to the use of nuclear warheads or will have definitely
been committed to such escalation. A Soviet stress on the offensive
is coupled, in these analyses, with Moscow's perceptions of the importance of preemption.[3]

If we, however, remember the many Soviet attempts to delegiti-
mate the introduction of nuclear weapons for a war in Europe or anywhere else, including the Stockholm Peace Petition and the Rapacki
Plan, and Moscow's continuing espousals of a no-first-use policy bind-

ing all the sides, we are back into synchronization with the objective geopolitical situation. Moscow has normally stood to gain from making conventional war possible in Europe and from making escalation to nuclear war less likely. The NATO countries have stood to gain from the reverse, as long as this deters a Soviet initiation of warfare in the first place. And the various Soviet maneuvers and Soviet military handbooks do not change this objective fact.[4]

One can think of but one short period of history where the objective situation might indeed have been more markedly reversed: this came at the end of the 1950s, when the Berlin Wall had not yet been erected and the Soviets were intent on somehow eliminating the threat to East German stability posed by the West Berlin escape hatch. While contemplating only a new blockade of West Berlin and no overt military offensives against West Germany, Moscow would for that time have been in a situation of welcoming the military status quo. The likelihood of nuclear escalation discourages conventional military offensives, just as the possibility of limited conventional war encourages such offensives. It would not have taken a military offensive act to close the autobahns and interfere with air access to the enclave. It would instead have taken a military offensive act for NATO to try to open a corridor again to Berlin.

Some of the Soviet commentary by which any war in Central Europe will go nuclear emerged in this period, before the Berlin Wall solved Moscow's problem, negating any need to run the risks of trying to swallow West Berlin. The rest of Soviet commentary suggesting that nuclear escalation is likely then also reflects the success of Western commentaries in the same direction.[5]

To repeat, we are in a competitive game of self-confirming prophecies here. If NATO talks enough about the likelihoods of nuclear escalation and if Soviet forces advance any distance across the Elbe, then such likelihoods become real.

THE ACTUALITY OF LIMITED WAR

What is the actual truth about whether a nuclear war can be limited? The truth, of course, is that we have some chance that new firebreaks and barriers to all-out escalation can be maintained, but we have no guarantee and must run serious risks that limits will cease to apply.

What is the actual truth about whether a war in Europe can be kept to conventional war, as nuclear weapons are entirely withheld? Again the truth, of course, is that we have some chance that no nuclear weapons will be fired, that each side will adhere to a no-first-use policy, but we have no guarantee of this, for there are a number of ways in which nuclear weapons could come into use in such a war.

The categorical statements about such matters are thus analyti-
cally wrong, as compared with more cautious statements about mixtures of probabilities. But the pattern shaping which side should issue
such categorical statements is clear, as noted above, matching very
nicely the probable strategic interests of the two sides. What one does
not see, on the U. S. government side, are any categorical statements
that nuclear war cannot be limited. What one does not really see, on
the Soviet side, are categorical statements that conventional war in
Europe could never be limited. Each side has made the errors of
categorical statements that serve its own bargaining position and not
the errors of the categorical statements that serve its adversary's
bargaining position; hence we might suspect there is less real error
here, and more strategy about strategy, as each side engages in strategically appropriate posturings and dissimulations about what it believes in.

WORRIES OF THE PAST

What makes the above issues still more interesting is a specula-
tive possibility that we may see a dramatic reversal of roles and
situations by the 1990s and that this could produce a reversal of
obfuscations in strategic pronouncements.

Will we see the United States proposing a no-first-use agreement
on nuclear weapons in the future and the Soviets turning it down? Will
we see American statements categorically pretending that every first
use of nuclear weapons would have to escalate to all-out thermonuclear
war, with the Soviets instead pretending to see attractive options for
a limited use of nuclear weapons, without uncontrolled escalation?
Will we see the Soviets insisting that Europe could never sit still for
a limited conventional war, applying the various coupling mechanisms
developed by NATO over three decades to make it all the more plausible that any conventional war in Europe would become a nuclear war?

The basic makeweight here, it will be argued, is what has shaped
the strategic dialogue ever since 1950, the general assumption about
whether conventional force comparisons and conventional warfare possibilities favor the East or the West. For decades, Moscow's hold
over its Eastern European satellites, or at the very least over their
armies, has been presumed to generate a strength that NATO could
not match. For decades, Moscow's investment in tanks has been presumed to constitute a military force that NATO would have great difficulty in holding back in any conventional combat.

Yet what if new conventional force augmentations in NATO and
new developments in antitank weaponry cancel out this latter Soviet
advantage in military hardware? And what if major unrest spreads

through Eastern Europe in the 1990s, on the model of Solidarity in
Poland, but spreads as well to Czechoslovakia and East Germany and
Hungary?

Predicting the outcome in any conventional war is a most difficult
task. In some ways, this presents a paradox.

We have had many conventional wars in our history and many
short bursts of such war since World War II (what we call limited
war, because various weapons, above all nuclear weapons, do not
get used). By comparison, we have had no nuclear wars (or just one,
if we cite Hiroshima and Nagasaki as an example of nuclear war).

Yet nuclear war is now basically very predictable, in that the
levels of destruction are assured of being very, very horrendous. By
comparison, the conventional wars with which we have had so much
experience are basically unpredictable, as each new round of warfare
in the Middle East somehow fails to resemble the last round, as the
electronic countermeasures that worked so well the last time do not
work this time, as new tanks and new antitank weapons are tested
against each other, as new fighter-bombers are tested against new
surface-to-air missiles, and so on.

With regard to a possible war in Central Europe, several kinds
of confusion and unpredictability are thus intertwined with one another.
As in the wars of the Middle East, it will be difficult to anticipate
whether the weapons systems of NATO will be outclassed by those of
the Warsaw Pact or whether the situation will be dramatically the reverse, with NATO tanks and antitank guided missiles (ATGM) and
helicopters and fighter-bombers proving to be much better than those
designed in the Soviet Union.[6] Related to this East versus West uncertainty will be questions about whether the defense or the offense
will be generally favored, whether either side can expect to win a
victory by striking first, or whether the side that has been struck
first will reap the advantage.

Obviously, then, compounding these uncertainties of the battlefield will be political issues about how the war began. Was it a revival
of Nazism in West Germany followed by a blatant German aggression
(in which case Polish and Czech troops might be more reliable from
a Soviet standpoint)? Or was the war caused by a brutal Soviet intervention in Poland or Rumania or Yugoslavia (in which case one would
not envy any Soviet commander who had divisions from Eastern Europe
assigned to his flanks)?

We know less than we would like to know about the probable loyalties and fighting qualities of all the East European armed forces in the
Warsaw Pact.[7] It would be a fair guess that Moscow also knows less
than it would like to know. We do know that Eastern Europe is going
to be prone to unrest for the remainder of this century and beyond, if
only because the average East European will see these affiliations with

the Soviet Union as standing in the way of the affluence and well-being that a freer political system produces in Western Europe.

We have lived through decades after World War II in which the outcome of a conventional war was (pessimistically) rated as much more predictable, as the Soviets were credited with having 175 divisions or 300 divisions, and it was feared that "Asian hordes" would roll forward to the Bay of Biscay once a war broke out. Such a pessimistic certainty may have simplified the analytical problem for U.S. and NATO planners in an earlier time, as the threat of nuclear escalation would seem indispensible for heading off Soviet threats of invasion.

Advocates of a greater reliance on conventional forces for NATO have at various times tried to debunk this Soviet superiority, arguing that there is no need for the United States to rely on threats of nuclear escalation.[8]

Yet such advocates of a NATO conventional force approach have tended to radiate an alternative certainty that might be more than the facts could support; the arguments of Alain Enthoven and Robert McNamara and others have seemed too patly optimistic to be convincing when suggesting that NATO forces could surely repulse a Soviet tank attack.

The West Europeans who have been skeptical of the conventional defense proposals offered by McNamara and his associates in the 1960s and now again in the 1980s[9] have been questioning the analysis;[10] they have also been questioning the sincerity of the motivation. From the viewpoint of Paris or Bonn, such arguments have exaggerated the security of Western Europe, in part because the proponents of those arguments would prefer to lose Western Europe if a war came, rather than losing all U.S. cities as well in a nuclear exchange. If this is a perfectly rational choice for Americans, it would be a choice that left Western Europe more exposed to threats and to possibilities of conventional invasion if Moscow now was freed of the fears of nuclear escalation and if U.S. national leaders were now ready to state that they believed in a conventional war in Europe.[11]

THE TRENDS AND SOME NEW WORRIES

Predictions that NATO can defend itself using only conventional weapons may thus be subject to worrisome uncertainties. But this is only a part of the difficulty with the conventional option, for (as we have noted) limited wars may be unpredictable in both directions. In addition to removing a reliance on U.S. nuclear weaponry, might not an enhancement of NATO conventional strength pose new threats to the Soviet position in Eastern Europe?

Our debate about predictions of conventional war has run on for more than three decades, but it has settled into a pattern that may be somewhat misleading for our analytical needs here. If we assume that NATO must inherently be on the defensive and stay on the defensive, then a large fraction of what is possible (and what is worrisome for Moscow) is ruled out of bounds. The issue then becomes the simpler and narrower debate of what is needed to keep Soviet tanks from rolling to Luxembourg or on to Paris, with one faction contending that a threat of nuclear escalation is indispensable for holding back this threat and another faction saying it can be done with conventional forces. But the arguments for conventional preparations have perhaps been far too modest in speaking only of NATO defense, when all of the considerations they bring to bear might one day also pose the threat of a NATO-supported liberation of Eastern Europe.

And here, of course, is the rub. If McNamara and like-minded analysts are correct about the possible inappropriateness of a U.S. posture committed to nuclear escalation, they may be forecasting an appropriateness of a Soviet posture generating escalation. Unless the conventional force posture heavily favors the defense (that is, heavily favors the status quo in punishing military forces when they are moving in either direction and rewarding them when they elect to sit still), one side or the other will feel threatened, and that side may then conclude that it should play dumb about the possibility of a limited conventional war.

In the past, all the scenarios tended to assume that a Warsaw Pact invasion of Western Europe would succeed relatively easily and straightforwardly if nuclear weapons were not introduced. Some skepticism about this assumption has been much overdue, and such skepticism is a key premise of all our arguments here. Yet what then would be counterprediction? It cannot be that we surely will have a stalemate on the lines of World War I trench warfare, whereby each side continues to hold its own.

If a conventional war were to break out in Central Europe, this author would predict a wide and uncertain range of possibilities, including rapid Soviet progress to Frankfurt and Brussels and beyond, a stalemate along the current front lines, rapid NATO counterprogress toward Magdeburg and Prague, or the like. Everything is possible here, just as everything is possible for the next war between Israel and Syria.

It is certainly true that the average of such predictions is more favorable for NATO than were the standard predictions of the past. And the trend of predictions thus reinforces the position of those Americans who favor a clearer endorsement of the possibilities of conventional war, with an elimination of the obfuscations that have characterized U.S. statements about limited nuclear war and flexible response in the past.

Yet if the trend continues, we may see very few references to "Asian hordes" in the future and rather more references to the identification of Europeans with each other, in a way that puts the Soviet Union very much more on the defensive. If this moves along far enough, will we then see some of the new posturings and obfuscations on the Soviet side that we are predicting here?

Putting the Soviets on the defensive has good and bad elements.[12] It might very much ease worries about the safety of NATO. It might seem like elementary justice, the natural punishment for Moscow's unreasonable dominance of its European neighbors and a historical verdict on the appropriateness of Marxist solutions. At the same time it could drive Moscow into worried and dangerous behavior. If it led Moscow to move away from any and all endorsements of no first use, adopting instead a posture that in a self-confirming away seems to guarantee first use, we might have a result that we would regret. The problems of extended nuclear deterrence and nuclear umbrellas and credibility (amid the dangers of bluffs being called in a way that would lead to nuclear escalation neither side wanted) would all remain in place, having simply gone through a symmetrical reversal of the two sides' positions.

THE CHINA FACTOR

One can think of a variety of reasons why all the references to "Asian hordes" will be out of date. To begin, China has almost switched sides since the 1960s. In an earlier day, when anyone had conjured up some way for NATO to deploy enough conventional battalions to block all the battalions of the Soviet Union and the Warsaw Pact, a pessimist could then cite the possible introduction of Chinese troops into the Communist force array, somehow transported in by the Trans-Siberian Railway, to make the difference. Today we instead see a substantial force of Soviet troops tied down along the Soviet and Mongolian borders with China, with at least some chance that any all-conventional war between NATO and the Warsaw Pact might see Sino-Soviet conventional force battles along these frontiers as well, battles that would see the Soviet forces doing well because of their superiority of equipment but that would see the Chinese doing well by sheer numbers (again with the results in terms of battlefield outcomes hardly being predictable).

It should be remembered that the Chinese were the first in the world to issue a categorical no-first-use statement, repeating over

and over again that China would never use nuclear weapons unless
some other country had used them first.[13] This might simply reflect
a sincere Chinese awareness of the destructive capabilities of such
weapons; nonetheless, it would seem to throw away some not so very
extended nuclear deterrence, if any military analysts have feared a
Soviet all-conventional invasion threat for Inner Mongolia and the rest
of China as much as they have feared it for NATO. What Robert Mc-
Namara and his colleagues have proposed for U.S. commitments on
behalf of NATO is in effect nothing different from what the Chinese
have enunciated for their own military defense situation ever since
Peking acquired nuclear weapons in 1964, and all the questions that
might seem relevant to the trade-offs for NATO ought to be at work
for the Peoples' Republic of China as well.

People who take the nuclear deterrence phenomenon seriously
might be skeptical in any event about the categorical nature of the
Chinese statement. It is one thing for the United States to consider a
policy of no-first-use of nuclear weapons for any remote corner of
the world, or even for NATO, or for the Soviet Union to offer such a
pledge for Central Europe, but it is quite another for any nuclear-
weapons state to promise such a policy for all of its interior territory.
A country whose capital is being occupied and whose entire country is
being overrun would normally feel that it had nothing left to lose and
would thus fire off nuclear weapons at the cities of the other side as
a last gasp of retaliation. A policy of no-first-use anywhere will be
heavily dependent on a matching policy of nondeployment, for if theater
nuclear weapons are deployed in the NATO area, or wherever, they
are likely to come into use willy-nilly when a war erupts. But to
where are the Chinese then to withdraw their nuclear weapons, if
their no-first-use pledge is to be taken so seriously?

The Chinese no-first-use pledge might conversely reflect some
kind of confidence (well founded or badly founded) about how a conventional war would go, as Beijing hopes to repulse Soviet armies at the
frontiers or expects to harass invading Soviet armies guerrilla-style,
just as Japanese armies were harassed earlier. No first use makes
sense for a country that expects to hold its own in a conventional war.
(In terms of overall rationality, it might, of course, make sense under
all circumstances, even if an adversary were going to win all the conventional victories; but here one at least may head off such defeats by
pretending not to be this rational, pretending not to believe in no first
use.)[14]

DEMOGRAPHIC TRENDS

Leaving aside the analogies between China's declaratory policy
on nuclear weapons and the possible future declaratory policies for

NATO or Moscow, the base fact is in any event that Chinese conventional forces are no longer to be interpreted as probable reinforcement echelons for the Warsaw Pact, but rather as forces loosely and informally allied instead with NATO.

Turning to the rest of the force comparison, it is always relevant to refer to elementary considerations of demography. Few variables in the social sciences are quite so predictable as the number of eighteen-year-old males there will be four or six years hence, since the birth patterns determining this are long settled.

Pessimists about the prospects of an effective NATO conventional military instrument often point to the demographic patterns in West Germany and elsewhere in much of Western Europe that will make it more difficult to muster full strength ground forces over the next decade. (A reliance on nuclear escalation is by contrast not dependent on totals of people.) The raw totals of age cohorts are then made even more worrisome after we factor in social trends of urbanization and drug culture and counterculture rebellion, all of which have probably reduced the fraction of each cohort that is militarily fit.

Yet many of the same trends have their equivalent in Eastern Europe and the Soviet Union as well, with a slight lag compared with the West, as birth rates have declined and as various forms of urbanization and societal trends are also at work to worry the military recruiter. The Soviet Union does not yet have a drug problem, but it has long had a major alcoholism problem. The tools of societal discipline available to the state preclude any youth rebellions as open as what we see in the United States or West Germany or the Netherlands, but more subtle manifestations raise some of the same worries about military discipline, bravery in combat, and the like.[15]

If anyone wished today to cite the Asian character of Soviet military strength, it would more probably be a reference to weakness instead of strength. By the natural process of comparative birthrates, Great Russians are no longer a majority of the total of people living in the Soviet Union. It might seem reasonable to regard Ukrainians and Byelorussians as close to being Great Russians, especially since these nationalities are increasingly speaking Russian rather than their own Slavic languages, and this then heads off the ethnic crisis of the Soviet Union a while longer. Yet all these Slavic groups, along with the other non-Slavic European nationalities (the Estonians, Latvians, Lithuanians, and Moldavians), have undergone marked drops in their birthrates, while the Asian nationalities continue to have large families. By the end of the twentieth century, the Slavic peoples will constitute less than a majority of the total, and it is even possible that the total of all Europeans will be close to 50 percent within another decade.[16]

There is ample evidence that this changed nature of the Soviet pool

for recruitment has caused concern among military planners in the
Soviet Union, even while the broader ramifications of the change also
cause some concern among Russians in general. A fair number of
military draftees are turning out to be barely capable of speaking and
understanding Russian. At the least this creates problems for effective
communication, command, and control, just as the appearance of non-
English-speaking Hispanics causes such concern in the U.S. Army.
Despite pretensions of being above all considerations of ethnic chau-
vinism, moreover, the Soviet Union has in a number of respects shown
concern for, and a dependence on, such national characteristics,
relying on Russian as the language linking all the Soviet Socialist
Republics together and tending mainly to trust Great Russians, or
at least other Slavs, in the most important positions of political and
military command.

The Soviet planner for a conventional war thus confronts problems
comparable to those of a NATO planner, fearing that his pool of recruits will not match the bravery and endurance and military prowess
of the troops who fought in World War II. Far more of such troops
than before will be of non-European, non-Russian origin, perhaps
undereducated, perhaps undermotivated, certainly a problem where
clarity and intensity of communication play an important role in battle.
Among the Great Russians and other Europeans, far more recruits
will now come from urban environments and will be less accustomed
to roughing it, less capable of moving great distances on a diet of
black bread and borscht. Soviet authorities have more generally expressed some anxiety about the jadedness and softness and lowered
motivation of their youth, who are apparently sometimes intent only
on acquiring a bigger apartment or a set of blue jeans or an Elvis
Presley record and are bored with tales of the Great Patriotic War
defending the motherland against Hitler's aggression or the general
accomplishments of socialism.

One should be on his guard about accepting at face value such
pessimistic impressions of diminished fighting prowess on either
side. Today's Bundeswehr may look like a much less dedicated and
disciplined fighting force than the World War II Wehrmacht, and today's Soviet army may look less committed to combat than that of
World War II. Yet one would hardly wish to try to beat a division of
the Bundeswehr with a division of the Wehrmacht or to beat a 1985
Soviet tank division with one of 1945. The sheer improvement in technical equipment and firepower would make the modern fighting force
overwhelming.

Technology and education count for a great deal today in gauging
the prowess of army units committed to conventional warfare, so
much that this may more than make up for any passing away of the
traditional societal attitudes that produced a warrior mentality. And

the preliminary symptoms of any such societal change can also be misleading. Many of the Royal Air Force pilots who performed so well in the Battle of Britain had only a decade earlier resolved that they would not fight for king or country.

HORIZONTAL ESCALATION

Just as with the effectiveness of ATGMs against tanks or the future loyalty of Polish infantry battalions, predictions of the fighting skills of Soviet forces or NATO forces add one more layer of unpredictability. Much of the news is that the Soviets will not have such an easy or sure venture in trying to roll into Frankfurt or Brussels with a conventional attack. Yet this might translate into two very different alternatives. One is that neither side can contemplate attacking the other for an easy conquest. The other is that NATO forces might in the next decade have an easy venture in trying to roll into Dresden or Warsaw.

One part of our conclusion here might thus amount to simply another lamenting of all systems and situations loaded toward the offensive and a hope for those more favorable to the defense. The European central front might one day see both sides disowning nuclear weapons, if whoever attacked conventionally in either direction were truly to be at a disadvantage, as compared with whoever sat still to be attacked. Here we would at last have a decent measure of crisis stability for this region and a chance that both sides might feel able to deemphasize nuclear escalation.

Unless this is achieved, however, the prospect remains that Western Europe will be of such great importance to the United States and that Eastern Europe will be of such great importance to the Soviet Union that one or the other will feel driven to extend all the threats of nuclear escalation it can to such prizes, treating them as "the fifty-first state" or the "sixteenth Soviet Socialist Republic."

Some of the conventional warfare possibilities we are considering here will seem the same as what has recently been much discussed as "horizontal escalation." This phrase broadly covers those retaliatory responses for a Soviet conventional aggression that do not involve escalation to nuclear warfare but involve some retaliatory escalation, nonetheless, in the addition of another round of conventional warfare of our choosing, in a theater where we presumably can win, thus punishing the Soviets for having grasped for victory in any theater of their initial choosing.

Where then would we find these theaters so conducive to a conventional retaliatory stroke on our part? Simple geography suggests that Communist-governed areas in the Western Hemisphere might be just

as militarily vulnerable as the democratically governed countries
on the Eurasian land mass. Perhaps we would thus retaliate for an
invasion of Austria by an invasion of Nicaragua. Perhaps we will
respond to a Soviet invasion of countries bordering the Persian Gulf
by finally terminating Castro's governance of Cuba.

Looking more narrowly at the European central front, Samuel
Huntington has captured a fair amount of attention by suggesting that
the logical response to a Soviet conventional invasion of West Germany would come in a NATO conventional ground force counterstroke,
carrying the war back into Czechoslovakia and East Germany and
Poland.[17] It is not entirely clear whether this would amount to an
offensive flank movement bypassing the advancing Soviet force, so
that Western troops were liberating Prague just as Communist forces
were entering Frankfurt, or instead a head-on blunting of the Soviet
advance, followed by an exploitation of this blunting, seizing a fair
amount of Eastern European territory as follow-on punishment for
Moscow.

The argument here, unlike Huntington's, is intended more to be
an exercise in prediction, rather than policy prescription. Yet the
proposals of analysts like Huntington are certainly symptomatic of
the premises for this argument in suggesting that augmented Western
conventional forces will have augmented opportunities for liberating
Communist-governed territory. The concern is that such a trend of
shifting of capabilities may soon enough lead to a shift of declaratory
postures and professed doctrine on nuclear war and conventional war.
We may not ever see the day when the Soviet Union threatens nuclear
escalation in defense of Nicaragua or (to achieve the same thing) pro-
fesses to see no possibility of a purely conventional war if Nicaragua
is attacked, any more than we have lately seen such U.S. threats or
professions of belief where Thailand is concerned. But we may see
such Soviet declarations where Czechoslovakia or East Germany are
concerned.

Horizontal escalation might become an option for the West because NATO has developed much better prospects in a war on the
European central front or because Marxist regimes have taken over
one more country such as Nicaragua. In the latter case, the emergence of such an option merely reflects a prior setback for the West
and the development of a new vested interest for the Communists.
And it does not have much impact on what either side would say or
do about nuclear weapons. In the former case, it may amount to a
real enhancement of Western military strength and political position,
but this can come at the price of applying real pressure on Moscow,
the kind of pressure that shapes nuclear strategy and nuclear doctrine
in the first place.

SOME CONCLUSIONS

Let us record the predictions that have been advanced here. We may see much less chance in the 1990s of a Soviet tank advance on West Germany. And we may see much more chance of a NATO tank advance into Eastern Europe, perhaps coming to the aid of movements like Solidarity.

As a direct result of this, we may then see the day when NATO is advocating, and even possibly unilaterally proclaiming, a no-first-use policy and at the same time warning that any tactical use of nuclear weapons cannot be limited. At the same time, we may see the Soviet Union rejecting any such no-first-use doctrine, simply presenting its new analytical conclusions that any war in central Europe would have to go nuclear, perhaps after an unspecified pause, perhaps as part of a Soviet policy of flexible response. To close the picture, the Soviets would offer scenarios for limited nuclear war, arguing that all-out escalation would not necessarily have to follow.

Such a 180-degree reversal of Soviet and U.S. positions on nuclear war might seem altogether too strange to be thinkable. Yet one might note the Soviet and U.S. reversal of positions on antiballistic missiles (ABM), from Glassboro to today's debate about Reagan's "Star Wars" Strategic Defense Initiative, and then conclude that all things are possible.

NOTES

1. A good overview and sorting out of the classic NATO problem can be found in James M. Garrett, "Conventional Force Deterrence in the Presence of Theater Nuclear Weapons," Armed Forces and Society 2 (Fall 1984): 59-83.

2. William W. Kaufman, Military Policy and National Security (Princeton: Princeton University Press, 1956); and Bernard Brodie, Strategy in the Missile Age (Princeton: Princeton University Press, 1959).

3. For examples of analyses by which the Soviets plan an early escalation from conventional to nuclear war, see Joseph D. Douglass, Jr., and Amoretta M. Hoeber, Conventional War and Escalation: The Soviet View (New York: Crane Russak, 1981). See also Ilana Kass and Michael J. Deane, "The Role of Nuclear Weapons in the Modern Theater Battlefield: The Current Soviet View," Comparative Strategy 4 (Fall 1984): 193-213; and Dennis Gormley and Douglas Hart, "Soviet Views on Escalation," Washington Quarterly 7 (Fall 1984): 71-84.

4. For a statement of views (parallel to this author's) that the Soviets have all along much preferred a European conventional opinion,

see Phillip A. Peterson and John G. Hines, "The Conventional Offensive in Soviet Theater Strategy," Orbis 27 (Fall 1983): 695-740.

5. A comprehensive examination of the details of the ins and outs of Soviet statements and actions on strategic nuclear policy can be found in Stephen M. Meyer, Soviet Theater Nuclear Forces, Adelphi Papers nos. 187-88 (London: International Institute for Strategic Studies, Winter 1983/84).

6. On the likely interactions of weapons systems in a conventional battle, see Boyd D. Sutton, John R. Landry, Malcolm B. Armstrong, Howell M. Estes III, and Wesley K. Clark, "Deep Attack Concepts and the Defense of Central Europe," Survival 26 (March/April 1984): 50-69. See also Phil Williams and William Wallace, "Emerging Technologies and European Security," Survival 26 (March/April 1984): 70-78.

7. The uncertain loyalties of East European armies are discussed in Dale Herspring and Ivan Volgyes, "How Reliable Are East European Armies?" Survival 22 (September/October 1980): 208-18; and A. Ross Johnson, Robert W. Dean, and Alexander Alexiev, East European Military Establishments: The Warsaw Pact Northern Tier (New York: Crane, Russak, 1982).

8. For example, Alain C. Enthoven and K. Wayne Smith, How Much is Enough? (New York: Harper and Row, 1971). See also Robert Komer, "Is Conventional Defense of Europe Feasible?" Naval War College Review 34 (September/October 1982): 80-91.

9. McGeorge Bundy, George F. Kennan, Robert S. McNamara, and Gerard Smith, "Nuclear Weapons and the Atlantic Alliance," Foreign Affairs 60 (Spring 1982): 753-68; and Robert S. McNamara, "The Military Role of Nuclear Weapons," Foreign Affairs 62 (Fall 1983): 59-80.

10. Karl Kaiser, Georg Leber, Alois Mertes, and Franz-Joseph Schulze, "Nuclear Weapons and the Preservation of Peace," Foreign Affairs 60 (Summer 1982): 1157-70. See also Colin Gray, "NATO's Nuclear Dilemma," Policy Review no. 22 (Fall 1982): 97-116.

11. See Stephen J. Cimbala, "Theater Nuclear and Conventional Force Improvements," Armed Forces and Society 11 (Fall 1984): 115-29. For some healthy skepticism on whether conventional force preparations can be reliable, see also Daniel Goure and Jeffry Cooper, "Conventional Deep Strike: A Critical Look" Comparative Strategy 4 (Fall 1984): 215-48. Also, Alan Ned Sabrosky, "America in NATO: The Conventional Delusion," Orbis 25 (Summer 1981): 293-306.

12. Some of the concerns about posing conventional military threats to Moscow's grip on Eastern Europe are outlined in Fen Osler Hampson, "Groping for Technical Panaceas: The European Conventional Balance and Nuclear Stability," International Security 8 (Winter 1983/84): 57-82.

13. On the Chinese evolution of nuclear posture, see Johathan D. Pollack, "China as a Nuclear Power," in <u>Asia's Nuclear Future</u>, ed. William H. Overholt (Boulder, Colo.: Westview, 1977), 35-66.

14. For an extended discussion of no first use sponsored by the Stockholm International Peace Research Institute, see F. Blackaby, J. Goldblat, and S. Lodgaard, eds., <u>No-First-Use</u> (Philadelphia: Taylor and Francis, 1984). See also Richard Ullman, "No First Use of Nuclear Weapons," <u>Foreign Affairs</u> 50 (July 1972): 669-83.

15. The demographic trends in military manpower for NATO and the Warsaw Pact are discussed in Gilbert Kutscher, "The Impact of Population Development on Military Manpower Problems," <u>Armed Forces and Society</u> 9 (Winter 1983): 265-73.

16. Michael Rywkin, "Central Asia and Soviet Manpower," <u>Problems of Communism</u> 27 (January/February 1979): 1-13.

17. Samuel Huntington, <u>The Strategic Imperative</u> (Cambridge: Ballinger, 1982).

Approaching Armageddon: Nuclear Proliferation and Nuclear War in the Middle East

Louis René Beres

INTRODUCTION

A dreadful irony haunts the Middle East. Enveloped by insecurity, the states of this unfortunate region may seek remedies that can only make them less secure. Fearful for life, they may take steps to encourage the remorseless embrace of collective disintegration.

The problem is nuclear proliferation. Although nuclear weapons can never offer real safety, each state finds itself in a dilemma. Gripped by uncertainty over the nuclear intentions of adversary powers, it may feel compelled to go nuclear itself. That the cumulative effect of such thinking must be radical insecurity for all is of little or no consequence. Since nuclear restraint by adversary states is problematic, only one judgment may appear sound: the benefits of becoming a nuclear power are apt to exceed the costs. This is because each state may calculate that the rationality of remaining nonnuclear is contingent upon the expectation of regionwide reciprocity.

There is another aspect to the problem. The nuclear arms race between the superpowers has endured for two generations without catastrophic failure. As a result, several prospective nuclear weapons states in the Middle East are likely to overestimate the stability of a regional balance of terror.

It is too soon to claim success for nuclear deterrence between the United States and the Soviet Union. Although it has worked thus far (a characterization that leaves out the overwhelming economic and ethical costs of nuclear terror), there is no reason to assume that it will work indefinitely. Indeed, at one time or another, in one way or another, the manifestly apocalyptic possibilities that now lie latent in Soviet and U.S. nuclear weapons are almost certain to be exploited. Whether by design or by accident, by misinformation or by miscalculation, by lapse from rational decision or by unauthorized decision, the system of deadly logic will fail.

Nuclear deterrence is a dynamic process, one that changes continually with momentous and unforeseen effects. Displaying a complex transfiguration unplanned by generations of strategists, the current superpower arms race bears little resemblance to its original forms. Instead of the relatively stable pattern of mutual assured destruction (MAD), nuclear deterrence between the superpowers now rests upon a presumed capacity for nuclear war fighting.

Still another aspect of the problem concerns rationality. The durability of any system of nuclear deterrence is based upon this notion. Yet, there is certainly no reason to believe that leadership in the Middle East must conform to this assumption. On the contrary, the prospect of irrationality seems especially significant in this area.[1]

This is not to suggest, however, that irrationality is synonymous with the "crazy leader" scenario. Should a new nuclear weapons state fall under the leadership of a person or persons suffering from severe emotional stress or major physiological impairment, that state might initiate nuclear first strikes against other nuclear-armed states even though enormously destructive retaliation would be expected. It is even plausible that irrationality would be exhibited by a leader free of madness, stress, or any other mental impairment. As revealed by the actions of President John F. Kennedy during the 1962 Cuban missile crisis, irrational behavior can be displayed by perfectly cool, calm, intelligent, and self-preservation-minded leaders. Kennedy, we may recall, imposed his quarantine on the assumption that it carried a fifty-fifty chance of nuclear war.

A final aspect of the problem lies in the overriding egotism of national leaders, a pattern of hubris that points numbingly toward radioactive silence. By denying their own mortality, their own susceptibility to oblivion, states in the Middle East may more readily turn to nuclear weapons. By insulating themselves from reasonable fears of annihilation, these states may make extinction imminent. Understood in terms of the imperative to halt proliferation, this suggests that leaders in the Middle East learn to associate nuclear war with the cessation of life. Only by rejecting the lethal and humiliating delusions of survival in a nuclear crowd can survival be possible.

HAZARDS OF A NUCLEARIZED MIDDLE EAST

Living in a regional nuclear crowd, the states of the Middle East would be confronted with multiple sources of danger:

● The expanded number of nuclear powers would undermine the idea of a stable balance of terror. There would simply be too many players, too much ambiguity, for any sense of reliable nuclear deterrence to be meaningful.

- The expanded number of nuclear powers would shatter the relative symmetry of strategic doctrine between nuclear weapons states. Some of the new nuclear powers would shape their strategies along the lines of assured destruction capabilities. Others would seek more ambitious objectives, including a nuclear war fighting or counterforce capability. As a result, nuclear weapons might lose their image as instruments of war avoidance, a situation that would surely be accelerated by the first actual use of nuclear weapons by a secondary nuclear power.

- The expanded number of nuclear powers would ultimately create the conditions whereby first-strike attacks could be unleashed with impunity, whatever the condition of the intended victim's willingness to retaliate or the security of its retaliatory forces. This is the case because in a region of many nuclear powers, it would become possible for a nuclear-armed aggressor to launch its weapons against another state without being identified. Unable to know for certain where the attack originated, the victim state might lash out blindly. In the resulting conflagration, a worldwide nuclear war enveloping even the superpowers might take place.

- The expanded number of nuclear powers would create the conditions for a chain reaction of nuclear exchanges. Even before it became possible to launch a nuclear strike anonymously, a strategic exchange might take place between two or more new nuclear weapons states that are members of opposing alliances. Ultimately, if the parties to such a clash involve clients of either or both superpowers, the ensuing chain reaction might consume the United States and the Soviet Union along with much of the rest of the world.

- The expanded number of nuclear powers would create major asymmetries in power between rival states. Where one rival would find itself in possession of nuclear weapons and another rival would be denied such possession, the new nuclear state might find itself with an overwhelming incentive to strike. The cumulative effect of such inequalities of power created by the uneven spread of nuclear weapons could be an elevated probability of nuclear aggression against nonnuclear states.

- The expanded number of nuclear powers would create the conditions whereby microproliferation—the spread of nuclear weapons capabilities to insurgent groups—might be accelerated. A possible outcome of such microproliferation might be not only nuclear terrorism but also an anonymous terrorist detonation that could be mistakenly blamed upon another state by the attack victim. In this way, microproliferation could actually spark regional or systemwide nuclear war between states.

    How might such far-reaching consequences of microproliferation come about? Perhaps the most likely way would involve a nuclear

assault against a state by terrorists hosted in another state. For
example, consider the following scenario:

> Late in the 1980s, Israel and several of her Arab-state
> neighbors finally stand ready to conclude a comprehensive
> peace settlement for the entire region. Only the interests
> of the Palestinians, as defined by the Palestine Liberation
> Organization (PLO), still seem to have been left out. On
> the eve of the proposed signing of the peace agreement,
> half a dozen crude nuclear explosives in the one-kiloton
> range detonate in as many Israeli cities. Public grief in
> Israel over the many thousand dead and maimed is matched
> only by the outcry for revenge. Responding to public senti-
> ments, Israel initiates strikes against terrorist strongholds
> in surrounding Arab countries, whereupon the governments
> of these countries retaliate against Israel. Before long, the
> entire region is embroiled in nuclear conflict.

In this scenario, nuclear terrorism spawns nuclear war. Of
course, such a war could encompass even wider patterns of destruction. How would the United States react to these events? What would
be the Soviet response? Depending upon the precise configuration of
superpower involvement, the war possibilities are myriad.

There are other ways in which nuclear terrorism might ignite a
nuclear war. For example, if regional proliferation in the Middle East
becomes a fait accompli, insurgent groups might try to hide their responsibility for acts of nuclear destruction. Here, by creating the
impression that another state was responsible, a nuclear retaliation
would be directed against an innocent country. Nuclear war, in this
case, would be catalyzed by a nonstate actor exploiting the confusion
of international life in a nuclear crowd.

Regional nuclear proliferation also gives rise to the prospect of
accidental nuclear war and nuclear weapons accidents. The reason for
this hazard is not simply a function of number (that is, the more nuclear weapons states, the greater the number of existing risks). It is
also a consequence of the need to compensate for vulnerable nuclear
forces by utilizing imprudent command and control measures. In addition, new nuclear powers are unlikely to invest the time and expense
needed to equip the nuclear weapons themselves with interlocking
safety mechanisms.

Today, U.S. (and presumably Soviet) nuclear forces are safe-
guarded from accidental firings by a considerable array of features
built into both the chains of command and the weapons themselves.
These features are highlighted by the two-man concept whereby no
single individual has the capability to fire nuclear weapons; by a con-

trol system whereby each individual with a nuclear weapons responsibility has been certified under the Human Reliability Program; by the use of secure, split-handled codes; by the employment of coded locking devices that prevent firing in the absence of specific signals from higher command; and by use of environmental sensing devices that prevent unwanted detonations through the operation of switches that respond to acceleration, deceleration, altitude, spin, gravity, and thermal forces.

It would be the height of folly to expect all new nuclear powers in the Middle East to undertake similar precautions against inadvertent firings of nuclear weapons. To be effective, safety measures would have to apply to all available nuclear weapons and to all pertinent nuclear-weapon operations throughout the stockpile-to-target sequence, that is, storage, maintenance, handling, transportation, and delivery. Moreover, specific provisions would be needed for all unique nuclear weapons system operations, that is, alerts, operational posturing, maneuvers, exercises, and training.

When one considers both the complexity and cost of such safety systems and the fact that new nuclear powers will find it necessary to disavow certain safeguards in the interest of preventing preemption, the prospect of accidental nuclear war is undeniably significant in a proliferated region. This prospect is magnified by the specter of catastrophic accidents that do not give rise to nuclear war but that still produce a nuclear yield. Since even the U.S. record of "broken arrows," or nuclear-weapon accidents, has included a number of very close calls, one cannot help but anticipate a new rash of broken arrows among the forces of new nuclear powers. What would happen when their bombers crash, when the nuclear payloads that they carry are accidentally dropped or intentionally jettisoned, or when these nuclear bombs or missiles are burned in a fire on the ground? With the proliferation of nuclear powers in the Middle East, such accidents could be expected to occur at an increased rate.

As with accidental nuclear war and nuclear-weapon accidents, regional nuclear proliferation would also increase the probability of the unauthorized use of nuclear weapons. This is the case, again, not only because of the expanded number of existing risks, but because the new nuclear powers would almost certainly lack the safeguards now in place in superpower arsenals. In response to the need for a quick-reaction nuclear force that can be fielded as soon as possible, new nuclear powers would inevitably turn to automatic or nearly automatic systems of nuclear retaliation that are not encumbered by complex and costly command and control checks.

The new nuclear weapons states would also be likely to increase the number of national decision makers who are properly authorized to use nuclear weapons. As long as their early warning networks are

unreliable and as long as concern exists that field officers might not
be able to respond to a first-strike attack if central authorization is
required, these secondary nuclear powers may predelegate launch
authority to selected commanders. Such launch-on-warning strategies
would increase the probability of all forms of both authorized and unauthorized nuclear attacks. In this connection, we must include the
prospect of intranational nuclear weapons seizure via coup d'etat, a
prospect that has particularly ominous overtones in such coup-vulner-
able potential proliferators as Iraq, Iran, and Pakistan.

The probability of unauthorized use of nuclear weapons that ac-
crues from nuclear proliferation can also be expected to increase
because of premeditated false warnings. The larger the number of
nuclear-weapon states, the greater the likelihood that personnel who
man early warning satellite or radar systems will deliberately falsify
information about hostile action, especially since the new nuclear
powers may enforce less than the highest standards of human and
mechanical reliability. The results of such falsification, of course,
might well be nuclear first strikes that are disguised as retaliation.

THE EFFECTS OF NUCLEAR ATTACKS

In the final analysis, everything points to the imperative avoidance of nuclear war. Even the most limited nuclear exchange would
signal unprecedented catastrophe. The immediate effects of the
explosions—thermal radiation, nuclear radiation, and blast damage—
would create wide swaths of death and devastation.[2] Victims would
suffer flash and flame burns. Retinal burns could occur in the eyes
of persons at distances of several hundred miles from the explosion.
People would be crushed by collapsing buildings or torn by flying
glass. Others would fall victim to raging firestorms and conflagra-
tions. Fallout injuries would include whole-body radiation, produced
by penetrating, hard gamma radiation; superficial radiation burns
produced by soft radiation; and injuries produced by deposits of radioactive substances within the body.

In the aftermath, medical facilities that might still exist would
be stressed beyond endurance. Water supplies would become unusable
as a result of fallout contamination. Housing and shelter would be unavailable for survivors. Transportation and communication would
break down to almost prehistorical levels. And overwhelming food
shortages would become the rule for at least several years.

Since the countries involved would have entered into war as modern industrial economies, their networks of highly interlocking and
interdependent exchange systems would now be shattered. Virtually
everyone would be deprived of a means of livelihood. Emergency fire

and police services would be decimated. Systems dependent upon electrical power would cease to function. Severe trauma would occasion widespread disorientation and psychological disorders for which there would be no therapeutic services.

In sum, normal society would disappear. The pestilence of unrestrained murder and banditry would augment the pestilence of plague and epidemics. With the passage of time, many of the survivors could expect an increased incidence of degenerative disease and various kinds of cancer. They might also expect premature death, impairment of vision, and a high probability of sterility. Among the survivors of Hiroshima, for example, an increased incidence of leukemia and cancer of the lung, stomach, breast, ovary, and uterine cervix has been widely documented.

Such a war could also have devastating climatic effects. It is now widely believed that even the explosion of a mere one hundred megatons (less than 1 percent of the world's arsenals) would be enough to generate a prolonged epoch of cold and dark. As we have learned, the threshold for a nuclear winter might be very low.[3]

HALTING NUCLEAR PROLIFERATION
IN THE MIDDLE EAST

The present nonproliferation regime is based upon a series of multilateral agreements, statutes, and safeguards. The principal elements of this series are the Atomic Energy Act of 1954; the Statute of the International Atomic Energy Agency (IAEA), which came into force in 1957; the Nuclear Test Ban Treaty, which entered into force on October 10, 1963; the Outer Space Treaty, which entered into force on October 10, 1967; the Treaty Prohibiting Nuclear Weapons in Latin America, which entered into force on April 22, 1968; the Seabeds Arms Control Treaty, which entered into force on May 18, 1972; and the 1978 Nuclear Nonproliferation Act.

The single most important element of the nonproliferation regime, however, is the Treaty on the Nonproliferation of Nuclear Weapons (NPT), which entered into force on March 5, 1970.[4] Since Article 6 of this treaty calls for an end to the nuclear arms race between the superpowers,[5] the current U.S.-U.S.S.R. negotiations on arms control must also be counted as part of the nonproliferation regime. Before the world's nonnuclear powers can begin to take nonproliferation seriously, the United States and the Soviet Union will have to take prompt steps to limit their own nuclear armaments.

In the view of the nonnuclear weapon states, a bargain has been struck between the superpowers and themselves. Unless the Soviet Union and the United States begin to take more ambitious steps toward implementation of the Article 6 pledge, they, too, may move in the direction of nuclear capability. The nonnuclear powers consider this bargain the most prudential path to safety.

From the standpoint of controlling nuclear proliferation, this suggests that the superpowers must restructure their central strategic relationship. Such restructuring must be oriented toward a return to strategies of minimum deterrence: a comprehensive nuclear test ban, a joint renunciation of first use of nuclear weapons, and a joint effort toward creating additional nuclear-weapon-free zones.

Additional incentives, however, would also be needed. The IAEA must be granted greater authority to inspect nuclear facilities, search for clandestine stockpiles, and pursue stolen nuclear materials. Ultimately, such authority must be extended to all nuclear facilities of all states without nuclear weapons. Without such a tightening of IAEA safeguards, a number of nonnuclear-weapon states can be expected to calculate that the benefits of nonproliferation are exceeded by the costs.

The strengthening and expanding of IAEA safeguards and functions is essential to nonproliferation. These goals can also be served by an improved international capability for gathering covert intelligence. In the future, many of the intelligence capabilities that now rest entirely with national governments will need to be pooled and coordinated.

A final arena in which the nonproliferation regime can be improved is nuclear export policy. This is the case because access to nuclear weapons capability now depends largely on the policies of a small group of supplier states. In the years ahead, these states—which carry on international commerce in nuclear facilities, nuclear technology, and nuclear materials—will have to improve and coordinate their export policies.

The crux of this problem is the duality of nuclear exports. Although they contribute to the spread of nuclear weapons, these exports are also an exceptionally lucrative market for the supplier states. Therefore, unless every supplier state can be convinced that its own commitment to restraint in the export of sensitive technologies will be paralleled by every other supplier state, the hazards of a worldwide plutonium economy may be irrepressible.

To avert these hazards, two systems are required: a system for verification of compliance with common nuclear export policies, and a system of sanctions for noncompliance in which the costs of departure from such policies are so great as to outweigh the anticipated benefits of export revenues. Without such systems, the obligations on nuclear exports now imposed by the IAEA and the NPT will have no meaningful effect.

Ultimately, the effectiveness of nonproliferation will depend largely upon a cooperative effort by the United States and the Soviet

Union to control limited aspects of their respective alliance systems. Moreover, it will depend upon an extension of such superpower control to all prospective proliferator states that fall under the orbit of U.S. or Soviet influence. While this statement seems to exhibit characteristics of a new elitism, the effect of such control would be to bolster world order rather than primacy. Rather than reassert an earlier form of duopolistic domination, a selective tightening of bipolarity in world power processes could significantly enhance the promise of nonproliferation. This is the case because a tightening of superpower control over prospective entrants into the nuclear club could make it very difficult for these states to go nuclear. The tighter the dualism of power, the greater the ability of the superpowers to assure broad compliance with nonproliferation goals.

As we have already seen, an important part of the nonproliferation problem is the control of too large a number of independent national wills. Such control is an instance of the more general problem of decision that arises when the benefits of common action are contingent upon the expectation that a particular number of parties will cooperate. Nonproliferation efforts in the Middle East will always be problematic to the extent that they rely upon volitional compliance. They may, however, be successful if the superpowers move with determination to assure the compliance of other states with the NPT and its associated norms and restrictions.

THE REAGAN POLICY ON NON PROLIFERATION

From its very beginnings, the Reagan administration has backed off from the antiproliferation stance of the Ford and Carter administrations. In this connection, it has not only failed to dissuade certain allies from their shortsighted excursions into nuclear commerce, it has also reversed efforts to defer reprocessing of civilian fuel and the use of plutonium here and abroad. Indeed, within the space of ninety days, the administration approved nuclear sales to India, Argentina, and South Africa—nations that refuse to open all of their nuclear facilities to international inspection; that refuse to ratify the NPT; and that either have, or are developing, means to set off nuclear explosions.

Curiously, the Reagan policy opposes U.S. law as well as international law. According to the terms of the 1978 Nuclear Nonproliferation Act, this country established sanctions against any state that subsequently supplies reprocessing technology to a nonnuclear-weapon state. By acting contrary to the rules of national and international law, the administration makes it next to impossible to sustain a viable nonproliferation regime.

Why does the Reagan policy take such a dangerous and lawless form? The answer appears to lie in the cynical view that proliferation is inevitable. Yet, there is certainly no evidence that this is the case. Moreover, as Paul Leventhal, president of the Nuclear Control Institute points out, "to assume proliferation is inevitable helps to ensure that it will be—a self-fulfilling prophecy of apocalyptic proportions."[6]

In the final analysis, the Reagan policy is a function of its overriding commitment to Realpolitik. Forced to compare nonproliferation objectives with presumed considerations of power, the administration consistently favors the latter. Thus, when India requested spare parts for its Tarapur nuclear power plant and when South Africa asked for assistance with its Koeburg nuclear power plant, the president agreed to help. Similarly, he acquiesced when Britain and France requested approval to retransfer 143 tons of U.S.-produced heavy water to Argentina's Atucha II nuclear power plant. On November 18, 1983, Argentina announced that it was capable of enriching uranium, a capability that gives it direct access to atomic bomb material.

To improve its policies to halt proliferation, the United States must first begin to comply with its own nuclear-export and plutonium-use standards. Although this country should continue as a nuclear supplier to reliable national customers, it should refuse to supply states that reject essential safeguards or pursue plutonium economies. As Paul Leventhal has pointed out, "This necessarily involves linking U.S. non-proliferation objectives to a wide range of political, economic and security issues with other nations, and not confining nonproliferation discussions to the narrow area of nuclear commerce, as is now largely the case."[7]

IF REGIONAL NONPROLIFERATION FAILS

Regrettably, although the advantages of expanded controls over nuclear weapons and nuclear exports as they concern the Middle East are self-evident, they are unlikely to be imposed. It follows that nuclear proliferation in the region may be inevitable. What, in that case, would need to be done?

In the first place, steps would need to be taken to slow down the rate of proliferation. As long as a number of potential proliferators had not yet attained membership in the nuclear club, efforts would have to be undertaken to inhibit further nuclear spread.

In the second place, steps would have to be taken to ensure the stability of nuclear power relationships and to spread information and technology pertaining to nuclear weapons safeguards. This means that an all-out effort would have to be mustered to prevent intense crises in the region and that such an effort would have to be supported by technical assistance to Nth-country nuclear forces. Since many, if not all, of the new nuclear states would be especially vulnerable to accidental, unauthorized and preemptive firings, the superpowers would have to take seriously the prospect of helping these states to develop safe weapon systems and reliable command, control, and communications procedures.

The need for such assistance would be dictated by a number of factors. For one, new nuclear powers, in response to the need for survivable forces, would almost certainly turn to quick-acting systems of retaliation. For another, new nuclear powers would be unlikely to invest the enormous amounts of money needed to equip the nuclear weapons themselves with trustworthy safety design features. It would be essential, therefore, in a proliferated regional setting, that the superpowers share many of their safeguard strategies with the newer members of the nuclear club. At a minimum, such sharing would have to include information about (1) making accurate identification of an attacker, (2) rendering nuclear forces survivable for a second strike, (3) ensuring human reliability in the command and control setting, and (4) ensuring weapon-system reliability through such means as coded locking devices and environmental sensing techniques.

In addition to offering technical assistance to Nth countries, the superpowers would also have to influence the strategic doctrines of these new nuclear weapons states. At a minimum, such efforts would have to be directed at underscoring the deterrence function of strategic force, reinforcing the idea that nuclear weapons must not be considered for actual war waging. Special emphasis would have to be placed on the centrality of minimum deterrence and on the disavowal of first-strike options and capabilities.

ISRAEL AND REGIONAL NUCLEAR PROLIFERATION

Medieval maps often portrayed Jerusalem at the center of the world. From the perspective of regional proliferation, such a portrayal has even greater validity today. Confronted with difficult choices concerning military preparedness, Israel's decision on the nuclear option will have especially far-reaching implications for peace in the Middle East. And since world order is strongly affected by what happens in this volatile area, this decision may have genuinely global consequences.

For more than twenty years, speculation that Israel has a bomb in the basement has been widespread.[8] With recent news that Israel had been receiving from a U.S. company devices that can be used to trigger nuclear weapons, such speculation appears increasingly correct.[9] It follows that other states in the region may now hasten to acquire the military benefits that allegedly reside in nuclear technology. With the atomic secret torn from nature, these states may see no compelling reason to refrain from full membership in the nuclear club.

What exactly, should Israel do now? If there is a "bomb in the basement" (that is, an undisclosed force of nuclear weapons or components that could be assembled rapidly into such weapons), should it remain there? Or would Israel (and perhaps the entire region) be better served by moving beyond its current policy of deliberate ambiguity to one of an explicit declaration of nuclear capability? If Israel has never actually moved to implement a nuclear weapons option, should it now exercise that option? And if it does, should the necessary steps be taken under the mantle of obscurity, or should they be accompanied by public disclosure?

These are difficult questions. Israel's leaders understand that adversary states may choose to go nuclear apart from any direct response to Israeli actions. Because there are many axes of conflict in the Middle East, Israel's enemies may feel substantial incentives to proceed with nuclear weapons technologies irrespective of Israel's strategic posture.

The value of nuclear forces has already been openly alleged by several other states in the region. Several years ago, Ismail Fahmi, President Anwar Sadat's Minister of Foreign Affairs, suggested that nuclear status would not only neutralize the ever-present possibility of Israeli nuclear threats, but it would also neutralize the possibility of threats from other aspiring nuclear states in the area (for example, Libya and Iraq). Moreover, noted Fahmi, such status would lead to a technological, scientific, and strategic revolution in Egypt, making it a leading power in that part of the world.[10]

A special problem is the Gulf. This is one of the few areas in the developing world where surplus funds exist to support proliferation or to purchase nuclear weapons from a third party. Perhaps just as significantly, the Gulf states are exceptionally vulnerable to a nuclear attack. According to Anthony H. Cordesman: "One well-placed bomb on a capital could destroy the national identity and recovery capability of most of the smaller southern Gulf states, and only five to seven such strikes could probably destroy the national identity of Iraq, Iran or Saudi Arabia. This makes the Gulf states vulnerable to both attack and nuclear blackmail."[11]

One possible Israeli move would be to shift from deliberate ambiguity to disclosure but to couple this posture with an unprovocative countervalue nuclear strategy. Yet even if Israel were to develop such a strategy, there is no assurance that it would not evolve (as it did between the superpowers) into a counterforce targeting doctrine.[12]

Moreover, the subtle intellectual distinctions between countervalue and counterforce may have little meaning in the Middle Eastern theatre, where distances are close and intentions often indecipherable.

Some argue that Israel's security would be high as a nuclear power even if it coexisted with several adversary nuclear powers in the region. This is the case, it has been alleged, because there would be little reason to strike first in a nuclear crowd. In Shai Feldman's words: "Since nuclear weapons enjoy a high cost-exchange ratio against answering or neutralizing weapons, the incentives for preemption have drastically decreased."[13]

But why? Even if preemption could not prevent an overwhelmingly destructive retaliation, it could have some damage-limiting benefits. Hence, it might well be rational for nuclear armed states to preempt against other nuclear states if they believe the only alternative is to be struck first—an alternative that could never be dismissed in a nuclearized context, especially where counterforce strategies are augmented by defensive measures.

It should not be assumed from all of this, however, that Israel would necessarily acquire safety if it had a regional nuclear monopoly. Even if it were the only regional nuclear power, Israel's nuclear arsenal might have little or no deterrent effect on "small" assaults upon its people or territory, because the prospective aggressors (state or nonstate) would be unlikely to believe Israel's willingness to use nuclear force under any but the most nation-threatening conditions.

One must also understand that Israel's nonnuclear enemies might achieve significant counterdeterrent effects by means of other highly destructive weapons technologies (for example, chemical, biological, or nerve weapon systems), technologies well within the grasp of all states. For example, a nonnuclear adversary of Israel might, after absorbing an Israeli nuclear assault, be able to retaliate against Israeli cities with chemical or biological agents. Knowing this, would Israel's threat to make use of its nuclear inventory be credible?

It is conceivable, of course, that Israel might move to accompany nuclear disclosure with a parallel weakening of its conventional forces—a move designed to signal a heightened Israeli willingness to resort to nuclear weapons. Although such a move would also carry significant economic benefits, it would have the effect of reducing Israeli options to calamity or capitulation. Hence, it would almost certainly be deemed contrary to Israel's security interests.

Violence is not power. Sometimes they are opposites. Understood in terms of the requirements of peace in the Middle East, Israel and all other states in the region must soon begin to recognize the overriding obligation to avoid nuclearization. By substituting the dignity of cooperation for the folly of mortal competition, these actors could create the conditions for a general and graduated process of de-escalation and conflict reduction. Rejecting the self-defeating lure of relentless hostility, they could acquire real lucidity, a pattern of coexistence replacing delusionary imaginings with pragmatic partnership.

NOTES

1. Even if we could assume that leadership behavior were always rational, this would say nothing about the accuracy of the information used in rational calculations. Rationality refers only to the <u>intention</u> of maximizing specified values or preferences. It does not tell us anything about whether the information used is correct or incorrect. Hence, rational actors may make errors in calculation that lead them to nuclear war. Daniel Frei speaks of these errors in terms of "unintentional nuclear war." According to Frei: "What is being envisaged here is not accidental nuclear war, but rather nuclear war based on false assumptions, i.e., on misjudgment or miscalculation by the persons legitimately authorized to decide on the use of nuclear weapons. Substandard performance by decision-makers in crisis situations is particularly common." (Daniel Frei, <u>Risks of Unintentional Nuclear War</u> [Geneva: United Nations Institute for Disarmament Research, 1982], ix).

2. The indiscriminacy and the extent of nuclear explosions also raise the standards of international law as they pertain to nuclear war. According to these standards, any resort to nuclear weapons would be contrary to the principles of <u>jus in bello</u> (justice in war). Although no specific treaty exists that outlaws nuclear weapons per se, any use of these weapons would be inherently indiscriminate and disproportionate, characteristics that violate the codified and customary laws of war. Further support for the argument that any use of nuclear weapons would be in violation of international law can be found in Book 3, chapter 11 of Hugo Grotius's <u>The Law of War and Peace</u>. Here, Grotius speaks of the need to allow innocents an opportunity to escape from carnage, an imperative that is itself drawn from Old Testament accounts of ancient Israel. According to Grotius: "The Jewish interpreters note that it was a custom among their ancestors that, when they were besieging a city, they would not completely encircle it, but would leave a sector open for those who wished to escape, in order that the issue might be determined with less bloodshed." A similar argument was made by Polybius (<u>Punic Wars</u>) with his account of Scipio Aemilianus's proclamation upon the destruction of Carthage: "Let those who wish, flee." And, in the judgment of Tacitus, "To butcher those who have surrendered is savage."

3. For additional information on the concept of a nuclear winter, see Richard P. Turco, Owen B. Toon, Thomas P. Ackerman, James

B. Pollack, and Carl Sagan, "The Climatic Effects of Nuclear War,"
<u>Scientific American</u> 251 (August 1984): 33-43; Paul R. Ehrlich et. al.,
"Long-Term Biological Consequences of Nuclear War," <u>Science</u> 222
(December 23, 1983): 1293-1300; R. P. Turco et. al., "Nuclear Winter: Global Consequences of Multiple Nuclear Explosions," <u>Science</u>
222 (December 23, 1983): 1283-92; Carl Sagan, "Nuclear War and
Climatic Catastrophe: Some Policy Implications," <u>Foreign Affairs</u> 62
(Winter 1983/84): 257-92; Curt Covey et. al., "Global Atmospheric
Effects of Massive Smoke Injections from a Nuclear War: Results
from General Circulations Model Simulations," <u>Nature</u> 308 (March 1,
1984): 21-25; and Carl Sagan, <u>The Nuclear Winter</u> (Boston: Council
for a Livable World Education Fund, 1983). See also <u>The Effects on
the Atmosphere of a Major Nuclear Exchange</u> (Washington, D.C.:
National Academy of Sciences Research Council, 1984). Commissioned
by the Department of Defense, this report supports the main lines of
argument and the principal findings of the 1983 nuclear winter research
team headed by Carl Sagan. The National Academy of Sciences research panel, chaired by Dr. George F. Carrier of Harvard University, stressed that its findings implied no threshold. A smaller war
would produce smaller effects, but the study did not disclose exactly
how small a nuclear exchange would have to be to avoid a nuclear
winter.

4. The third review conference for the Treaty on the Nonproliferation of Nuclear Weapons (NPT) was held in September 1985. A
fifth review conference will be held in 1995 to decide whether the
treaty shall continue in force indefinitely. For information on the
history and background of the NPT and on the 1985 review conference,
see Robert L. Beckman and Warren H. Donnelly, <u>The Treaty on the
Non-Proliferation of Nuclear Weapons: The 1985 Review Conference
and Matters of Congressional Interest</u>, Congressional Research Service, Library of Congress, Report no. 85-80 S, April 22, 1985. For
additional information on the background of the current nonproliferation regime, see Warren H. Donnelly, <u>The International Non-Proliferation Regime: A Brief Description of Its Precursors, Present Form,
and United States Support for It</u>, Congressional Research Service,
Library of Congress, Report no. 83-127 S., June 1983.

5. According to Article 6 of the Treaty on the Nonproliferation
of Nuclear Weapons: "Each of the Parties to the Treaty undertakes to
pursue negotiations in good faith on effective measures relating to
cessation of the nuclear arms at an early date and to nuclear disarmament, and on a treaty on general and complete disarmament
under strict and effective international control."

6. See Paul Leventhal, "Getting Serious About Proliferation,"
<u>Bulletin of the Atomic Scientists</u>, March 1984, 8.

7. Ibid., 9.

8. For a detailed discussion of these issues, see Louis René Beres, ed., Security or Armageddon: Israel's Nuclear Strategy (Lexington, Mass: Lexington Books, 1985).

9. These devices, described as krytrons or pentodes, are a type of cathode tube with primarily military applications. According to Israeli officials, they were not used for any nuclear applications. See Thomas L. Friedman, "Israel Offers to Return Some of the Trigger Devices Usable in Making Nuclear Arms," New York Times, May 17, 1985, p. 6.

10. See Uri Bar-Joseph, "The Hidden Debate: The Formation of Nuclear Doctrines in the Middle East," Journal of Strategic Studies 5 (June 1982): 208.

11. See A. H. Cordesman, The Gulf and the Search for Strategic Stability: Saudi Arabia, the Military Balance in the Gulf, and Trends in the Arab-Israeli Military Balance (Boulder, Colo.: Westview Press, 1984): 760.

12. Even if its strategy remained countervalue, Israel's perceived willingness to use nuclear weapons would be problematic, since civilian populations would be intentionally targeted (unlike a counterforce strategy, where civilian injuries and fatalities are "collateral damage").

13. See Shai Feldman, Israeli Nuclear Deterrence: A Strategy for the 1980s (New York: Columbia University Press, 1982), 46.

Part III
The Geopolitical Dimensions of Deterrence: Implications for U.S. Strategy

The Evolving Geopolitics of Nuclear-Strategic Basing for the 1990s

Robert E. Harkavy

INTRODUCTION

The advent in the 1960s of long-range intercontinental ballistic missiles (ICBMs) and submarine-launched ballistic missiles (SLBMs) has since served somewhat to obscure the continuing importance of external basing access in relation to the superpower nuclear strategic balance. That importance had earlier been more obvious, highlighted among other things by the U.S. requirement for forward basing of the B-47 reflex bomber force, the ill-starred Gary Powers U-2 flight and, above all, by the origins of the Cuban missile crisis, including the previous U.S. emplacement of medium-range missiles in Turkey and Italy.

Nowadays, newly emerging political and technological developments may again be bringing to the fore the politics of access for nuclear strategic-related forces. A now seeming ineluctable trend toward decoupling of some U.S. alliance relationships—and the concomitant increasing precariousness of U.S. basing access—has been underscored by recent events in, among other places, New Zealand, Australia, Spain, Greece, even Canada.[1]

Meanwhile, the seeming inevitability of Star Wars and also more mobile and dispersed launching systems on both sides of the superpower divide may presage still newer basing requirements, as yet but dimly perceived. Increasingly, the geopolitics of the nuclear balance has assumed the nature of a very complex game played out in the crucially interrelated realms of outer space, the underseas, and the land and sea surfaces of the earth, though in some important respects too, it retains the spatial character of a Mackinderian heartland/rimland pattern of a struggle between continental and maritime power. So far, this game has remained an essentially bipolar one, reflecting the less-than-global nature of British, French, and Chinese nuclear forces, as well as their relatively limited extraregional power projection requirements.

BACKGROUND: EARLY POSTWAR PERIOD

The U.S. was early on very dependent on overseas bases for its nuclear deterrent posture, across the board involving offensive and defensive systems and a host of related technical facilities now commonly subsumed under the vague rubric of C^3I (command, control, communications, and intelligence).

Up to around 1952/53, the United States—then having something close to first-strike capability—relied heavily on forward bomber bases in the United Kingdom. Later, during the 1950s, the B-47 bombers became the backbone of Strategic Air Command (SAC), and although their effective range was greatly extended by then new aerial refueling techniques, the United States determined on forward deployment to enhance their chances for penetration and to lessen their vulnerability to a Soviet first strike.[2] This reflex force rotated between U.S. home bases and those in the United Kingdom, Morocco, Spain, Greenland, Bermuda, and in the Pacific. Its related tankers (mostly then the KC-97s) were based primarily at Thule, Greenland, and Goose Bay, Labrador. Though the subsequently deployed B-52s that began entering inventories in 1955 did not require forward basing, they too utilized trans-Arctic refueling points as well as hypothetical postattack recovery bases in Spain and elsewhere.[3]

The Soviets had no matching forward bases during this period, for strategic deterrence or anything else. Their early bombers, such as the three-thousand-mile-range TU-4, could only reach the U.S. Pacific Northwest from Siberia, and even then, by giving away some four hours' warning time to presumably alerted U.S. radars.

During this period and continuing to today, the United States also relied on foreign access, primarily in Canada and Greenland, for strategic defense. During the early 1950s, the United States and Canada built the $500 million Distant Early Warning (DEW) radar picket line across the Arctic, which the U.S. relied upon for its two to four hours' warning of a Soviet attack. The system was later made three-tiered, added to by the Mid-Canada and Pinetree strings of electronic listening posts, all under the U.S. Air Defense Command, which worked closely with SAC.[4] Some U.S. interceptor aircraft were deployed as well at Canadian bases such as Goose Bay, Labrador for perimeter early defense.

The mid to late 1950s saw the development in the United States of the famed missile gap scare, highlighted by the leaking of the Gaither Report toward the end of the Eisenhower administration. Soviet testing first of intermediate-range ballistic missiles (IRBMs) and then ICBMs (1956) and the launching of the first Sputnik (1959) gave rise to fears about a "technological Pearl Harbor."[5] This gave rise in turn to U.S. development of Thor and Jupiter IRBMs, Atlas and Titan ICBMs, and then the solid-fuel Minuteman ICBMs and Polaris submarine missiles, which were to become the backbone of the U.S. strategic nuclear forces of the 1960s.

As these programs developed, the United States came to foresee in the late 1950s a dangerous period from about 1959 to 1961 (a window, in current jargon) during which Soviet ICBMs might threaten the U.S. B-52 and B-47 bomber bases, vitiating their deterrent potential. The short-term solution, pending development and deployment of U.S. ICBMs, was to emplace the shorter-range U.S. Jupiter and Thor IRBMs in the United Kingdom, Italy, and Turkey, from where they could reach the major cities of the Soviet Union; this was done around the juncture of 1959 and 1960. Two Jupiter squadrons were deployed in Italy, another in Turkey, and Jupiters and Thors in the United Kingdom to supplement the still considerable deterrence threat of the deployed SAC B-52 and B-47 force.[6] Later during 1960, the United States deployed the first three of its Polaris submarines, and almost simultaneously, Atlas and Titan ICBMs were ready-based in the United States, so that the missile gap was quickly on the way to being bridged. The IRBMs nevertheless remained in place for a few years; those in Italy and Turkey were later eliminated after the Cuban missile crisis, their removal having figured in its precarious denouement.[7]

Alongside the importance of the missile and bomber bases provided to the United States overseas was the perhaps equivalently crucial role played by overseas facilities in the surveillance and detection of the Soviet strategic bomber and missile buildup. Specifically, this involved in the 1950s the use of U-2 surveillance flights and the ferret activities of electronic surveillance aircraft; later also the ground activities related to satellite reconnaissance.[8]

The U-2, a high altitude sailplane with long, extended wings, began its career in 1956, and its activities were gradually expanded thereafter for the next four years over Soviet airspace. The United States, of course, suffered then, as now, from a distinct disadvantage vis-à-vis the Soviet Union with respect to strategic intelligence, given the closed nature of Soviet frontiers and society and its enormous penchant for security and secrecy, which disadvantage could only in part be made up for by human-source intelligence (HUMINT).[9]

In the spring of 1957, U-2 flights operating out of Peshawar, Pakistan, discovered a new Soviet missile test site at Tyuratam near the Aral Sea, some seven hundred miles east of the older, main launching site at Kapustin Yar. The flights revealed the progress of the Soviet ICBM program, which earlier had been monitored by a giant radar at Diyarbakir on the Turkish Black Sea coast near Samsun. These flights continued on through 1960, ending that year when Gary Powers's plane, en route from Peshawar to Bodo, Norway (but having originated at Adana, Turkey), was shot down by Soviet missiles near Sverdlovsk.[10]

During this period, U-2 flights were flown from a number of bases overseas, primarily in Pakistan, Turkey, Norway, and West Germany (Wiesbaden); additionally, the use of Iranian air space along the southern Soviet frontier was apparently critical. Other U-2s operating out of Atsugi, Japan, were vital to reconnaissance activities in the Far East. Aside from overflights of Soviet territories, these bases also allowed for reconnaissance flights using oblique-angle photography from the side windows of high-flying planes, which could take pictures of airfields as much as one hundred miles distant.[11]

During the late 1950s and early 1960s, the United States and the Soviet Union were engaged in parallel development of satellite technology, which also was to entail new external basing requirements (the first Soviet Sputnik went up in 1957; fifteen months later the U.S. launched its first Vanguard satellite).

To recover satellite photos, the United States utilized both radio transmission and midair physical recovery procedures, and as the latter initially encountered difficulties, the former was crucial for rapid and assured transmission of the pictures to analytical laboratories in Washington. For that purpose, the United States deployed ground stations not only in the continental United States (in New Hampshire and California) and in Hawaii, Alaska, and Guam, but also in the British-held Seychelles Islands and in at least one African country.[12] Several shipboard stations with thirty-foot long antennas were used in addition, beginning later in 1964, but these, too, presumably relied on overseas port facilities for refueling, food, and water.[13] In this area, as in many others, there was a growing need for foreign facilities to provide esoteric technical intelligence activities, at the very time the advent of ICBMs was lessening the need for forward overseas bomber bases.

By the late 1950s, Soviet ICBM developments had rendered somewhat obsolete the three-layered radar early warning system across the Canadian Arctic, which had been constructed originally to provide several hours' warning of approaching Soviet bombers. To cope with the new missile threat, the United States built, beginning around 1958 the Ballistic Missile Early Warning System (BMEWS), the three hinges of which were in Fairbanks, Thule, and Yorkshire, England.[14] Here too, foreign access was crucial to America's nuclear deterrence posture.

Complementary to BMEWS and perhaps more important for warning of an impending missile attack is the new class of early warning satellites developed by the United States to double the warning time provided by BMEWS. This involved the MIDAS (Missile Defense Alarm System) satellite program, which came to rival in importance the somewhat earlier developed SAMOS (Satellite Missile Observation System) satellite reconnaissance system. MIDAS was based on the combined

capability of infrared sensors and telephoto lenses to immediately
detect missile launching tracks and to transmit this information immediately to U.S. decision makers.[15] Launched by Atlas/Agena D
missiles, advanced MIDAS satellites deployed later in 1969 could be
parked in synchronous orbits that allowed for continuous coverage of
both the western Soviet Union and the China-Siberia region, as well
as of the Atlantic and Pacific ocean areas where Soviet submarines
lurked in firing positions. According to one source, information from
the MIDAS satellites' infrared systems is radioed to monitoring stations in Alice Springs, Australia, and in Guam and then immediately
relayed via communications satellites or by underseas cables to
Washington, NORAD (North American Air Defense) headquarters in
Colorado, and SAC headquarters near Omaha.[16]

Two other elements of the strategic deterrence system came to
depend upon overseas access: fighter-interceptor defense and long-
distance and protracted deployment of the Polaris nuclear submarine
force. By now, of course, the United States has largely abandoned its
air defense system against bombers, having also jettisoned the once
complementary antiballistic missile (ABM) system designed to protect the Minuteman missiles against Soviet ICBM attack. But earlier,
as implied by the three-tiered radar system in the Canadian Arctic,
fighter defense against incoming bombers was deemed both viable and
important, echoing earlier geopolitical theories about the crucial
nature of air superiority over the Arctic. Fighter-interceptor bases
under control of the U.S. Air Defense Command ringed numerous
major American cities. Also, they were stationed in Iceland, Greenland, and at various locales in Canada, particularly in Labrador and
Newfoundland, along the trans-Arctic route Soviet bombers would
have to fly on the way to the United States.[17]

The Polaris submarines were initially deployed early in the Kennedy administration. The percentage of the fleet that the United States
was able to deploy at any given time was enhanced by replenishment
and repair facilities at Holy Loch, Scotland; Rota, Spain; and at Guam.
Indeed, the asymmetries provided relative to the Soviet Union, once
the latter deployed its SSBNs, allowed the United States to negotiate
the Strategic Arms Limitations Talks (SALT I) treaty, which gave the
Soviets a sixty-two to forty-four advantage in submarines but which
was claimed nullified by the efficiencies accruing to the United States
from its overseas replenishment facilities. Later, the advent of the
longer-range Trident submarines would lessen the importance of overseas submarine facilities, allowing the United States to negotiate the
closing of the Rota base in Spain.

Throughout the entirety of the early postwar period, the Soviet
Union was bereft of overseas access that might have served to rectify
the unfavorable strategic balance it faced. Its deterrent capability was

long (up to the late 1950s) based upon bombers that might only have
been able to achieve one-way missions against the United States.[18]
The Soviets also long lagged behind the United States in aerial refueling technology. Early, Soviet development of ICBMs during the late
1950s seemed to augur an at least temporary Soviet strategic advantage, causing the United States to compensate with its hurried overseas deployment of IRBMs while development of the Atlas, Titan,
Minuteman, and Polaris programs was hurried along. But what was
expected to be a Soviet strategic advantage, at least temporarily
around 1960, was quickly turned into a massive U.S. advantage when
the aforementioned systems were deployed and while the Soviets still
had fewer than one hundred ready ICBMs. The shoe was quickly shifted
to the other foot, and to compensate, Nikita Khrushchev gambled with
the introduction of IRBMs into Cuba, hence precipitating the Cuban
missile crisis.[19] The rest is history, but it is worth noting that only
by 1960 did the Cuban revolution avail the Soviet Union of its first valuable overseas points of access applicable to the strategic nuclear
balance. In ensuing years, even despite the forced withdrawal of Soviet
IRBMs in 1962, Cuba would become a very valuable Soviet base, its
proximity to the United States providing irreplaceable assets related
to intelligence, surveillance, and naval replenishment.

During the 1950s and early 1960s, overseas facilities became increasingly important for the United States in relation to other technical
operations (again primarily in the areas of surveillance and intelligence), not all of which related solely to the nuclear strategic balance.
Again, the balance of overseas assets was entirely to the favor of the
United States, serving to compensate for the closed nature of Soviet
society, which denied easy surveillance and penetration via open
sources or through human-source intelligence. Most notable here
was the use of aircraft for electromagnetic reconnaissance and intelligence (ELINT) conducted around the periphery of the Soviet Union,
China, and North Korea, as well as of numerous ground-based intercept stations around the Eurasian periphery for communications intelligence (COMINT).[20]

Further in the strategic nuclear arena, both U-2s and other aircraft, primarily the RB-47, were long flown from bases in Europe
and Asia to "tickle" Soviet early warning radars; the U-2 flights were
used to test radars deep inside the Soviet Union that might be of different types than the Soviets' peripheral early warning systems. By doing
so, U.S. planners might ascertain weaknesses, ranges, and scan patterns in the Soviet radar system that could be valuable for planning
the penetration routes for a nuclear bomber attack.

The game of tickling, begun in the 1950s, apparently even involved
mock raids mounted by U.S. units in Turkey and elsewhere to penetrate Soviet airspace in order to compel Soviet radar technicians to

turn their sets on and hence to reveal their capabilities.[21] These exercises in low-level brinkmanship, all mounted from foreign bases, resulted in some serious incidents in which U.S. ferret aircraft were shot down and their crews killed or captured. Some flights originating at Brize Norton in the United Kingdom apparently traversed the entire northern Soviet coastline, emerging at the Barents Sea.[22] The area between the Caspian Sea and Sea of Azov was apparently a particular focus of U.S. surveillance, with the United States flying frequent reconnaissance missions over Turkish and Iranian airspace, some staged originally from West Germany and Cyprus. Soviet ferrets, on the other hand, mostly operating out of Siberia toward Alaska, are believed rarely to have penetrated U.S. airspace, in part because U.S. radar stations apparently kept their sets on at all times.

Later, the use of ferret aircraft for ELINT purposes was apparently replaced in part by large ferret satellites. This function is, however, apparently not easily handled by satellite, owing to size and weight problems and the need for human operators in utilizing complex equipment.[23] Still, such activities were apparently begun around 1962 or 1963 and presumably also required overseas facilities for rapid transmission of data to home processing facilities.

In addition to the above, the United States has long made use of numerous facilities for its ground-based radio-intercept network (COMINT). Patrick McGarvey reports that earlier this involved some fifty stations in at least fourteen countries, ranging from small mobile field units to sprawling complexes such as the Air Force security headquarters in West Germany.[24] According to him, these facilities have been operated by some thirty thousand men worldwide, with a minimum of four thousand radio intercept consoles in operation in such varied locales as northern Japan, the Aleutian Islands, the Khyber Pass in Pakistan, and an island in the Yellow Sea off the coast of Korea.[25] Further, according to McGarvey, these COMINT land stations had to be supplemented by numerous flying and seaborne radio intercepts, particularly after Communist military units massively switched to VHF (very high frequency) radios during the 1950s, whereinafter complete coverage demanded getting closer to transmitters and circumventing terrain features such as mountains.[26] Early use for this purpose was made of Kimpo airfield in Korea, Clark Field, and many others; at any time, several dozen airborne listening posts were said to have been in intermittent operation. Added to these were some twelve to fifteen spy ships, such as the ill-fated Pueblo and Liberty, which also presumably required routine replenishment access to foreign ports.[27] These combined assets were used for interception of even encoded or otherwise unintelligible communications and to monitor merchant shipping, foreign trade, internal transportation, and so forth.

From 1945 to 1960, amid striking developments in electronic and communications intelligence and in side-angle and overhead photography, the United States had an enormous advantage over the Soviet Union owing to its strategic overseas assets, with reciprocal access for the Soviets then altogether absent. Later, newer technological advances, particularly in satellites, might somewhat but not altogether reduce the need for these overseas facilities.[28] This was later indicated by the reports about the holes created in the U.S. intelligence effort by the (temporary) loss of Turkish facilities and then of those in Iran and was also highlighted by the still heavy use of U-2 and SR-71 (successor to the U-2) reconnaissance flights all over the world well after the full development of seemingly sophisticated satellites for reconnaissance and monitoring purposes. And, of course, the U-2 and SR-71 flights also needed overseas staging bases.

The Soviets had, of course, long been aware of and unhappy about the strategic advantage given the United States by its system of overseas access. In 1958, when President Dwight Eisenhower first proposed a ban on the use of outer space for military purposes, the Soviets insisted that such a measure be accompanied by liquidation of foreign military bases in Europe, the Middle East, and North Africa.[29] At the time, such a mutually agreed upon measure would have been very asymmetrically disadvantageous to the United States, given its strategic reliance on B-47 and related tanker refueling bases and the whole vast network of facilities devoted to ELINT, COMINT, air space detection, and what not. But the Soviets would later be much more competitive in acquiring overseas bases for similar functions, and hence also later more reserved about suggesting formal arrangements that might mutually do away with overseas facilities.

EXTANT BASING FACILITIES CONNECTED WITH THE NUCLEAR BALANCE

By extension from the earlier period, there has been a further elaboration of rival U.S.-Soviet basing requirements, in connection with nuclear deterrence, to the present. This is true despite the reduced overseas dependence of both sides for the basing of launching systems per se.

In some cases, the role of external bases is obvious and direct, for example, the U.S. forward SSBN base at Holy Loch, Scotland. In others the relationship may be a bit more indirect, for example, contingent refueling points for aircraft, surface ships, or even attack submarines (SSNs) of potential value to antisubmarine operations vis-à-vis SSBNs. Then, too, to the extent arms-control regimes remain vital or at least relevant strategic nuclear calculations, those facilities used to monitor compliance of SALT I and II, the Threshold Test-Ban Treaty (TTB), and so forth, are also part of this equation, however indirectly. Further along the spectrum are overseas research facilities involving a variety of locales and functions that, ultimately, will importantly affect the rivals' strategic postures as they are reflected in the quality of nuclear forces. Further, numerous facilities serve multiple functions (co-location), only some of which may relate specifically to the strategic nuclear equation; tanker aircraft, for instance, refuel cargo aircraft in arms resupply operations as well as strategic bombers on alert, and a facility such as Rota has co-located basing functions related to antisubmarine warfare (ASW) and communications as well as (earlier) having been used as a forward base for SSBNs.

These myriad facilities can be categorized in any of numerous ways.[30] A breakdown might involve air, land, and naval facilities, or space-related, intelligence, communications, and research facilities. Another might be organized along combat/functional lines: platforms or bases for long-range nuclear delivery, communications, air defense, ballistic missile defense (BMD), ASW, antisatellite systems (ASAT), early warning, arms-control verification, nuclear explosion detection, and so on. A hypothetical division between prewar and intrawar functions might in some cases also be appropriate. The list in figure 4 draws from both such categorizations. It lists primarily those basing requirements now fulfilled on the U.S. side; a corresponding Soviet list would be shorter, as later noted, because of the asymmetries produced by geography (large Soviet land mass), greater Soviet use of ships, asymmetries in weapons systems, C^3I, and the like, and the still more limited Soviet network of external clients willing to provide them access, recent trends notwithstanding.[31] We shall here discuss these functions in tandem, the basic data being summarized in figure 4.

As earlier noted, there is now a lesser requirement, for both the United States and the Soviet Union, for basing actual launching systems outside their respective homelands. Both sides' ICBMs are, obviously, fully home-based. American SSBNs previously were heavily dependent on forward basing (provisions, maintenance, crew rotation) at Rota (Spain), Holy Loch (Scotland), and Guam (not an external basing matter); in a short time, only Holy Loch among these will remain in use as the United States transitions to longer-range Tridents that will be based solely on the continental United States. It was this forward-basing of SSBNs, incidentally, that allowed the United States to concede a quantitative advantage to the Soviets in SALT I in allowed numbers of SSBNs: Soviet submarines must return to homeports in Severomorsk and Petropavlovsk; hence, a smaller proportion of them can be kept on station at any given time. It is important to note, how-

FIGURE 4   Types of Strategic Nuclear-related Facilities

Platforms
   Launching delivery systems, associated functions
   SSBN provisions, maintenance, crew rotation (Holy Loch, Scotland,
      or Rota, Spain earlier)
   Long-range or medium-range bombers: dispersal, recovery, or
      en-route transit; refueling (KC-95, KC-135, KC-10); C^3I (fail-
      safe, i.e., Scope Signal)
   IRBMs, MRBMs (Western Europe; earlier, Turkey, Taiwan),
      GLCMs
   SLCMs: ship refueling, resupply by air, etc., now including battle-
      ships
   FBS: land-based aircraft (Turkey, United Kingdom, Japan, South
      Korea [F-4, F-15, F-16, F-111]), sea-based aircraft (Mediter-
      ranean, Pacific, North Atlantic)
   Weather stations related to bombers
Navigation Aids, Precise Positioning
   Omega; Loran-C; Loran-A; TACAN; ground stations related to
      NAVSTAR and MILSTAR
ASW
   Aircraft bases, i.e., P-3Cs
   SSNs: repair, maintenance, provisions, crew rotation (La
      Maddalena, Italy)
   SOSUS or barrier sonars: ground terminals
   SURTASS: port access for ship refueling, etc.
   AWACS bases: assisting nuclear-capable P-3Cs

(Figure continued on page 157.

ever, that while newer SSBNs may not require forward bases for provisioning and maintenance, they may retain external basing requirements for navigation/positioning, communications, and so forth.
   Both sides' long-range bombers are also primarily home-based;
the U.S. B-52 force uses a string of main bases across a lengthy
swatch of the northern United States from Maine to the Dakotas. But
U.S. bombers have scattered dispersal and recovery bases outside
the United States, mostly in northern locales such as Greenland and
Iceland, but also in Spain; their legs are lengthened by extensive tanke:
refueling capabilities (KC-95, KC-135, KC-10), also mostly located
along trans-Arctic routes. These requirements will only partly have
been lessened by the stand-off strike capabilities provided by air-
launched cruise missiles and the older air-to-surface missiles. The
B-52 force also utilizes external C^3I facilities, particularly the Scope
Signal System used in fail-safe communications in connection with pos-

Figure 4, continued

Missile and Antiaircraft Defense

  BMEWS; DEW line, Pinetree; OTH-B (U.S. based); Pave Paws (U.S.
    based); aircraft interceptors (Canada, Iceland); nuclear weapons
    storage: prepositioned fuel for nuclear-related functions

Satellites

  SPADATs: Baker-Nunn telescopes, GEODSS, radar sensors;
    STADAN: radars; satellite film recovery: HC-130 bases; early
    warning: MIDAS, data relay; satellite control facilities

Communications

  Various, overlapping systems: DCS (Defense Communication Sys-
    tem) and FLTSATCOM transmitters; relays (troposcatter relay;
    VLF, ELF, etc.); Tacamo aircraft and their bases

SIGINT

  Ground stations: COMINT, ELINT; aircraft access: RC-135, EA-38

PHOTINT

  U-2, SR-71 air-base access

HUMINT

  Agreed access (on Soviet side involving Aeroflot access)

Seismology

  Long-period arrays; microbarographs

Research

  Test ranges: eastern and western test ranges; missile calibration;
    geodesy: Tranet, SSBN accuracies, Pageos; underwater research:
    calibration of SSBN systems, ASW, etc.; seismology; nuclear
    testing; solar laboratories; riometers; SOFNET (predict radio
    blackouts)

---

sible recall of en-route bombers. Navigation aids and meteorological
facilities located offshore are also important. By contrast, one may
note the presumed use of Cuban facilities for Soviet bomber recovery:
that capability was debated at length during the SALT II negotiations
in connection with the range of Backfire bombers and the question of
whether they should be counted as strategic bombers.

    Theater nuclear weapons, though often demarcated from strategic
ones in general categorizations and in arms-control discussions, are
also effectively part of the strategic equation. They require, in the
U.S. case, foreign bases. The ongoing installation of GLCMs and
Pershing IIs in Western Europe is familiar enough—in West Germany,
Italy, Belgium, the Netherlands, and the United Kingdom. (Earlier,
the United States had based Thor and Jupiter missiles targeted on the
Soviet Union in Turkey, Italy, and the United Kingdom; Matador missiles aimed at China in Taiwan; and Mace missiles targeted either on

China or Soviet Siberia on Okinawa). And units of the U.S. Navy will
now be armed with SLCMs that, in the event of war, will be targeted
on the Soviet Union proper, for instance, on the key Kola Peninsula
area. Ships carrying those missiles, including newly refurbished battleships, while homeported in the United States, will presumably require external facilities for refueling, provisioning, aerial resupply,
and so on, so as to allow for lengthy on-station deployment.

The United States now deploys forward-based aircraft (FBS) capable of launching nuclear weapons into the Soviet Union in numerous
nations—the United Kingdom, West Germany, Turkey, Japan, South
Korea, and so forth; additionally, its aircraft carriers bearing other
nuclear-armed aircraft utilize various overseas ports in Europe and
in the Mediterranean, the Far East, and the Indian Ocean areas. The
aircraft involved—F-4, F-15, F-16, F-111, and so on—have not been
counted in strategic arms negotiations. By contrast, the Soviet Union
deploys few if any such forward-based systems but, in a crisis, could
deploy nuclear-armed aircraft to Cuba capable of conducting strikes
on military targets, particularly in the southernmost United States.

Perhaps of greater importance than launching sites to the overall
nuclear equation are the numerous and varied combat support or technical facilities used by both superpowers. Many are vital, near irreplaceable. And their functions span the domains of navigation aids,
antisubmarine warfare, satellite tracking and control, various types
of intelligence gathering (SIGINT, PHOTINT, HUMINT), seismology,
and research. Again, the United States utilizes far more such external
facilities than does the Soviet Union; the latter compensates by use of
shipboard facilities as well as by spatial utilization of the huge Soviet
land mass.

Antisubmarine warfare (directed both at SSBNs and SSNs and also
extensively conducted by the latter) in particular dictates a variety of
external basing requirements. Both sides have global deployments of
ASW aircraft—in the U.S. case, mostly now involving P-3C craft deploying an array of detection capabilities, for instance, sonobuoys.
Storage of related nuclear depth charges also requires forward basing,
if not in normal peacetime periods, then on a contingency basis for
crises or wars. The SSNs used for ASW work also require forward
bases for repair, maintenance, and provisions; those in the U.S.
Mediterranean fleet, for instance, are based at La Maddalena in
Sardinia, Italy. Vital to ASW, particularly on the U.S. side, are the
networks of SOSUS facilities (underwater sonar cable grids linked to
ground data-processing and transmission facilities), which are ranged
along vital coastlines; across important straits, chokepoints, and sea
lines of communication (SLOCs); and on strategically located islands.
Aside from the SOSUS nets along both U.S. coasts, other important
locales are the Greenland-Iceland-United Kingdom (GIUK) gap and the

Norwegian coast, the Azores and Bermuda, the Gibraltar exit, the
Straits of Indonesia, and the long coastal littoral stretching from
Japan's northern islands down through Korea, Okinawa, and Taiwan.[32]
The SOSUS ground terminals constitute potentially visible and vital
targets for intrawar interdiction or sabotage, which will be discussed
later.

Somewhat more indirectly, there are additional basing functions
that can be linked to nuclear-related ASW ships bearing towed sonar
arrays (SURTASS) that require fuel and maintenance overseas; nuclear
capable P-3Cs on submarine-hunting missions may be vectored to
their prey by AWACs aircraft themselves based at, or transiting
through, foreign facilities.

The nuclear submarines themselves (SSBNs) require use of overseas facilities both for navigation/positioning crucial to precise targeting and for land-based communications. In the former category
are Omega and Loran-C stations organized in fairly elaborate global
networks (also the subject of prior political controversies in Norway
and elsewhere);[33] in the latter, VLF and ELF communications transmitters and relays. Strategic-related aircraft as well require navigation aids—Loran-C, Loran-A, TACAN, and the like; they and ships
will be availed of the newer NAVSTAR (Navigational Satellite System)
and MILSTAR (Military Strategic and Tactical Relay) satellite navigation and positioning systems, themselves presumably requiring overseas data down-links.

Satellite tracking, involving both the tracking of rivals' space
systems and the control and tracking of one's own systems, is an important segment of the nuclear balance, presumably to be rendered
still more important in the apparently impending era of ASATs and the
Strategic Defense Initiative (SDI). In the former category is the U.S.
SPADATs monitoring system, earlier based largely on Baker-Nunn
telescopes, now abetted by GEODSS (Ground-Based Electro-Optical
Deep Space Surveillance) and other radars. (The Soviets have similar
systems, one apparently involving use of lasers.) The U.S. STADAN
system incorporates a global system of radars used to track down-
range launches of U.S. satellites. Several very crucial U.S. overseas
facilities are used to control satellites, querying them for data, receiving down-linked data and photographs, and steering the satellites
into altered orbits. Others deploy HC-130 aircraft used to recover
satellite films. Also very crucial are the ground links for early-warning satellites, the MIDAS (Missile Detection and Alarm System) system, which can relay warning of the infrared signatures of the plumes
of rising missiles in their boost phases. Overall, despite increasing
capabilities for over-the-horizon satellite data transmission and the
use of multiple satellite systems to transmit data, the ground links
overseas subject to basing diplomacy remain vital. Finally, note is

made of ocean surveillance satellites, which will be vital, for instance, in tracking the movements of surface cruise missile carriers as well as ships performing ASW work.

There are, of course, a variety of communications requirements related to nuclear forces; some, such as ELF for submerged submarines and another for bomber recall, have been mentioned. Otherwise, open sources mention a plethora of (perhaps overlapping) communications facilities—for example, transmitters and relay stations—associated with FLTSATCOM, the Defense Communications System (DCS), and so on.[34] Some of these presumably have functions related to nuclear deterrence. And, to supplement ground-based communications with submarines, the U. S. Navy utilizes its TACAMO aircraft, which drag communications gear through the water; they, too, often require overseas facilities.

Although the crucial SIGINT function (usually taken to subsume communications and electronics/radar intercepts) has largely been taken over by satellites (themselves requiring ground down-links), the United States still retains numerous ground intercept stations around the world, particularly along the Eurasian rimland close to the Soviet Union. These and also the aerial SIGINT interceptors (RC-135, EA-35) further require basing access. The U-2 and SR-71 Blackbird photographic aircraft, which can be programmed for quick-focused photography in a crisis, have in the past been stationed in Atsugi, Japan; Bodo, Norway; Adana, Turkey; and Akotiri, Cyprus, among other places.

Human intelligence (HUMINT) access may also be counted as an aspect of strategic basing; note the mounting fears about Soviet Spetznaz forces' penetration of the United States and Western Europe, with the associated capability for sabotage actions that, in some instances, could alter the nuclear strategic equation during a crisis or protracted war. Some such operations are, of course, covert; some operations in allied countries are done covertly but with the connivance of domestic intelligence agencies. The Soviet Union has additionally long used access for Aeroflot aircraft to enable emplacement of human operatives.[35]

Seismological facilities overseas (long-period arrays, micro-barographs) are usually thought of in connection with the monitoring of nuclear tests related to the test ban or nonproliferation regimes or both. These are important. And, if a nuclear war should occur between the superpowers, such facilities could be used to pinpoint nuclear explosions, which would be all the more valuable if ASATs should eliminate overlapping satellite sensor capabilities.

Though often not receiving a lot of publicity, overseas locales are often the sites of research facilities crucially tied to the nuclear arms race. The United States, for instance, makes external use of the eastern (Caribbean and Atlantic) and western test ranges—the latter, hinged on Kwajalein, has recently been utilized for testing antimissile systems. Missile calibration, missile test recovery, geodesy (science of the earth's surface, related to missile accuracies), underwater ASW and other research, nuclear testing, solar laboratories, riometers, and SOFNET (predicting radio blackouts) are other relevant areas of investigation with nuclear strategic implications. Some related overseas facilities are chosen or sought because of particular locations on the globe (down-range missile test sites based on ICBM or SLBM ranges, for instance).

Last but not least are the various forms of access and facilities required in connection with strategic defense directed against both aircraft and missiles. As noted, the earlier main requirement for intercepting bombers spawned the DEW and Pinetree picket lines across Canada and aircraft interceptors there and in Iceland. The advent of long-range ICBMs resulted in the U.S. BMEWS system. It now appears that SDI may in turn produce still newer requirements for defense against bombers and cruise missiles. That may require additional access in Canada to abet the over-the-horizon (OTH-B) and Pave Paws systems being introduced within the United States itself to cope with potential Soviet bomber or cruise missile threats. It could also involve foreign facilities for ground-based laser ASATs, point defenses against missiles within the NATO area, and so forth.[36]

MACROPOLITICAL TRENDS: THE NUCLEAR BALANCE,
ACCESS, AND THE EMERGING INTERNATIONAL SYSTEM

Amid the minutiae of ongoing, current political events (how, for instance, will the Greek and Spanish elections affect U.S. strategic force postures?) it is almost too easy to ignore long-term, secular, systemtic shifts that fundamentally affect the major powers' access to strategic facilities. One refers here to macropolitical trends (terminology preferred by futurologists) or, in a more theoretical vein, to the variables commonly used in international systems analysis. These might be used, for instance, to explain why the United States has experienced a long-term, seemingly ineluctable reduction in its access to bases over the past several decades or cautiously to predict whether those trends are likely to be continued.

On a historical note—one at the same time obvious but not widely recognized—it should be pointed out that the postwar phenomenon of extensive U.S. and now Soviet basing access within fully sovereign, independent nations (hence the term facilities as distinct from bases as a matter of formal definition) is an altogether new and novel phenomenon. There is virtually no evidence of such access asymmetrically or reciprocally being granted among sovereign states during the whole swath of modern diplomacy preceding 1945 (correspondingly, nothing equivalent to the structured, long-term alliances such as NATO and the Warsaw Pact).[37] Hence, if it is the case that the United States (and perhaps now also the Soviet Union) is finding it ever more difficult to acquire and maintain such access, even despite the proffering of extensive quid pro quo, that is, security and military/economic aid, it should be recognized that historically speaking, this represents nothing more than a return to a past norm.

There are a number of areas in which macropolitical or systemic trends would appear particularly germane to basing diplomacy:

- broad changes in the global political climate for big-power basing (superimposed upon local idiosyncrasies), including a complex web of essentially subjective, psychological factors revolving about the themes of sovereignty, national dignity, dependency, humiliation, and the like
- changing global political structure, involving such factors as polarity (bipolarity versus relative multipolarity), the continuing role of ideology in determining alignments, propensities toward or against neutralism on the part not only of developing countries but also of nations now firmly within the Western or Eastern military blocs (tight versus loose bipolarity)
- the nature of arms-control regimes: SALT/START (Strategic Arms Reduction Talks), test bans, outer space; perhaps also MBFR, arms transfers, nuclear-weapon-free zones, nuclear nonproliferation, and so on
- the remnant decolonialization of the Third World, that is, how many and what additional new nations might be created from presently remaining nonindependent island groups
- trends in intra-Third World warfare: how many wars, frequency by region, their types (that is, conventional versus unconventional), extent of big-power involvement, and the related impact on basing access
- trends in conventional weapons developments and their relationship to arms transfers and warfare in the Third World
- changes in nuclear proliferation, particularly if involving a large-scale expansion of the number of nuclear-armed states
- shifting conditions of international economics, variously involving north-south, east-west, intra-OECD (Organization for Economic Cooperation and Development) dimensions and incorporating trade, investment, raw materials (specifically, how do changes affect the overall leverage of big powers for base acquisition?)

A comprehensive analysis of the myriad interrelationships among the above areas would, of necessity, be beyond the scope of this chapter. Some illustrative points, however, are here offered, again as they might relate specifically to basing requirements in connection with the strategic nuclear balance.

Generally, regarding the climate for big-power access, it is clear that recent years have seen an increasingly less permissive environment for foreign access. A foreign presence is, for obvious reasons, almost nowhere welcome, except where it can be construed as contributing directly and visibly to the host's protection. But, indeed, almost everywhere, both in the Third World and within the U.S. orbit of Western democracies, governments are subject to pressures regarding a foreign presence. Bruised dignities and compromised sovereignties are here involved, often at the level of rivalry over local women in areas adjacent to bases or over wages paid local personnel (witness the present U.S. problems in Greece). In Western countries and in U.S. clients in the Third World, the Soviets conduct a daily onslaught of propaganda (see any daily issue of the regional FBISs), which takes its toll.[38] Bases are a very visible political target.

Further, there is now a lot of lateral pressure among Third World countries involving superpower basing presences, echoed in United Nations resolutions and, for instance, in such manifestations as the Iraqi Charter floated several years ago, which called on all Third World countries to eliminate foreign bases.[39] Some of these pressures are global; some are regional (for example, discussions among Indian Ocean littoral countries about demilitarization of that region, in reality, specifically directed against Diego Garcia; intra-Arab pressures linking U.S. bases in Oman, Morocco, and so on, to the Israeli issue). And, of course, the United States seems to be targeted—asymmetrically, relative to the Soviet Union—by these pressures, for all of the usually cited reasons, that is, the legacy of Western colonialism, the failures of U.S. public diplomacy, the irrationalities of anti-Americanism. The moves toward closure of the seas and overland air space as evidenced by the Law of the Sea regime is, of course, further illustrative of this general pattern.

Additionally, recent years have witnessed the spread of anti-nuclear and environmental movements throughout the Western world and elsewhere, generally associated with the radical left or various domains of Luddite-like idealism. The recently arisen U.S. problems in New Zealand (needless to say involving broader political issues) well illustrate how such factors can constrain U.S. basing access even in connection with an old U.S. ally and one rather remote from the cold war front lines.[40]

For the future, it is difficult to tell whether these trends will continue. Pressures have been felt in the United States and Canada as well. It is likely that the psychological environment, generally, for foreign military access, particularly that involving nuclear weapons or even nuclear-powered vessels, will become even less permissive. That trend could presumably be reversed, in some circumstances, by increased global tensions, which at least in some places make a U.S. protective presence more desirable. That in turn could depend upon perceptions of U.S. strength and resolve, though paradoxically, that same strength can induce resentment. Otherwise, it is also possible that in the future, Soviet basing access will suffer from the same pressures as now apply more seriously to the United States. Soviet problems in Egypt—there clearly related to issues of national pride and independence—could be the forerunners of a more general phenomenon.

It is, of course, difficult to predict just what macroeconomic trends, possible economic crises or cataclysms, and changes in the global economic power balance will unfold over the next two decades, much less what impact they will have on basing access. The difficulties are no more obvious than in the light of the various recent surprises: oil glut replaces oil shortage, the resurgence of the U.S. dollar vis-à-vis European currencies, the Latin American debt problems in countries earlier thought to be on the verge of takeoff, and so forth. But some possibilities are worth discussing.

Whether the debt crisis can or will in some instances be used by the United States so as to acquire leverage for basing access is not clear. The United States now appears to have increasing leverage in dealing with central north-south economic issues, based on its influence within the International Monetary Fund (IMF) and World Bank and its economic wherewithal, which can be translated, howsoever indirectly, into debt bail-out and rollovers. Could basing access quietly be acquired sometime as part of the bargain? Would that have to be done covertly, in view of the aforementioned issues of pride and sovereignty? Could this apply at least to less visible, small technical facilities, that is, SIGINT, satellite tracking, contingency weapons storage?

The Organization of Petroleum Exporting Countries (OPEC) may or may not wane or collapse. If it does, would this provide additional leverage for U.S. basing access, say, in Egypt or Oman? And, if Saudi largesse can no longer be used to aid, indirectly, U.S. basing access in Somalia, Pakistan, Morocco, and others, does this mean that increased direct U.S. aid could achieve such leverage? Of course, a further collapse of OPEC would assist the economic conditions in oil-dependent states, such as some of the debtor nations in Latin America, hence, perhaps, lessening U.S. leverage there. Generally, however, U.S. economic leverage should improve.

It is now widely argued that Western Europe is in the process of irreversible secular economic decline and that a U.S.-Asia, Pacific Basin dominant economic node is forming. Others, on the contrary, see Europe's present economic disarray as merely temporary, the failures of European integration notwithstanding, and see many of its cultural problems as merely time-lagged from the now nearly disappeared U.S. Age of Aquarius; hence, also, as imminently to evaporate. If, however, Europe is to undergo a lengthy period of economic problems (for example, chronically higher unemployment than the United States, failure to compete in "hi-tech," "Finlandization," youth alienation cum pacifism and counterculturalism, maintained strength of U.S. dollar, and a new burst of buy-outs of European businesses by U.S. multinational corporations), then just what impact that might have on U.S. basing access in Europe (clearly only one subset of the broader matter of the future of NATO) is unclear. It could mean more security dependence on the United States and a new respect and confidence translating into improved access. It could also spell resentment, withdrawal, expansion of the current malaise of the successor generation, neutralism, and the focus on removal of nuclear weapons, or the denuclearization of Europe.

There are any number of possible broad structural changes in the international system that could impact on basing structure. Though it is unlikely, Western Europe and the United States could split, perhaps dramatically (this could, of course, involve partial split-offs). Germany's Ostpolitik could be pushed much further, perhaps even to a second Rapallo. The People's Republic of China (PRC) could become more closely aligned with the United States; contrariwise one might envision a revival of the Sino-Soviet alliance. Historically, long-term, stable, ideologically based alliances have been more conducive to basing access; multipolar global systems with more rapidly shifting alignments have been less so. There seems now an overall trend toward alliance decoupling; if so, access will presumably become more precarious and tenuous, or at least more costly, all around. Alliances based on pragmatic (hence, also probably more unstable) rather than ideological grounds are probably less conducive to access.

The overall future of arms control is now very unclear, both generally and with respect to specific arms-control domains. (It is also presumably subject to volatile short-run as well as long-run political shifts within the United States and the Soviet Union.) Whether the now frozen SALT structure will survive is unclear. Also unclear are the futures of test bans and ASAT. The outcomes clearly will affect basing requirements in response to changing (that is, allowed) weapons deployments: laser battle stations in space, C^3I requirements for ASAT warfare, SDI, cruise missile deployments, newer deployments of bombers, numbers of deployed SSBNs all are at issue, along with their research and testing in the context of basing. Hence, U.S. planning

must be conducted all along the spectrum, from assumptions that
SALT will fundamentally hold as the basic structure of the U.S.-Soviet
nuclear balance to an all-out, unconstrained arms competition, whether
stabilizing or not according to various criteria. The test ban issue
will determine other basing requirements, that is, seismology and
verification. So, too, will NPT, outside the direct superpower context, but related. Certain arms-control arrangements that might be
envisioned, howsoever dimly, for Central Europe—MBFR, nuclear-
weapon-free zones—might also critically affect basing issues, that
is, might reopen the Pershing/GLCM/SS-20 issue or reopen the question of U.S. FBS in Central Europe or the Mediterranean or both.

Decolonialization is, it would appear, nearly complete, save a
few remnant, nagging issues, such as Namibia, and aside from dis-
ingenuous Third World definitions of such situations as Puerto Rico
as fitting the rubric. But there may be further pressures in international forums that could involve Diego Garcia, Ascension, the Falklands, Bermuda, Greenland, the quasi-independent states of the several former U.S. trusteeships in the Central Pacific, the Canary
Islands, Mayotte, and Gibraltar, to cite a few salient problems. [41]
Some of these involve important Western basing assets (note Ascension's crucial importance in the Falklands war as well as for space
tracking and tanker refueling) related to the strategic balance.

Regarding Third World warfare, it is important to note that some
of these wars, particularly because of the diplomacy of big-power
arms resupply, have had a large impact on basing access. Enhanced
Soviet access to Vietnam was almost explicitly bargained for in the
context of Soviet aid to Vietnam during its war with the PRC in 1979.
Soviet access to Syria has been enlarged as a result of the crisis in
Lebanon. U.S. access to Argentina has now been curtailed because
of Washington's tilt toward the United Kingdom in the Falklands crisis.
And, of course, there is the matter of Soviet bases in Afghanistan,
and maybe later in Central America. Soviet and U.S. bases were
reversed after the Horn war of 1977/78 involving Ethiopia and Somalia.

The future of arms transfer diplomacy, related to the foregoing,
will be important, both generally and with reference to specific cases,
to the future of basing diplomacy. As indicated, it has become overwhelmingly (modified by the ideological component of alignments) the
major coin of basing diplomacy. There are few cases indeed where
significant basing access has been granted either superpower without
a significant arms transfer relationship, though the reverse of this
proposition does not necessarily hold, that is, arms transfers do not
always or automatically translate into access. Overall leverage is
here critical. Current analyses of the presently evolving trends in
arms transfers tend to coalesce around some of the following points,
all germane to the future of basing access diplomacy.

The overall volume of transfers to the Third World may now be declining, owing mainly to OPEC's decline (note the huge proportion of arms transfers recently accounted for by oil states) and also to the debt problems of other states. Otherwise, the near saturation of some arms markets and the vastly increased unit costs of modern weapons, such as high-performance aircraft and main battle tanks, have been important factors.

The United States seems to be overtaking the Soviet Union as an arms supplier, as measured by new orders, reversing the trend of recent years. This has resulted in part from the relaxation of self-imposed U.S. restraints as earlier embodied in PD-13 (Carter Administration Arms Transfer Policy). It may also have resulted from the successes of U.S. arms in Lebanon and the corresponding Soviet debacle, that is, from a perception in the Third World that U.S. arms technology is ascendant.

Superpowers may increasingly be able to tilt some local arms balances with infusions of qualitatively more advanced systems, such as ECM, ECCM, precision bombing technology, and FLIR. If so (if that is one lesson of Lebanon) it may result in greater big-power leverage in bargaining for bases via arms sales, that is, the quality and sophistication of those sales may be paramount. Contrariwise, the Iran-Iraq war points to the problem of absorption as often overriding that of technology.

More and more developing countries, as well as some developed ones, are demanding technology transfer in the form of assistance to indigenous arms production programs. As the case of the recent U.S.-Turkey agreement may indicate, this too may become part of the arsenal of leverage available to a major power seeking basing access, perhaps even in cases where political cross-pressures might inhibit a forthcoming U.S. response to a request for resupply in the case of conflict. The latter point might well direct more attention to transfer of technology involving consumables—ammunition, spare parts, quartermaster supplies, and the like—than to relatively sophisticated end-item systems.

PROTRACTED CRISIS, PROTRACTED CONVENTIONAL
PHASE, AND BASING ACCESS: DECOUPLING
AND HOSTAGE TARGETS

Much of the previous discussion has dwelt upon nuclear strategic basing access during normal times, that is, peacetime conditions that focus attention on the usual requirements for deterrence. But the discussion on progressive decoupling of numerous U.S. basing relationships also raises questions about how those relationships would work in more extraordinary circumstances, such as those of protracted crisis or even a lengthy U.S.-Soviet conventional war.

It ought not be forgotten that in 1973, Arab oil leverage forced numerous U.S. allies—most formally aligned with the United States in NATO—to deny staging bases and overflight rights important to arms resupply of Israel (the Soviets were more successful in this regard, not only within the Warsaw Pact but in dealing with Yugoslavia and Turkey). Portugal was a reluctant exception under pressure (it has since hinted it would not allow a repeat performance in another such crisis) in connection with landing rights at its Lajes air base in the Azores; Germany, too, appears covertly to have allowed some shipments of U.S. Army materiel from its ports, public pronouncements to the contrary. Earlier, during the 1962 Cuban missile crisis, U.S. pressures apparently persuaded Guinea to deny the Soviets important air and naval access to Conakry.

There are other such examples. The point is that access during normal times is one thing, access under duress during a crisis another. If U.S. access was denied by close NATO allies because of fears about an oil embargo (which, at any rate, could only have had a major impact after two or three months), it might be assumed that such access would be far more contingent and precarious under the threat of a nuclear attack. Hence, the seeming importance of a careful look at the possibilities of nuclear blackmail related to threats during crisis.

If the United States were to be involved in a lengthy conventional phase in central Europe (or perhaps a broader scenario also involving the Persian Gulf), what might be the status of crucial facilities related to nuclear deterrence: ASW aircraft bases in the Azores (Portugal) and Iceland, SAC and submarine facilities in Spain, SOSUS facilities in Norway, FBS aircraft bases in Turkey, early warning satellite relay facilities in Australia? What if the Soviets were to enunciate, as no doubt they would, strong nuclear threats against countries allowing such U.S. access? (The United States could do the same vis-à-vis, for instance, Cuba.) Would the alliance hold or would it crumble, in whole or in part? This involves, incidentally, some interesting questions related to fundamental issues of international relations theory, for instance, dealing with coalition behavior during wars and crises and the impact of technological developments on alliance stability.

Strategic bases might play still another role in lengthy crises, alerts, or conventional warfare, for example, that of mutual hostages in relation to an escalation ladder. Both the United States and the Soviet Union would presumably, in a conventional phase, have an incentive to improve, relatively, their nuclear strategic postures vis-à-vis each other, perhaps by degrading the other side's strategic posture. One way to do this would be by picking off or eliminating key strategic basing assets, which, assuming this were done with conventional weapons, would constitute a form of horizontal escalation. One might imagine, for instance, an escalating situation in the Persian Gulf area in which a Soviet attack on U.S. facilities in Oman would provoke a U.S. response against Soviet facilities in South Yemen or Ethiopia. Just how such a scenario might relate to questions of crisis stability is an interesting theoretical point.

The above matters are, of course, highly hypothetical. But the recent flow of current events does appear to provide some clues that might concern a U.S. defense planner, if not a defense planner in Moscow. All the signs point to decoupling of U.S. alliances and to a tendency for U.S. allies to consider opting out in a crisis or war. No one, of course, wants to be a focal target of nuclear war. Overall, the events in New Zealand, Australia, Greece, Spain, and elsewhere raise serious questions about what nuclear-related access the United States might obtain in the event of a serious crisis that involved pointed Soviet nuclear threats. There are strong hints that the traditional bifurcation of deterrence and defense is germane here, that much of the U.S. basing system remains useful and germane for deterrence in ordinary times but might be far less useful in a real crisis. That raises some interesting questions for international relations theory as well as for U.S. foreign policy. In turn it reinforces the impression—often noted in discussions of SDI—of an ineluctable trend toward "fortress America"; actually on both sides of the central balance, a trend toward strategic autarky. That may require a wholesale bifurcation of geopolitical imagery into its (hypothetical) intrawar and interwar components.

NOTES

1. Some of the recent press discussions of U.S. problems with New Zealand suggest the broader problem of a decoupling effect and see it as somewhat of an epidemic-like phenomenon, which in turn further explains the tough U.S. reaction. See "New Zealand Rebuff: A Baffling Furor," New York Times, February 7, 1985, A10.

2. See Johan Jorgen Holst, "Comparative U.S. and Soviet Deployments, Doctrines, and Arms Limitation," Occasional Paper of the Center for Policy Study (Chicago: University of Chicago, 1971), 31-32; and Philip Klass, Secret Sentries in Space (New York: Random House, 1971), 30. Klass notes that the B-47 force had grown to fifteen hundred aircraft by 1958; along with the B-52s, they were later supported by a tanker fleet of over six hundred KC-135 jet tankers and nearly two hundred propeller-driven KC-97s.

3. Holst, "Comparative U.S. and Soviet Deployment," 35-36; Klass, Secret Sentries, 5; and in particular, Clifford B. Goodie, Strategic Air Command (New York: Simon and Schuster, 1965), 12, 14, 24, 42, 52. The requirement for overseas bases for the B-47 resulted from its range of only slightly more than three thousand miles without refuel. According to Goodie, "For many years, until April 1965, B-47 crews flew their planes on a continual shuttle across the Atlantic Ocean to European bases in an operation known as 'Reflex'" (p. 24). Similar flights were made across the Pacific Ocean to Guam until 1964, when B-52s assumed the Pacific role.

4. See, in particular, Stanley L. Englebardt, Strategic Defenses (New York: Thomas Crowell, 1966), chap. 10. See also U.S. Senate, Committee on Foreign Relations, United States Foreign Policy Objectives and Overseas Military Installations, (Washington, D.C.: Congressional Research Service, Library of Congress, 1979), 18, which lists 21 U.S. DEW line stations in Canada and a total of 31 in Greenland, Canada, and Alaska, stretching four thousand miles roughly along the seventieth parallel north, from Alaska to the east coast of Greenland, providing NORAD forty-thousand-foot high-altitude and five-hundred-foot low-altitude radar surveillance throughout.

5. Klass, Secret Sentries, 15.

6. Ibid., 17, 42.

7. See Graham Allison, "Conceptual Models and the Cuban Missile Crisis," American Political Science Review 63 (September 1969): 696.

8. See Klass, Secret Sentries, chaps. 8 and 9, for a discussion of the role of the U-2 during this period; and Glenn B. Infield, Unarmed and Unafraid, chap. 10. For a discussion of ferret activities, see Klass, 188-95; and Patrick McGarvey, CIA: The Myth and the Madness (Baltimore: Penguin, 1972), chap. 11.

9. Infield, Unarmed and Unafraid, chap. 10.

10. Klass, Secret Sentries, 50-51.

11. Ibid., 84.

12. Ibid., 136.

13. Ibid.

14. Ibid. BMEWS's construction was said to have cost $800 million to provide a fifteen-minute warning of any Soviet missile attack, enough time for a portion of the U.S. SAC bomber force to become airborne. For further analysis of U.S. BMEWS access outside the United States, see Englebardt, Strategic Defenses, 105-22, which includes, on p. 110B, a map showing the BMEWS, DEW, and Mid-Canada line radar coverages. Here there is a discussion of the choice of the BMEWS site near Thule, Greenland, which was located optimally to meet a variety of combined criteria.

15. Klass, Secret Sentries, 91, 104-5, 124.

16. Ibid., 182.

17. Ibid., 6, which discusses the manner in which F-102 interceptors, by 1954, could be guided by radar and air defense computers on optimum intercept paths for intercepting Soviet bombers.

18. Ibid., 5-6.

19. Ibid., chap. 12; and Graham T. Allison, "Conceptual Models and the Cuban Missile Crisis," 689-718.

20. McGarvey, CIA, 42-49.

21. Ibid., 50.

22. See John Carroll, Secrets of Electronic Espionage (New York: Dutton, 1966), 175.

23. Klass, Secret Sentries, 190. "Aircraft used for this type of ferret work normally carry several human operators whose judgment is needed to operate the complex receiving equipment. Furthermore, aircraft can carry many hundreds of pounds of ferret receivers. In a satellite, space and weight were at a great premium in the early 1960s, and the function of human operators would need to be automated." See pp. 190-95 for further discussion of the development of the ferret satellite program up to 1971.

24. McGarvey, CIA, 42-49.

25. Ibid., chaps. 2 and 5.

26. Ibid., p. 47.

27. Ibid., p. 49.

28. Klass, Secret Sentries, 136-37 reports as follows. "For a typical radio-transmission-satellite orbit, with an inclination of approximately 80 degrees, the spacecraft's first daylight pass over Communist territory occurs at the eastern tip of Siberia. Soon the satellite comes within range of the Guam station and can transmit down its photos. Two orbits later, the satellite passes over the east coast of Red China and shortly afterward comes within range of the New Boston, N. H. Station. Pictures taken over central Siberia or Red China's missile test range may be radioed to New Boston, or perhaps a shipboard station in the Indian Ocean. As the satellite begins to pass over western Russia, where many of the most important military installations are located, many more photos will be taken and radioed down to stations at Vandenberg, Seychelles and in east Africa. Pictures taken as the satellite passes over Russia's Communist neighbors to the west will be radioed to the stations at Kodiak and Hawaii. . . . The received radio signals are recorded on magnetic tape at the station but are not reconstituted into pictures until they have been flown by special USAF jet courier aircraft to Washington and turned over to the National Photographic Interpretation Center. . . . For shipboard stations, the tape-recorded photos can be transferred to a specially outfitted aircraft by playing back and transmitting the signals to the airplane as it circles the ship."

Germane to the question of the extent to which the use of overseas facilities can be circumvented is a note that says the "maximum range at which a station can receive transmissions from satellites depends on spacecraft altitude and the topography of ground-station locations. For radio-transmission satellites, maximum range is typically about 750 miles."

29. Ibid., 34.

30. This breakdown was inspired in part from the data format devised by Owen Wilkes at the Stockholm International Peace Research Institute, which in turn is providing a guide to my broader research effort in this area. Much of the subsequent information in this paper derives from that source, as well as from R. E. Harkavy, Great Power Competition for Overseas Bases (New York: Pergamon, 1982), especially chap. 5.

31. Soviet use of ships in lieu of land facilities for purposes related to satellites is discussed in U.S. Senate, Committee on Commerce, Science, and Transportation, Soviet Space Programs: 1976-80 (Washington: GPO, 1982), 123-37. Generally, see also Bradford Dismukes and James McConnell, eds., Soviet Naval Diplomacy (New York: Pergamon, 1979).

32. One purportedly relatively comprehensive map of U.S. SOSUS coverage is provided in John Tierney, "The Invisible Force," Science 4 (November 1983): 69-78. See also Norman Friedman, "SOSUS and U.S. ASW Tactics," U.S. Naval Institute Proceedings, March 1980, 120.

33. See Albert Langer, Owen Wilkes, and N. P. Gleditsch, The Military Functions of Omega and Loran-C (Oslo: Peace Research Institute, 1976).

34. See Phil Lacombe, "The Air Force Satellite Systems," Air Force Magazine, June 1982, 52-59; Edgar Ulsamer, "C^3 Survivability in the Budget Wars," Air Force Magazine, June 1985, 38-58; Tony Velocci, "The State of the Nation's C^3I," National Defense, October 1982, 19-25; and Michael B. Perini, "Managing Change in Telecommunications," Air Force Magazine, June 1983, 78-87.

35. See Ralph Ostrich, "Aeroflot: How Russia Uses its 'Civil' Airline for Covert Activities," Armed Forces Journal 118 (May 1981): 38 ff.

36. See "'Space Wars' Bases Likely in Europe," London Daily Telegraph, July 10, 1984.

37. This is elaborated upon in Harkavy, Great Power Competition, at various points in chaps. 1, 3, and 7.

38. See ibid., 233-34, in a section devoted to base denial strategies.

39. Ibid., 236; and Robert Weinland, "Superpower Access to Support Facilities in the Third World: Effects and Their Causes" (Paper

delivered at the annual meeting of the International Studies Association, Philadelphia, March 18-21, 1981).

40. See references in n. 1.

41. See Harkavy, Great Power Competition, 235.

U.S. Naval Strategy:
A Global View

John Allen Williams

INTRODUCTION

With extensive global commitments and capabilities, the United States remains the preeminent maritime power in the world. At the same time, the most important commitment of the United States outside the Western Hemisphere is to the defense of Western Europe under the umbrella of the North Atlantic Treaty Organization (NATO). The task for military planners is to meet both sets of obligations as effectively and as economically as possible.

If defense resources are abundant or threats are low, balancing these commitments does not present a problem. In a time of constrained budgets and increased challenges, however, ways must be found to meet these European obligations in ways that contribute as much as possible to the protection of U.S. global interests, many of which are important to our NATO allies, as well. In addition, the relative priority to be given these interests is affected by a Eurocentric bias in U.S. defense policy that is only partially explained by strategic realities and that may have an inappropriate influence on U.S. defense planning.

The U.S. Navy's Forward Maritime Strategy has emerged as a strategy for balancing these commitments. The Maritime Strategy originated as a strategy to deter, and if necessary to fight, a pro-

---

This chapter was prepared while the author was in residence at the Center for Naval Warfare Studies, Naval War College, Newport, Rhode Island. I am grateful for the intellectual stimulation of the Center and particularly for the advice and assistance of James R. Kurth, Robert S. Wood, and Donald C. Daniel. The responsibility for the analyses and conclusions presented here remains with the author.

longed conventional war with the Soviet Union, emphasizing the likely
global scope of such a conflict. It has expanded to include other uses
of naval power, such as responses to Third World crises unrelated
or tangentially related to U.S.-Soviet relations. The Maritime Strategy
is a global strategy that is applicable to the defense of Europe, rather
than a European defense strategy applied globally, and the forces
required for its execution can be used in non-European contexts more
easily than Continental Strategy forces can be. The utility of the
Maritime Strategy as a basis for European deterrence and defense
has been widely discussed and will not be the primary focus here.[1]

If its force structure implications are properly understood, the
Maritime Strategy can serve as a basis for security planning that will
maximize U.S. ability to protect its global interests, while at the
same time meeting its vital commitment to the defense of Western
Europe. The challenge is to improve those capabilities that are most
useful in both contexts. Emphases consistent with the Maritime Strategy that are also appropriate for Third World operations should be
considered.

THE THIRD WORLD AND UNITED STATES INTERESTS

Economic Interests

One dimension of the Third World's importance to the United
States is economic. The United States imports large quantities of
raw materials to sustain its economy and has a great interest in their
continuing flow. These include strategic minerals not found in the
United States, or at least not found in sufficient quantities, and the
oil needed to meet U.S. energy needs. The Third World is also a
significant market for U.S. manufactured goods and, to some extent,
U.S. agricultural products. Whether U.S. policies in the Third World
amount to "imperialism" is open to dispute, but it is not necessary to
be a Leninist to realize the area's economic importance to the United
States.

Anomalies abound, however: Cuban troops in Angola protect Gulf
Oil facilities from guerrillas supported by anti-Communist South
Africa. In 1973, a U.S. ally, Saudi Arabia, sponsored an oil boycott
of the United States, and pro-Soviet Iraq did not fully participate. Iran,
also a U.S. ally at the time, then quadrupled the price of oil—an action
that remained after the boycott ended. Yet in 1985, one of the reasons
oil-producing nations were unable to enforce oil prices was price
cutting by Iran, by then a bitter opponent of the United States. It is
also possible to overstate U.S. wartime dependence on Third World
resources; stockpiling and the judicious expenditure of scarce com-

modities can mitigate the effect of shortages if they do not continue
indefinitely. Nevertheless, it is clear that for the long run the United
States will continue to depend on Third World resources and markets
to sustain its standard of living.

Military Interests

More serious challenges to the United States posed by the Third
World are military in nature and may or may not be linked to superpower rivalry. Many developing nations have severe internal difficulties that cause great distress among the people directly affected and
that can sometimes be exploited by outside powers for their own advantage. Ethnic disputes, elite conflicts, underdevelopment, unemployment, and malnourishment all contribute to Third World unrest,
and instability can pose problems for a country such as the United
States that is relatively advantaged by the status quo.

Strategic Locations. Comprising as it does most of the land mass
of the globe, the Third World contains areas of vital strategic importance to the United States and its allies by virtue of geography alone.
Areas near the United States, the Soviet Union, and their allies are
potentially useful for intelligence gathering facilities or as bases for
military action in the event of war. A maritime nation such as the
United States requires the freedom of the seas, which could be restricted by Third World nations able to interdict access through strategic choke points and narrow seas—or who allow the use of their
territory to more powerful nations who have that ability. Concern for
freedom of the seas (quite aside from the desire to send a message
about state-supported terrorism) explains the strong U.S. reaction
to Libyan attempts to claim the Gulf of Sidra as part of its territorial
waters, even though it is not a strategic waterway for the United States.

Bases for Soviet Power. By far the most serious problem the
United States faces in the Third World for the foreseeable future is
the establishment of Soviet military colonies there. Soviet forces in
Cuba and the increasingly powerful Cuban forces pose problems for
U.S. military planners concerned about the resupply of Europe in the
event of general war there. Approximately 60 percent of the reinforcement materiel for Europe flows from U.S. ports on the Gulf of Mexico
and passes through straits that could be interdicted by Cuban forces
or Cuba-based Soviet forces. Increased Cuban military capabilities,
including ground forces, high-performance fighter aircraft, and capable diesel-electric attack submarines, give that country the ability to
intervene militarily on behalf of the Soviet Union in areas of Latin
America and Africa where the Soviets would prefer not to operate

directly. If Soviet reconnaissance aircraft were stationed in Nicaragua, they could conduct surveillance of the West Coast of the United
States, including the access routes to the new Trident submarine base
in Bangor, Washington.

Outside the Western Hemisphere, Soviet or Cuban technical advisors are stationed in nineteen African, nine Asian, and three Latin
American countries.[2] The Soviet attempt to pacify Afghanistan, however costly it has been for them, has put Soviet fighter aircraft within
range of the Persian Gulf and, coupled with a destabilization of the
Baluchi region of Pakistan, could be the first step toward direct Soviet
access to the Gulf itself.

To be sure, Third World allies are not necessarily permanent
ones. Who could have guessed in 1965 that in twenty years the pillar
of the U. S. position in the Arab world would be Egypt, or that the
United States would be concerned about Soviet weapons in Nicaragua,
or that the Soviet navy would increase its Southeast Asian presence
significantly by means of U. S.-built facilities in Cam Ranh Bay, Vietnam? On the other hand, the Soviets can be quite hard to dislodge once
they have been established. Who could guess that the United States
would acquiesce in the slow but steady buildup of the Cuban military,
not to mention Soviet reconnaissance, communications, and other
capabilities there?[3]

Bases for U. S. Power. It is not only the Soviet Union that uses
Third World nations to expand its military power. U. S. bases in such
places as the Philippines, Korea, and Central America and access to
facilities worldwide, possibly including the Persian Gulf, greatly extend the global reach of U. S. armed forces. Combined with a navy
capable of independent operations at sea, these facilities give the
United States the ability to undertake prompt and sustained combat
operations virtually anywhere at will. Such bases are good force
multipliers while they are available, but the transitory nature of
some Third World alliances just noted enhances the importance of
mobile maritime forces that are not so dependent upon land bases.
And if changed political situations cause the withdrawal of U. S. forces,
the navy and the Marine Corps will become even more important for
global military operations.

Conventional Warfare. The conventional military threat to U. S.
interests is posed by Soviet forces based in the Third World and by
the forces of the Third World nations themselves. The primary wartime problem with respect to the Soviet forces deployed there is in
the context of a global war, when they could hamper U. S. operations
such as the covert sortie of U. S. submarines or the resupply of
Europe. In conflicts short of global war, the Soviets already assist

their host nations in military operations, for example, the air defense
of Syrian forces in the Bekaa Valley. These operations could be at the
expense of U.S. or allied interests if, for example, the United States
or Israel thought it necessary to undertake antiterrorist air strikes
in that area or to attack Syrian forces directly.

Not all Third World military challenges can be blamed on the
Soviet Union, however much they might try to take advantage of problems existing there. The flow of high-technology weapons to the Third
World from the West and the East has greatly increased the potential
costs of U.S. or allied intervention there, given the damage that precision-guided munitions can do and the extent to which they have proliferated. For example, the most serious risk to Western shipping
in the last several years has been from Exocet missiles supplied by
France, as the British discovered in recapturing the Falkland Islands
and as oil tankers in the Persian Gulf discovered when they were
attacked by Iraqi aircraft. It is not impossible to conceive of another
attack by North Korea against South Korea, and given the size of the
attacking forces this would be difficult to repel. Similarly, the powerful armaments of Vietnam, partly underwritten by U.S. taxpayers,
are a threat to occupied Cambodia and to neighboring Thailand.[4]

Unconventional Warfare. The increased susceptibility of U.S.
citizens to terrorist attack has focused attention on international terrorism, including that sponsored or tolerated by states such as Iran,
Syria, Libya, North Korea, and Cuba. Splinter groups pursuing their
own agendas have received assistance from these countries, among
others, who have found the disruption engendered by terrorist operations to be in their own interests (one of the tasks of antiterrorist
military actions must be to change this perception).

In the long run, however, it is not episodic terrorist actions that
will pose the greatest threat to U.S. interests, but other unconventional warfare operations that are included in the generic term, low-
intensity conflict. The most difficult of these are politically grounded
guerrilla conflicts. Even when governmental forces have the assistance of powerful friends, these movements can be extremely difficult
to root out, especially if they are based on genuine social injustices
and are supported by countries on the border of the target state. The
British experience in Malaya and, one hopes, the U.S. experience
in El Salvador stand as two of the few examples of successful antiguerrilla operations.

The question for military planners is what contribution military
force, especially nonindigenous military force, can make to the ultimate resolution of these conflicts. Short of physical annihilation of
the guerrillas and their supporters, an action with moral as well as
practical difficulties, the only way such conflicts will end is when the

guerrillas decide to stop fighting. One way to achieve this is some
sort of political accommodation to meet their legitimate grievances,
a task that is much easier if they are not being supported by external
forces that have their own interest in continuing the fighting and if the
pro-U.S. government is willing and able to compromise.

Military force is useful, and sometimes necessary, to buy the
time needed for political resolutions and to lower the guerrillas' expectations about what can be achieved, but its short-term utility
should not deceive one into believing that it is equally effective over
the long run. The example of El Salvador illustrates the importance
of political as well as military responses to such conflicts.

Western democracies have particular problems in fighting unconventional wars. It is difficult, and perhaps ultimately impossible, for
open societies to conduct aggressive antiguerrilla operations and to
do so for a period of years in the full glare of publicity. U.S. actions
in this area would be more credible if opponents could plan on the
forceful implementation of consistent antiterrorist and antiguerrilla
policies once these were decided upon by the political authorities.

<u>Possible Nuclear Proliferation</u>. Nuclear proliferation is an area
in which it is difficult to fault the Soviets. They have been most cir-
cumspect in the transfer of nuclear technology, which is more than
can be said about the French and West Germans. Whatever the source
of their capability, several Third World nations could conceivably join
the nuclear club within a few years. This is mainfestly not in the
United States' interest, for several reasons. First, the possibility
that a Third World nation is about to achieve a nuclear capability
could be very destabilizing for that area of the world. (In that connection, one thinks of the reaction of India to an incipient nuclear
capability by its archenemy, Pakistan.) Second, there is no certainty
that the new nuclear powers would show the same degree of restraint
in the use of nuclear weapons that the current nuclear powers have
shown since the end of World War II. They might actually use them,
possibly against another Third World rival. Third, the use of these
weapons against the forces or even the territory of the United States
or its allies could not be excluded if the nations felt sufficiently
threatened (and it may be in the U.S. interest to instill just such feelings from time to time). Fourth, further proliferation becomes more
likely as the ability to build nuclear systems is more widely dispersed,
including the possible accidental or deliberate proliferation to nonstate
terrorist groups. Finally, the detonation of a nuclear weapon by a
Third World nation could be mistaken by the United States or the
Soviet Union as the responsibility of the other, with the possibility
of calamitous escalation. Indeed, such a result could have been the
intent of the original detonation.

The Nature of the Threat. Sometimes a military challenge will
be so apparent as to cause immediate agreement within a threatened
country on its seriousness and sometimes on the course of action to
be taken. The Cuban missile crisis was such an occasion, although
there were some opinions from the right and the left that the Kennedy
administration should have been either more aggressive or more restrained.

Generally, however, the nature of Third World military challenges is not that clear-cut. If the Cuban armament of the last ten
years had been carried out more quickly, there would have been a
pronounced U.S. response, perhaps even a military one. As it happened, the buildup of Soviet and Cuban arms on the island occurred
gradually, with time for the American people to adjust to the relatively small incremental changes as the costs of taking effective military action against Cuba rose ever higher. A country traumatized by
Vietnam found it convenient to rationalize the military buildup, which,
as noted earlier, poses a genuine problem for the United States in
connection with the reinforcement of Europe, not to mention the problem of Cuba's penchant for disturbing the domestic tranquility of Latin
American nations friendly to the United States when it can. It might
have been better for the United States if it had found a way to over-
throw the Castro regime in 1961; the military and diplomatic costs
of doing so would have been high even then, but they are now pro-
hibitive.

As a result of the ambiguous nature of the threat, coupled with
the moral uncertainties inherent in some types of Third World situations, military actions are unlikely to have strong and consistent
political support, either domestically or internationally. This is
especially true if the connection with the U.S.-Soviet rivalry is
absent or not apparent or if the forces that U.S. political leaders
would like to oppose have political support in the United States (as
is the case with respect to the guerrillas in El Salvador and the
Sandinista government of Nicaragua).

EUROCENTRISM IN U.S. DEFENSE POLICY

During the Carter administration defense priorities reflected the
high priority given to forces immediately useful to stop a Warsaw
Pact assault across the central front at the inter-German border.
Forces were judged primarily by their contribution to this mission.
The result was a reduced emphasis on the defense of NATO flanks in
Norway and in southern Europe and less concern with U.S. interven-
tion capabilities in the Third World. This continental strategy recog-
nized the importance of the central front, but its preoccupation with

that area of NATO resulted in a misallocation of defense resources
and a strategy inappropriate for a nation with global interests and
commitments. With the fall of the Shah of Iran, the taking of American hostages there, and the Soviet thrust into Afghanistan, the administration shifted priorities somewhat, and the Rapid Deployment Joint
Task Force (RDJTF, now the Central Command) was created to implement the Carter Doctrine to defend the Persian Gulf.

Nonstrategic Reasons for the European Emphasis

Not all of the reasons for the U.S. reluctance or inability to deal
with the Third World can be explained by a rational judgment that
European priorities are so important and the situation there so precarious that it must consume a disproportionate share of U.S. attention. There are some nonstrategic reasons that help to explain this
phenomenon. They relate to the relative unfamiliarity of the Third
World to U.S. observers, bureaucratic politics and inertia, and the
moral ambiguities inherent in U.S. actions there.[5]

Unfamiliarity of the Third World. Most people find it difficult to
understand cultures that are significantly different from their own,
and Americans are no exception. Many events in the Third World are
hard to comprehend even by specialists who have made such a study
their profession, and it is unlikely that busy decision makers and
attentive publics will fully comprehend situations there.

Despite their disparate ethnic origins, Americans remain remarkably homogeneous in important ways. U.S. political institutions
are overwhelmingly British, and the common law can be traced across
the Atlantic to Blackstone and beyond. Socially, Americans are more
diverse, but even so, the predominant origin of those who feel bound
to foreign cultures is European. In general, Americans are far more
comfortable with European art, music, literature, and even political
institutions than with those of other areas. Europe is easier to deal
with because it is more familiar; even the Soviets seem familiar to
Americans, who quite possibly do not understand them as well as they
think they do. It may be that increased Hispanic immigration will increase U.S. attention to and understanding of Latin America, but this
has not yet had a decisive effect.

One factor that compounds this tendency to be unfamiliar with the
Third World is the relatively greater number of contacts Americans
have with Europeans than with people from the Third World. This is
increased by, and in turn increases, Americans' relative familiarity
with European culture, institutions, and ultimately people, as noted
above. Americans are far more likely to travel to Europe than to

Africa, Asia, or even South America. Some of the explanation for this is geographic and economic, of course; it is easier and cheaper to travel to Europe than to Asia, and the result is increased familiarity with Europe compared with other areas.

A large number of European contacts is evident in the military as well as the civilian area. Senior military officers in the United States are likely to have had extensive interactions with their counterparts in the navies of the NATO countries. This is owing partly to the requirements of the NATO alliance and partly to the feeling that U.S. officers are more likely to have something to learn about naval operations from naval officers of relatively developed countries. (Since the functions of Third World navies more closely approximate those of the U.S. Coast Guard than those of the U.S. Navy, this perception is often accurate.) There are some useful exceptions to this tendency found at the U.S. military war colleges, where highly capable officers from around the world are brought to study professional subjects and, not incidentally, mix with U.S. officers and one another. A number of these students will become the heads of their services later in their careers, which enhances the importance of developing friendly contacts with them at this point.

Organizational and Technological Inertia. Old patterns become difficult to change, even uncomfortable and dangerous ones. Some U.S. Eurocentrism can be explained by force of habit, perhaps even by a perpetuation of the cold war syndrome. A European war originating with a Soviet attack on Western Europe has been war-gamed since the 1940s, and the necessary U.S. and allied responses, although difficult, are known. A good case can be made that the United States fought the Vietnam War the way it did—primarily as a conventional war—because how to fight such a war was well understood, whereas how to conduct an unconventional war was not. The fact that the war ended conventionally with armored assaults from the north should not obscure the essentially unconventional character of the war in its early, and perhaps manageable, stages.

It is also true that technological considerations have their effect. The heavy armored forces developed—and required—for European defense are less useful in most Third World situations, even if they could be transported there. (This is the stated rationale for the army's interest in light divisions, which would not have the armor support of the European heavy divisions. Elements of bureaucratic politics are apparent, as the army uses the national concern with oil supplies from Southwest Asia as a force builder.) The equipment and doctrine available can have an effect on strategy if they determine the way in which a war would be fought, rather than strategy determining what equipment and doctrine are most appropriate for various situations.

Moral Ambiguities. More than most people, perhaps, Americans prefer their military conflicts to be moral crusades. Politico-military policies based on pragmatic considerations are likely to receive less enthusiastic assent. This is especially true when the policies call for sacrifice or when the object of the sacrifice is not clearly seen to relate to the national interest. The difficulty of the United States in providing consistent, long-term support for friendly governments is further exacerbated by the lack of perfection of the governments in question. Even when the alternative forces appear to have similar vulnerabilities, as seems clearly to be the case in Central America, public support is hardly assured, even for policies of low U.S. sacrifice.

Given the ambiguous nature of many threats to U.S. security, intervention is often hard to justify. There is a tendency to suspect that a policy based on both worthy and unworthy motives is really grounded only on the latter, with the other intentions merely serving as a smokescreen for the true U.S. purposes.

Strategic Reasons for the European Emphasis

Despite the inappropriate reasons that help to explain the relative priority given to Europe in American defense planning, it does not follow that the European commitment should be reduced. Rather, the attention given to Third World contingencies should be increased. Except for the defense of North America, there should be no more important priority for the United States than the defense of Western Europe. Unrestricted Soviet access to the technology and productive capacity of that area would swing the world balance of power away from the United States, with eventual results that cannot be predicted. A Soviet victory in a European war, or even the successful political intimidation of the Western European nations by a Soviet Union so powerful as to be able to do so, would have the most serious long-term consequences for the United States. If the results of a conflict or political intimidation were shifts in military alliances or even Soviet military bases in Western Europe, the consequences would be incalculable.

The vital importance of European defense should not obscure the importance of U.S. interests in the Third World, however. The necessary European commitment should be met in ways which are most transferable to Third World contexts, and increases in U.S. military capability should be made with Third World operations in mind.

THE MARITIME STRATEGY AS A
BASIS FOR GLOBAL INFLUENCE

Given the importance of the Soviet challenge and the primary
European emphasis of recent administrations, navy strategic thought
has been most concerned with the requirements of a Europe-centered,
but global, conventional war with the Soviet Union. The strategic requirements of such a war have been carefully considered, and the
result has been the evolution of the Forward Maritime Strategy. Other
maritime strategies are conceivable that would differ significantly
from the strategy that the navy is developing, of course.

The Maritime Strategy and Global War

Consistent with National Security Decision Directive 32 (NSDD-
32), which it supports, the Maritime Strategy assumes that the
Soviets are the primary military threat the U.S. faces and that a
war with them would probably be a global one. In peacetime it is
also necessary to have a forward posture to support national objectives. In addition to being global and forward, both national military
policy and the Maritime Strategy emphasize joint (multiservice) and
combined (interallied) operations.[6]

The Maritime Strategy is more than a framework of analysis to
aid the thinking of strategic planners as they plan their campaigns,
although it is that, too. It gives directions about the types of operations that would be necessary and their sequence, although specifics
are left to the commanders responsible for particular theaters of
operations. The navy has not been hesitant to discuss the outlines of
the Maritime Strategy openly, perhaps because it feels it has the best-
developed strategy of all the services. The most recently declassified
discussions describe three phases of a possible conflict with the Soviet
Union:[7]

Phase 1 is "Deterrence or Transition to War." The most important goal during this period is deterrence, so that this transition would
not occur. Whatever time is available during this phase would be used
to increase readiness, position forces, and deter or control crises.

Phase 2 is "Seize the Initiative." If war should come, this phase
might include placing aircraft carrier battle groups (CVBGs) north of
Iceland in the Norwegian Sea and very likely would see the early forward movement of U.S. nuclear-powered attack submarines (SSNs) to
war patrol stations. These decisions would be made by the National
Command Authority and the particular theater's unified commander
in Chief (CINC).

Phase 3 is "Carry the Fight to the Enemy." This phase has the

potential for serious escalation if, for example, the United States
were to use several CVBGs to attack the Soviet Union or use its SSNs
to reduce the number of Soviet ballistic missile-firing submarines
(SSBNs) in the Arctic.[8] The question of timing is important for the
possibility of success, and this could vary by theater. It cannot be
predicted in advance how long would be required for moving from one
phase to another, and different theaters of operations could well be in
different phases simultaneously. Although it is difficult to attack the
Soviets' Kola Peninsula early in a war (even if this should be judged
desirable), it may be that certain targets in the Pacific could be
attacked successfully relatively early.[9]

The goal of these phases is an early war termination, without the
use of nuclear weapons and on favorable terms. At the end of the war,
if navy plans are realized, the seas would be swept clean of Soviet
maritime forces, and the United States and its allies would be in a
position to maintain their global interests.

The Maritime Strategy and the Third World

Since U.S. military operations in the Third World have generally
involved the navy, it has long understood the necessity for operations
there. Unlike the army, which until the recent emphasis on rapid deployment forces and light divisions was primarily concerned with
European requirements, the navy has maintained a global perspective.
This was seen even in the early iterations of the Maritime Strategy,
which, although concerned with the European theater, developed ways
in which conventional naval power could be brought to bear against
Soviet forces worldwide. The navy has resisted being relegated to
specialized roles in support of war in Europe, for example, if it were
limited to close-in defense of the sea lanes. Such an emphasis, navy
leaders feel, degrades the offensive potential of naval forces that could
be useful in crisis situations at various levels of violence.

This latter point is important as the navy expands the Maritime
Strategy to deal more explicitly with Third World challenges that occur
outside the context of global war. Soviet or Soviet surrogates (such as
the Cubans) may be involved in these situations directly or indirectly,
and they may even provide the forces that are used. It is also possible
that the navy would have to react to crises that have little or no Soviet/
surrogate involvement. Whatever the occasion of the U.S. intervention,
the navy has long felt that it needs to build balanced forces, useful for
a wide range of contingencies. Thus, for example, the antisubmarine
warfare (ASW) mission should not become so dominant that it drives
out other forces necessary for power projection ashore. Operations
in the Third World increasingly require forces of high capability, given

the proliferation of sophisticated weapons and training to the most
remote areas of the globe.

Developing a strategy for the Third World, or expanding the
Maritime Strategy so it better applies there, is a difficult task. The
Maritime Strategy was created to deal with a complex, but explicit,
scenario of global, conventional war. The probable opponents are
assumed, and the likely courses of action are predicted. Intelligence
and warning indicators are chosen to help national leaders anticipate
hostile actions, and the possible courses such a war could take are
considered. The range of conceivable Third World contingencies, on
the other hand, is so much more diverse as to make predictions extraordinarily difficult.[10] If strategy means the development of comprehensive, overarching plans for the employment of forces in projected military campaigns, the use of the term to describe planning
for Third World contingencies may not be appropriate. A strategy of
flexibility is not a strategy at all, but the antithesis of strategy.[11]

FORCE INVESTMENT IMPLICATIONS

It must be noted at the outset that navy thinking on strategic
policy does not occur in a vacuum, and Henry Eccles' distinction
between the student of strategy, responsible only to the demands of
intellectual rigor, and the executive authority, which must devise
actual plans with real consequences, is quite germane.[12] Navy
authorities charged with the responsibility of developing strategies
for the employment of their forces can be sensitive to criticism from
those whom they regard as irresponsible in the sense that they do not
have the responsibility for creating policy. Former Secretary of the
Navy John Lehman, for example, sometimes referred to critics of
the Maritime Strategy as "parlor-room Pershings." [13]

It is also apparent that strategic choices affect budget priorities.
Indeed, critics who perceive weaknesses in existing policies are likely
to believe that these are proof of the influence of vested institutional
interests on the part of the military, rather than being the result of
genuine intellectual disagreements. The author suggested the possibility in an earlier work that several nonstrategic factors may unduly
affect navy priorities.[14] My views about the Maritime Strategy itself
have changed as the strategy has evolved (it seems more sensible now
than it did earlier), but the possibility remains that these nonstrategic
factors may have an inordinate influence on strategy development.

But even though strategic considerations can never completely
dominate other, more immediate, factors in the real world of institutional interests and constrained resources, it is also important not
to underestimate the influence of abstract strategic thinking on the part

of those charged with developing navy strategy. The process of thinking through how a war should be fought is enormously important for
the preparation of specific operation plans and very useful for crys-
tallizing ideas for the most effective employment of military forces.

Missions and Forces for Global War

Necessary Missions. The most important decision to be made
with respect to navy missions against the Soviet navy is the choice
between what the author terms offensive and defensive sea control[15]
or a combination of the two, which the author terms forward area
sea control. The U. S. Navy clearly prefers the former, which requires offensive operations to seek out and destroy Soviet naval forces
(including their SSBNs) wherever they might be found, even in Soviet
home waters. The navy rationale for this position is that it is better
to destroy as many Soviet forces as early in the battle as possible,
and Soviet knowledge of this intention could be a useful deterrent, the
escalatory potential of such actions notwithstanding.

Another mission that could be included in offensive sea control
is a direct attack on the Soviet Union by naval forces. This possibility
has been widely misunderstood to mean that U. S. aircraft carriers
are required by the Maritime Strategy to sail close to Soviet defenses
early in a war, before Soviet forces have been reduced by previous
actions, and launch kamikaze-like attacks on the mainland. The possibility of CVBG attacks on the Soviet homeland is contemplated as an
option and is one thought useful for deterrence purposes, but these
are not required, especially in the first phases of a war. Early movements by U. S. Navy forces would more likely be by the attack submarines (which will also have the capability to attack land targets,
using Tomahawk cruise missiles).

One alternative approach would be to use available naval forces
in barrier operations at critical choke points through which Soviet
forces would need to pass to attack allied shipping (such as between
Greenland, Iceland, and the British Isles; the Dardanelles; the
Skagerrak and Kattegat; and the outlets from the Sea of Okhotsk and
the Sea of Japan). Proposals to adopt this defensive sea control orientation are not received warmly in naval circles. The bureaucratic
politics argument often advanced (including by the author in the article
just cited) is that the navy really needs the offensive orientation to
justify the continued procurement of aircraft carrier battle groups,
rather than needing the CVBGs because of the orientation. The navy
response to this has a good deal of merit: offensive sea control is
much more effective than defensive, because if significant numbers
of Soviet naval forces get loose in the sea lanes, the task of finding

and destroying them will be much greater, especially if earlier operations have degraded U.S. ocean surveillance systems.

A third alternative, forward area sea control, combines defensive operations with forward operations short of home water attacks and attacks on Soviet bases themselves. This has the advantage of recognizing the necessity of forward operations for sea control, but without the escalatory potential of some of the offensive sea control missions.

Required Forces. Given the difficulty of the missions to be performed in implementing the Maritime Strategy, there is no obvious upper limit to the number of forces required to carry them out or to the degree of sophistication needed in ships, planes, and equipment. Discussion of force levels has centered around the most visible stated requirement of the Maritime Strategy, the fifteen deployable carrier battle groups. Even in the third phase of a global war, carrying the fight to the enemy, Soviet defenses could be formidable, and only the most capable units would have a chance to return home after a strike. In fact, it might require more than fifteen carriers to fight a war with the Soviets: a study by the Brookings Institution reports that the Joint Chiefs of Staff would really like not fifteen, but twenty-two carrier battle groups by 1991.[16] This is physically impossible, of course, and even getting up to the fifteen CVBGs the navy wants is by no means certain. It is also possible that as new carriers authorized are built, older carriers will be retired, thus saving the cost of building entirely new battle groups and air wings. The result would be to maintain the same number of deployable battle groups, but centered on more modern and capable carriers.

But too much public attention has been paid to the implications of the Maritime Strategy for the aircraft carrier controversy, and too little to the requirement for improved amphibious warfare capabilities. One of the strengths of the Maritime Strategy is its emphasis on control of the flanks of NATO: Norway and Denmark to the north and the Aegean area to the south. Powerful and mobile amphibious forces are a wild card whose effect the Soviets would have difficulty in predicting, and navy plans call for expanded amphibious lift capability (to one Marine Amphibious Force and one Marine Amphibious Brigade) and new equipment (such as air cushion landing craft and tilt-rotor aircraft).[17] Beyond the effect on deterrence of complicating the Soviet calculation of the correlation of forces, this amphibious capability could determine whether or not the Warsaw Pact could successfully turn the NATO flanks. Soviet control of Denmark, for example, would greatly complicate the defense of the rest of continental Europe and of Britain. Soviet control of northern Norway would make it easier for the Soviet navy to project itself further south into the sea lanes required for the resupply of Europe. Control of the Aegean area would make U.S. Navy operations in the eastern Mediterranean even more hazardous then they would otherwise be, and it would move Soviet forces closer to the Middle East.

In the final analysis, it is probably not possible to reach agreement on the appropriate levels for the various military forces. Even on an analytical basis devoid of bureaucratic considerations (if that were possible), required force levels differ for various contingencies and scenarios and are sensitive to numerous questionable assumptions regarding system capabilities, the intentions and capabilities of opponents, and the projected exchange ratios in engagements.

Missions and Forces for Third World Contingencies

Necessary Missions. Individual missions required for wartime operations in the Third World are as varied and difficult to plan for as one would suspect from the large number of possible contingencies. These range from a large-scale conventional war, such as in Korea, through protacted low-intensity conflicts, to hostage rescue and counterterrorist operations.

Missions for a large-scale conventional war in the Third World would resemble most closely those envisioned in the Maritime Strategy, although the opponents would differ. Control of the seas sufficient to transport required supplies and troops would be necessary, as would air superiority in the battle area. Large amphibious operations such as Inchon in Korea might become necessary (and might have been used in Vietnam if that war had been fought differently).

Low-intensity conflicts, discussed above, present serious problems, especially for nonindigenous military forces. Conventional naval forces can be useful for interdicting outside supplies and for attacking tangible military assets when these can be located, but they are not directly useful in the crucial political dimensions of such conflicts. Counterinsurgency units, including special warfare forces from all branches of the U.S. military, can be useful for small-unit operations and for training host nation forces. Amphibious operations can be mounted to seize the military initiative, capture enemy forces and strongholds, and disrupt lines of communication.

Hostage rescue and counterterrorist operations have become the recipient of increased public support in the wake of recent incidents involving U.S. citizens. The special units involved in some missions are rarely discussed publicly because of the sensitivity of their operations, but even these may require support from more conventional forces to carry out their assignments. The abortive Iranian hostage rescue mission, for example, involved forces from all services for its implementation (in fact, problems of interservice planning and coordination may have contributed to the failure of the attempt). Other counterterrorist operations could involve conventional military attacks on strongholds and staging areas.

Required Forces. Although Third World military forces are hardly as formidable as those of the Soviet Union, many are capable enough to cause serious problems for a nation attacking them. This was shown clearly in the Falklands, when the relatively small British ASW carriers and their limited-performance Harrier vertical/short takeoff and landing (V/STOL) aircraft proved unable to control the air reliably during operations against Argentina in the South Atlantic. U.S. Navy analyses of the war note the importance of defense in depth and larger, more survivable warships. A major study concludes, "Most of what happened in the South Atlantic supports the judgments that underlay all that is being done in the Administration's naval recovery program."[18] While opponents of increased investments in surface forces emphasize their demonstrated vulnerability, both perspectives are correct. The most important lesson of the war is that as sophisticated defensive weapons proliferate, a certain number of the more capable vessels required to implement the Maritime Strategy will be needed for these lesser contingencies as well.

Given the importance of control of the air for military operations, the battle group centered on a large-deck aircraft carrier is essential for almost all operations there. It is arguable whether fifteen aircraft carrier battle groups are required purely for Third World contingencies, but a certain number of them would certainly be required. (Recall, though, that the goal should not be to optimize naval forces for the Third World, but rather to design a force structure that is useful for both Third World and European contingencies. It is the more demanding scenario of global conventional war against the Soviet Union that sets the higher number required.)

Powerful amphibious forces are also required for Third World operations, just as they are for operations in Europe. This is a very expensive capability, of course, involving specialized amphibious shipping, Marine Corps forces, naval gunfire support (now available from the reconditioned battleships), air support, and supplies provided by strategic air and sealift.

Specialized forces may also be required for certain Third World operations, particularly those involving low-intensity conflict or counterterrorist actions. Perhaps the most important requirement in such situations is a sophisticated understanding of the social and political forces shaping events and a realization that military actions may be only symptoms of deeper problems that must be resolved before peace can be attained.

Both the Eurocentric and the Third World perspectives call for capable naval air forces, although the size, and to some extent the degree, of sophistication necessary is determined by the more demanding requirements of a war centered in Europe. A more significant overlap is in the importance of amphibious power projection forces in both instances. This is not an argument for the atrophy of other capabilities, but an emphasis on the amphibious requirements of a truly global Maritime Strategy that is applicable to the Third World as well as to Europe.

CONCLUSION

The defense of Western Europe remains a crucial interest of the United States, but strategic arguments often reflect a Eurocentric bias that is not entirely appropriate. U.S. interests in the Third World are also crucial, and they require a review of military capabilities to see if they can be made more responsive to foreseeable challenges there, without damage to European interests. This paper has argued that the U.S. Navy's Forward Maritime Strategy offers a basis for this evaluation that balances U.S. European and Third World interests and increases the likelihood that limited defense expenditures will be used to the best advantage. At a time of increased concern with budget deficits and the possibility of defense cutbacks, this is of crucial importance.

The United States must ensure that the commitment to defend Western Europe is met, but it is prudent to do so in ways that are applicable to other U.S. interests as well. An examination of the requirements of each shows that improvements in amphibious insertion capabilities, already part of the implementation of the Maritime Strategy, can enhance the U.S. ability to perform Third World operations in ways that are also relevant for the defense of NATO Europe. The buildup of such forces offers the hope of better protecting U.S. interests worldwide.

NOTES

1. The best annotated bibliography on these questions is Peter M. Swartz, "Contemporary U.S. Naval Strategy: A Bibliography," supplement to U.S. Naval Institute Proceedings, January 1986, 41-47.

2. The Organization of the Joint Chiefs of Staff, United States Military Posture for FY 1986 (Washington: GPO, 1986), 4-7.

3. The key distinction between Cuba and Egypt is the perception of the national leaders on the desirability of the Soviet presence. So long as the Soviets are helping to prop up the regime or to protect it from outside attack, their military presence will be welcome.

4. Speaking to the utility of maritime as opposed to land-based forces, Admiral Thomas Moorer remarked that when the United States left Vietnam, it did not leave any aircraft carriers behind for the North Vietnamese to use. Would that the United States could have sailed Cam Ranh Bay away as easily.

5. I am indebted to John Lovell for many of the ideas in this section.

6. Senate Armed Services Committee, Department of Defense Authorization for Appropriations for Fiscal Year 1985, Part 8: Sea Power and Force Projection, 98th Cong., 2nd sess., (March 14, 1984), 3851-3900 (hereafter cited as FY 1985 Hearings.)

7. FY 1985 Hearings, 3864-887; and Admiral James D. Watkins, "The Maritime Strategy," in U.S. Naval Institute Proceedings (January 1986 supplement), 3-29.

8. See Barry R. Posen, "Inadvertent Nuclear War? Escalation and NATO's Northern Flank," International Security 7 (Fall 1982): 28-54.

9. The Chief of Naval Operations, Admiral James Watkins, has testified that the navy and the air force could attack the Soviet homeland in the Northwest Pacific rather early in a war. See FY 1985 Hearings, 3887.

10. Harlan K. Ullman, "Naval Uses, Naval Strategies, and Naval Budgets," in Harlan K. Ullman and Thomas H. Etzold, Future Imperative: National Security and the U.S. Navy in the Late 1980s (Washington, D.C.: Georgetown Center for Strategic and International Studies, 1985), 21.

11. Or, as Illinois Senator Everett McKinley Dirksen remarked, at least partly in jest, "I am a man of principle. And my first principle is flexibility."

12. Rear Adm. Henry E. Eccles, "The Basic Elements of Strategy," in B. Mitchell Simpson III, ed., War, Strategy, and Maritime Power (New Brunswick, N.J.: Rutgers University Press, 1977), 67.

13. John F. Lehman, Jr., "Posture Statement by the Secretary of the Navy," FY 1986 SECNAV Report, (Washington, D.C.: Navy Internal Relations Activity, 1985), p. 8.

14. John Allen Williams, "U.S. Navy Missions and Force Structure: A Critical Reappraisal," Armed Forces and Society 7 (Summer 1981): 499-528, and "Rejoinder" to Rear Adm. John A. Baldwin, Armed Forces and Society 8 (Summer 1982): 521-23.

15. Williams, "U.S. Navy Missions and Force Structure," 501-3.

16. William W. Kaufmann, The 1986 Defense Budget (Washington, D.C.: Brookings Institution, 1985), 27.

17. Lehman, "Posture Statement," 23.

18. Department of the Navy, Lessons of the Falklands: Summary Report (Washington, D.C.: GPO, February 1983), 1.

Europe's Conventional Defense

Jeffrey Record

INTRODUCTION

Any discussion of Europe's defense must be guided by the premise that Europe's defense, vital though it is to the United States, can never be as important to Americans as it is, or at least ought to be, to Europeans. For Americans, Europe is not home, and for American force planners, the North Atlantic Treaty Organization (NATO) is but one of several demanding overseas military commitments. Moreover, geography continues to deny a complete unity of U.S. and European strategic interests. There is no Group of Soviet Forces Canada or Mexico hovering along U.S. borders, and if one has to fight, it is always better to do so on someone else's territory. It is thus in the strategic interest of the United States to confine any war in Europe to that continent.

How to defend Western Europe without resorting to nuclear fire has been a major preoccupation of NATO force planners ever since the early 1960s, when the Soviet Union acquired the ability to strike the U.S. homeland with nuclear weapons. The development of viable conventional defenses became all the more imperative in the 1970s as the Soviet Union achieved a rough parity in intercontinental nuclear weapons, gained a pronounced superiority in so-called theater nuclear weapons, and continued to expand its long-standing advantage over NATO in conventional forces.

Yet here the alliance is, headed for the 1990s with conventional defenses, according to the testimony of NATO's own supreme commander, inadequate to hold against a major Warsaw Pact attack for more than a few days without the use of nuclear weapons that, given the altered nuclear balance, would be self-defeating and probably suicidal. Flexible response has been a dead letter ever since its official adoption by NATO, because the alliance has steadfastly refused to act effectively on the military implications of the loss of American nuclear superiority. That loss dictated the creation of a truly viable conventional leg of the NATO triad, which, in turn, required a willingness to think beyond deterrence. Neither has been forthcoming.

Nor, more specifically, has the alliance come to grips with the force structural and operational implications of a forward defense doctrine that calls for, in effect, a rigid, linear, meter-by-meter defense of German territory against fast-moving and numerically superior Soviet armored forces. The Federal Republic understandably has rejected a defense in depth that, though seemingly dictated by the nature of the Warsaw Pact armored threat and by deficiencies in NATO's conventional force posture, would serve in advance to write off at least that one-third of Germany's population living within one hundred kilometers of the inter-German border. An effective forward defense is not impossible. But history (for example, the Finnish Mannerheim Line of 1939/40 and the Israeli defense of the Golan Heights in 1973) shows that a successful forward defense of the kind envisaged by NATO force planners requires at least two things: (1) robust fortifications and other barrier defenses along the line to be held and (2) the availability of substantial operational reserves to contain and destroy inevitable breakthroughs. If the Maginot Line lacked sufficient operational reserves behind it and failed to cover the Franco-Belgian border, it at least had fortifications. NATO's forward defense has neither; indeed, of the Bundeswehr's twelve divisions, only one is not assigned to a forward position along the inter-German border. In short, what NATO has today in the way of conventional defenses is about what it had in the era of massive retaliation, though many refuse to admit it: a nuclear tripwire.

It was this conclusion that prompted submission of the Nunn amendment before the U.S. Senate in 1984. While that amendment angered many in Europe, the logic behind the amendment remains unassailable. If the alliance remains unwilling to muster the conventional force wherewithal required to avoid an early first use of nuclear weapons in the event of war, then U.S. ground forces in Europe sufficient to trip the nuclear wire need not be as large or as costly as they are now. The wire could as easily be tripped by 200,000 or even 150,000 U.S. troops in Europe as by 350,000. Indeed, the fewer the better, since the refusal of key allies to stockpile enough ammunition for more than a few days or weeks of combat and to provide needed shelters for reinforcing U.S. aircraft would condemn U.S. troops in Europe, whatever their number, to probable defeat or destruction. Although Europe's defense consumes more than one-half of the U.S. defense budget, the United States has never been in a position to defend Europe in the absence of sufficient allied investment.

It might be noted in passing that U.S. complaints about the reluctance of European allies to bear their fair share of the common defense burden are often rejoined by allied complaints about U.S. performance. European allies, most of whom rely upon conscription, point out, for example, that the United States is unwilling to make the political and social sacrifices entailed by conscription, an unwillingness that contains potentially disastrous consequences for the ability of the United States to deliver U.S. reinforcements pledged to Europe's defense in a timely fashion. The Nixon administration's decision in the early 1970s to replace the draft with an all-volunteer force (AVF) unattended by even a semblance of a standby draft system was taken for purely domestic political reasons and without any concern for the decision's strategic implications. That the AVF has survived at all can be ascribed primarily to high unemployment in the civilian economy, to substantial reductions undertaken in authorized active-duty service end-strengths, and to a willingness to countenance levels of reserve component manning that are woefully inadequate to sustain a major or protracted war in Europe. General Bernard W. Rogers, NATO's supreme commander, has justifiably called for a return to conscription. Indeed, the U S. military's manpower crisis is certain to worsen in the coming decade, as the number of American males of military age continues to decline.

The only intellectual deficiency of the Nunn amendment, which may well be resubmitted in the future, is a deficiency common to almost all promptings for improved conventional defenses, namely, an underlying assumption that more effective conventional defenses would raise the nuclear threshold. This assumption is not at all self-evident, at least with respect to a Soviet Union that had already decided on war in Europe. NATO's own doctrine of nuclear first use reflects a willingness to substitute nuclear fire for conventional inadequacy. Would not the Soviet Union, if confronted with otherwise unbreachable NATO forward conventional defenses, also be sorely tempted to use nuclear weapons as a means of swiftly overcoming those defenses? While it can be persuasively argued that improved NATO conventional defenses would reduce the chance of war in Europe, it can also be argued that such defenses, by diminishing Soviet force planners' confidence in a quick conventional victory, would serve to lower the nuclear threshold for the Warsaw Pact in the event of war. There have always been two nuclear thresholds in Europe, one for NATO and one for the Warsaw Pact.

None of this line of thought is to belittle the continuing deterrent power of nuclear weapons, even in the absence of credible nonnuclear defenses. More than any other factor external to the Soviet Union, it has been the very presence of thousands of U.S. nuclear weapons on European soil that has kept the peace in Europe. Even were NATO to renounce its long-standing doctrine of nuclear first use, it is doubtful that the most unregenerate of hawks in the Kremlin would feel appreciably more inclined to opt for war in the event of a crisis. The Soviet military is nothing if not Clausewitzian in its appreciation of war's friction and inherent unpredictability. Could the Group of Soviet Forces Germany make it to the English Channel ports without someone, somewhere, first-use doctrine or no, firing off at least a few of NATO's tactical nuclear weapons, thereby sparking uncontrollable events that could lead to mutual suicide? One is tempted to ask those who would denuclearize Europe, for centuries a cauldron of interstate violence and the cockpit of both world wars, to explain four decades of peace in a place where the density of nuclear weapons is greater than anywhere else in the world. They might also explain the absence of any kind of war—nuclear or nonnuclear—between the United States and the Soviet Union, which possess the largest arsenals of nuclear weapons.

CAN EUROPE BE DEFENDED?

With respect to the present debate within the alliance over how best to improve NATO's conventional defenses, the first question to be addressed is whether Western Europe is in fact conventionally defensible against a large and determined Warsaw Pact assault. If Western Europe is militarily defensible without a resort to nuclear fire, then the next question is: Is a viable conventional defense politically feasible? Within the alliance there has always been an uneasy, and at times bitterly antagonistic, relationship between the militarily necessary and the politically acceptable. Indeed, the history of NATO's conventional defenses since the adoption of flexible response has been for the most part a history of the subordination of military imperatives to political considerations—an inability to reconcile deterrence and defense. Such a situation might be tolerable if NATO enjoyed the major strategic, operational, and geographic advantages over its potential adversary that the Warsaw Pact enjoys.

First there is the Warsaw Pact's numerical superiority in both standing forces and forces readily available upon mobilization. What makes this superiority potentially decisive is a second advantage, geography. Unlike NATO, which is bifurcated by three thousand miles of water, the Warsaw Pact is a compact, contiguous alliance whose principal member and source of reinforcement, the Soviet Union, enjoys comparatively short land lines of communication with central Europe.

Even shorter are the distances that Soviet forces would have to cover to gain a decisive victory. NATO Center lacks great depth, which, operationally, means that it lacks the ability to trade a lot of space for a lot of time. Yet the history of modern, mechanized warfare has shown that, in the absence of barrier defenses, both the capacity and the willingness of a defender to trade space for time is essential in defeating an attack preceded by little warning and characterized by rapid, deep thrusts of large concentrations of armor. The success of the German blitzkriegs of 1939 and 1940 against the relatively shallow states of central and western Europe could not be repeated in the vast expanses of Russia against an opponent able and prepared to retreat over a thousand kilometers. However, the distance from the inter-German border to Antwerp is less than five hundred kilometers (and from the border to the Rhine, less than three hundred) and NATO has not seen fit to erect barrier defenses worth the name.

To these numerical and geographic advantages must be added the inestimable operational advantages associated with the initiation of hostilities. By virtue of its purely defensive strategy, NATO has ceded to the Warsaw Pact the choice of time and place. While not for a moment suggesting that NATO should adopt an offensive or preemptive strategy, it is prudent to recognize the operational penalties incurred by its present posture. Against an intended victim lacking barrier defenses and robust operational reserves, an attacker that achieves surprise need not possess any margin of numerical superiority, to say nothing of the mythological three-to-one advantage. Moreover, modern military technology and operational doctrines have increased the traditional military benefits of surprise attack against an unready defender. A mobilization command structure that relies confidently on the ability of sophisticated surveillance technologies to provide early, unambiguous warning of an impending blow ignores major improvements in means of deception that might well render it a victim of surprise.

Also ignored by Western strategists is perhaps the weakest link in the entire chain of NATO's conventional defenses, namely, the lack of any assurance that political decision makers will act effectively in time, or even act at all, on whatever warning is received. Unlike the Warsaw Pact, which is an alliance of forced and enforced loyalty, NATO is a voluntary organization of sovereign, democratic states. As such, it lacks both the military commonality and the political cohesion of the Warsaw Pact. And given recent events in Western Europe, including the capture of both the British Labour and German Social Democratic parties by political movements hostile to the United States, to nuclear weapons, and even to the very idea of NATO, the possibility of political paralysis in time of crisis cannot be dismissed. One can envisage some political leaders in Europe refusing to agree on such indispensable crisis measures as the dispersion of nuclear warheads and the movement of ground forces to their general defensive positions. Such action, they will argue, are provocative and could spark the very war NATO seeks to prevent; never mind that the Soviets have already moved the Group of Soviet Forces Germany out of garrison, that they have called up Category II and III divisions inside the Soviet Union, and that they have sent most of their submarines to sea. Thus, the continuing debate over how much warning NATO will have of an impending Warsaw Pact military move misses the point. Even six months' warning would count for nothing if NATO disintegrated politically.

To be sure, the Soviet Union, too, would be plagued by a number of political and military disadvantages in a violent contest for Europe. However, some of those disadvantages have been grossly overstated, while others probably would prove irrelevant to the outcome of a NATO-Warsaw Pact war. It is said, for example, that some of Moscow's East European allies are politically unreliable and that the Soviet Union could not count on them to provide assured political and military support for an attack against Western Europe. This may well be true, but it also may well be inconsequential. It can be argued that the Soviet forces deployed in Europe and readily available for combat in the theater are alone sufficient to overwhelm NATO's defenses and that, therefore, the only wartime tasks Moscow need ask of its allies are the purely defensive ones of parrying potential NATO counterattacks on East European territory and of maintaining secure lines of communications for Soviet forces passing through Eastern Europe. (And let it also be recognized that not all members of NATO can be regarded as assuredly reliable in the event of an East-West military confrontation in central Europe. Could the alliance count on Greece or Spain in circumstances where their own territories were not directly threatened? Would Denmark offer more than token resistance, even if attacked?)

It is also said that the Soviet Union lacks unrestrained access to high seas. There can be no doubt on this point. The very geography that works to the Soviet Union's benefit in a land war on the Eurasian landmass has conspired to place the Soviet Union at a distinct disadvantage in a naval war with the West. The question is whether the outcome of the struggle at sea would be decisive in determining Europe's fate in the event of war. Let us assume that on the first day of hostilities NATO succeeded in sweeping every Soviet ship from the high seas and in demolishing all Soviet home and overseas naval bases. Would this prevent the Soviet army from overrunning Europe? For the Soviet Union, whose war economy and ability to conduct military operations in Europe are not dependent on maritime communications, sea power is a luxury, not a strategic imperative. Indeed, Admiral S. G. Gorshkov's transformation of the Soviet navy from a coastal appendage of the land battle into a powerful "blue water" force may be regarded as an inherently unnatural development, as was Admiral Alfred von Tirpitz's creation of a German High Seas Fleet in the decades before World War I. The Soviet Union, like Wilhelmenian Germany, is a con-

tinental power with continental military experiences and traditions,
and it possesses none of what Alfred Thayer Mahan defined as the
basic elements of sea power, including geographical position.

It is further said, although less so now than in the past, that the
Soviet Union is technologically inferior and that its inferiority deflates
the significance of its numerical advantage. To be sure, the Soviet
Union does lag behind the West in a number of military technologies,
including some of the so-called emerging technologies related to
"smart" area and precision-guided munitions, sensors and other long-
range surveillance and target-acquisition devices, and advanced data-
processing and information distribution systems. On balance, however,
the Soviet Union during the past two decades has managed to eliminate,
and in some cases surpass, the West's qualitative lead in most of the
technologies critical to both the land and tactical air battle. Far more
significant has been the Soviet Union's success in doing so without an
enormous sacrifice in numbers of deployed systems. Unlike NATO,
the Soviet Union, with its proportionally far greater investment in
things military, has not permitted quality to become the enemy of
quantity.

What conclusion can be drawn from these multiple circumstances?
Namely, that any discussion of how best to improve NATO's conventional defenses must be predicated on recognition that the alliance
would enter a conflict in Europe profoundly (though by no means hope-
lessly) disadvantaged and that those disadvantages—political and military—are not even remotely offset by the disadvantages, real or
imagined, attributed to the Warsaw Pact.

THE ROGERS PLAN

Before addressing the question of what measures are necessary
to provide reasonable credibility to NATO conventional defenses, it
is important to recognize what is not essential. Take, for example,
the Rogers Plan for follow-on force attack (FOFA), which not only is
of doubtful operational validity and political feasibility but also fails
to address the most serious deficiencies in NATO's present conventional defenses. Those deficiencies are lack of barrier defenses along
the inter-German border; lack of sufficient operational reserves; lack
of sufficient war reserve stocks of ammunition, spares, and other
combat consumables; the lack, on the part of the supreme allied commander in Europe (SACEUR), of prehostilities mobilization authority
commensurate with his responsibilities.

Few of the premises on which the Rogers Plan rests are self-
evident. Many are questionable, and some are just plain wrong. For
example, the FOFA concept, which was officially endorsed by NATO

in 1984, presumes that NATO has, or would be willing to create, the necessary conventional military wherewithal to engage the pact's initial attacking forces and follow-on echelons effectively and simultaneously. To be sure, NATO collectively possesses an economic, industrial, and technological base sufficient, at least on paper, to mount concurrent and successful attacks on the pact's first and follow-on echelons. But the real issue is a political one: resource allocation. The alliance has never chosen to devote resources to the military sufficient to stop the pact's first echelon well forward, to say nothing of decisively engaging follow-on echelons, and, if present defense budgetary trends are indicative, NATO is not likely to do so in the future. Given the current and likely future political constraints on the actual military resources made available to the alliance, strategic and operational choices must be made, and NATO cannot afford to disperse its finite forces over too many objectives. This disparity between assets and ends means, in short, that top or perhaps sole priority must be accorded to defeating the first echelon.

This is not to suggest that NATO refrain altogether from striking targets in Eastern Europe: aerial strikes across the inter-German border have always been a feature of U.S. and NATO war plans for Europe's defense. It is only to argue that choices cannot be avoided between the immediate defense of German territory and the engagement of more distant pact follow-on forces. To put it another way, it is unreasonable to expect annual real increases in national defense expenditure of 6 to 7 percent (the cost, according to General Rogers, of implementing his plan) from the alliance, most of whose members have failed to honor past pledges of 3 percent and whose principal member is unlikely to enact any real increases in annual defense expenditure during the coming half decade.

The heart of the FOFA concept is its operational presumption that the success of a Warsaw Pact offensive against NATO Center hinges on the timely arrival intact of follow-on forces in the battle area—on a delicate, exacting, and complex plethora of timetables and programmed march rates reminiscent of the inflexible and over-centralized Schlieffen Plan of 1914. However, many observers question this portrayal of Soviet ground-force offensive doctrine, claiming that it reflects a fundamental misinterpretation of the nature of the problem and of recent Soviet force improvements that suggest a declining operational significance of follow-on echelons. In any event, the stacking of follow-on Soviet echelons behind forces initially committed to the attack presupposes the inability of first-echelon forces to achieve a decisive breakthrough, a presupposition that would seem at odds with General Rogers's own gloomy assessment of NATO's initial conventional force sustainability.

A second and no less suspect, if admittedly implicit, operational premise of the Rogers Plan is that effective countermeasures to follow-on force attack are either unavailable to the Soviets or, if available, unlikely to be adopted, due to assumed rigidities in Soviet theater force doctrine and structure. A recent major study conducted at the U.S. National War College concluded, however, that a host of effective potential countermeasures to the Rogers Plan are available to the Soviets and that the Soviets are in some cases moving toward their implementation. Countermeasures identified by the study include increasing the combat power of the first echelon either by reallocating units from the follow-on echelons or by increasing the strength of existing first-echelon units across the board; decreasing the time required to commit follow-on echelon forces; improving counterair capabilities or the ability to interrupt air-ground coordination through physical and electronic attacks on command, control, communications, and intelligence (C^3I) systems; and preparing the battlefield to facilitate rapid movement forward, support of forward echelons, defense of the rear area, and quick recovery from interdiction via such measures as forward deployment of additional engineer units and prepositioned bridging and road construction equipment and supplies.

Indeed, the Soviets have for at least a decade been increasing the combat power of their first-echelon forces in Eastern Europe, notably the Group of Soviet Forces Germany. This has been accomplished largely by the addition to existing divisional force structures of mechanized infantry, self-propelled artillery, air defense, and other combat support forces. Moreover, the Soviets have developed so-called Operational Maneuver Groups (OMGs) and an associated doctrine designed to decrease the amount of time required to commit second-echelon forces. The OMGs are charged with immediate exploitation of breakthroughs obtained in NATO's forward defenses; their mission is to bypass islands of resistance and wreak havoc in NATO's soft and comparatively undefended rear areas. Additional countermeasures available to the Soviets include heightened investment in camouflage, smoke, decoys, flares, chaff, aerosols, and other items designed to deceive and confuse NATO sensors and other target acquisition devices, as well as electronic jamming, spoofing, and other actions designed to impede, disrupt, or block the flow of real-time information critical to NATO strikes, especially on moving targets. The Soviets continue to pay far more attention to night operations than do most NATO armies and have long been masters of battlefield deception. A properly devised large-scale deception could completely destroy the integrity of the computer-based intelligence system on which NATO's follow-on force attack concept depends.

The Rogers Plan's third operational premise—that effective interdiction of pact follow-on forces can be accomplished by aerial (manned aircraft and missile) strikes alone—also is questionable. In many respects the plan is little more than the latest expression of the old forlorn hope of victory through air power. Past aerial interdiction campaigns, notably in Europe, Korea, and Vietnam, failed to achieve decisive results in the absence of attendant large-scale offensive ground operations, and their costs, in terms of munitions expended and lives and aircraft lost, have often exceeded, in some cases vastly so, both the monetary and the operational value of targets destroyed. For example, during the air interdiction campaign in Vietnam known as Rolling Thunder, the United States destroyed targets estimated at less than $1 billion in value at the cost of $6 billion worth of lost aircraft. More to the point, an aerial campaign against pact follow-on forces in Eastern Europe is likely to encounter air defenses far more formidable than those of North Vietnam in the 1960s and early 1970s.

Even the eventual substitution of ballistic and cruise missiles for manned aircraft as the principal means of carrying out the Rogers Plan promises no significant alteration in the dismal cost-benefit ratios characteristic of most past air interdiction campaigns. Missiles are individually cheaper and would possess far greater system survivability than aircraft in the hostile air defense environment of Eastern Europe, but their lack of reusability would compel their purchase in greater numbers to cover the same target array, and the unit cost of their advanced conventional munitions is expected to far exceed the cost of current munitions carried by manned aircraft.

If many of the strategic and operational premises of the Rogers Plan are questionable, so too is its political feasibility. Despite the adoption of the follow-on force attack concept by the NATO Defense Planning Committee in 1984, many Europeans privately question its operational desirability and validity, and most allied governments have registered little willingness to undertake the substantial real annual increases in national defense expenditure deemed necessary by General Rogers himself to implement the plan. No less a political obstacle to the plan's implementation has been the absence to date of a doctrinal and procurement consensus within the U.S. military itself regarding the wisdom and affordability of the plan. Indeed, the U.S. Army's lukewarm response to the Rogers Plan may in the end prove the most formidable political obstacle to its adoption. The army strongly objects to the plan's emphasis on striking distant rather than close-in targets, as well as the plan's centralization of tactical air assets at the theater level, which the army feels would deprive ground commanders of adequate and timely close air support. And neither the army nor the U.S. Air Force, which endorses the plan at least in principle, has extended to the associated emerging technologies a preferential position in their respective procurement policies, despite strong pressures to do so by the office of the Secretary of Defense and key members of the Senate Armed Services Committee. The army's

other military modernization programs, which entail the purchase of
fourteen new systems, including the M-1 tank, the Bradley fighting
vehicle, and the AH-64 attack helicopter, have clear priority over the
emerging technologies program. Similarly, such air force big-ticket
procurement programs as the F-15, F-16, B-1, and MX programs
enjoy a marked preference over emerging technologies. The air force
also is reluctant to pour its limited resources into deep-strike technology, since many of these systems are designed ultimately to replace manned aircraft missions.

There are, finally, serious doubts about the Rogers Plan's technological feasibility and cost. The history of high-technology, smart
weapons has been a history of cost overruns and of often disappointed
expectations in terms of actual operational effectiveness. The ultimate
performance of many follow-on force attack technologies remains
clouded by technical and budgetary uncertainties, and it can be argued
that the Rogers Plan is excessively dependent on complex technologies
of questionable operational effectiveness and maintainability in the
stress and chaos of actual combat. As for the costs of procuring those
technologies, estimates range from $10 billion to $30 billion. If experience is any guide, however, these estimates will rise not by per-
centages but by multiples. Even if the Rogers Plan were feasible, however, it would still be subject to condemnation on the grounds that it
seeks a solution to the wrong problem. It is the Warsaw Pact's high-
quality and already reinforced first-echelon forces, not its more distant and less capable follow-on forces, that would most threaten
NATO's political and military integrity in the event of war. What good
would it do to defeat the pact's second echelon in Eastern Europe while
losing to its first echelon in Western Europe?

REMEDIES

To defeat the Warsaw Pact's first-echelon forces, at least four
alterations in NATO's present conventional defense posture are required, all but one of them notable for their absence in the Rogers
Plan's scheme of operations. The first is fortification. The creation
of barrier defenses along the inter-German border—employing bunkers, tank traps, mines, explosives prechambered in bridges or along
key defiles, afforestation, and a more deliberate orchestration of
NATO's numerous water obstacles—would serve to canalize and re-
tard the momentum of a Warsaw Pact attack. In so doing, barrier
defenses would enhance target acquisition and, more important, buy
time necessary to form up operational reserves for the purpose of
counterattacking breakthroughs. Additionally, because barrier defenses could be manned by reserve units and territorial forces, they

would contribute directly to the formation of operational reserves by freeing at least some of those mobile, first-line, and comparatively costly NATO forces now allocated to the inter-German border's forward defense. Given the Warsaw Pact's possession of both the initiative (courtesy of NATO's purely defensive strategy and operational doctrine) and numerical superiority, the issue is not whether first-echelon pact forces could breach NATO's forward defenses, even forward defenses augmented by barriers, but rather whether, when, and where inevitable penetrations could be halted and subsequently eliminated. Even the Mannerheim Line, a model of what forward defense ought to be, was ultimately breached, although it took the Russians six months and staggering losses to do so.

The question may well be asked as to why NATO has refused to do something so militarily beneficial as to construct barrier defenses. The answer is, as usual, political. Even though proper barrier defenses could be had for far less cost than the Rogers Plan and even though they might mean the difference between victory and defeat in wartime, Bonn has opposed them on the grounds that fortifications along the inter-German border would somehow encourage the permanent division of Germany. This argument is mystifying, at least to many Americans. The Federal Republic of Germany (FRG) already recognizes the German Democratic Republic (GDR) as a separate, independent, and politically sovereign state, and the GDR is a member of a military alliance that poses the only threat to the Federal Republic's own independence. Has not the German Democratic Republic fortified its own side of the border? And are the consequences of the French fear of offending the Belgians by extending the Maginot Line along the Franco-Belgian border to be forgotten?

The second measure required to confer credibility on NATO's conventional defenses is related to the first: more operational reserves, the lack of which many observers regard as NATO's gravest military weakness. Barrier defenses are one means of increasing the alliance's operational reserves, but there are others. David Greenwood has proposed replacing the current, front-loaded "layer cake" of national force dispositions with a "piano keyboard" disposition that would withhold larger forces farther back. Steven Canby has called for a more effective utilization of NATO Europe's vast pool of trained military manpower no longer on full-time active duty. Again, the point must be made that the goal is not an impregnable forward defense of the inter-German border, which is impossible even with barrier defenses and plentiful operational reserves. The objective is rather a successful defense of Western Europe as a whole, including Germany. To attempt to defend every square meter of Germany, irrespective of overriding operational considerations, is to lose every square meter of Germany.

A third prerequisite for any effective conventional defense is, of course, sufficient war reserve stocks of ammunition and spares. Any scheme of defense, be it follow-on force attack, a linear defense, or a modified defense in depth, is by definition doomed to defeat if the defender runs out of ammunition before the attacker. Although the question of how much is enough is a matter of varying opinion (sixty days' supply would seem to be a prudent minimum), it is patently non-sensical for one country to stockpile forty-five or sixty days' worth while other key allies keep but a week or two's worth on hand. This matter is admittedly a tired old issue, but it cannot be simply wished away through inaction and unfulfilled promises. The history of modern warfare has been a history of shell shortages.

Finally, there can be no confidence in an effective conventional defense of Western Europe if, in a crisis, those charged with the responsibility for defense are denied authority to undertake essential preparatory measures. No one has suggested that SACEUR or any NATO military body be granted de jure or de facto authority to plunge Europe once against into war. No one wishes to return to the summer of 1914, although only the Soviets could make it happen. Simple prudence, however, argues strongly for giving SACEUR more authority than he now has to undertake certain prehostilities military measures in the face of an impending Warsaw Pact attack. Such measures would include dispersal of nuclear weapons and tactical aircraft, most of which are now concentrated at a relatively small number of main NATO airbases and therefore exceedingly vulnerable to preemption; movement of NATO ground forces, many of which are inexcusably maldeployed, out of garrison to their general defensive positions; and call-up of certain categories of reservists as well as civilian resources such as militarily useful trucks.

It might be added parenthetically that judgment of hostilities as likely or imminent is as much a military decision as a political one. And it can be argued that SACEUR, by virtue of his already transnational military role and limited mobilization authority, represents a far more reliable and effective repository for making certain critical preparatory military decisions during a crisis than the present collection of more than a dozen sovereign political authorities who find consensus difficult in the comparative quietude of peace. May it be further added, to dispel suspicions that endowing SACEUR with greater authority would lead to greater American influence within the Atlantic alliance, that there is nothing sacrosanct about the notion that SACEUR should always be an American. Indeed, were France to resume military participation in NATO, one could even envisage a French SACEUR.

The time is long overdue for NATO to face—and to act effectively on—the unpleasant reality that conventional deterrence and defense are inseparable under conditions of nuclear parity. Conventional force deficiencies that were tolerable in the days of pronounced nuclear superiority are no longer so. At this stage in the history of the alliance, the only argument for tokenism is the one, now often heard in Europe, that the Soviet Union does not now, if it ever really did, pose any military threat to Western Europe. If this argument is valid, however, there is no need for NATO itself.

Japan's Role in Deterrence

Stephen P. Gibert

INTRODUCTION

Throughout the history of the nation-state system, wherever the interests of the great powers intersected and collided, war was often chosen as the ultimate arbiter. Thus today status quo nations must adopt some means of deterring aggression on the part of hostile revisionist states. The North Atlantic Treaty Organization (NATO) provides that function for Western Europe. Indeed, it has furnished such a robust deterrence, despite its failures to live up to all the expectations hoped for it, that it is frequently observed that superpower war is least likely to occur in Europe. When it is recalled that both of the twentieth century's great global wars originated in the Europe now claimed to be largely immune from conflict, this is a remarkable testament to the utility of deterrence and the faith placed in it as a means to preserve the peace.

In contrast, Northeast Asia does not enjoy a NATO alliance to maintain adequate deterrence of those nations that would disturb the status quo. Earlier, China was perceived to be most likely to conduct aggression against other Asian states. In recent years, however, as the Soviet Union has steadily strengthened its overall military capabilities and expanded its forces in the Far East, Moscow has taken Peking's place as the chief threat to the noncommunist Asian nations. So far, however, the Soviet Union, the world's great revisionist power, has been held in check by a strong U.S. military presence in the western Pacific and in Northeast Asia and by the enmity of China, the other great Asian communist power. Should either of these two conditions change—should there occur a further erosion of the Soviet-U.S. military balance in the area, occasioned by the continuation of the Soviet military buildup in the Far East, or a rapprochement between Moscow and Peking—deterrence in Northeast Asia would become fragile indeed.

Unfortunately, a NATO-type solution to enhancing the deterrent posture of the noncommunist states is not feasible. And U.S. worldwide commitments, economic difficulties, and the necessity to prevent further unfavorable shifts in the superpower nuclear balance argue against a greater U.S. security role in Northeast Asia to counteract the lengthening Soviet military shadow in the region. Furthermore, China's policy of equidistance between the two superpowers (although in reality tilting toward the United States) and ideological and other obstacles make a Sino-American alliance aimed at the Soviet Union highly improbable.

Of course it makes sense for Washington and Peking to maintain the kind of relationship that gives Moscow pause. But the United States should not, as it presently does, rely on a communist nation as its principal vehicle for deterring the Soviet Union in East Asia. A different country needs to play that role. There can be only one candidate for the job and that is Japan; the only feasible solution for a viable and enduring free world deterrent posture in East Asia is for Japan to improve significantly its military capabilities. Tokyo must unilaterally provide that additional measure of defensive strength that deterrence requires, thus ensuring that East Asia, like Europe, is free from Soviet bullying, political coercion, and even possible military aggression. Japan, with the world's most vigorous economy, and China, the world's most populous nation, even though not in alliance and even if occasionally pursuing policies at cross-purposes with each other, can together maintain the power balance in Northeast Asia. China presently, whether willingly or not, contributes significantly to deterring Soviet adventurism. Japan, in contrast, is not an important factor in keeping the peace in Asia. This situation is no longer acceptable.

This chapter approaches the subject of an enhanced deterrent role for Japan by addressing the following topics: the necessity to restore the Eurasian balance of power and the contribution Japan could make to this; an appraisal of Japan's military posture and the true nature of the Japanese-U.S. alliance; and finally, policy implications for the United States in order to cope with a situation that is not (or should not be) acceptable to the U.S. government and the American people.

RESTORING THE EURASIAN BALANCE OF POWER

Objectively speaking it should be relatively easy to deter the Soviet Union. Moscow's potential enemies are not only numerous but in combination overwhelmingly stronger. Yet it is one of the great ironies of the twentieth century that the Soviet Union since 1945 has successfully intimidated much of the world despite the fact that Western

Europe, the United States, China, and Japan could in concert bring
irresistably superior power to bear on the Soviet Union. Furthermore,
except for the military, the Soviet Union remains essentially an under-
developed country. A stagnant economy, a discredited ideology, a dis-
illusioned and cynical population, and hostile nationality groups, both
within and outside the borders of the Soviet empire, hardly are the
ingredients that make for success. Yet today no one is confident that
the Soviet Union is successfully deterred; the world remains in constant nervous tension hoping against hope that Mikhail Gorbachev and
the new team in Moscow will be less belligerent than past Soviet leaders and will accord high priority to the Soviet Union's domestic needs
rather than continuing to pour money into its armed forces.

There are many reasons why the Soviet Union's potential enemies
have been unable to persuade or coerce the Soviet government into
more acceptable behavior. China, however, has proved willing to resist Moscow, despite the large Soviet military forces arrayed on its
border. And Western Europe, although constantly pursuing its version
of détente, has contributed creditably to making NATO into a significant
deterrent force. The United States, certainly, has borne more than its
share of the collective defense.

In contrast, Japan does not undertake commensurate efforts to
preserve the free international system from which Tokyo has so
greatly benefited. If the Soviet Union can be described as a nation in
arms, Japan may be characterized as a nation in yen. While the Soviet
Union seems to care primarily about military strength, Japan seems
to care little about anything other than commerce and becoming the
world's dominant economic power.

Yet history teaches that Japan could contribute very importantly
to deterrence. In the late fall of 1941, for example, despite that fact
that German armies were at the gates of Moscow, the Soviet government maintained the elite Far Eastern Army with some thirty to forty
divisions in Siberia to guard against Japanese attack, even though a
desperate Stalin had persuaded Japan to sign a nonaggression pact the
previous April. When the Soviet government became convinced that
Japan was going to strike the United States and Britain instead of the
Soviet Union, some eighteen divisions with seventeen hundred tanks
and fifteen hundred aircraft were transferred from the Soviet Far East
to the western front. This enabled the Soviets to deliver the counterstroke that would save Moscow.[1]

So it is today that Japan as a military power would become in
terms of the military balance a de facto member of the NATO alliance,
contributing significantly to deterring a Soviet invasion of Western
Europe as well as helping to maintain stability in Northeast Asia. If
Japan were to make military efforts comparable to those of the Western Europeans, it is not an exaggeration to say that the Soviet Union,

confronting possible conflict on multiple fronts, would have to come
to terms with the noncommunist world. Then the mellowing process
that George Kennan nearly forty years ago predicted might occur in
the Soviet Union in ten or fifteen years might actually begin to happen.[2] Détente then would be transformed from hopeful myth to political reality.

   Any world balance of power has to mean, first and foremost,
balance on the great Eurasian continent. That balance was destroyed
in 1945 with the total defeat of Germany and Japan. Now the European
portion of the balance is at least partially restored; it remains to be
seen whether Japan will play its vitally necessary role. Should Japan
do so, the American contribution to maintaining the Eurasian balance
could be limited primarily to a nuclear guarantee, thus freeing U.S.
assets to contribute to a broader global stability. If Japan does not,
the Soviet Union can be balanced in Eurasia only by continuing the
very substantial American military contribution. This is an outmoded
strategy, becoming a less and less satisfactory solution to deterrence
and the maintenance of peace.

AN APPRAISAL OF JAPAN'S MILITARY POSTURE

   At the end of World War II the United States was determined to
put an end to Japanese militarism. And (unlike the case in Germany)
U.S. occupation officials held unchallenged sway over the entire country. While the Soviet Union and the other victorious allied powers
were represented on the Control Commission that supposedly was to
advise the Supreme Commander, in fact General Douglas MacArthur
exercised complete and final authority. In all particulars, U.S. policy
could be implemented without the consent of any other nation. Thus it
was the U.S. Supreme Commander for the Allied Powers who in 1946
drafted and put into effect a new constitution for Japan aimed at ending
its alleged martial propensities forever. This "peace constitution"
contains a now justly famous clause, Article 9, which declares that
"the Japanese people forever renounce war as a sovereign right of
the nation" and, accordingly, "land, sea and air forces . . . will
never be maintained. The right of belligerency of the state will not
be recognized." Beyond this particular clause, the entire constitution
is cast in a framework of war renunciation. For example, in the pre-
amble, one finds in the second paragraph this sentence: "We, the
Japanese people, desire peace for all time and are deeply conscious
of the high ideals controlling human relationships . . . trusting in the
justice and faith of the peace-loving peoples of the world."

   A little over three years later, during the height of the Korean
War, the same General MacArthur who had so firmly insisted on

abolishing Japanese militarism now told the Japanese people that there
might be times when the ideal of renouncing war had to give way to the
duty of acting "in concert with others who cherish freedom to mount
force to repel force." This new U.S. attitude was reflected in the 1952
allied Treaty of Peace with Japan. In that document Japan is required
to "refrain in its international relations from the threat or use of force
against the territorial integrity or political independence of any state."
However, the "Allied Powers . . . recognize that Japan as a sovereign
nation possesses the inherent right of individual or collective self-
defense . . . and that Japan may voluntarily enter into collective
security arrangements."

Thus the U.S. legacy bequeathed to Japan is a dual one. On the
one hand, a unique peace constitution was created in an idealistic era
when the central international political problem was viewed as preventing the rebirth of German and Japanese military power. By 1949/
50, however, this concern had given way to containing Soviet expansionism and restoring a balance of power in Eurasia. Naturally, this
entailed making allies out of the two former enemy countries since
the destruction of Germany and Japan had created a political vacuum
that was viewed as dangerous, given Soviet military strength, the
communization of Eastern Europe, and the successful communist
revolution in China. First peace treaties, then the establishment of
alliances and mutual security pacts, and finally rearmament of Germany and Japan became the order of the day. This U.S. policy largely
succeeded in Germany; in Japan there remains much to be accomplished. In fact, whether one thinks of the situation in purely military
terms or in the legal language of the Mutual Security Treaty of 1960
between Tokyo and Washington, Japan is in essence a military pro-
tectorate, not an ally, of the United States.

The Japanese Self-Defense Forces (JSDF) originated in 1950 as
a seventy-five-thousand-man National Police Reserve, legally established as the JSDF in 1954. But it was not until 1957, with the pro-
mulgation of the Basic Policy for National Defense, that Japan began
to build a military capability. Between 1956 and 1976, Japan under-
took four five-year defense plans. But these plans lacked clear-cut
defense objectives and were designed more to mollify the United States,
which was pressing Japan to rearm, than to provide realistic military
capability. Rather, Japan relied for its security on the 1952 Security
Treaty with the United States, which was revised in 1960.

In October 1976, at the end of the fourth five-year defense plan,
the Japanese government adopted the National Defense Program Outline (NDPO). The NDPO allegedly was to provide Japanese force levels
capable of conducting an "unyielding resistance" to any aggressor
attacking Japan "until such time as cooperation from the United States
is introduced, thus rebuffing such aggression."[3] In short, Tokyo would

continue under the NDPO, as it had the previous thirty years, to rely upon the United States to defend Japan. The most recent (1985) Japanese Defense Agency White Paper affirms Japan's continuing dependent status in its review of the NDPO guidelines: "Japan will repel limited or small-scale aggression by itself in principle. In case this is difficult because of the scale or type of aggression, Japan will repel the attacking force with the cooperation of the U.S."[4] That it is likely to be "difficult" for Japan to defend itself was illustrated in a recent military exercise, in which Japanese forces were defeated in seventeen minutes.

The NDPO also replaced the five-year plans with a flexible system intended to decide details of the defense buildup for each year, consistent with the longer-term National Defense Program Outline. This results in a Defense Agency intradepartment document whose purpose is to serve as a reference when the Defense Agency draws up its annual programs and budgetary requests. Two such documents, each entitled Mid-Term Defense Program Estimate, have been formulated since 1976. The first such document was known as Fifty-six Chugyo; the current Mid-Term Program Estimate, established in FY 1984, is known as Fifty-nine Chugyo, and covers a five-year period from 1985 through 1990.

Whether one compares the contemplated force levels in each of the original five-year plans or in Fifty-six Chugyo and Fifty-nine Chugyo, it is clear that even the modest military improvements in the Japanese Self-Defense Forces those documents called for have not been obtained. This results from the decision, also taken in 1976, to hold Japanese defense spending to 1 percent or less of gross national product. At the end of the first defense plan in 1961, the Ground Self-Defense Forces (GSDF) were short of the plan's goals by one brigade, the Maritime Self-Defence Forces (MSDF) were short three submarines and ten major surface ships, and the Air Self-Defense Forces (ASDF) were short 130 aircraft. Failure to meet force goals continued throughout the years.[5]

The failure to meet the force goals stipulated in Fifty-six Chugyo was anticipated, since successive Japanese governments have adhered to the 1 percent of GNP limitation on defense expenditures. In 1982 the U.S. Undersecretary of Defense for Policy testified that to reach the force goals set in 1976 by 1987, Japanese defense spending would need to approximate 1.3 percent of GNP in the 1983-87 period. Of course the amount of money spent on defense represents an input, not an output. Nevertheless, it takes money to raise and equip military forces and, however crude as a measurement, resource allocation ultimately determines the acquisition of both weapons and personnel. As the undersecretary stated:

While the fulfillment of the 1976 outline would increase significantly Japanese capabilities, it would not provide air and naval forces adequate to defend Japan's territory or its sealanes against the threats of the 1990s.[6]

Successive Japanese Defense Agency White Papers confirm this judgment: indeed, there is no attempt on the part of Japanese officials to conceal their utter dependence for national security on the United States. Military analysts, both Japanese and American, with a numbing monotony and consistency, find the JSDF seriously deficient in virtually all aspects of war-fighting capabilities. A former chief of the Secretariat of the Japanese National Defense Council declared in 1973 that the SDF "could hold out for no more than a matter of days against the Soviet Union."[7] A year later, a staff member of the Japanese defense college would warn that the SDF's wartime role was simply one of "buying time until the United States steps in to mediate Japan's surrender."[8] In 1975 a U.S. analyst asserted that

the United States may hold that conventional defense of Japan "is entirely now a Japanese responsibility," but this is not even remotely possible against a conventional Soviet attack or even a significant Soviet attack on Japan's air defense or sealanes. Japan could not retain supremacy in the air and command of the seas even around the home islands during the early stages of an air attack.[9]

In 1980 two government reports, one American and the other Japanese, pointed in a clear and unambiguous fashion to the extensive deficiencies of the JSDF.[10] In a 1981 study prepared by the Japanese Center for Strategic Studies, it was argued that, given the current deficiencies, it was quite conceivable that a major portion of Japan would be devastated in the early stages of a war.[11] In 1982 an assistant secretary of defense testified that owing to significant shortcomings, "the Self-Defense Forces do not constitute effective deterrence."[12] In 1983 the outgoing U.S. Commander in Chief, Pacific (CINCPAC) testified that

the Japanese military forces have insufficient stocks of equipment to sustain combat. They also have inadequate force levels, particularly in air defense and in anti-submarine warfare. The modernization of their ground forces is not adequate to handle a high threat situation today. They also do not have the necessary command and control, in my judgment, to effectively fight and sustain a war in their own self defense.[13]

Vital to Japan's security is an air defense capability. But the Japanese Defense Agency admits that air defense capabilities are very inadequate; this was dramatically illustrated in 1976 when a defecting Soviet MiG pilot was able to penetrate Japanese airspace and land unhindered at a Japanese airfield.[14] Not only are the twenty-eight fixed radar sites antiquated, some of them dating back twenty years, but they are very vulnerable to attack. As the latest White Paper puts it, "such ground radar watches are incapable of detecting any invading hostile aircraft . . . at altitudes lower than their view-lines. . . ."[15] The interception of intruding aircraft is adversely affected not only by the poor detection capabilities, but also by an outdated airforce; as of March 1985 the ASDF had only 56 F-15s. The remaining fighter aircraft are 1960s-vintage F-104s and F-4s.[16] Even if the Japanese could detect and intercept incoming aircraft, the supply of air-to-air missiles would only last a few sorties. Even after one sortie, however, the returning aircraft would be lucky to find their airbases still intact because the limited air defense provided by the obsolete Nike-J surface-to-air missile (SAM) system is entirely inadequate.[17]

Under the current defense plan, if implemented, by March 1991 the ASDF will significantly increase its F-15 force; 53 F-15s are currently on order.[18] It is also anticipated that the six E2C airborne early warning aircraft will be increased to twelve.[19]

Even if these improvements occur, however, the Japanese government intends to continue to rely on the United States for forward air defense through attack on Soviet bases in the Far East. For this purpose, in 1985 the United States deployed eleven F-16 fighter bombers at Misawa in northern Honshu. It is intended that this U.S. force total 52 F-16s by 1987. It is the Japanese position that its peace constitution does not permit it to "possess weapons systems which . . . are used exclusively for the total destruction of other countries, such as ICBMs and long-range strategic bombers."[20]

Current Japanese-U.S. naval cooperative arrangements assign two important missions to the Maritime Self-Defense Forces (MSDF) in the event of war with the Soviet Union: closing three straits connecting the Sea of Japan with the Pacific Ocean, thus preventing passage of Soviet ships to the open waters of the Pacific, and protecting the sea-lanes out about one thousand miles south of Tokyo. This latter task is exceptionally important since it includes the vital oil routes from the Persian Gulf and Southeast Asia to Japan. But there is unanimous agreement that the Japanese armed forces cannot now, nor can they in the foreseeable future, successfully undertake either of these burden-sharing tasks. Furthermore, even in the unlikely event that the goals outlined in Fifty-six Chugyo and Fifty-nine Chugyo are met by about 1991, Japan's contribution to deterrence would still be wholly inadequate. This is because, of course, one cannot assume that the Soviet Union will stand still in Northeast Asia. For example, the former U.S. CINCPAC, Admiral Robert Long, testified in 1983 that "in each of the last two years the USSR has replaced more of their fighter and interceptor force with new generation aircraft than we have fighters in the entire U.S. Pacific Air Forces."[21] And, as has been frequently noted, the Pacific Fleet is the strongest of the four Soviet navies, with about 825 major combat ships as of 1985. There are 24 nuclear submarines in the Pacific Fleet, 2 aircraft carriers, and 11 guided-missile cruisers. It is estimated that 135 of the 1985 total of 414 SS-20s are in Asia, with a further 10 SS-20 missile sites under construction, of which 3 are in East Asia. About a quarter of the entire Soviet Air Force, some 2,220 aircraft, are in the Far East. These include about 300 bombers and 1,600 fighters and fighter-bombers, about three-quarters of which are third-generation.[22] Against these forces, Japan's defense efforts are pathetic indeed.

Finally, the United States has no assurance that Japan will assist the United States in the event of war with the Soviet Union. Specifically, Article 5 of the 1960 Mutual Security Treaty denies its mutuality in that the United States bears an obligation to defend Japan but Japan does not have a similar obligation to defend the United States, even against open aggression against U.S. military forces, provided the attack occurs outside of Japan: "Each party recognizes that an armed attack against either party in the territories under the Administration of Japan would be dangerous to its own peace and safety and declares that it would act to meet the common danger in accordance with its constitutional provisions and processes."[23]

This nonreciprocated U.S. obligation to Japan stands in sharp contrast to U.S. mutual security treaties with other nations. In the NATO treaty, for example, also by coincidence in an Article 5, the signatories "agree that an armed attack against one or more of them in Europe or North America shall be considered an attack against them all" and consequently will require common action by all the treaty participants.[24]

If this fully described the legal situation it would be, from the U.S. point of view, bad enough. But in fact it is worse. This is because, despite the wording of the 1960 treaty, the Japanese government may not be fully committed to assist the United States even if an attack upon U.S. forces occurs within the geographic scope of Japan's land, sea, and air space, provided the attacker struck only U.S. forces. As the most recent Defense Agency White Paper observes:

> Under international law, it is considered that a state has
> the right of collective self-defense, that is, the right to use
> armed force to stop an armed assault on a foreign country

with which it has close relations, even if the state itself is
not under direct attack. . . . However, the government is
of the view that the use of the right of self-defense as permissible under Article 9 is authorized only when the act of
self-defense is within the framework of the minimum limit
necessary for the defense of this nation. The government
therefore believes that [to] exercise the right of collective
self-defense exceeds the minimum limit and is constitution-
ally not permissible.[25]

For several decades Japan has shown a stubborn unwillingness
to undertake a fair share of the burden of defense in Northeast Asia.
Japan, with nearly half the U.S. GNP, is currently spending about
$13 billion on defense. U.S. defense outlays, in contrast, are antici-
pated this fiscal year to be about $292 billion. In other words, with
slightly over twice Japan's GNP the United States is spending about
twenty-two times as much on defense.

Coupled with this penurious attitude on defense resource allocation is a denial that Japan has a mutual security obligation to the
United States. If Japan were unwilling to commit itself to defending
the United States in areas under U.S. territorial jurisdiction, it would
stand in sharp and unfavorable contrast to NATO's definition of the
collective defense geographical area. But to cast doubt on its willingness to assist the United States, even if the attack on U.S. armed
forces occurs within Japan's territorial jurisdiction, is surely to
call into most serious question the value of continuing the alliance
with Japan.

POLICY APPRAISAL

Any policy recommendations must begin by acknowledging that
much of the blame for the deplorable state of Japanese defense must
be laid at the door of the United States. The United States insisted on
and actually drafted and thrust upon the Japanese government and people the so-called peace constitution. This curious document clearly
demonstrated at that time a greater fear of future Japanese militarism
than of the potential danger of the Soviet Union. This fallacious notion
persisted for some thirty years, punctuated, to be sure, with occasional lapses into reality, as when Secretary of State John Foster
Dulles urged a greater Japanese defense effort. It was as if no important U.S. political leader had any notion of what is today a geopolitical truism: by destroying both Germany and Japan, the logical
bulwarks against Soviet expansionism were removed, thus making
U.S. containment of the Soviet Union infinitely more difficult. Whether

it was necessary to insist upon the unconditional surrender of both
Germany and Japan, thus ensuring that the war would be fought until
both countries were in ruins, remains today a debatable point, and it
is not certain that a different course would have yielded more feliciti-
tous results. Nevertheless, within five years of the war's end the
necessity for integrating Germany into the containment ring had been
fully accepted. In the case of Japan, however, this rather obvious requirement was not recognized for an additional generation; indeed, it
can be argued that many do not recognize the essentiality of a militarily stronger Japan even today. Yet there can be no question that a
militarily strong Japan would contribute so significantly to deterrence
as to, in essence, end the cold war on terms satisfactory to the noncommunist world. But successive U.S. governments have failed to be
either convinced of this themselves or to persuade Japan. As for the
Reagan government, it has been reluctant to put pressure on Japan
because it believes Prime Minister Yasuhiro Nakasone is the best
possible Japanese leader from the U.S. point of view. While this is
true, no Japanese government, including that of Nakasone's, will
undertake a meaningful role in western Pacific defense unless the
United States exerts unremitting pressure for it to do so. It is unfortunate, but that is the reality.

Nothing illustrates U.S. vacillation and downright incompetence
more than the U.S. response—or rather failure to respond—to the
Japanese repudiation of the Suzuki-Reagan summit communique in
1981 and the subsequent backtracking in Tokyo on the commitment to
increase Japan's share of the defense burden. In the face of really
outrageous behavior on the part of Japan's political leaders that spring,
Washington did not press the Japanese security issue at the Ottawa
economic summit. This was unfortunate but possibly understandable
given the economic emphasis at the conference. Inexplicable was the
public pronouncement by a state department spokesman in August 1981
that the United States was "not dissatisfied" with Japan's policy on the
defense question.[26]

Not dissatisfied? Not dissatisfied that Japan's defense spending
as a percentage of its GNP remains at about 1 percent? Not dissatisfied with the repudiation of the joint communique? Or with the anti-
American and openly hostile sentiments expressed by the foreign minister? Not dissatisfied with Japan's refusal to acquire the capability
that the prime minister agreed is essential to carry out even the limited role assigned to Japan in the western Pacific? Or with the failure
to achieve agreement in the annual Honolulu security meetings? What,
one is compelled to ask, would have caused dissatisfaction on the part
of the state department?

Of course, the gratuitous declaration that the United States was
not dissatisifed made the front pages of the newspapers in Tokyo.[27]

Prime Minister Zenko Suzuki's supporters breathed a sigh of relief
that he had managed to "manage the Americans." Foreign Minister
Sunao Sonoda's followers felt smugly vindicated and the U.S. embassy
in Japan continued its placid and flaccid business-as-usual routine.
Undoubtedly they were pleased that their complacent attitude received
approbation from former Secretary of State Cyrus Vance who on August
14, 1981, told his New York Times readers that he had stood fast
against those "well-meaning but misguided people who wanted us to
'lower the boom on Japan.'" Lowering the boom, he informed us, includes among other things asking the "impossible of the Japanese in
the military area." As to why it is impossible, Secretary Vance must
have assumed it was self-evident, since he did not advance any reasons for this unhelpful conclusion other than the warning that U.S.
pressure on Japan would "only backfire."

It is of course true that so many things backfired on the United
States during President Jimmy Carter's years—especially those during
which Secretary Vance served—that he must be forgiven his rather
jittery attitude. It is hard to understand, however, why asking Prime
Minister Suzuki to implement a communique that he agreed to with
President Reagan should backfire on Washington. It should be observed
also that the U.S. failure to hold Japan's leaders accountable on the
defense issue backfires on those Japanese who want Japan to improve
its national security posture. Japan, after all, is a democracy, and
there are a number of informed people—both former and present members of the Defense Agency, professors, analysts in think tanks, and
commentators—who feel very strongly about the Soviet threat and
Japan's need to counter it and who disagree with Japan's official policy.[28] These people, to be sure, are a minority but nevertheless a
significant element in the defense debate in Japan. Their position is
weakened when the United States acquiesces in the Japanese government's retreat from its commitments to the United States.

It is now time to put aside the mutual recriminations of the past,
to readily admit that U.S. policies toward Japan contributed mightily
to the present situation in which an unarmed Japan confronts the growing strength of the Soviet Union in Northeast Asia and the western
Pacific. It is now essential that Japan make a much greater effort in
the security sphere, acquiring the conventional capability to defend
not only Japan itself by itself, but the western Pacific, as was agreed
to in the spring of 1980, out to a distance southward of about one thousand nautical miles to the west of Guam and to the north of Luzon.[29]
This is a modest contribution and the absolute minimum currently
acceptable role for Japan. The United States should continue to extend
nuclear protection to Japan; all other aspects of Japanese defense
should be borne by Japan and by Japan alone.

This expanded role for Japan is well within its potential capability.

There are a number of reasons for this. First, Japan is distant from the heart of Soviet power—Soviet forces in the Pacific are at the end of a very long logistical lifeline. Second, it is undeniably the case that the Soviet military buildup in Northeast Asia is and likely will continue to be directed primarily at China, not Japan. That this is so should not be an excuse for Japan to remain unarmed; rather, the Chinese factor enables Japan to proceed with an increase in its military forces confident in the knowledge that it is not a useless exercise against an overwhelmingly stronger opponent. Neither geography nor circumstance dictates Soviet domination of Northeast Asia and the western Pacific.

Third, anything the Japanese undertake they do well. If the Japanese decided to acquire a military capability to defend Japan and the Pacific waters out to about one thousand nautical miles, it can be taken for granted that the forces created would be competent, well equipped, efficient, and disciplined.

Finally, it is true that currently Japan is running a budgetary deficit. But there is nothing to suggest that Japan cannot, from an economic point of view, more easily improve its defenses than any other great power. To the contrary, Japan's economic growth rate has been higher, productivity greater, technological advance more spectacular, unemployment lower, and inflation rate lower than that of any of the other major industrial countries. It is, quite simply, ridiculous to argue that economic conditions prevent a substantial increase in Japan's defense spending.

No matter how reasonable the idea is that Japan should shoulder a greater share of the defense burden, this may not happen. No matter what policies Washington adopts, Japan may remain essentially unarmed. U.S. pressures against Japan may, in the end, prove counterproductive. Japan is a democratic state with all the difficulties democracies customarily confront in coping with totalitarian enemies. The Japanese people, through their elected leaders, may choose to remain militarily helpless, even in the face of the growing might of the Soviet Union. Nothing the United States does may alter this situation.

But the United States is also a democracy. It is intolerable to expect the American people, whose defense burden already is greater than that of the other members of NATO and vastly larger than that of Japan, to make the sacrifices entailed in the current administration's attempt to rectify the military imbalance without greater exertions on the part of the other rich, industrial countries. The enormous U.S. budget and trade deficits and the continuing decline in American heavy industry argue for greater U.S. governmental attention to the American economy. This is critical not only for economic but for security reasons as well. A service economy cannot defend the nation. But the United States can devote more resources to improve the economy only

if further increases in defense spending are held to modest levels.
This, in turn, is possible only if other countries—most especially
Japan—undertake a much larger defense role. Otherwise, the corre-
lation of forces will continue to shift in favor of the Soviet Union.

President Reagan came into office pledged to tell the truth about
the Soviet-U.S. military balance. He courageously repudiated the end-
lessly repeated phrase that the United States would remain "second to
none" in defense, and he is attempting to convert the untrue assessment into reality by seeking a margin of safety for the United States.
It is now time for the Reagan administration to inform the American
people of another unpleasant fact of life: the Japanese alliance on which
U.S. security policy in East Asia has been based for many years is in
the most serious difficulty. It serves no useful purpose to continue to
ignore this elementary fact.

NOTES

1. John Keegan, Barbarossa (New York: Ballantine Books, 1970),
154-58.

2. See "X" [George Kennan], "The Sources of Soviet Conduct,"
Foreign Affairs (July 1947).

3. "The National Defense Program Outline," in Japanese Defense
Agency, Defense of Japan 1985 (Tokyo: Japanese Defense Agency,
n.d.), 248.

4. Ibid., 203.

5. International Institute for Strategic Studies, The Military Balance, 1961/62, 23; 1966/67, 34; 1972/73, 49-50; 1976/77, 56.

6. Fred C. Ikle, in U.S. Senate, Committee on Foreign Relations,
East-West Relations: Focus on the Pacific, June 10, 1982, 23.

7. Osamu Kaihara, in Mainichi Shimbun, January 13, 1973, cited
in Frank B. Weinstein, ed., U.S.-Japan Relations and the Security of
Asia: The Next Decade (Boulder, Colo.: Westview Press, 1978), 59.

8. Makoto Momoi, "Pax Russo-Americana and its Theoretical
Impact on Japan's Defense Concept," in Robert Pfaltzgraff, Jr., ed.,
Contrasting Approaches to Strategic Arms Control (Lexington, Mass.:
Lexington Books, 1974).

9. Fred Greene, Stresses in U.S.-Japanese Security Relations
(Washington, D.C.: Brookings Institution, 1975), 80.

10. Japanese Defense Agency, Defense of Japan 1980 (Tokyo: Japa-
nese Defense Agency, n.d.); and U.S. Senate, Committee on Foreign
Relations, Japan's Contribution to Military Stability in Northeast Asia
(Washington: GPO, June 1980).

11. Japanese Center for Strategic Studies, The Defense of Japan: An Alternative View from Tokyo, trans. Heritage Foundation (Washington, D.C.: Heritage Foundation, 1981), 13.

12. Francis J. West, Jr., in U.S. House of Representatives, Committee on Foreign Affairs, Hearings, March 1, 1982.

13. Admiral Robert Long, in U.S. House of Representatives, Committee on Armed Services, Hearings on Military Posture, March 8, 1983, 1231.

14. Japanese Defense Agency, Defense of Japan 1977 (Tokyo: Japanese Defense Agency, n.d.), 140.

15. Japanese Defense Agency, Defense of Japan 1985 (Tokyo: Japanese Defense Agency, 98.

16. Ibid., 258.

17. Ibid., 99-101.

18. International Institute for Strategic Studies, The Military Balance 1985-1986 (London: International Institute for Strategic Studies, 1985), 126.

19. Nine E2C aircraft are contemplated upon the completion of Fifty-six Chugyo. According to Pacific Defense Reporter (1986 Annual Reference Edition), 47, the E2C force will total twelve in 1991.

20. Japanese Defense Agency, Defense of Japan 1985 (Tokyo: Japanese Defense Agency, n.d.), 59.

21. Admiral Robert Long, in Hearings on Military Posture, 996.

22. All of the figures are from the Research Institute for Peace and Security, Asian Security 1985 (Tokyo: Brassey's Defense Publishers, 1985), 52-56.

23. For discussion of both the 1952 and the 1960 agreements, see Greene, Stresses in U.S.-Japanese Security Relations, chap. 3.

24. A recent very critical discussion of the premises of NATO may be found in Theodore Draper, "The Western Misalliance," Washington Quarterly, Winter 1981, 2-4. But at least North America is included in the defense area, unlike the case in the treaty with Japan.

25. Japanese Defense Agency, Defense of Japan 1985, 60. Emphasis added.

26. Mainichi Daily News (Tokyo), August 8, 1981; and Japan Times (Tokyo), August 8, 1981.

27. Ibid.

28. The author and a colleague interviewed a number of leading figures in the think tank, the University, the Diet, and the foreign and defense ministries in Tokyo in August 1981. While not wishing to go on record, a number (although, of course, not all) of these persons both acknowledged the Soviet threat and expressed a desire to significantly improve Japan's defense. See William M. Carpenter and Stephen P. Gibert, "Japanese Views on Defense Burden-Sharing," Comparative Strategy 3 (1982).

29. Shortly before the Suzuki-Reagan summit meeting in the spring of 1981, the director general of the Japanese Defense Agency, Joji Omura, and Foreign Minister Masayoshi Ito reaffirmed Japan's commitment to defend the area north of Luzon and west of Guam. See Foreign Broadcast Information Service (FBIS), <u>Daily Report, Asia and Pacific</u>, March 30, 1981, C-1, C-2.

Part IV
Future Force Structures and Deterrence Stability: Issues of Cost and Strategy

Midgetman Small ICBM: Issues for Deterrence in the 1990s

Jonathan E. Medalia

INTRODUCTION

On December 19, 1986, President Reagan decided that the United States will begin the final stage of research and development on the "Midgetman" small ICBM based in a hard mobile launcher. Midgetman is scheduled for initial deployment in 1992. The President's decision is important for deterrence in the 1990s because Midgetman, arguably more than any other strategic weapon system, was conceived and is intended to enhance stable deterrence.

Midgetman was transformed from a concept into a high-priority funded development program upon the recommendation of the Scowcroft Commission, which was appointed by President Reagan in January 1983 in the wake of a continuing inability by Congress and several administrations to decide on a basing mode for the MX missile. The commission's charge was to review U.S. strategic forces and in particular to make recommendations for the U.S. ICBM program. The commission recommended deploying about one hundred MX missiles in Minuteman silos, developing a small ICBM for initial deployment in the early 1990s, and seeking arms control agreements that would promote stability.

The commission defined stability as:

> The condition which exists when no strategic power believes it can significantly improve its situation by attacking first in a crisis or when it does not feel compelled to launch its strategic weapons in order to avoid losing them.[1]

In the commission's view, "stability should be the primary objective both of the modernization of our strategic forces and of our arms control proposals."[2] The recommended elements were linked as follows: MX, by threatening Soviet ICBMs, would make the Soviets more willing to negotiate stabilizing arms control agreements; such agreements would help Midgetman survive by limiting the Soviet threat to it; and Midgetman would promote stability by reducing the incentive for the Soviet Union, and the pressure on the United States, to launch strategic forces preemptively. MX, Midgetman, and arms control were thus means to an end, stability.

How is Midgetman's design intended to promote stability? The missile will be based in a mobile mode in order to be survivable. It will carry one warhead, on the grounds that a single-warhead missile would be lighter and a less attractive target than a multiple-warhead missile. Light weight is thought to facilitate survivability by enabling the missile to be carried by a smaller and more maneuverable mobile launcher. Light weight also makes for flexibility in basing. That is, the missile could be shifted from one basing mode to another more readily than, say, a ten-warhead MX in response to changes in Soviet ability to threaten U.S. ICBMs. By being a less attractive target (because it would carry one warhead instead of several), the theory holds, the Soviets would be less tempted to attack it. By being survivable, the Soviets would realize that the United States would feel less pressured to strike preemptively out of fear that a Soviet attack would destroy it. Even though Midgetman is to have the accuracy and yield needed to destroy Soviet ICBM silos, and thus would put pressure on the Soviets to launch their ICBMs preemptively in a crisis, the Soviets would realize that Midgetman is not intended as a first-strike weapon because most of its cost goes for survivability.[3]

Since 1983, strong congressional support and air force and industry effort have advanced Midgetman rapidly. As a result, the program quickly reached the point of decision on whether or not it should enter full-scale development (FSD), the last stage of research and development (R&D), when individual technologies—for missile, guidance, basing, command and control, and the like—are combined into a producible, functioning weapon system.

The FSD decision is consequential for at least three reasons. First, it involves a commitment, reversible only at high cost, to a specified system so that contracts can be let and the components will fit together.

Second, FSD involves greatly increased yearly cost. Figure 5 shows funds requested each year for MX, Trident II, and Midgetman, exclusive of supplementals. For MX and Trident II, the request rose sharply when the program started FSD, in 1980 (excluding a small 1979 supplemental) for MX and in 1984 for Trident II, and continued to rise thereafter.[4] For 1987, Midgetman's first year of FSD, the cost jumped from several hundred million dollars a year to $1.2 billion. The defense department has requested $2.2 billion for Midgetman in fiscal year 1988, and the same amount in fiscal year 1989. Its cost can be expected to rise further in later years, as the development progresses and procurement begins.

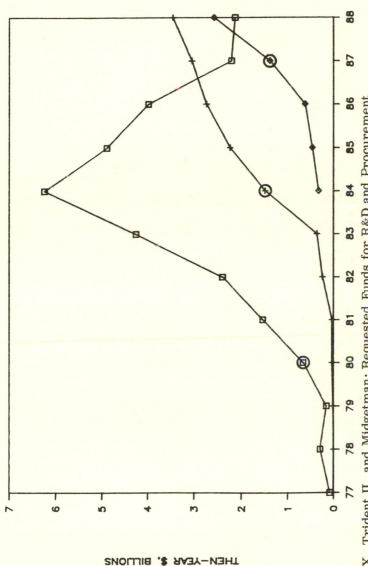

FIGURE 5 MX, Trident II, and Midgetman: Requested Funds for R&D and Procurement
(□ = MX; + = Trident II; ◇ = Midgetman; ○ = start of full-scale development.

Source: Department of Defense Annual Reports, various years.

Note: Fiscal year 1988 data are projections submitted with the fiscal year 1987 defense budget, not actual requests.)

Third, FSD implies a commitment to deploy a system. The money spent by the time it is ready for production, the constituencies mobilized on its behalf, and the lack of an alternative at that point argue for a system to continue once it has started FSD.

The decision on whether to begin FSD hinged not just on the state of the technology for Midgetman, which is apparently progressing well, but also on whether to proceed with Midgetman at all, and if so, if it should have one warhead or several.

There was a possibility that the United States would not continue with Midgetman. In November 1985, the administration proposed to the Soviets a ban on mobile ICBMs. This proposal grew out of several concerns:[5]

● Mobile missiles might be hard to verify.
● The Soviets have much sparsely populated land available for deployment.
● The Soviets lead in mobile missiles: They have deployed the SS-25 and are about to deploy the SS-24 mobile ICBMs, while Midgetman deployment is not anticipated until late 1992.
● Congress might withdraw support given Midgetman's high cost.
● Mobile Midgetman might weaken the case for the Strategic Defense Initiative (SDI) because it is intended to survive without defense.

While Midgetman could have been deployed in silos under this policy, Congress would probably have objected, given its concern for survivability and mobility. As a result, a ban on mobile ICBMs could have terminated Midgetman.

A decision not to proceed with FSD would have been consequential. An administration decision to this effect would have violated a 1983 agreement in which several congressional moderates promised to support MX in exchange for an administration promise to support Midgetman.[6] Congress might then have retaliated against MX and SDI, systems the administration favors but that many in Congress oppose. On the other hand, Congress could at some point withdraw support from Midgetman given its high cost. Since Midgetman, MX, arms control, and stability are linked elements in the Scowcroft package, a decision by Congress or the administration not to proceed with Midgetman could disrupt the consensus on strategic policy as articulated by the Scowcroft Commission.

It is also possible that the United States will later choose to proceed with a MIRVed Midgetman (one carrying multiple independently targetable reentry vehicles), on grounds that it would be more cost-effective and at least as survivable as a single-warhead missile, as discussed later in this chapter. The Defense Science Board, in a report of March 1986 on small ICBM modernization, favored a missile initially configured to carry a single warhead.[7] Two Under Secretaries of Defense, however, commenting on that report, recommended examining a MIRVed missile.[8] Senator Pete Wilson suggested delaying FSD by a year to study a three-warhead missile.[9] And in April 1986, President Reagan directed that a MIRVed mobile missile, weighing more than twice as much as Midgetman, be studied.[10]

Does it make sense for the United States to proceed with Midgetman, and if so, with which version? To help the reader judge, this chapter presents arguments on five key questions: Is Midgetman survivable? Is it stabilizing? Does it promote stabilizing arms control agreements? Are Midgetman and other mobile ICBMs verifiable? Is Midgetman cost-effective? This paper describes the Midgetman system, then turns to these questions.

MIDGETMAN: MISSILE AND BASING

The Midgetman system includes a missile and a basing mode. Congress mandated in 1983 that the missile have a maximum weight of 33,000 pounds, with 30,000 preferred, and carry one warhead. That is a "small" missile. In 1986, Congress permitted the weight to grow to 37,000 pounds to permit Midgetman to carry penetration aids, devices to help its warhead penetrate any Soviet ballistic missile defenses. In comparison, the currently deployed Minuteman III weighs 78,000 pounds and carries three warheads, while MX weighs 192,000 pounds and carries ten warheads. Midgetman will be highly accurate so that, combined with the reported yield of perhaps 300 kilotons (KT), each warhead will have a high probability of destroying a Soviet silo-based ICBM.[11] The air force has estimated costs for a system of 500 deployed missiles, but no decision has been reached on quantity.

A basing mode selection was part of the FSD decision. Midgetman will be based in the hard mobile launcher, or HML (pronounced "hummel"), a vehicle designed to withstand nuclear weapon effects. The design goal is for the HML to withstand a minimum blast force of 30 pounds per square inch (psi) and all the other weapon effects (such as heat and radiation) accompanying that level of blast force. For comparison, a large truck can withstand 1 to 2 psi, and a tank, 10. A 500-KT warhead, typical of the Soviet inventory, can generate 30 psi at about 1 mile.

Midgetman/HML will be deployed in two ways. Some HMLs will be stationed on large military reservations in the Southwest. In peacetime, HMLs would be dispersed on parts of the reservations. On higher alert, they would disperse over the entire base area. In crises, some would disperse off the reservation over a large area, many thousands of square miles. Other HMLs will be stationed within the 2- to 3-acre enclosures that contain Minuteman ICBM silos or Minuteman launch control bunkers (see Figure 6). On warning of attack, they would dash into the surrounding countryside.

The idea of using both deployment modes is that Southwest basing, with its continuous peacetime deployment, provides some deterrence against a "bolt from the blue" attack, as the Soviets would have to use a substantial number of warheads to destroy the Midgetmen. In contrast, the Soviets could destroy each Minuteman-based Midgetman/ HML with only one or a few warheads in a "bolt from the blue," before they could disperse, and the Soviets would target the Minutemen anyway. Minuteman basing, though, enables HMLs to disperse on warning of attack, generating a vast dispersal area and helping deter a preemptive attack in a crisis. Minuteman basing also costs less than Southwest basing, and interferes less with other military land uses.

In both deployments, the United States would use various methods to try to prevent the Soviets from targeting individual HMLs, such as moving some at random, giving them a high dash speed, and making them maneuverable. In theory, decoys could be used if necessary. These measures would force the Soviets to barrage the entire deployment area to destroy all the Midgetmen. If the area is large enough, the Soviets would not have enough warheads to barrage it. In that case, the system should deter attack or, if it is attacked, some Midgetmen would survive.

Another basing mode that has been considered is superhard silos. Current Minuteman silos can withstand perhaps 2,000 psi. New designs, using more steel and special shock isolation and egress systems, might withstand 50,000 psi. This basing mode appears less attractive than HML basing. It is somewhat more costly. In addition,

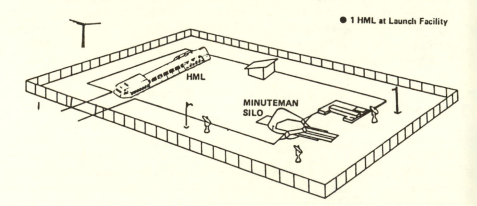

FIGURE 6   Midgetman Basing in Hard Mobile Launchers at Minuteman Silos (Drawing by Boeing Aerospace Company)

Soviet ICBM accuracy has continually improved over time. The Soviets seem sure to continue this trend to enhance their ability to destroy U.S. silo-based ICBMs. Substantial further improvement, which is quite possible by the time Midgetman is fully deployed in the late 1990s, would threaten Midgetmen in superhard silos.

SURVIVABILITY

Many of Midgetman's supporters see the most important attribute of that missile as being a high likelihood of surviving a Soviet attack if deployed in a mobile mode. The Midgetman's survivability—the ability of some missiles to remain operational after attack—and thus its ability to deter attack hinges on the balance between the number of warheads the Soviets have and the number of warheads required to destroy Midgetman.

- If the Soviets do not have enough warheads to destroy the entire Midgetman force, then some missiles will survive any attack.
- If the Soviets have enough warheads to destroy the entire Midgetman force but not most other critical strategic targets as well, then they would conclude that, by attacking, they would put themselves at severe risk. As a result, they would be deterred.
- If the Soviets have enough warheads to destroy Midgetman and most other strategic targets, then they would in theory not be deterred even with Midgetman.

Midgetman's critics assert that the Soviets could improve this balance in various ways by increasing the first element and reducing the second.

The Soviets could deploy many more modern warheads than they have now. According to Central Intelligence Agency (CIA) testimony of June 1985, the Soviets have over 8,000 warheads deployed on ICBMs and submarine-launched ballistic missiles (SLBMs), the forces able to attack Midgetman promptly.[12] By 1990, remaining within SALT II (Strategic Arms Limitation Talks) quantitative sublimits, they could have about 11,000 ICBM and SLBM warheads. The CIA estimates that without arms control the Soviets could deploy about 15,000 to 18,000 ICBM and SLBM warheads by the mid-1990s. This force (assuming average yield to be the current standard, 500 KT) is sufficient for attacking all U.S. land-based strategic offensive forces including Midgetman deployed over many thousands of square miles.[13]

The Soviets could add even more missiles for barraging Midgetman.[14] They could readily deploy spare missiles, space boosters (which are very similar to ICBMs), and new production missiles.

Under the CIA's mid-1990s no–SALT scenario, the Soviets would re-
tire almost all of their currently deployed ICBMs. These missiles,
if redeployed, would enable the Soviets to barrage approximately
18,700 square miles at 30 psi.[15] The Soviets have also retired over
1,000 ICBMs since 1974. While there is no indication as to what the
Soviets have done with them, the Soviets typically do not scrap retired military equipment.[16] Perhaps they could redeploy these missiles, which could barrage 14,000 to 18,000 square miles at 30 psi.
(See Table 3.)

The Soviets might reduce the number of warheads required for a
barrage by selectively targeting only those areas where HMLs could
travel. It would take 9,500 500-KT warheads to barrage 28,000 square

TABLE 3   Barrage Area of Retired Soviet ICBMs against 30-psi
           Hard Mobile Launchers

Missile	Number	Barrage Area (in square miles)
Retired ICBMs		
SS–7	190	1,849 to 2,942
SS–8	19	185
SS–9	308	9,935 to 10,537
SS–11	510	2,307 to 4,523
Total	1,207	14,276 to 18,187
Currently Deployed ICBMs*		
SS–11	520	4,611
SS–13	60	196
SS–17	150	1,774
SS–18	308	9,104
SS–19	160	3,016
Total	1,198	18,701

Sources: Missile data: John Collins and Patrick Cronin, U.S./
Soviet Military Balance: Statistical Trends, 1975-1984, Rept. 85-83
(Washington, D.C.: Library of Congress, Congressional Research
Service, 1985), 10-12, and U.S./Soviet Military Balance: Statistical
Trends, 1970-1983, Rept. 84-163 S (Washington, D.C.: Library of
Congress, Congressional Research Service, 1984), 14. Barrage area
was calculated by the author.
Note: This table uses the idealized assumptions made in note 15
with respect to accuracy, reliability, and timing, so overstates
actual barrage area of these missiles.
*These are currently deployed ICBMs that would be retired by
the mid-1990s, according to the CIA no-SALT projection.

miles, the area considered for Midgetman/HML deployment in a
Southwest-only basing plan, at 30 psi, assuming the area is a smooth
plane. But in reality, the areas of the Southwest under consideration
for Midgetman (including areas outside military reservations) contain
mountains, rivers, training areas where live ammunition is used,
and other features on which HMLs could not operate. For instance,
Luke Air Force Range, Arizona, a proposed deployment area, contains parts of at least eight mountain ranges.

Espionage and sabotage might reduce the barrage requirement.
Regarding Southwest basing, Soviet agents might be able to implant
sensors on the bases that would help locate HMLs. In that case, the
Soviets could narrow the area where HMLs might be. Regarding
Minuteman basing of Midgetman, the air force prohibits access only
to the small enclosure around each silo. Could saboteurs shoot antitank weapons at HMLs, mine the roads leading from silos, or place
radio beacons on these roads that would attach to HMLs and transmit
radio signals on which Soviet warheads might home?

Futuristic technologies could in principle enable the Soviets to
attack individual HMLs. These technologies, by allowing the Soviets
to avoid a barrage, would greatly reduce the number of warheads
required to attack Midgetman. Even though these threats are many
years away, they are worth mentioning because Midgetman deployment is also many years away: The air force indicated that tentative
plans call for deployment to be completed in 1999 (assuming a force
of 500 single-warhead missiles in HMLs). The Soviets might develop
maneuvering warheads that would scan the terrain for HMLs and home
in on them. U.S. deployment of HMLs on deserts or prairies, where
there is little cover, would ease the Soviets' task. The Soviets might
attack HMLs with depressed-trajectory submarine-launched ballistic
missiles (SLBMs). These missiles would reach their targets quickly
by flying special low trajectories. The reduced warning time, combined with the time needed to begin moving the HMLs after receipt of
warning, might allow HMLs only three to six minutes of travel time.
Since the Soviets could not have enough of these missiles to barrage
thousands of square miles, as they would have to build hundreds of
submarines, this technique would require the Soviets to locate individual HMLs. This would be easy for HMLs deployed at Minuteman
silos. For Southwest basing, the Soviets might need to use satellites
or implant sensors to find HMLs.

Critics also question whether we could have high confidence in
HML survivability. A HML designed to withstand 30 psi of blast pressure would be intended to survive at about a mile from ground zero,
or about three-quarters of a mile from the fireball, of an airburst
500-KT weapon. At that distance, it would be exposed to intense heat,
electromagnetic pulse, and radiation and to winds of 1,000 miles per

hour that could hurl debris against it. Designing a HML to withstand such effects in combination is a demanding task. While components could be tested for vulnerability by using underground nuclear tests, Midgetman/HML could not be tested against above-ground nuclear explosions because atmospheric tests are prohibited by treaty.

Midgetman's supporters see the Midgetman force as highly survivable against the current threat, or against a future threat of similar size and capability, as the Soviets would not have enough warheads to barrage Midgetman and attack other targets. Midgetmen are vulnerable in their peacetime deployment, dispersed over parts of military reservations or undispersed at Minutemen silos. But when the HMLs start to disperse, the area over which they disperse, and hence the number of warheads required to attack them, expands rapidly. If the Soviets attack Midgetmen with the current force of ICBMs, then the travel time available to the HMLs before the ICBM warheads detonate, probably 20 to 25 minutes,[17] would in theory permit them to disperse over more than 28,000 square miles.

Supporters see a future threat in which the Soviets add thousands of missiles as unlikely because the United States would surely detect some of the millions of actions needed to deploy these missiles. This nation could respond by increasing Midgetman survivability in several ways. The fastest and cheapest way would be to expand the deployment area by deploying HMLs at more Southwest bases or Minuteman silos or by dispersing some HMLs on public land in peacetime. The Soviets would then have to use many more warheads to attack Midgetman.

Launcher hardness might be increased beyond current levels. The harder the launcher, the smaller the area over which a warhead can destroy it, so the more warheads would be needed to barrage a given area. Hardness might be augmented by preparing thousands of austere concrete shelters into which the launchers could drive for added protection; the Soviets would then have to barrage the entire deployment area and target individual shelters.

Some suggest that antiballistic missiles (ABMs) could increase Midgetman's deterrent value through a concept called preferential defense. The concept is that by using all one's ABMs to defend a fraction of one's missiles (or other targets), one forgoes the survival of part of one's force in exchange for giving the defended forces high survivability. The attacker, not knowing which missiles would be defended, would in theory have to attack each of them as if they were defended. Several times as many warheads would thus be needed for a successful attack, making an attack more difficult and uncertain and enhancing deterrence.

Preferential defense was considered for MX in a multiple-shelter system.[18] In one variant of that basing system, each of 200 MX missiles would be stationed in one of 23 shelters connected by a loop road, or racetrack. One ABM unit, consisting of a radar, one or more missiles, and a computer, would be placed in a shelter near the MX. In a Soviet attack, the theory was, the ABMs would shoot only at Soviet warheads going toward shelters that held MX. The possibility that each ABM unit would knock down one attacking warhead would have compelled the Soviets to launch a second wave of warheads at each shelter, since they would not know which ones had the MX but would know that the ABM system could save many MX. By defending only one out of every 23 shelters, preferential defense would have provided the defense with significant leverage: 200 ABM units would compel Soviets to use another 4,600 warheads.

A preferential defense of Midgetman/HML would work as follows. The ABM units would probably be mobile, in violation of the ABM treaty.[19] The ABM units, containing one or two short-range interceptor missiles, a radar, and a computer, would be placed inside HMLs to provide mobility, nuclear hardness, and deception.[20] On warning, a fraction of the Midgetman/HMLs at each base, and all the ABM/HML units, would dash to a small part of the deployment area. In theory, the ABMs concentrated in that area would save many of the defended Midgetmen.

Preferential defense would provide even more leverage for Midgetman than it would for MX in multiple-shelter basing. With MX, the Soviets could readily calculate the increase in warheads the ABM would require. With Midgetman, however, the Soviets would not know whether Midgetmen would concentrate on a fifth, tenth, or twentieth of the area, or where they would concentrate, or what fraction of the Midgetmen would concentrate there. These uncertainties would prevent the Soviets from calculating the results of their attack. One wave of warheads barraging the deployment area might destroy only half the HMLs, but two waves might have almost the same result. Unless the Soviets could allocate extra warheads to the area of concentration—which they could not do because they would not know where it was—they would have to barrage the entire deployment area several times to be sure of destroying the Midgetmen. This very high price to attack, and the uncertain effectiveness of attack, would enhance deterrence.

The United States could avoid the foregoing responses if the Soviets accepted (and observed) arms control agreements that limited to current levels the number of missiles and warheads they could deploy or if the United States thought the Soviets would be deterred from barraging Midgetman by the prospect of creating a self-destructive nuclear winter.

STABILITY

The Scowcroft panel's recommendation that "stability should be the primary objective both of the modernization of our strategic forces and of our arms control proposals"[21] was the foundation of the 1983 strategic agreement between congressional moderates and the administration. With stability, neither side would feel impelled by hope of gaining a military advantage or compelled by fear of destruction of its strategic forces to launch a nuclear strike in a crisis. As a result, deterrence would hold.

Midgetman's supporters see that missile as promoting stability in two ways. First, because the Soviets would know that Midgetman is survivable, it would reduce any Soviet incentive to preempt. Second, because the United States would know that Midgetman is survivable, it would reduce pressure on this nation to launch its ICBMs for fear of losing them.

Supporters hold that it is stabilizing for U.S. ICBMs to evolve toward carrying only one warhead. With single-warhead missiles, an attacker would have to use at least one warhead, and probably more, to destroy one of the defender's warheads. As a result, the attacker would gain no strategic advantage by attacking and would be deterred. On the other hand, if each side has roughly equal numbers of silo-based ICBMs carrying MIRVs (multiple independently targetable reentry vehicles), then one side could in theory destroy all the other side's ICBMs with a fraction of its own, providing an incentive for each side to preempt. Moreover, a single-warhead missile, being lighter than a MIRVed missile, would be more maneuverable (for example, could travel on lighter-duty roads and have better off-road capability). As a result, supporters hold, it could disperse over a larger fraction of a deployment area and would force the Soviets to use more warheads to attack it.

Supporters believe stability is promoted by maintaining survivable forces in all three triad elements, since the differing strengths of each complicate attack and hedge against vulnerabilities in other elements. They hold that forgoing new survivable ICBMs, in the belief that bombers are modestly vulnerable and missile submarines are virtually invulnerable, would be most unwise. On the contrary, they argue, it is critical for deterrence to hedge against unforeseen contingencies. If the United States abandons Midgetman and the Soviets find a way to detect missile submarines, then, given massive Soviet air defenses, the United States would have no assuredly survivable forces. This extraordinarily unstable situation, they hold, must be avoided at all costs.

Midgetman's critics could argue that if Midgetman is vulnerable, as discussed earlier, then it would be a use-or-lose system and thus

would be destabilizing, precisely the opposite of what Congress and
the Scowcroft Commission sought with Midgetman. Vulnerable Midgetmen cannot hedge against unforeseen future vulnerability of missile
submarines; rather, continued R&D on antisubmarine warfare will
provide the needed hedge, as will the vast array of other U.S. strategic and intermediate-range nuclear weapons.

If the United States must use Midgetman as a hedge, its critics
could argue for keeping it in R&D only. The program could be modeled
on the U.S. ABM program of the early 1980s, in which the Advanced
Technology Program pushed the technological state of the art while
the Systems Technology Program designed a system that could be
deployed on several years' notice. The advances from the former
would be incorporated into the system designed by the latter, so that
new technology would be continually incorporated into a deployable
system. The army called it a rolling hedge. This approach to Midgetman could save billions of dollars because it would permit Midgetman
to be deployed only if needed. It would enhance effectiveness because
the system deployed would be more closely tailored to whatever threat
ultimately emerges.

In the view of Midgetman's critics, supporters make a fundamental error in assessing the stability implications of Midgetman when
they assert that the Soviets would be deterred by having to use several
warheads to destroy each Midgetman warhead. The error, critics
argue, is the implicit assumption that the Soviets assign the same
strategic value to each of their warheads. Yet missiles differ in strategic value. SS-18s and SS-24s are accurate enough to destroy silo-
based ICBMs; refurbished SS-9s would have poor accuracy and low
countersilo capability but massive payloads suitable for barrage. If
the Soviets deployed old missiles and spares to attack Midgetman,
they could easily afford to use several warheads from these missiles
to destroy each Midgetman warhead (an adverse exchange ratio) because they would not be sacrificing countersilo capability. As a result, the adverse exchange ratio could prove of minor concern to the
Soviets.

Midgetman's critics argue that mobile ICBMs need not carry only
one warhead apiece to be stabilizing. If a force carrying a given number of warheads compels the Soviets to barrage a given area, then it
doesn't matter how many warheads each missile carries. For example, if a force of 167 three-warhead missiles or a force of 500 single-
warhead missiles can each compel the Soviets to barrage 28,000 square
miles at 30 psi, then both forces are equally stabilizing. The basis for
deciding on numbers of warheads per missile would shift from stability
to cost. Life cycle cost per warhead is estimated to be 40 to 50 percent less for mobile three-warhead ICBMs than for mobile single-
warhead ICBMs, assuming each force carries about 500 warheads,[22]

because the MIRVed force would need fewer missiles, guidance sets, HMLs, and personnel.

Midgetman's supporters would argue that the MIRVed force could not draw the same barrage as a larger force of single-warhead missiles. Increased size would make the HMLs easier to detect. HMLs with heavier MIRVed missiles would have less off-road capability. Even if each HML could disperse over a given area, the MIRVed force, with one-third as many HMLs, could only disperse over a third of the area that the MIRVed force could when measured from the location of the HMLs at the moment the Soviets launched an attack. This drawback would be important if the Soviets could use real-time intelligence to retarget their missiles at launch, as it would not require as large a barrage. These difficulties are particularly severe in combination.

Midgetman's opponents would respond as follows. Added funds could offset some limitations of the MIRVed system. Larger engines and tires could improve the HMLs' off-road capability, and roads could be upgraded and expanded to reduce the need for off-road capability. The ability of the single-warhead system to generate more deployment area by virtue of having more HMLs is unimportant. If a HML can travel 15 miles in the half-hour flight time of an ICBM, then the 167 HMLs of the MIRVed force could in theory disperse over 118,000 square miles, so should in practice be able to disperse over more than 28,000 square miles. Dispersal over three times that area would be unnecessary unless the Soviets added thousands of missiles. In that case, an ABM defense of Midgetman could prove preferable to an open-ended proliferation of Midgetmen and deployment area and might be paid for with some of the billions a MIRVed system would save. On the other hand, if the Soviets could locate HMLs in real time and retarget warheads in flight against individual HMLs, they could destroy each HML with a few warheads. Neither the requirement to use, say, 1,500 warheads against 500 single-warhead missiles nor the requirement to use 501 warheads against 167 three-warhead missiles would reliably deter attack.

ARMS CONTROL

The Scowcroft Commission felt that arms control agreements permitting the United States, and encouraging the Soviet Union, to move away from MIRVed ICBMs toward systems with fewer warheads would be stabilizing because they would reduce the temptation to preempt in order to gain a military advantage or to avoid losing one's weapons.[23] At the same time, Midgetman survives most assuredly, and thus contributes most reliably to stability, if agreements limit Soviet forces to numbers insufficient to attack Midgetman and other targets. Will Midgetman promote stabilizing agreements?

Supporters say that Midgetman should make the Soviets more amenable to negotiating away their silo-based ICBMs because Midgetman, being survivable, reduces the offensive value of these Soviet missiles, while at the same time they are threatened by Midgetman, MX, and Trident II.

Midgetman's supporters argue that the question of whether Midgetman promotes arms control misses the point. Midgetman's primary objective is not to promote arms control per se. The pieces of the Scowcroft report were MX, Midgetman, arms control, and stability. They fit together as follows: MX promotes arms control by threatening Soviet ICBMs; arms control enables Midgetman to survive by limiting the threat; and Midgetman promotes stability. Arms control and Midgetman are thus means to an end—stability—not ends in themselves.

Critics hold that Midgetman would not promote stabilizing arms control agreements because it would put the United States in an unacceptable bargaining position. If the Soviets add ICBMs to counter a mobile Midgetman force, the United States would have to increase deployment area, launcher hardness, numbers of missiles, or some combination. Otherwise, Midgetman would become vulnerable and destabilizing, as discussed earlier. The Scowcroft Commission recognized this requirement, albeit obliquely:

> During that period [before Midgetman is deployed] an
> approach toward arms control, consistent with such
> deployments [of Midgetman], should also seek to en-
> courage the Soviets to move toward a more stable ICBM
> force structure at levels which would obviate the need to
> deploy very large numbers of such missiles [i.e., Mid-
> getman].[24]

Conversely, the Soviets would know that, by deploying many more missiles, they could compel the United States to spend more money (for more missiles or harder launchers) or incur political opposition (by expanding deployment area) to protect its investment in Midgetman. Accordingly, they could exact major concessions from the United States in exchange for agreeing to limit their forces.

For Midgetman to provide bargaining leverage before it is deployed, the Soviets would have to believe it would be deployed. Yet they would have many reasons to believe the opposite: the administration's willingness to bargain mobile Midgetman away, the system's high cost, its requirement for an open-ended commitment to preserve its survivability, and the history of MX.

A force of MIRVed mobile ICBMs might promote stabilizing arms control agreements in the sense that these missiles could be built to comply with SALT II. That treaty permits each side to build only one new type of ICBM but permits modifications of existing ICBMs. A missile weighing between 74,000 pounds and 82,000 pounds, approximately, and having certain other characteristics, would meet the definition of a modification. A missile of this weight could carry much more than a single warhead and penetration aids, so would probably be MIRVed.

Few protagonists in the Midgetman debate seem eager to raise the SALT-compliant aspect of a MIRVed mobile ICBM, however, because it conflicts with positions many of them hold on arms control. Those who see a single-warhead missile as promoting stability favor compliance with SALT, while those who favor a MIRVed Midgetman tend to be less insistent on SALT compliance or advocate that the United States cease compliance with SALT. Moreover, the United States has asserted that the Soviets have violated the one-new-type provision by testing two new types of ICBMs, the SS-24 and the SS-25.[25]

VERIFIABILITY OF MOBILE ICBMs

Can the United States verify deployment of Soviet mobile ICBMs? If it cannot, the Soviets could cheat by building many missiles beyond what is permitted, threatening U.S. strategic forces, making a mockery of arms control, and undermining stability.

Mobile ICBMs pose an arms control dilemma. To survive, their moment-to-moment locations must remain unknown to the other side. Otherwise, they could be attacked individually instead of requiring a barrage, thus greatly reducing a mobile system's deterrent effect. At the same time, unless some way is found to give the other side confidence in the number of mobile missiles deployed, no agreement could be reached limiting them.

Midgetman's supporters hold that agreements could be constructed that would permit mobile ICBMs to be counted without revealing their precise locations. Agreements could limit deployment of these missiles to designated areas and could require each side to notify the other of movements outside these areas (such as to and from factories or repair facilities). Finding even one missile outside a deployment area without notification would constitute a violation. The United States would be highly likely to detect large-scale or continuing violations and could respond, while a few undetected violations would not affect the strategic balance.

Another possible agreement, though one that would be harder to negotiate, would be to provide for on-site inspection at factories to count missiles and launchers produced. Under this regime, the Soviets might be deterred from building covert factories by the possibility of detection by national technical means, agents, defectors, accidents, or even analysis of flows of materials between factories.

Midgetman's critics, including some in the administration, counter that the Soviets have many advantages compared with the United States if they wished to cheat on such agreements. The Soviets could hide these missiles in the central part of the Soviet Union. This vast, sparsely populated area is densely forested and often overcast. Midgetman, however, would be deployed on smaller areas and on deserts or prairies, which provide much less cover. The Soviets control access to these large areas. The United States, in contrast, could at best control access to military reservations, not to the areas on which Midgetmen would deploy in crises: at most 20,000 square miles outside Southwest military bases or the area outside Minuteman silos. While both sides could build covert factories, it would be easier for the Soviets to do so successfully.

COST-EFFECTIVENESS

Midgetman will be expensive. The air force estimates that it would cost $44 billion (1982 dollars) for acquisition and 15 years of operation of 500 Midgetmen in HMLs (see Table 4). Would the money be well spent?

To measure cost-effectiveness, one could hypothesize equal-cost forces (that is, Midgetman and something else), attack each force with the same number of warheads, and see which one lets more U.S. warheads survive. In this case, though, it is difficult to judge which force is more cost-effective. The choice of unit of account is debatable. Midgetman supporters present their strongest case by measuring cost-effectiveness in terms of cost per surviving warhead. This case presumes that the Soviets would not have enough warheads available to barrage the entire deployment area; if they did, then in theory they could destroy all Midgetmen and the cost per surviving warhead would be infinite. The MX missile looks promising, in contrast, when one considers cost per deployed warhead, especially if one argues that the MX would be launched promptly in the event of Soviet attack, before they could be destroyed.

Cost-effectiveness evaluations require making many assumptions, such as Midgetman system cost, launcher hardness, deployment area, and, for a silo-based MX, silo hardness and Soviet missile accuracy. Any analysis is sensitive to each factor, thus making it possible to construct examples showing Midgetman to be more or less cost-effective than MX missiles in superhard silos.[26] Finally, cost estimates for Midgetman and for MX missiles in superhard silos are preliminary.

TABLE 4   Life-Cycle Cost per Warhead

System	Life-Cycle Cost (in billions of dollars)	Life-Cycle Cost per Warhead (in millions of dollars)
100 B-1B with 16 weapons each	33.5 (FY81$)	21
100 MX in Minuteman silos	18.7 (FY82$)	19
1 Trident with 24 Trident II	5.4 (FY83$)	28
500 Midgetmen on HMLs	44 (FY82$)	88

Sources: B-1B: Office of Legislative Liaison, U.S. Air Force, January and February 1986. The B-1B figure includes a rough estimate, derived by the Congressional Research Service from air force data, of the life-cycle cost of the weapons, assuming an average load of 16 weapons per aircraft. MX: Office of the Special Assistant for ICBM Modernization, U.S. Air Force, February 1986. Trident II: Office of Legislative Affairs, U.S. Navy, February 1986. Midgetman: U.S. General Accounting Office, Status of the Intercontinental Ballistic Missile Modernization Program, Report no. GAO/NSIAD-85-78, p. 7; and Office of the Special Assistant for ICBM Modernization, U.S. Air Force, January 1986.

Note: Life-cycle cost includes acquisition and operation. These figures exclude Department of Energy costs for the nuclear devices; they include 15 years of operation for B-1, MX, and Midgetman, and 30 years for Trident II.

Midgetman's supporters argue that the system's high survivability lowers its cost per surviving warhead and makes it cost-effective. Cost-effectiveness can be further increased, supporters note, by expanding the deployment area, which could significantly increase the number of Midgetmen surviving for little added cost. Others suggest that changing the basing and operating concepts for mobile Midgetmen and pressing the air force to maintain competition among contractors can further reduce cost per surviving warhead and increase cost-effectiveness.[27]

Midgetman's supporters point out that it is just a matter of time until superhard silos would become vulnerable. Both sides have been improving ICBM accuracy ever since these missiles were introduced. This trend will continue. Accuracy of 300 feet or so would enable the Soviets to destroy superhard silos. Then, the cost per surviving MX warhead based in superhard silos would be immense.

Midgetman supporters stress that the decision on Midgetman's fate should not hinge on cost-effectiveness. Without Midgetman, a breakthrough in Soviet ability to find U.S. submarines would leave no assuredly survivable U.S. forces. Deterrence could then collapse. Why run that risk when we can avoid it by buying Midgetman?

Midgetman's opponents counter that obtaining a given effect for the least cost is important, especially in a time of fiscal austerity. They note that just as it may be possible to lower Midgetman's cost, it should be possible to lower the cost of alternatives. For example, the air force indicates that the life-cycle cost of 100 MX in Minuteman silos is $18.7 billion (1982 dollars) versus $16.7 billion for 50.[28] Thus the United States could add 500 MX warheads (50 missiles) for $2 billion or 500 single-warhead Midgetmen for $44 billion (15-year life-cycle cost for each in 1982 dollars).

If the United States intends to buy a mobile ICBM, Midgetman critics hold, it is worth investigating whether a single-warhead or MIRVed mobile ICBM is more cost-effective.

Building more Trident submarines than current plans envision and arming them with Trident II SLBMs is another alternative to Midgetman. As noted, the 15-year life-cycle cost of 500 single-warhead Midgetmen in HMLs is $44 billion (1982 dollars). For comparison, a force of 750 Trident II warheads has a nominal 30-year life-cycle cost of $21.2 billion (1983 dollars)—750 multiplied by the $28.3 million life-cycle cost per warhead. This force would permit 500 warheads to be at sea at any time. Those who are confident of the survivability of the Trident force would see it as more cost-effective than Midgetman: all 500 at-sea Trident II warheads would presumably survive, while not all Midgetmen would, yet the Trident force would cost tens of billions of dollars less. Trident's costs also are more predictable than Midgetman's costs, reducing the risk of fiscal surprise: Trident submarines are operational and the first flight test of a Trident II occurred in January 1987, while mobile Midgetman is a new system in an earlier stage of development. In a time of fiscal austerity, predictability of costs is especially important.

Midgetman's critics would see it as more cost-effective for this nation to compete with the Soviets in submarine systems, an area of U.S. advantage, than in mobile ICBMs, an area of Soviet advantage. Reports indicate that U.S. submarines are quieter and U.S. antisubmarine warfare capabilities better. Geography also aids the survivability of U.S. missile submarines. In contrast, land-mobile ICBMs should be more cost-effective for the Soviet Union. The state has firm control over the population, which reduces the cost of missile security and prevents public opposition of the sort that faced MX. Labor costs are low, which benefits labor-intensive mobile ICBMs. The Soviets have much more land available for deployment, increasing the number of warheads the United States would require for barrage. Even the deployment areas favor the Soviets, as noted earlier, simplifying covert deployment of mobile ICBMs and rapid targeting of the other side's mobile ICBMs for the Soviets.

Supporters of the Trident alternative believe Trident offers other advantages claimed for Midgetman beyond cost-effectiveness. It is survivable. It is stabilizing, as it neither tempts the Soviets nor pressures the United States to strike first. Deployment of Trident instead of Midgetman would encourage the Soviets to negotiate limits on their ICBMs by threatening those missiles and removing their targets. Trident is verifiable. Trident's supporters believe the system meets U.S. needs, so that spending billions more for Midgetman than Trident is not justified.

NOTES

1. U S. President's Commission on Strategic Forces, Report of the President's Commission on Strategic Forces (Washington: GPO, 1983), 29.

2. Ibid., 3.

3. For comparison, the United States could in theory deploy an additional 50 MX missiles (500 warheads) in Minuteman silos and operate them for 15 years for $2 billion (1982 dollars) versus $44 billion (1982 dollars) to deploy 500 Midgetmen in hard mobile launchers and operate them for 15 years. MX missiles in Minuteman silos provide the offensive capability, but not the survivability, of Midgetman.

4. MX funding requests dropped sharply after fiscal year 1984 following a decision in 1983 to base MX in Minuteman missile silos, the least expensive basing mode, and fiscal year 1986 legislation stating that 12 to 21 MX missiles should be procured for fiscal year 1987, compared with the 48 that the administration had intended to request for that year.

5. See Don Oberdorfer and George Wilson, "Offer to Ban Mobile Missiles Draws Fire," Washington Post, November 22, 1985, 1, 16; and Albert Gore, Jr., "Design Concept of the Midgetman," Congressional Record, daily edition, November 22, 1985, S 16403.

6. "We will promptly undertake a major effort to bring the proposal of a small, single-warhead ICBM to fruition on a high priority basis. . . . I am seeking a clear show of support from Congress to signal U.S. resolve. A case in point is the clear necessity of approving funds promptly to procure Peacekeeper missiles," letter from Ronald Reagan to Albert Gore, May 11, 1983, reprinted in Congressional Record, daily edition, November 4, 1985, S 14735.

7. U.S. Office of the Under Secretary of Defense for Research and Engineering, Defense Science Board, Report of the Defense Science Board Task Force on Small Intercontinental Ballistic Missile Modernization (Washington: GPO, March 1986), 17.

8. Fred Ikle, Under Secretary of Defense for Policy, and Donald Hicks, Under Secretary of Defense for Research and Engineering, memorandum for the Secretary of Defense on the Defense Science Board Task Force report on ICBM modernization, March 26, 1986, 1.

9. Pete Wilson, "Wilson Says Immediate Full Scale Development of Single Warhead Midgetman Missile Would Waste $22 Billion," news release, February 12, 1986, 1-2.

10. Michael Gordon, "Reagan Orders a Study to Decide If U.S. Should Build New Missile," New York Times, April 25, 1986, 1, 36.

11. One kiloton equals the explosive force of 1,000 tons of TNT.

12. U.S. Central Intelligence Agency, Soviet Force Developments, testimony by Robert Gates and Lawrence Gershwin before a joint session of the Subcommittee on Strategic and Theater Nuclear Forces of the Senate Armed Services Committee and the Defense Subcommittee of the Senate Committee on Appropriations, June 26, 1985, fig. 5.

13. If, as anticipated, the Soviets remain unable to detect at-sea missile submarines, they could not target them.

14. The number of warheads added can be immaterial to barrage potential. A missile has about the same barrage potential whether it carries a few high-yield warheads or many lower-yield ones. Thus barrage potential can be increased by adding missiles, not by having existing missiles carry more lower-yield warheads. See U.S. Congress, Office of Technology Assessment, MX Missile Basing (Washington: GPO, 1981), 258-60.

15. This calculation sums the areas over which the individual warheads could generate 30 psi of blast pressure. For these warheads to barrage this total area, the attack would require perfect accuracy, reliability, and timing. Use of realistic assumptions would increase the number of warheads needed to barrage this area. Accuracy is imperfect, and warheads that miss their aimpoints would leave gaps in the intended barrage coverage. Other gaps would result from imperfect reliability, with some warheads not reaching their targets or not detonating. The calculations assume that warheads are detonated so that the rings of 30-psi blast pressure that they generate just touch and that HMLs in the areas between 30-psi rings are destroyed by the simultaneous convergence of several blast waves. This convergence would increase the barrage area beyond that of the 30-psi rings but requires the warheads to be detonated simultaneously and at about the same altitude. Such detonation is difficult to achieve, and failure to achieve it would create still more gaps in barrage coverage. "Fratricide," an effect in which warhead detonations interfere with following

warheads, could result if detonations are not simultaneous, creating further uncertainty for the attacker.

16. "Soviet leaders . . . rarely reduce force levels, and winnow out stocks only when they cease to serve useful purposes." John Collins, U.S.-Soviet Military Balance: Concepts and Capabilities, 1960-1980 (New York: McGraw-Hill, 1980), 194.

17. This figure assumes that the HMLs begin to disperse several minutes after the Soviets launch their ICBMs, and that the HMLs require several minutes to anchor themselves to the ground to attain maximum hardness.

18. For a discussion of defense of MX missiles, see Ashton Carter, "Ballistic Missile Defense," in U.S. Office of Technology Assessment, MX Missile Basing, chap. 3, 111-43.

19. The ABM treaty and its 1974 protocol permit deployment, at only one site with a 150-km radius, of 2 large and 18 smaller radars and only 100 interceptor missiles. They forbid mobile land-based (and certain other) ABM systems or components.

A treaty-compliant ABM system to defend Midgetman/HML would face many difficulties. A fixed ABM system limited to one site could in theory defend wide areas by intercepting Soviet ICBMs in midflight, while they were still thousands of miles from their targets. Such a defense would face at least two difficulties in particular. First, it is well beyond the state of the art. For example, it would require greatly improved discrimination (i.e., the ability to differentiate between warheads and penetration aids, which are devices such as chaff and decoys that help the warhead penetrate an ABM defense) and target acquisition and tracking. Second, in a barrage of many thousands of warheads, plus vast quantities of penetration aids, it would be extremely difficult for the defense to pick out all and only those warheads traveling toward the area to be defended.

A defensive system that intercepted warheads a few hundred miles from their targets would mitigate these problems. The system's shorter range would limit the area it could defend, but as a result it would only have to contend with those warheads and penetration aids heading toward that area and would do so late in the missiles' flight, when their targets were more precisely known to the defense.

A system with a range of several miles would mitigate these problems still more because the lower atmosphere, by slowing penetration aids more than warheads, would facilitate discrimination. But with a short-range system deployed in small numbers at a fixed site, the Soviets would know exactly which area it could defend and could overwhelm it by using a few hundred more warheads against that area. Moreover, a treaty-limited system would face two special problems. First, the number of interceptors is much too small. One hundred could at best destroy 100 warheads, which (assuming a yield of 500

KT and HML hardness of 30 psi) could barrage only about 300 square miles. Second, being at a fixed site, the Soviets could attack the defense directly, forcing it to use some of these few interceptors to defend itself. Given the limited and uncertain effect of this system, it would probably be more cost-effective to spend the funds that it would require on increasing HML hardness.

20. If the ABM units were placed in vehicles other than HMLs, the Soviets might be able to learn where the Midgetmen were concentrated by observing where the ABM units were concentrated. That information would be of particular value to them if they could retarget their missiles in flight.

21. U.S. President's Commission on Strategic Forces, Report of the President's Commission on Strategic Forces (Washington: GPO, April 1983), 3.

22. Les Aspin, Midgetman: Sliding Shut the Window of Vulnerability, House Armed Services Committee, February 10, 1986, 22–23; and Pete Wilson, "The Sad Tale of the Too-Small Missile," Congressional Record, daily edition, February 17, 1986, S 1240–41.

23. Report of the President's Commission on Strategic Forces, 3, 14–15, 23–24.

24. Report of the President's Commission on Strategic Forces, 15.

25. See U.S. White House, Office of the Press Secretary, The President's Unclassified Report on Soviet Noncompliance with Arms Control Agreements (Washington: GPO, December 23, 1985, mimeo), 3–4. The Soviets counter that the SS–25 is a modification of the SS–13 and is thus permitted by SALT II.

26. Superhard silos are a possible basing mode for MX. They would be many times more resistant to nuclear weapon effects than are the current Minuteman silos in which the first 50 MX missiles will be deployed.

27. Albert Gore, Jr., "Administration Misgivings on Midgetman," Congressional Record, daily edition, November 13, 1985, S 15364.

28. Information provided by the Office of the Special Assistant for ICBM Modernization, U.S. Air Force, Feb. 1986. The figures are so close because the figure for 50 includes the cost of research and development on missile and basing mode, 20 R&D missiles, and 123 spare missiles (for operational test and for surveillance of aging). The added 50, in contrast, require mainly the costs of building the added missiles and modifying silos and launch control equipment for them.

Trident and Credible Deterrence: The Sea-Space Link

D. Douglas Dalgleish and Larry Schweikart

INTRODUCTION

The primary challenge to sea-based deterrence in the 1990s will quite naturally focus on the ballistic missile submarine leg of the Triad of U.S. strategic forces, including land-based missiles and bombers with cruise missiles. Certainly, carrier-based aircraft and ship-to-shore missiles constitute a part of the overall deterrent mix, but submarines will continue to carry the burden of the seagoing deterrent and may assume preeminence in the future Triad. This chapter, then, concentrates on four major concerns regarding sea-based deterrence that specifically affect submarines: the development and production of the D-5 missile for the Trident submarines, the continued threats to command, control, communications, and intelligence (C^3I), other threats to submarine survivability, and the potential for using submarines within the framework of the Strategic Defense Initiative (SDI). As a result of this focus, deterrent considerations related to the impact of cruise missiles, battleships, aircraft carriers, or other cruise-missile-firing surface ships will not be discussed, although many of the conclusions reached here can be applied to those areas.[1] Nor does this chapter deal with arms control, as it is assumed that threats to deterrence should be considered apart from unpredictable developments in this area.

TRIDENT CHARACTERISTICS

No development will have a more immediate impact on the deterrent forces of the United States than the introduction of the D-5 (Trident II) missile in December 1989. This missile, to be deployed beginning with the SSBN (nuclear-powered ballistic-missile-firing submarine) 734 (the ninth Trident submarine to be built), is now classified as having a range of over 4,000 miles. It will deliver 8 to 14

Mk-5/W-88 warheads of 475 kilotons, or 10 to 12 Mk-4/W-76 100-kiloton warheads each. Trident submarines now carry 24 C-4 (Trident I) missiles and will accommodate the same number of D-5s, despite their larger diameter and greater weight and height. Currently, the C-4s can deliver 8 Mk-4/W-76 100-kiloton warheads. But the point that generates the greatest criticism about the D-5 is its accuracy: estimates suggest that it can drop a warhead within a circular error probable (CEP) of 100 meters. (This represents an average; actually, accuracy error depends on the particular warhead deployed and could conceivably drop to as low as 35 meters.)

This accuracy and warhead mix has already held significant implications for the uses of D-5. First, all ranges have been reduced to 4,000 nautical miles in order to put to sea more warheads. Originally, the navy had planned to move Tridents farther out to sea through the increased range of the D-5, thus making the submarines more survivable. In the last few years, however, the Soviets have not demonstrated advances in their antisubmarine warfare (ASW) sufficient to necessitate longer-range deployments of U.S. SSBNs. Trident's range has seemed adequate to handle the ASW threat, and thus the navy altered its plans for the D-5 to have a 6,000 nautical mile range, although either the D-5 or the C-4 can attain 6,000 nautical mile ranges, given a reduction in the number of warheads.[2] (This implication, like a Chinese puzzle box, implies yet something else: with a shorter range, the missile can be still more accurate.)

Second, the greater throw weight and megatonnage of the D-5's warhead make it more useful as a counterforce weapon than the previous generation of Poseidon (C-3) missiles. A Trident II can deliver 5,075 throw-weight pounds, as opposed to Trident I's 2,900 throw-weight pounds. Using their superior accuracy, these missiles indeed constitute "silo busters."

Third, the maximum D-5 load allows a per-submarine improvement of 96 warheads over the 192 load of the Trident I (minimum load using the larger W-88 warhead would be the same). A significant increase in megatonnage also accompanies the addition of warheads: D-5-equipped vessels have 28.8 megatons per ship, while a Trident loaded with C-4 missiles can deliver 19.2 megatons. An alternate D-5 loading would permit launch of as much as 91.1 megatons. In megatonnage ratio, any single Trident loaded with the D-5/W-88 combination is nearly equal to all of the first eight Tridents loaded with C-4s.

ISSUES AND CONTROVERSIES

Arguments against deployment of the D-5 cite the accuracy and powerful warheads as being destabilizing by threatening the Soviet

land-based missile forces and other hardened targets. The corrollary
to this criticism is that the temptation to launch makes the missile a
first-strike weapon. A second but less often invoked contention is that
the D-5s represent a more expensive route toward deterrence than
the C-4.

First Strike

The argument that the silo-busting capabilities of the D-5 make
it a first-strike weapon admits by implication that the ICBM force is
not considered dependable for missions requiring prompt, hard-target
counterforce. This line of thought assumes that intercontinental ballistic missile (ICBM) modification is futile because the United States
is too far behind to update the ICBM program, implying that the MX
program, too, has been futile. Therefore, the argument contains paralyzing logic: because we did not modernize the ICBM force, we cannot modernize the submarine-launched ballistic missile (SLBM) force.
Consequently, this logic also leads to a greater distortion of planning,
as the navy intended the Trident I only as a transition missile to extend
the life of twelve of the least overage Poseidon subs. But the C-4 was
never considered as anything other than an interim measure for the
Ohio class. What came as a concession to extend the life of the Lafay-
ette submarines has now worked its way into policy argument to abandon the very weapon for which the Ohio class was designed.[3]
    Still, this discussion must deal with the question: "Does a high-
accuracy, heavy-payload weapon have to be a first-strike weapon?"
Such an approach assumes that technology drives strategy, a poor
presupposition indeed. At Jutland, Waterloo, Leipzig, or even Pearl
Harbor, tactical deployment and weapons development followed the
political intentions to pursue certain objectives. Moreover, the accuracy question begs for a threshold: When is accuracy too good? Again,
to argue that a 300-meter CEP warhead is a second-strike weapon but
a 150-meter CEP warhead is a first-strike weapon is illogical, because strategy determines the objective for either weapon. Moreover,
is a highly accurate (10-meter) conventional weapon a first-strike
weapon? Applying such questions illuminates the illogic of the first-
strike argument.
    The D-5 is a response to the clearly stated Soviet strategy of
using a first strike to incapacitate the U.S. ICBM force, and then re-
loading the silos with the intention of threatening the U.S. population.
No matter what else D-5 might be able to do, its development is based
on a strategy that calls for a second strike to destroy refilled silos
before they can be used to refire on U.S. cities and other countervalue
targets.

Such an approach to D-5 implies that if the submarine force used its missiles in a first strike, there would be no second-strike capability. In other words, the United States, with no remaining submarine-based launchers and no land-based launchers capable of refiring, would have no retaliatory capacity. Although the critics accept the logic of using the D-5 as a first-strike weapon, they seem to miss this implication. In fact, SSBNs have recently had increasingly more so-called first-strike missions by default, because without MX, the role of counterforce must be met in some other way. In the absence of ICBM modernization, no need exists to differentiate between C-4-equipped and D-5-equipped Tridents in strategic targeting. Identical functions need not be performed by all submarines.

As Walter Slocombe has noted, "All new systems will inevitably have substantial hard target capability."[4] To selectively attack the Trident II for being too accurate ignores the fact that even bombers using conventional cruise missiles will have much improved accuracy. Moreover, since some capability to attack all varieties of targets is critical to deterrence, that capability should reside in the most survivable part of the Triad, namely, SSBNs. As the Soviets have placed so much of their strategic punch in land-based missiles, in the critics' eyes anything that makes these units obsolete will threaten to be destabilizing. But that suggests only that the United States punish itself because the Soviets were so short-sighted as to put the bulk of their deterrence in land-based missiles.

Some psychological considerations are also in order, the most fundamental of which is the nature of the Soviet command structure. "Launch under attack" may be a realistic policy option in a decentralized system, but less so in a totalitarian, controlled government that avoids delegation of authority like the plague. In other words, to whom would Mikhail Gorbachev give the authority to launch under attack? The top Politburo officials? Generals in the Soviet rocket forces? A tightly controlled political system would in fact reduce the temptation to launch under attack. Instead, a sensible policy, even from the Soviet viewpoint, would be to take corrective action before launch under attack ever became a policy option. The Soviets have done this by deploying their own SSBNs and have made a transition from fixed ICBMs to mobile ICBMs. Thus the D-5 poses a less than comprehensive first-strike threat.

Despite these sensible responses to the first-strike critics, the most overwhelmingly overlooked point is that accuracy is a function of distance as well as technology. If a Trident submarine fired a C-4 from the North Sea, it is likely to be much more accurate than a D-5 fired from the maximum range, regardless of inertial guidance advances. Thus, not only has high accuracy been available in the past, to the Soviets as well as to ourselves, but it will continue to improve because of improvements in inertial guidance technology. So will Soviet ASW. Consequently, increased accuracy will be necessary merely to offset gains in Soviet ASW range. Soviet antiballistic missile (ABM) and SDI developments prospectively threaten to cut down the number of retaliatory missiles severely, thus making it more critical than ever to "make your shots count." These same ABM/SDI developments will also require development and deployment of MARV (maneuverable reentry vehicles) and AMARV (advanced maneuverable), so that the decrease in MARVed accuracy must be offset by the increased platform and booster accuracy. Finally, D-5's greater throw weight and accuracy make it possible to offset Soviet ABM/SDI by being able to carry more penetration aids than C-4.

Cost

Perhaps the most feeble objection to Trident II deployment arises from the program's cost. Through 1986, the D-5 costs for research and development (R&D), construction, and procurement will total $7.33 billion, out of a total estimated program cost of $38.1 billion; roughly one-fifth of the money has already been spent, and another $3.6 billion will be spent by 1987. Given the dynamics of the legislative process, virtually no program can be effectively curtailed in a year. Thus, before any significant policy change could be made, almost one-third of the total already would be spent. However, more important, of the final R&D cost of $10.3 billion, more than $6 billion has been spent—almost two-thirds of the final figure. Since procurement constitutes $27 billion of the $38 billion total, and since some missile—a C-4 or D-5—must be purchased, how much would procurement of a different missile save? The cost of a C-4 has been placed at $12.3 million (1980 dollars), compared with an estimated cost of $30.9 million per missile for the D-5 (1986 dollars). Subtracted from this, however, was a one-time conversion savings of $680 million that would have been lost if Trident II submarines 9 to 13 were reoutfitted for C-4s after being outfitted for D-5s (including costs such as those associated with tearing out the C-4 cradles). This would require $1 billion for refit, plus the purchase of 120 C-4 missiles (put at a cost of almost $12.3 million each, or $2.3 billion to refit the Trident submarines 9 through 13. However, even this is low: the navy puts the cost of refitting submarines 9 (SSBN 734) and 10 (SSBN 735) at $1.2 billion together. Added to the $2.3 billion should then be $680 million for the first conversion, or $2.9 billion. Associated costs include changes in existing submarines for equipment such as firing mechanisms, launchers, and a host of other expenses, especially related to shipbuilding and delivery extension on five ships. If each is extended by a year, this compounds the original year's delay incurred when the cradles were first changed and increases costs.[5]

The D-5 can, in fact, do double duty by replacing the MX and the Midgetman in providing survivable prompt counterforce. Currently, the plan to deploy 100 MX missiles (put at a cost of $20 billion) is an unnecessary replication of R&D and procurement costs that can be assumed by the D-5. In short, the Trident II missile can do virtually everything that the MX can, and there is little debate about the concept of accurate land-based missiles, if they are survivable. Thus, the D-5 critics would have to find acceptable its deployment in survivable land basing. Meanwhile, early arguments for the Midgetman have floundered. As of 1986 (in 1982 dollars), the cost over a twenty-year life cycle for 500 Midgetman missiles was estimated at $44 billion by expert analysts (see the chapter by Jonathan Medalia).

Overall, then, D-5 viewed as a replacement for MX and Midgetman would save between $43 billion and $63 billion, less the $31 billion cost of the 100 D-5 missiles themselves, or a total savings of $12 billion to $22 billion. Replacing D-5 with the Trident I would mean losing not only this, but also the $6 billion in already expended D-5 R&D. To discard the D-5 would thus throw certainly $8.9 billion down the drain and forsake potential savings of $12 billion to $22 billion, compared with deploying MX and Midgetman but not Trident II. Navy estimates place the costs of backfitting at $1 billion for the ships alone. But there is no Trident I production line, making restart costs an integral part of any consideration. Missile restart costs, changes in the warhead production line, and modifications to the King's Bay, Georgia, facility would add $2.5 billion, by navy estimates. Restarting the production line alone would cost $1.3 billion. During that time, SSBN construction would have to be halted. All together, navy sources put the conversion cost from D-5 to C-4 at $4 billion to $6 billion, on top of the $8.9 billion already spent, or $12.9 billion to $14.9 billion total, not counting the $12 billion to $22 billion that can be saved over MX-Midgetman. Thus, abandoning the D-5 at this point would involve total real and potential losses of between $14.9 billion and $36.9 billion over and above the cost of MX.[6]

Finally, the underutilization of the Trident submarine hull, which was specifically built for the larger D-5 missile, would result in underutilization of the presently planned twenty ships. Thus, there are yet other costs associated with manning and operating that further add to the overall savings of the D-5. When these savings, real and potential, are considered, the D-5 is not only the weapon of the navy's future, but that of the air force as well. U.S. plans to deploy D-5 are further strengthened by the British program to adopt the D-5. The British, in fact, are leaping over two interim stages, past C-3 and C-4, to the Trident II. More important, the United States has a commitment to produce and sell Trident II missiles to the United Kingdom. Alliance unity would be seriously damaged in a repetition of the Skybolt type of episode if the United States abandoned D-5.[7]

Command and Control

Just as serious, but not as dramatic in its impact on the deterrent force, is the further hardening and reinforcement of C^3I. Whereas survivability is a submarine's strength, communication is its weakness. This will not significantly change in the 1990s. However, improvements in a host of communications techniques and media will occur by the year 2000, providing partial correctives for deficiencies in C^3I.[8]

Daniel Ford, one critic of the U.S. strategic communications networks, has detailed the series of procedures that a submarine must perform to receive its communications, first from VLF (very low frequency) radio transmissions, which provide the defense condition reports as long as the transmitters function, then to HF (high frequency), using other antennae. There are a small number of navy broadcasting stations to perform these duties.[9]

Submarines also will continue to receive messages from Tacamos (radio relay planes) in the 1990s. These are E6-A C-130 aircraft modified to act as flying relay stations, but they transmit commands only from other authorities; they do not originate them. These aircraft have UHF (line-of-sight voice transmission), HF (longer-range voice transmissions), and LF (long-range teletype transmissions) capabilities. Their maximum six-hour flying time and 4,530 nautical mile range currently limit their ability to transmit signals to all ballistic missile submarines. Never designed as radio stations and having a short on-station endurance, many units are needed just to make sure that one is operational at all times in each ocean. Earlier aircraft did not have a duplex antenna, meaning they could not receive and transmit simultaneously, creating the potential for self-jamming in an attack situation. Since those planes could not undergo airborne refueling, their range was fairly well confined. At least one is on patrol in the Pacific and one in the Atlantic at all times, but it is difficult to reach all of the submarines with an alert message at the same time, with the aircraft range limitations. Worse, for a submarine to get its instructions from Tacamo, until 1983, it had to sail into the aircraft's broadcast range. That can give ASW forces (especially those using barrage techniques) a much greater chance of hitting a higher percentage of the U.S. SSBN force. Because some Tacamo aircraft are forward based at Guam, Wake Island, and Western Europe, they are also vulnerable to engagement by cruise missiles, sabotage, or tactical aircraft. One source cited the fact that of the SSBNs on high alert—50 percent of the total force—only a fraction came within receiving range of Tacamos at regular intervals. In 1983 the navy began to double the inventory of Tacamos to coincide with the Trident deployment and to improve the radio equipment. Each aircraft was also equipped with more powerful transmitters. As a result, the aircraft and the subs had a better chance of receiving the messages.[10]

A parallel access to Tacamo, from the top down, comes from Looking Glass, which is the name given to the principal airborne command post of the Strategic Air Command. Looking Glass can send messages to Tacamo that will then be sent by radio, if the ground stations are knocked out. Looking Glass's ability to contact Tacamo, however, is seen by expert analyst Bruce Blair as being extremely limited, to the extent that even if the Emergency Rocket Communications System (ERCS)* and Tacamo platforms both made it into position—a dubious proposition, according to Blair—the radio link would not have a high chance of reaching the Atlantic Tacamos. The risk of isolating submarines even under alert conditions is greater in the Pacific. The primary communication path from the National Emergency Airborne Command Post (NEACP) through Postattack Command and Control System (PACCS) aircraft to Tacamo-Pacific relies upon an easily disrupted LF channel. The ERCS offers an alternative way to reach Tacamo, but its survivability is doubtful.[11] In 1986, the C-130 Tacamos will begin to be replaced by ECX, a Boeing 707/C-137/E-3. Eventually, fifteen of these aircraft will be acquired, will be electromagnetic pulse (EMP) hardened, and will have twice the speed of the C-130s, as well as refueling capability to permit endurance of several days.[12]

Without Tacamo, the Ohio class submarines must rely on either ELF (extremely low frequency) transmitters or on a variety of space-based communications satellites. Normal satellite communication includes AFSATCOM (Air Force Satellite Communications) and FLTSATCOM (Fleet Satellite Communications), but in the event of an attack, ERCS can be put into orbit to transmit for up to half an hour if ERCS silos survive attack. It has been previously speculated that each Trident can have dedicated one of its tubes to its own individual communications satellite missile. But without this option, ERCS remains as the primary satellite emergency replacement system. Located at Whiteman Air Force Base in Missouri, the number of ERCSs is classified, but one source puts it at eight. The ERCS missiles count against the United States in the SALT I treaty.[13]

---

*ERCS is launched from Minuteman silos and provides transattack communications in an Emergency Actions Message.

Space-based communications possibilities for the 1990s include use of the blue-green laser, but tuning the lasers so that their beams can pass through water without diffusing, thus providing a signaling device, has not yet been perfected; nevertheless, it has great potential to reach submarines sailing at full speed. A space-qualifiable blue-green laser transmitter will be tested in 1986/87. A submarine receiver for laser transmissions is being readied. Even less likely to be ready by the 1990s, but holding out tremendous long-term communications potential, is a neutrino transmitter. Neutrino particles have no charge or mass, and thus make matter highly transparent. A neutrino accelerator could shoot neutrino beams through the earth to any spot in the ocean for collection and reading. The trouble is, however, that collection of neutrino particles is quite difficult, in that they make the collectors transparent, like anything else. For now, neutrino communication remains experimental.[14]

Space also now provides great opportunities for improving accuracy of missiles, both by improving the position fix of the platform and by feeding into each missile navigational information while it is in flight. NAVSTAR, which is the navigational satellite system consisting of eighteen satellites, however, may not be needed for SLBMs by the mid-1990s. Fiber-optics navigational positioning systems on board submarines will make NAVSTAR only a useful backup, and the evidence now suggests that submarines feed their own navigational data into missiles.

Reconnaissance provided by space will improve in the 1990s, and there is the possibility that open ocean surveillance information could be useful to SSBNs. However, it is doubtful that this space-to-sea link will be actively pursued. (Why, for example, would an SSBN endanger itself by surfacing, or even coming near the surface, for information on the enemy's position?) More important than the reconnaissance satellites are the Defense Support Program satellites (three in orbit at all times), whose job is to detect ICBM or SLBM launches. Fleet Ocean Surveillance Centers (FOSICs) also provide broad coverage of the seas. FOSICs receive information from SOSUS (undersea sonar lines), land-based intelligence, and other sources and feed into the several headquarters. These centers give warning of Soviet buildups and relay patterns in Soviet activity that might be threatening. The advantage to submarines of using FOSICs is threefold: (1) a high degree of Soviet submarine activity would trigger U.S. deployment of its own submarines, (2) FOSICs show Soviet SSBN deployment so that U.S. SSBNs can avoid those areas, and (3) FOSICs information will provide timely warning to shorten reprovisioning and maintenance cycles of U.S. SSBNs in port, at least those having some operational cycle left in their provisions.

But the most recent submarine communications system is not

space-based at all. ELF (extremely low frequency) transmitters operate two sites in synchronism. One, the Wisconsin system, has a 28-mile EMP-hardened antenna system operational as of 1985. A Michigan transmitter, with its 56 miles of antenna, will be operational by 1987. The sites can operate from Wisconsin alone or in unison. In an upgraded version, with the addition of 74 more miles of antenna in Michigan, the range is greatly expanded to send messages as far south as Argentina, through the central Pacific, and up to the Arctic, including three-fourths of the Mediterranean. ELF reduces the chance of Soviet detection of submarine antennas, since 200 feet of wire must be surface trailed to receive Tacamo messages (unless the submarine uses a buoy, in which case most speed is sacrificed). ELF can also deliver early-warning orders. With ELF, submarines can patrol at 300 to 700 feet at a 20 nautical-mile-per-hour speed and still receive transmissions.

Yet ELF is a peacetime system vulnerable to attack, with low data transmission rates. It would take hours via ELF to order a retaliatory strike. However, simple coded references to other instructions on board submarines can signal the submarines to monitor Tacamo, and nonalert submarines can be brought to alert status through ELF. This is especially helpful in the case of attack submarines carrying Tomahawk nuclear cruise missiles, because they usually monitor transmissions less frequently than the SSBNs. Moreover, the loss of the ELF system signal, which broadcasts continuously, would itself be a warning. Finally, new proposals for a van-transportable, reconstructable ELF grid are receiving attention. Such a grid would not necessarily be limited to the continental United States. New systems along these lines could even use railroad track or rock formations implanted with receivers as natural huge transmitting stations.[15]

First-strike scenarios devised by U.S. analysts have the Soviets knocking out many of the established strategic communications links with missile attacks specifically designed for that mission. As shown above, severe vulnerability in this area will continue to pose a threat to U.S. command and control in the 1990s. The Minuteman silos are thought to be of dubious survivability, and the assumption must be that ERCS would be completely destroyed by a three-to-one attack; it is not a highly survivable system unless fired on warning. On the other hand, SLBM attacks might overcome launch on warning. They can also destroy Tacamo; the commander in chief, Pacific (CINCPAC); the commander in chief, Atlantic (CINCLANT); and the National Emergency Airborne Command Post (NEACP) bases before reaction is possible. The survival of any ground-alert aircraft in an attack is dubious at best.[16]

Along with first-strike effects, electromagnetic pulse (EMP), by itself, threatens to disrupt most command and control aircraft, re-

stricting their communications under plausible transattack conditions.
The United States has, since 1973, put most of its eggs into airborne
command craft, which have become increasingly less survivable. The
Tacamo antennas are particularly susceptible to EMP. In any case,
Tacamo aircraft would have to be deployed on warning, but an order
to deliver a retaliatory attack, combined with the Tacamo's limited
endurance, could leave the effective time on station to issue orders
at only an hour or less. Some of these problems will be addressed by
the ECX aircraft, but readiness remains a concern. Likewise, ELF
would easily be knocked out, although, as noted, the end of its message alone would constitute a message. Perhaps by the year 2000
land-to-submarine and submarine-to-submarine communications will
permit deep-sea command posts to be set up, but before then communications links under water do not offer much hope for creating such
stations.[17]

Likewise, blue-green lasers or neutrinos or both may eliminate
many of these problems, but the survivability of transmission stations,
whatever the medium, will face the same problems as Tacamo, ELF,
or other systems in use. Nor are space-based platforms invulnerable:
antisatellite weapons, EMP, and enemy laser weapons all pose a threat.

Antisubmarine Warfare

Challenges to the underwater deterrent force will of course extend well beyond the threats to the C^3I links. Threats to the submarine
force can be divided into two major groups: those to the boat itself and
those to the security of the crew and/or base. As for the first group,
SSBNs face a threat only when detected, and therefore the primary
challenge to the SSBN fleet has been to avoid detection. New threats
to the fleet's undetectability in the 1990s will include side-looking
synthetic-aperture radar, visual/optical detection, sonar, magnetic
anomaly detection, electronic intelligence transmission detection,
shipboard compromises by human error, oceanic volumetric displacement, and tactical evidence during deployment.[18]

Submarines are warmer than the water in which they travel and
thus leave "thermal scars," even if the boat is barely moving. As
sensors improve, so will the Soviets' abilities to search with techniques that focus on thermal scars. Plankton destruction also creates
a scar. Finally, the faster the submarine travels, the brighter its
scar of thermal change. Commanders can offset advances in sensors
by making better use of thermal layers and reducing speed except in
emergencies. Areas of high plankton density can be avoided, and the
boats can take advantage of geological structures. Soviet use of side-
looking synthetic-aperture radar has been limited to cold-water areas.
U.S. testing of similar technology has occurred in space missions.

More standard forms of detection involve the use of satellites and aircraft. Defeating satellite detection relies on premission intelligence briefings on Soviet navigational orbits and satellite detection capability. Aircraft visual/optical will probably be a by-product of acoustic or magnetic anomaly detection rather than a valuable technique on its own, and visual means of detection are ineffective below 200 feet.

Advances in sonar, long the primary method to locate and identify a submarine, provide the most consistent chance of witnessing relative technology upgrading. Improvements in this area affect seabed-based sonar lines as well as on-board sonar systems. For seabed detection, rapidly deployed sonar systems (RDSS), while providing no new break-throughs, make possible a mobile deployment of seabed detection lines. American forces, for example, could use B-52s to drop RDSS, but its use requires a virtual certainty of enemy action, since the lines could be collected and their security compromised. Towed surveillance arrays are becoming tactically innovative forms of ASW, but there is limited evidence of Soviet adaptation of their use. The "ensonifica-tion" of the ocean by powerful, low-frequency sonars seems an even less likely Soviet approach to detection than towed-array sonars. Operational problems of widely based, large-area arrays involve huge processing problems. Many of these threats can be overcome through procedures for further quieting U.S. submarines.[19]

Once a general position is fixed, magnetic anomaly detection (MAD) is used, but improvements in MAD to make it more accurate beyond two thousand meters do not appear to be forthcoming. Like-wise, since electronic intelligence transmission (ELINT) can monitor only outgoing messages, it does not promise to be the breakthrough in ASW that the Soviets had hoped for. Nor do shipboard compromises, such as discharge of human waste products or human accidentally caused noises, constitute operational problems that cannot be solved by shipboard discipline. Oceanic displacement can be measured in volumetric change (through RORSAT and EORSAT [Electronic Ocean Reconnaissance Satellite]) in its two forms of manifestation: surface "hump" phenomena and widely evidenced internal waves of horizontal displacement. But radical Soviet breakthroughs in SSBN detection will depend upon computer ability to integrate and process all data detecting bioluminescence, wake turbulence, magnetic anomalies, thermal scarring of all forms, including coolant outflows, and navigational displacement in all of its forms.[20]

To confirm that a spectacular breakthrough will not occur, a $50 million ongoing R&D security program specifically checks Soviet ASW capabilities and fuels U.S. countermeasures. All nonacoustic threats are continuously reviewed, but to U.S. authorities sonar is ten times more important as a science than any other.

Base security offers a more substantial problem. Soviet trawlers

have harassed U. S. SSBNs within the twelve-mile limit but have
broken off before the submarine dived. At King's Bay, Georgia, light
private aircraft can now overfly the base, but this can be remedied
easily by closing the small airport or changing the runways. Operational patterns are regularly changed to keep patrols from becoming
predictable, thus aiding security. Striking at source suppliers, such
as the contractor for the screw, might enable the enemy to severely
disrupt production. Finally, an ingress/egress problem leaves the
possibility for a conventional war of attrition. At what point is there
too little left? For example, what if the Soviets knocked out 50 to 60
percent of the Trident force in conventional attacks? At present, because of sonar considerations, the United States does not bodyguard
SSBNs. As of 1986, the United States successfully "deloused" (evaded
a trailing hostile vessel) at a 98 percent rate, and only two of twelve
encounters in the last 3,000 missions were not random. All delousing
has been accomplished without external help and usually has been performed by simple dive maneuvers. Regular evasion practices against
SSN-688s are held to keep SSBN crews sharp in their ingress and
egress procedures.[21]

Possibly the least discussed potential aspect of seagoing deterrence in the 1990s is the coordination, integration, and interaction
of the submarine force, surface ships, and SDI (the Strategic Defense
Initiative). Policy analysts have understood the ICBM threat as strictly
a continent-to-continent problem. A second tendency—and an unfortunate one—is to conceive of submarines in a limited role because of a
lag in popular consciousness about these weapons' technical capabilities. Generally, a submarine's self-contained appearance is visually
deceptive; they are not overtly festooned with ordnance. But a more
serious question is: Why have not strategic thinkers, especially those
involved in the SDI program, seen the threat of SLBMs and the potential solutions offered by sea-based SDI? Again, the SSBN represents
a new weapon whose original form was makeshift. Deployment of a
thoroughly original SSBN system occurred only in 1981, with the com-
missioning of the Ohio. Against the background of prospective block
obsolescence of C-3-equipped SSBNs, navy attention has focused on
the limited production rate and hull availability of the 726 class to offset this problem. Likewise, SDI planners have narrowly viewed the
SDI platforms as space based. Politically, SDI proponents have no
need for more enemies, especially the navy, whose ire would be
raised by commandeering a scarce Trident hull for SDI research
purposes.[22] Since little engineering attention has been directed to the
exploitation of a highly adaptive system, no feasibility studies have
been undertaken to consider alternative SDI applications.

Perhaps the best way to view the Trident/SDI connection is to
simply look at the qualities possessed by a Trident:

- Speed. A 726 class boat can keep up with any battle fleet.
- Maneuverability. It can be deployed around a fleet maneuvering area.
- Submersibility. When surfaced, it presents a minimal target area. Only the sail is exposed, making the vessel well configured for the projection of any beam system (laser, particle, or kinetic). With minimal modifications, an appropriate component of the sail could be fitted with an EMP-hardened turret capable of dispensing beam fire in all directions and angles (except, obviously, immediately below itself). Such a turret has already been tested successfully on a KC-135 "flying laser laboratory." In one test, while in the air, it shot down six Sidewinder missiles traveling at varying speeds of up to 2,000 mph, with a 100 percent kill ratio.
- Launch capability. Tridents can launch C^3I rockets, mirrors, SDI-capable platforms, or homing overlay system defensive vehicles.
- Size. The Trident hull is huge (560 feet long, 42 feet in diameter) and can accommodate the large energy-generating equipment and still have missile-firing capability. However, even as large as the Trident hulls are, they could not carry C^3I rockets, SDI platforms, and the power-generating equipment simultaneously. Three options are available: strip the Trident of its own defensive weapons, provisions, and some of its crew, and add more hull sections; use some type of dual-hull arrangement; or trade off tubes for beam-generation capability.
- Navigational accuracy. Knowing exactly where it is allows a Trident to plot a more accurate intercept course.

Certainly, problems in redesigning the submarine for three purposes would arise, not the least of which would involve trade-offs between the provision of an independent power source for beam projection and reductions in either the number of missile tubes or the onboard horsepower of the power plant. This must be solved without compromising the tube capability for mirror launching and C^3I rockets.

Tridents thus adapted and armed would perform two missions. First, seagoing SDI would supplement, enhance, and indeed could resolve crucial weaknesses in the continental SDI. By picking up SLBM low-trajectory attacks, by providing additional coastal barrier defense, or by fending off sea-launched cruise missiles, a sea-based SDI can soak up much of the leakage from the space-based systems. Second, however, seagoing SDI could be converted into "TDI"—tactical, or theater, defense initiative—with a specific mission of providing cover for the aircraft carrier battle groups.

Cost limitations would determine the mix of the two missions, as well as the total number of hulls constructed. However, one can envision a force mix that would require five boats on patrol for continen-

tal defense duty, four to accompany the battle groups, and eleven for
reserve, refit, and resupply. A total force of twenty laser-armed and
C^3I-outfitted boats would be expensive by any standard. Adapting the
hull could run $600 million to $800 million per copy, with a final price
tag of $2 billion per outfitted boat. (For this reason, only a few could
be constructed). For fleet protection, four might be adequate. These
could act as floating umbrellas, launching a mirror constellation to
completely cover a perimeter, under which the entire battle group
would sail in safety. Soviet ASW would have no means to determine
in which battle group the SDI boat was. This uncertainty factor would
further deter an attack.[23]

The primary function of laser-equipped Trident hulls should be
SLBMs in the boost and postboost phase. A boat placed on wide-perim-
eter defense far from shore would have to receive a great deal of intelligence information and other data to position itself in the optimum
spot. Such a position might permit the destruction of SLBMs from
behind as well as in front. However, given beam weapons' limitations,
once the missile began to climb, it could quickly escape a defensive
weapon's range inside the atmosphere.

Related to this mission, a new strategic view that emphasizes
defense would seek to relocate as many important targets as possible
farther inside the United States to extend warning times of SLBM
launches. This is a different approach from that of the old ABM
"point defense of high-value targets" approach, whereby the window
of attack, and not warning time, was the crucial factor. In other
words, a truly dedicated SDI program will require a thorough rethinking of defense as a strategy.

Certainly, engineering and budget arguments can be massed
against any suggestion of seagoing SDI, but to ignore the potential of
the Trident hull for applications such as this seems unwise. The point
here is not to resolve these problems, but to raise them for engineers
and others to consider.

Another challenge to seagoing deterrence in the 1990s will come
from inadequate counterintelligence. The Walker espionage case
pointed out certain weaknesses in the security program, such as the
failure to provide clearance updates, inadequate classified materal
destruction capability, dual certification of destruction of classified
material on an "erratic assignment" basis, improved indexing of information on hand and of those with access to it, and the lack of a
positive counterespionage program to read the mail of future Walkers
on the appropriate Soviet desks.[24]

CONCLUSIONS

By the 1990s, the primary challenges to seagoing deterrence will come from strategists, engineers, and policy makers of limited vision; from budget restrictions by lawmakers of similarly narrow imagination; and from blind obedience to outdated arms-control agreements. Assuming that MX and Midgetman reach their well-deserved and, in the case of MX, overdue, graves, the seagoing deterrent force will be stronger than ever in the 1990s and will, relatively speaking, face less of a Soviet ASW threat, not more. This point seems implicit in two visible trends: the Soviets have continued to experience difficulty in mass producing either the Alpha class or the Oscar class subs, each of which purported years ago to demonstrate their submarine-building superiority; and the U.S. Navy has opted for heavier warheads on the D-5s at the expense of range, indicating that Soviet ASW has not yet reached the threat level that would require the additional sailing range over that offered by the C-4. Generally, the Soviets continue to flirt with technological disasters of all sorts, including the Lenin (the icebreaker whose reactor went "red" and was abandoned), the loss of at least two subs and the running aground of the Whiskey class submarine in Sweden, and the 1986 Chernobyl nuclear reactor incident. All of this is underscored in military terms by the greater down time of Soviet submarines and their unreliability. When was the last time a Los Angeles class submarine had to be towed to its patrol lanes?[25]

In short, the submarine leg in the 1990s will continue to represent the United States' best, most survivable deterrent, threatened only by possible communications disruptions. But the communications problems relative to SSBN missions must not be misstated by confusing worst case estimates with typical conditions. In the final analysis, U.S. SSBN commanders would have independent firing authority under very restricted circumstances, precluding retaliatory launches based on conjecture. This more than offsets the communications disadvantages. The SSBNs offer the opportunity to add layers to SDI and to introduce Buck Rogers to Captain Nemo. It is an introduction long overdue.[26]

NOTES

1. For a broad review of these threats, especially through the early 1980s, see D. Douglas Dalgleish and Larry Schweikart, Trident (Carbondale, Ill.: Southern Illinois University Press, 1984).

2. Material on the D-5 is summed up in two articles—Robert Norris, "Counterforce at Sea: The Trident II Missile," Arms Control Today, September 1985, 5-10; and Walter Slocombe, "Why We Need Counterforce at Sea," Arms Control Today, September 1985, 10-12—as well as in Jonathan Medalia, Trident Program, Congressional Research Service Issue Brief IB73001, June 27, 1985.

3. Criticisms of D-5 appear in Norris, "Counterforce at Sea," as well as Harold Feineson and John Duffield, "Stopping the Sea-Based Counterforce Threat," International Security, Summer 1984, 187-202; William Arkin, "Sleight of Hand with Trident II," Bulletin of Atomic Scientists, December 1984, 5-6; and Thomas Downey, "Against Trident II," New York Times, February 11, 1982.

4. Slocombe, "Why We Need Counterforce at Sea." 10.

5. Although the estimates used come from Jonathan Medalia's reliable series of issue briefs ("U.S. Navy Trident II Missile Data Sheet," in Trident Program, app. A), Medalia reported the estimates that the navy made in terms of 1985 dollars. Care must be used for several reasons: (1) The nation has experienced several quarters of deflation, whereas the estimates used by Medalia included inflation (to what degree, no one seems sure; the navy estimated that a figure of 4 to 5 percent was used, and Medalia, contacted by phone, said he used "then-year dollars," but did not say what the index was). Whatever index was used, if it included constant rates of inflation—unless a massive leap in the CPI occurs—the numbers are severely upward bound. Medalia noted, for example, that the Trident II per-unit cost, $46 million, was only $23 billion in 1983 dollars, or $13 billion if escalation over three years was built into estimates. Consider that if deflation, or no inflation, continues as a trend, all of the numbers will have to be substantially rewritten downward. One navy source pointed out that the price index dropped enough last year that the navy could buy an extra year's worth of missiles and still save money (unnamed source, Office of Legislative Affairs, May 6, 1986). (2) Norris, especially, seems to use per-unit costs and program costs as it suits him. The program cost of a D-5 is now (1986) estimated at $48 million each, compared with the per-unit cost of $30.9 million, whereas in 1986 the per-unit cost of the C-4 is $12.3 million. (3) Program costs included R&D, and per-unit costs do not drop until enough units have been built to defray the cost of R&D. Hence, one way that D-5 costs will drop is to build more of them.

6. Phone conversation with unnamed source, Office of Legislative Affairs, May 6, 1986. Costs on MX and Midgetman came from Dalgleish and Schweikart, Trident, 278-308; and in D. Douglas Dalgleish and Larry Schweikart, "Trident and the TRIAD: Systems Flexibility and Durability," U.S. Naval Institute Proceedings, June 1986, chart; and "Hot Debate on the Fate of Midgetman Missile Shapes Up in Congress," Wall Street Journal, March 4, 1986.

7. The rationale for building the Trident to handle D-5s from the outset appears in Larry Schweikart and D. Douglas Dalgleish, "The Trident Program in Bureaucratic Perspective," U.S. Naval War College Review, February 1984.

8. Overviews of command and control appear in Paul Bracken, The Command and Control of Nuclear Forces (New Haven, Conn.: Yale University Press, 1983); Bruce Blair, Strategic Command and Control (Washington, D.C.: Brookings Institution, 1985); and Daniel Ford, The Button (New York: Simon and Schuster, 1985), as well as in Dalgleish and Schweikart, Trident, 253-68 and chap. 8.

9. Ford, The Button, 41-44, 95-97.

10. Blair, Strategic Command and Control, 172-74; and Sea Power, March 15, 1986, 174.

11. Blair, Strategic Command and Control, 167, 174-75, 198-201.

12. Ibid., 268-69.

13. Dalgleish and Schweikart, Trident, 262.

14. Edgar Ulsamer, "C^{3}I Keeps Climbing," Air Force Magazine, July 1985, 150-6; "Laser Applications in Space Emphasized," Aviation Week, July 28, 1980, 62-63; R. J. Starkey, Jr., "The Renaissance in Submarine Communications, Pt. 5" and "Pt. 5 cont'd," Military Electronics and Countermeasures, March 1981, 48-54, and April 1981, 44-69; Roger A. Freedman, theoretical physicist at the University of California, Santa Barbara, interviews with authors, various dates, 1981-1982; and Dalgleish and Schweikart, Trident, 265-66.

15. Material on ELF appears in Blair, Command and Control, 269-72; "ELF Activation: Sending a Message to the Soviets," Sea Power, September 1985, 25-26; Department of Defense Appropriations for 1980, Subcommittee of House Committee on Appropriations, 96th Cong., 1st sess., pt. 6, 141-42; and Department of Defense Authorization for Appropriations for Fiscal Year 1979, Senate Committee on Armed Services, 99th Cong., 2d sess., pt. 9, 6722.

16. Blair, Strategic Command and Control, 175-76.

17. Ibid., 198; Dalgleish and Schweikart, Trident, 267-68; Nuclear Explosions in Space: The Threat of EMP (Electromagnetic Pulse) Issue Brief (Washington, D.C.: Congressional Research Service, May 4, 1982); and William Broad, "Nuclear Pulse (I): Awakening to the Chaos Factor," Science, May 1981, 1009-12; "Nuclear Pulse (II) Ensuring Delivery of the Doomsday Signal," Science, June 1981, 1116-20; "Nuclear Pulse (III): Playing a Wild Card," Science, June 1981, 1248-51. Bruce Blair, the most knowledgeable source on command and control, ran into trouble when he produced a report so frightening and sensitive that even he was forbidden to have a copy ("The Ultimate Secret: A Pentagon Report Its Author Can't See," Wall Street Journal, February 18, 1986).

18. Many ASW threats are dealt with in Dalgleish and Schweikart, Trident, chap. 8. Also see Congressional Budget Office, The U.S. Sea-Based Strategic Force: Costs of the Trident Submarine and Missile Programs and Alternatives (Washington, D.C.: GPO, February 1980).

19. J. R. Hill, Anti-Submarine Warfare (Annapolis, Md.: Naval Institute Press, 1985), 92-93.

20. Ibid., 37-59. MAD is the tactical detection of local magnetic changes in the oceanic dimension of the earth's magnetic field induced by the passage through it of the ferrous mass of the submarine hull. Displacement detection occurs when various processes measure volumetric changes caused by a submarine's tonnage, especially in motion. ELINT involves monitoring any radio transmissions from the submarine. The "humping" process consists of surface manifestations of active displacement by speed. Internal displacement is the process of horizontal wave generation radiating at more or less 90 degrees to the axis of the submarine's motion. Wake turbulence is the compound hydrodynamic disturbance caused by three phenomena: reconvergence of displaced water at the stern of the sub resulting from forward motion and hull shape of the sub; the propulsive disturbance of the ocean affected by the pitch, size, number, and speed of the screw(s); and cavitation (air turbulence created along the surface of the screw's blade during rotation). Bioluminescence is detectable displacement of microscopic sea creatures or organisms, especially plankton, which occurs during the ascent.

21. Interview with authors, director, Strategic Submarine Division, OPNAV (Navy command center), May 1985.

22. See, for example, Dalgleish and Schweikart, Trident, 275-77; William Wright, "Charged Particle Beam Weapons: Should We?" Proceedings, 28-35; Robert Jastrow, "The War Against 'Star Wars,'" Commentary, December 1984, 19-25; Clarence Robinson, Jr., "Panel Urges Defense Technology Advances," Aviation Week and Space Technology, October 17, 1983; Bruce Valley, "The Ultimate Defense," Proceedings February 1985, 30-37; Malcolm Browne, "Stopping Missiles with Energy Beams," Discover, June 1983, 28-32; SDI: the "Star Wars" Project (New York: The George C. Marshall Institute, 1985); Alex Gliksman, "Strategic Defense Business," National Defense, April 1986, 54-58; Gerald Yonas, "The Issues Faced by the Strategic Defense Initiative Programme," Defense Update 68 (1958): 8-16, 61; and "'Star Wars' Advances: The Plan vs. the Reality," New York Times, December 15, 1985.

23. Consider these arguments in light of the article by Alan Zimm, "The First Salvo," Proceedings, February 1985, 55-60. See also Joseph Adelman, "U.S. Navy Will Build Five Nimitz Carriers in 1990s," Jane's Defense Weekly, March 1, 1986, 351; and "Carrier

Power," _Time_, May 5, 1986, 18. Art Hanly puts the cost of a carrier battle group at closer to $28.12 billion, or a total outlay of $294 billion; see Art Hanly, "The Carrier Weapon," _Wings_, April 1986, 10-24.

24. James Bamford, "The Walker Espionage Case," _Proceedings_, May 1986, Naval Review, 111-19.

25. Robert Hutchinson and Antony Preston, "Soviet Submarine Accidents—New Details," _Janes's Defense Weekly_, January 19, 1985, 85.

26. Dalgleish and Schweikart, _Trident_, 267-68.

How Should We Retaliate?
Slow Down and Live

Stephen J. Cimbala

INTRODUCTION

Since the nuclear age began, strategists and statesmen have struggled to define ways of using those terrible weapons to prevent and fight war. American and other Western strategists settled upon "deterrence" as the preferred analytical model for explaining the use of nuclear weapons in war prevention and war fighting. Deterrence, as it came to be explained, was really nothing more or less than credible bluffing. One side bluffed that it might use nuclear weapons in the hope that the other would capitulate to its demands, whatever they were. The other side might bluff, too. Presumably this bluffing would always end in stalemate rather than war if it involved the United States and the Soviet Union, provided certain rather fundamental conditions were met.

These fundamental conditions were, first of all, that neither side could lose its retaliatory force to a surprise first strike of the opponent. Even the remote practical possibility of that unwanted event would deter the side that felt vulnerable to a counterforce attack against its nuclear missiles on land and sea and bombers.[1] Second, neither side could base or deploy its weapons in a provocative way. Provocative in this context means suggesting to the opponent the intention of striking first because either (1), you had no other option or (2), the advantage of striking first compared with striking second was great enough to interest a desperate president or premier during a crisis. Third, in the event deterrence failed and nuclear war began, neither side could defend its population from substantial and unprecedented damage, whatever the result of force exchanges might be. That is, the Soviet Union striking first against the United States might de-

The author gratefully acknowledges helpful comments from Bruce M. Russett on a draft of this paper. Views are solely those of the author

stroy more of our missiles and bombers than we would of theirs, but it would be thought irrelevant to do so if their successful counterforce attack unleashed a U.S. countervalue retaliation against Soviet cities and society.

The two superpowers did not always fulfill all of these conditions for what has come to be called stability, at least not with equal commitment at the same times. As to the first, it is now argued by some U.S. analysts, although disputed by others, that the Soviet Union has obtained a putative first-strike capability against the U.S. land-based missile force.[2] This is far from having a first-strike capability against the U.S. deterrent as a whole, given the proportions of U.S. warheads deployed on submarines and bombers.[3] The perception that the Soviet Union is moving toward such a capability against land-based missiles and that the United States cannot now reciprocate has helped to propel forward the Reagan administration modernization program for all legs of the Triad, including the proposed MX/Peacekeeper land-based missile (ICBM), the Trident II submarine-launched missile (SLBM), and the B-1B bombers. The perception of comparative counterforce vulnerability favoring the Soviet Union has also influenced the character of U.S. arms control proposals for the Strategic Arms Reduction Talks (START) between the Reagan administration and their Soviet counterparts.

The tabulations of comparative strategic nuclear capabilities have been perused more frequently than they have been correctly read. Perusal of the tables can always discover one indicator on which our side or theirs is deficient and another in which the superiority-inferiority ratio is reversed. This is to be expected given the size and complexity of the superpowers' arsenals. The more relevant questions are, "What can either the United States or the Soviet Union do with this colossal power? What political objectives can it support?"

These more pertinent questions are more difficult to answer, and it is therefore not surprising that they are answered tritely, if at all. It is said, for example, that the superpowers' nuclear weapons are useful in not being used. They exist to deter the other side's use of nuclear weapons. Or it is asserted that they are not useful at all. The level of destruction attendant to U.S.-Soviet nuclear war in many probable scenarios is beyond historical experience. Indeed, the "survivors might envy the dead" and the world be much worse off than before. Or, it is suggested that while general nuclear war would be absurd and preposterous, limited nuclear wars can be imagined in which less than total levels of destruction take place for both sides. After several preliminary rounds of nuclear slugging, both sides tote up their wins and losses, and the loser quits.

A large literature has just been surveyed, perhaps unfairly, in the last paragraph. But not too unfairly, if the summary has any sensitivity to what has been written about nuclear deterrence and war. It is not that gifted writers have not tried to do the job. Something else makes all answers to these questions about nuclear deterrence and war incomplete.

The incompleteness of much deterrence and nuclear war literature results from the comparative neglect of "why" or "for what" questions. Why would the United States and the Soviet Union attempt to fight a nuclear war? What issues would drive them to such desperation? One can imagine a continuum of answers to that question. At one polarity, almost inexhaustible lists of crises and circumstances provoking nuclear attacks can be conjured. At another end of the spectrum, one might argue that only direct attack against the homeland of one superpower would cause the other to engage in nuclear retaliation against the homeland of the other.

RATIONAL CHOICE

The difficulty in deciding where to roost on this continuum or spectrum of possibilities is that nuclear war, however chosen, does not meet any of the traditional criteria for rational choice. Rational choice theory, as developed by economists, sociologists, and others, implies that a choice is made by an individual or group if that individual or group's net welfare is maximized, or net misery minimized, by that particular choice. We all use this kind of reasoning to purchase automobiles or to select telephone companies.

But it is improbable that national leaders will choose nuclear war within a framework that meets such theoretically rational conditions. They will decide for or against war knowing that however it turns out, they will be worse off than before. Thus any decision for nuclear war will be subrational or nonrational under any conditions, because any nuclear exchange between the United States and the Soviet Union carries the strong probability of countercity exchanges reducing their societies to mere shells. Although analysts can posit nuclear wars in which large-scale devastation is followed by prompt recovery, no national leader can add up such a balance sheet favorably. Not the least among the reasons why the balance of any strategic nuclear war will appear unfavorable to leaders on either side is the possibility of their personal destruction. They might lose their own lives since both sides have apparently targeted leadership centers and command bunkers of the other; their postattack control would certainly be jeopardized.[4]

Instead of a rational decision to launch retaliatory or preemptive (first-strike) nuclear weapons, the best we can expect is a subrational or "satisficing" decision. This awkward term was coined by Herbert Simon and James G. March to describe the way in which most bureaucratic decisions are actually made.[5] Few real decisions in private management or government meet the value-maximizing criterion of rationality described above. Most search for the first one or few alternatives that seem acceptable. However semantically awkward, the satisficing approach is the better description of the choices facing national leaders who fear they are under nuclear attack.

There is still the matter of what to do if attack is feared or detected. This might seem like an irrelevant, even silly, point to raise. Surely if we are attacked we will respond. A nuclear strike by the Soviet Union against the forces or cities of the United States must call for an immediate retaliation against Soviet forces or cities or both. If the Soviets do not expect this, how will deterrence work?

But the matter is not so simple. First, it is not obvious that the United States should retaliate immediately, and grossly. This rather controversial assertion will be discussed at greater length below. Second, even if we do retaliate in response to a Soviet attack, there are important choices to be made about the targets of our weapons and the scale of our attack. There is also the issue of what we hope to accomplish.

Take the issue of retaliation per se, first. However shocking to our emotional sensibilities, it might not be the most prudent alternative for the U.S. president, or his or her successor, to order comprehensive counterforce retaliation in response to a Soviet nuclear attack, even a substantial attack including targets on U.S. soil. And the satisficing rationality of a U.S. retaliation against the Soviet Union for their nuclear or conventional attacks on Europe, Japan, or other American allies is even more dubious.

The three most common objections to withholding an immediate and substantial U.S. retaliation against Soviet targets after their first strike against U.S. targets are honor, psychology, and efficiency. The first, honor, demands that we react with fury and vengeance to the destruction of targets on U.S. soil and the resulting millions of fatalities. The assertion is <u>not</u> that it is in fact honorable to kill Soviet civilians. It is instead the Soviet expectation about our national reaction that is relevant to deterrence. The second, psychology, insists that the Soviet Union believes its prompt destruction is certain to follow any attack against our homeland. Only this way can deterrence work. The third, efficiency, argues that once war begins, the United States must attempt to destroy as many Soviet nuclear weapons as rapidly as possible so that they cannot be used against us. This might be the only way to terminate the war short of countercity holocaust.

Each objection has merit because we are dealing with a satisficing rather than a maximizing choice. No choice following a nuclear first strike against the United States by the Soviet Union (or vice versa for them) leaves us better off than we were before the war started. This

comparison with our prewar capabilities and societal cohesion is the
true measure of the credibility of our policy. The comparison between
prewar and postwar status is sometimes confused with another comparison. Writers sometimes compare the post-nuclear-war Soviet
Union with the post-nuclear-war United States. Depending on the scenario, more U.S. than Soviet citizens might survive, or more Soviet
weapons than U.S. weapons, and so on.[6] These comparisons may be
useful ways of computing the residual power left to a defender and an
attacker after they have exchanged nuclear weapons, for whatever that
calculation is worth. But postattack nuclear comparisons between
devastated Soviet and U.S. societies, whatever they show, are of
lesser importance than the fact that both have lost, compared with
where they started.

Given this understanding of proper and improper comparisons,
no value-maximizing nuclear wars are possible. Since satisficing is
the best we can do, national honor might demand some kind of prompt
and very destructive retaliation in response to any Soviet attack of
more than demonstrative scope.

But national honor also demands that policy makers do what is
most advantageous in the long run for their society. And what is most
advantageous may not be immediate destruction of Soviet society in
response to their attack against only part of ours, and the more limited
the Soviet attack, the more acute the dilemma. A limited Soviet attack
on the United States would leave more surviving U.S. forces with which
to retaliate or more U.S. society undestroyed (or both). The former
condition would tempt us to hit back quickly and with gusto, while the
latter (undestroyed society) might suggest that we do something else
(see below).

The second objection is psychological. It says that deterrence
cannot work if the Soviet Union disbelieves that the United States will
attack in response to its attack (assuming what is thought to be the
easier case for the moment, that the Soviet Union attacks us and not
one of our allies while sparing us). The objection has merit but conditional merit. To understand how far it is applicable, we must accept
the distinction between declaratory policy and employment policy for
U.S. strategic nuclear forces. Declaratory policy is publicly pro-
claimed policy by heads of state and their designees in which we spe-
cify officially what we will do under certain circumstances. Operational
or employment policy is what we actually can do given our capabilities
and will decide to do, under varying circumstances.

As declaratory policy, the threat of retaliation makes sense, although the kind of retaliatory threat the United States poses to the
Soviet Union, even at this level, is debatable. As operational policy,
dictated by the kinds of forces and command arrangements we actually
build and deploy, the problem is more open-ended. For the moment

we will concede that whatever declaratory policy says, it may not be prudent to plan to do or to do in the event.

The third objection on grounds of efficiency makes clearer the importance of the distinction between declaratory and operational policy. Efficiency seems to dictate that the United States respond to Soviet attacks with the most rapid and most comprehensive attack possible against remaining Soviet forces and other assets contributing to their capability to wage war. This might not mean immediate attacks against their cities, but it would certainly imply prompt attacks against their counterforce target base, nuclear weapons storage sites, and reconnaissance or navigation satellites that contribute to Soviet precision targeting of remaining U.S. forces.

The efficiency objection sounds persuasive until we return to the distinction between prewar-postwar and postwar-postwar comparisons. A putative value-maximizing logic of rational decision making suggests that we should fight a duel with the Soviet Union in the early stages of war to see who prevails after the arsenals of those weapons are exhausted. The side that succeeds in destroying the greater number of the opponent's military forces, or in more completely decapitating the opponent's command and control, will have "won" at least the early stages of war. If the Scowcroft Commission can be believed, these may be the decisive stages, at least as seen from the Soviet side. The commission asserted, in keeping with the logic of at least the last three administrations in Washington, that the Soviet Union valued most highly its forces and command bunkers to protect its leadership and not its citizens as such.[7] Thus U.S. threats to destroy promptly their surviving forces and leaders would provide the most credible deterrents.

No one can prove that the commission is not right. Given the absence of superpower nuclear wars and no confirming or disconfirming statements from Politburo leadership, it is difficult to prove or disprove assertions about what deters the Soviet Union. But two kinds of decisions facing U.S. leaders who are under attack, or expect to be, must be distinguished here. The first kind of decision is the decision about what deters. The second is what to do after deterrence fails. It is not obvious that the most satisficing decision for the first purpose is equally satisficing for the second.

In fact, the commission might have the matter backwards. If silos and command bunkers are the most valued targets in the Soviet Union, it might make sense not to hit them immediately. This seems plausible for two reasons. First, they might be the hardest targets to destroy and we might not be able to do it, at least not quickly. Second, it might be counterproductive. Destroying the Soviet leadership might prevent any resolution of the war before it spun totally out of control. However slim the chance that such a war could be terminated short of global catastrophe, even subrational policy makers would be obligated to try.

The objections of honor, psychology, and efficiency do not seem superficially convincing to the proponents of delayed or no retaliation. Perhaps they have received superficial treatment. It might be better to consider the questions of operational policy, or what we can do, and efficiency at greater length. The matter of national honor is so abstract that it defies further discussion, except to state that prudent Soviet planners would count it as a factor pushing us to do <u>something</u> (other than ignoring it) in response to their attack. Thus the following comments do not ignore the importance of national honor, but they assume its importance without knowing how that favors one alternative compared with another.

WARNING AND RESPONSE

From an operational standpoint, the U.S. president can be on the receiving end of three different kinds of warnings about Soviet nuclear attack. We might refer to these as conditions or states of warning. The first state is of course normal—peacetime, or "day-to-day" alert in Pentagon jargon. The second is ambiguous warning that we are under attack, although the precise character of the attack is not confirmed. We might, for example, have warning of Soviet missile launches from one set of sensors aboard satellites but not yet have received confirmation and analysis from other sensors and attack assessment centers.[8] Third, the president could have unambiguous confirmation that a Soviet attack on U.S. homeland targets was under way. There are, of course, in-between conditions.

Current U.S. <u>declaratory</u> policy is that we <u>may</u> attack in the second condition (launch on warning) and probably <u>will</u> attack in the third condition (either launch under attack or retaliate after absorbing the attack). Whether U.S. operational policy can fulfill these conditions is something else again. A growing literature has questioned whether the U.S. strategic nuclear command and control system could even absorb a Soviet counterforce attack and remain cohesive enough to guarantee prompt retaliatory destruction of Soviet cities or other targets.[9] Since worst-case pessimism is fashionable in defense analysis and since Soviet antisubmarine warfare capabilities are insufficient at the moment to destroy all U.S. submarines preemptively, we will assume that the United States can destroy Soviet cities in retaliation under the worst conditions of decapitation. But the controlled and prompt retaliatory destruction of Soviet command bunkers and silos could be precluded.

The famous "window of vulnerability" argument during the presi-

dential campaign was really about this capability for prompt retaliation against Soviet silos and command bunkers. It was alleged that
we were deficient compared with the Soviet Union in prompt, hard-
target capabilities and that this deficiency would weaken our deterrence. The analysis and the claim were hardly new, being based on
studies done by Paul Nitze and associates and published during the
Carter administration as a way of making the case for U.S. strategic
offensive modernization.[10] Partisans of the right tended to make much
of the window of (ICBM) vulnerability; those of the left saw the window
of vulnerability as a political polemic rather than a strategic insight.
The Reagan case for the MX/Peacekeeper missile is that it is needed
to rectify this perceived imbalance in prompt, hard-target capabilities.

Let us return to the three conditions or states of warning postulated above. They represent a gradient from normal conditions, in
which each side's forces are relaxed, to the highest condition, in
which they are poised to retaliate in the expectation of attack. Experts
might disagree about where to place the dividing lines between kinds
of warning conditions, but the direction of the gradient is clear.

In the first instance, normal day to day operations, U.S. forces
will not be expecting a Soviet attack and most will be destroyed. Most
of the land-based missile force, about 70 per cent of the bomber force
not on alert, and approximately one half of the fleet ballistic missile
submarine force in port will be lost. This is a worst-case scenario,
but worth understanding for benchmark purposes.

In this most stressful case, the prompt, hard-target weapons
are the least useful. They are based on U.S. ICBMs, which are the
least survivable portion of the strategic inventory. As we proceed
from normal conditions to ambiguous warning, more forces can be
alerted and higher proportions of those forces will survive. This will
improve the survivability of the bomber force more than it will ICBM
survivability, however, because bomber launch is appropriate under
conditions of ambiguous warning, since bombers can be recalled.
Land-based and submarine-launched missiles cannot be recalled after
launch.

The final case of confirmed attack follows a pattern similar to
that apparent in the cases of attack under normal conditions and attack
under conditions of ambiguous warning. The prompt, hard-target
weapons are deployed on delivery vehicles whose survivability is least
subject to improvement by increased warning. This seems counter-
intuitive to some strategists. The ICBMs have the unique properties
of secure command and control and rapid retargeting, compared with
other strategic weapons systems, and they are the only U.S. delivery
vehicles that now carry the warheads with sufficient yield and accuracy
to destroy Soviet command bunkers, silos, and other time-urgent hard
targets.

The reasons why increased degrees of warning cannot do much for the land-based missile force compared with other forces in the U.S. Triad are not obvious. They lie in the distinction between "critical time" and "control time" as understood by some military analysts, including Soviet ones.[11] Critical time, oversimplified, is the time it takes to complete a mission. Control time is the time it takes to make the relevant decision to activate a weapon or weapons system toward a prescribed mission. If control time exceeds critical time, the mission cannot be accomplished.

Unfortunately for the U.S. land-based missile force, control time is likely to exceed critical time. The time available for alerting U.S. land-based missiles and launching them under attack is not great if U.S. command centers are first attacked with Soviet submarine-launched ballistic missiles. If those Soviet SLBMs strike at Washington, D.C., and disconnect the National Military Command Center and other vital connective tissue in the postattack command and control system, U.S. land-based missiles and bombers might not get their orders, or all their orders, to retaliate. This is because the three conditions of warning are assumed to coincide with increasingly severe levels of Soviet attack. The warning in condition three will be less ambiguous than the warning in condition two, because the attack (presumably, unless sensors are deficient) will be more severe and destructive or because the attack has progressed further.

Even given adequate warning, it is somewhat doubtful that U.S. ICBMs can be launched under attack. A plausible Soviet pindown attack over the U.S. ICBM fields might preclude egress of U.S. ICBMs through their launch corridors. Of course, using SLBMs to attack ICBM fields would waste those weapons compared with assigning them to what are thought to be their primary targets for Soviet planners: U.S. bomber bases and command centers. The Scowcroft Commission noted that the Soviets have a timing dilemma in attacking the entire complement of U.S. strategic forces. Early SLBM attacks on the bomber bases followed by later Soviet ICBM attacks on U.S. ICBMs will allow more U.S. ICBMs to escape. On the other hand, if the Soviet Union chooses to attack U.S. ICBMs first and delays the launches of its SLBMs against bomber bases, more of the bombers will avoid destruction.[12]

However, this is not so much of a dilemma as it appears, for reasons discussed above. Since the U.S. prompt, hard-target counterforce weapons are not based survivably almost regardless of warning, they do not have to be attacked first. Bombers derive more added survivability from additional warning than do land-based missiles or submarine-launched missiles; therefore, attacking bombers first and ICBMs later (with excess SLBMs devoted to pindown) seems more sensible from the Soviet standpoint.

This analysis, whether deductively correct or not, aims at another point besides the logic of Soviet attack strategies. It is the logic of U.S. response. Let us assume for the sake of simplicity either of two kinds of attack by the Soviet Union on the United States. The first is a counterforce attack against U.S. missile silos, bomber bases, and submarine pens, with a piggyback component designed to destroy as many fixed command centers and communications as possible. The second is an all-out attack on U.S. forces, command centers, and all war-supporting economic infrastructure, whatever the consequences in prompt fatalities and city destruction. These are not the only two cases possible, and even they are hard to imagine. Nevertheless, the suspended animation required to contemplate them further should pay dividends.

COUNTERFORCE RETALIATION

A Soviet counterforce first strike against the United States would kill promptly an estimated 13 million to 34 million Americans. This does not include fatalities from delayed effects of nuclear detonations.[13] Whether U.S. warning and attack assessment could distinguish this more selective counterforce attack from one designed to destroy American forces, commanders, and war-related societal assets simultaneously is not clear. Whether the distinction, if believed, would make much difference in our response is also unclear. There are two aspects to the "make much difference" issue. The first is whether it would. The second is whether it should.

The scenario popularized by Paul H. Nitze portrayed Soviet first strikes against the U.S. ICBM force, bomber bases, and submarines in port. The United States was faced with two unpalatable alternatives: to retaliate, assuring a Soviet third strike against our cities, or to surrender.[14] But this scenario was somewhat incredibly described, even for analytical purposes. It was both too optimistic and too pessimistic. It was too optimistic about the probable survivability of our command and control (which is low) and too pessimistic about our ICBM survivability (only in the latter 1980s would the Soviet Union have those kinds of preemptive capabilities, assuming very high reliability rates for them).

But the thrust of the Nitze analysis and that of the Committee on the Present Danger and the Reagan 1980 Campaign, was not primarily technical. It was that the Soviet Union would perceive a relative disadvantage for the United States and coerce us in a crisis, such as the Cuban missile crisis in reverse. Deterrence might not actually fail, but only because we could do the sums, see our counterforce inferiority, and capitulate. The Soviets would have what they want without firing a shot.

The Nitze analysis had a point, although more persuasive as a diagnostic rather than a prescriptive one. Under conditions of assumed counterforce inferiority, and given the superpowers' targeting priorities as Nitze described them, it might be more rational for the United States not to retaliate. The numbers seemed to show that no matter what we did in retaliation following Soviet counterforce first strikes, their third strike would obliterate our cities more destructively than our second strike would demolish theirs. Moreover, U.S.-Soviet comparative counterforce capabilities would get more unfavorable for us and more favorable for them as the war progressed.

Clearly Nitze and the Committee on the Present Danger were not willing to draw the prescription of delayed retaliation from their diagnosis. What they wanted was an improvement in the U.S. prompt hard-target capabilities to match those of the Soviet Union and especially to close the gap in land-based missile warheads and throw weight. This was to be accomplished by a combination of arms control restraints on Soviet ICBM modernization together with an accelerated buildup of U.S. offensive forces, especially MX. Depending on its azimuth and length-of-delivery trajectory, Trident II (D-5) submarine-launched ballistic missiles might also provide prompt hard-target capabilities (as well as more delayed strikes) against some targets.

No one in the strategic debate argued that U.S. forces should be based so vulnerably that they invited attack. This issue had been settled with Albert Wohlstetter's classic analysis of potential U.S. bomber vulnerability in "The Delicate Balance of Terror."[15] Yet the emphasis placed upon prompt hard-target capabilities by MX advocates reveals an inescapable conclusion that ICBM survivability is not their major concern. Instead, their concern is to face the Soviets with a counterforce duel of uncertain outcome should the Soviets be bold enough to attack in the first place.

This judgment by some MX advocates may be correct if the Scowcroft Commission assumptions about what deters Soviet leaders is correct. But the applicability of that assumption to very large exchanges of nuclear weapons between superpowers is suspect. In a short war with tens of weapons exchanged, it could matter whether forces, commanders, or cities were targeted and what signals those targets were designed to send. In a protracted war involving thousands of weapons on each side, political direction of the war would dissolve into broken-backed calamity. Exhaustion or extinction rather than war termination would end it. Whether nuclear winter resulted or not, societies would not resemble their prewar status and might fall into total anarchy.

Given these arguments, the most "rational" course of action for the United States is obviously not to unleash a massive prompt counterforce response to a limited Soviet counterforce attack. If the United

States retaliates, it is worse off than if it doesn't, assuming fewer dead Americans are an "improved outcome" compared with more dead Americans. This could be called surrender by those who are concerned about national honor. Earlier we suggested that national honor is a long-run rather than a short-run consideration. Is it more honorable to have twenty million or more than one hundred million dead Americans? The choice is not obvious, and the decision to retaliate immediately is not obviously the rational one.

Following Soviet counterforce first strikes, the United States has substantial bargaining power in its strategic submarine force. These Poseidon and Trident submarines can obliterate every major Soviet city several times over. They now carry more than five thousand strategic warheads, and their missiles will be upgraded by addition of the Trident II (D-5) beginning in 1988 or 1989.[16] Other delayed counterforce and countervalue capabilities will reside in the U.S. strategic bomber force, now being modernized through the planned deployment of the B-1B and the follow-on Advanced Technology Bomber (ATB) during the 1990s. Newer bombers will carry advanced cruise missiles that will have stealth and possible supersonic speeds to improve their ability to penetrate Soviet defenses. And the land-based leg of the Triad may be made more survivable during the 1990s by the addition of Midgetman small ICBMs, which could be deployed in fixed sites or in mobile basing.[17] Even if most but not all of the Reagan modernization program is adopted by the Congress, as seems likely, the United States will have much more surviving counterforce after any conceivable Soviet first strike during the 1990s than it does now.[18]

Then, as now, the bulk of U.S. strategic counterforce will reside in slow rather than prompt counterforce systems. If what we want to do is to retaliate against remaining Soviet forces, then slow counterforce on bombers and submarines can accomplish most of the necessary missions. The time urgency of Soviet targets is contingent to some extent on the Soviet war plan. Those missiles not used in their first strike are possible targets for U.S. second-strike counterforce, but it is not obvious that they must all be attacked promptly. The Soviet Union must maintain some strategic reserve as long as it faces a potentially hostile neighbor in the People's Republic of China. Slow counterforce places those missiles at risk just as surely as prompt counterforce does. Soviet missiles already launched in their opening salvos against the United States will presumably be their most modern and capable, the SS-18 and SS-19 and their follow-ons. They will not be necessary prompt targets because they will be empty silos, unless a prompt reload capability can be demonstrated for those silos.

So we are discussing a finite set of prompt counterforce targets that would require an equally finite set of prompt counterforce responses, if we wanted to bother with them at all. It might make more

sense for the United States to threaten the <u>delayed</u> destruction of the
Soviet leadership and command and control, including KGB and party
headquarters, Soviet conventional forces, border patrols, and other
elements that are vital to postattack cohesion of the Soviet empire.[19]
But there is a limit to how much of this control infrastructure we can
destroy without also destroying the entire Soviet economic and social
base, which makes the issue of command destruction moot. As Robert
Art has noted, beyond a certain point the leadership is devoid of significance if it has no meaningful society over which to rule.[20] It has
been noted correctly that the Soviets are more tolerant of social dislocation than are Americans, who shoot one another in protracted gas
lines. But social dislocation even on the scale of the Bolshevik revolution is one thing, and the aftermath of nuclear war another.

In the final analysis, U.S. slow counterforce weapons (provided
they can penetrate Soviet defenses, which is not to be taken for granted)
hold at risk Soviet reserve forces and cities to the extent necessary
to deter any first strike. Until now we have had it easy, however. The
issue of defenses introduces complications into this optimistic picture
of reliance upon slow counterforce, as discussed further on. A second
fly in the ointment is that some slow counterforce weapons like cruise
missiles are not easy to count and verify for arms control purposes.
We will concede the second point without argument and pursue the first
as more immediately relevant to our discussion. Whether the United
States should retaliate, and how, after Soviet attacks depend upon the
character of the attack, the survivability of our forces and other assets, and the vulnerability of the Soviet forces and society to our
retaliation. Until recently it had been assumed that both sides' societies would remain vulnerable to retaliatory destruction even if they
attacked first. Renewed superpower interest in missile defense complicates the estimates, in some ways that are apparent, and others
that are not so obvious.

STRATEGIC DEFENSE

President Reagan's "Star Wars" speech of March 23, 1983, taken
literally was not very revolutionary. It called for a research and development program for the remainder of the 1980s to determine the
feasibility of deploying missile defenses in the 1990s or thereafter.
Actually, the superpowers have been studying missile defense and
developing prototype weapons for anti-ballistic missiles (ABMs) or
ballistic missile defenses (BMD) for several decades. The objective
is simple to state but difficult to achieve: to find a practical way to
destroy enemy missiles and warheads before they impact on your soil.
What is practical and what is not practical are major bones of conten-

tion; as Ambassador Nitze has stated on behalf of the Reagan administration, it means at least that any missile defense system must be survivable and cost-effective at the margin. That is, it must not be so vulnerable that it invites attack on itself, and it must not cost us a great deal more to add each increment of defense than it does for the Soviet Union to offset the incremental defenses with its own incremental offenses.

No one can object to a research and development program as such. There is the suspicion on the part of critics of the Strategic Defense Initiative (SDI), however, that the research and development might open the door to eventual U.S. and Soviet deployment of defenses. This in itself would not necessarily be bad for deterrence or stability. One can imagine, as Freeman Dyson has done, several international environments permissive of defenses. The most benign would involve the superpowers' gradual deployments of defenses together with corresponding reductions in their strategic offensive forces.[21] One can also imagine a mindless building of both offenses and defenses motivated by action-reaction or monkey-see, monkey-do imperatives. Both the United States and the Soviet Union have bureaucracies and interest groups with vested interests in developing weapons, whether or not they are essential for national defense and current war plans.

It might be useful to consider the potential effects of BMD on strategic stability, given the likelihood that both sides will deploy it or neither will. If both sides deploy, their deployments are likely to constitute more than a single phase of technology. The Reagan SDI program apparently envisions a series of defense filters that attack enemy missiles and warheads during the boost, postboost, midcourse, and terminal phases of flight. Futuristic technology such as lasers and particle beams would be most applicable to the boost phase, in which the destruction of a single Soviet missile early in its flight would cause the loss of all the warheads assigned to that missile. Thus, a Soviet SS-18, one model of which is now thought to carry ten warheads and might carry as many as thirty, could deliver those ten or thirty warheads to as many separate targets in the United States. The early-boost-phase filter, if successful, would get all the warheads because it would intercept the missile before the warheads were dispersed on separate trajectories during the postboost phase that follows. A second filter would work during the postboost phase, when the bus carrying multiple warheads disperses those warheads on preprogrammed flight paths. A third system would work during the midcourse phase of warhead flight through space, about twenty minutes. A final screen would be based on U.S. territory and consist of rockets with smart bullets capable of nonnuclear interception outside or within the atmosphere.[22]

Suppose that, in a notional system of the kind described, each layer were 80 percent effective: it shot down about four out of five possible warhead or missile targets. Assume also that the Soviets eventually deploy a comparably effective system. Now it appears that the age of defense dominance has truly arrived. Neither side can contemplate a successful first strike against the retaliatory forces of the other because the defense deployed by each side will protect a substantial proportion of its deterrent and its society as well.

This apparently benign scenario of defense dominance is deceptive. It leaves many questions unanswered. The most important unanswered question is, "Now that both sides have defenses, how will they use them?" A defense can be a denial force or an intimidation force. Used as a denial force, it allows the defender to sit behind assumed protection without feeling any necessity to place its offenses on a hair trigger to prevent their being lost in surprise attack. Used as an intimidation force, a defense is something different. It can be used to intimidate by threatening a first strike against the adversary and then planning to absorb the full weight of his retaliation without suffering unexpected or unbearable consequences.

If both sides deployed comparably effective defenses at exactly the same rates, it would be difficult for either to imagine that defenses could be used to intimidate. However, it might turn out that either side felt more confident about its defenses than technology warranted. It might also happen that each side would do worst-case estimates, assuming its own defenses to be much more flawed than those of its opponent. Two worst-case analyses of this kind would lead to disaster. Each side would expect the other's defenses to mop up its retaliation in the event that it were attacked first. The penalty for being pre-empted, or struck first in the expectation that one's adversary is about to strike, seems to rise as both sides "worst case" their own and their opponents' defenses.

This is why the transition from offense-dominant to defense-dominant deterrence is so tricky. The superpowers, in the absence of an appropriate treaty, cannot be depended upon to deploy exactly comparable defenses at equivalent rates. Each will probably deploy those systems that it can build and feasibly deploy, on earth and in space. A hodgepodge of deployments leaves each uncertain about the capabilities of its opponent. All that will be known with certainty is that the situation is more uncertain than it was before defenses were deployed. Uncertainty is not all that bad. To some extent we depend upon it for deterrence. If Soviet leaders were convinced that their surprise first strike would meet with certain success, U.S. leaders would be determined to restore the credibility of our retaliation. Stable deterrence thus depends on some uncertainty. Missile defenses introduce compound uncertainty on top of simple uncertainty. Simple uncertainty lies in the sizes and diversity of both superpowers' offensive

forces, which make them hard to eliminate in any first-strike secnario.
Defenses would compound this uncertainty with the additional uncertainty about how many offensive warheads would be destroyed by the
defenses. The conjoint uncertainty of offenses and defenses deployed
together might create more reasons for national leaders to pause before attacking. So far, so good.

Nevertheless, deterrence might fail. And we are back to the issue
of whether to retaliate and how. That issue is now more complicated
than it was without defenses. We will have to make assumptions about
what the opponent has defended and how strong those defenses are.
Indeed, we might have to attack the defenses and eliminate them before turning to the opponent's offensive forces. Precursor attacks
against the adversary's space-based defenses will in turn be expected
and defended against. If either superpower deploys space-based missile defenses, it will also equip those defensive satellites to defend
themselves or provide other satellites to do it.[23] Thus, protecting
one's defenses against preemptive attack (perhaps by the opponent's
satellites, or by other countermeasures) will become a strategic imperative, in addition to the protection of each side's offensive retaliatory forces.

One can imagine in theory, then, that preemptive attack becomes
a two-stage affair. The first stage involves destruction of as much of
the opponent's defenses as possible. The second follows the first and
attacks the opponent's offensive forces before they can be used against
us. Presumably the Soviet Union is reckoning as we are about the need
to attack defenses first and offenses second, or at least to attack them
simultaneously. It might also occur to both sides that very good defenses are also by implication potential offensive weapons. This is so
in several senses. First, if the defenses are based in space (partially
or totally, depending on the technology) and have boost-phase intercept capabilities, they may also be able to attack targets within the
atmosphere or on the ground. Second, defenses may be vulnerable to
one another if both superpowers deploy them. Third, the U.S. space-
based laser missile defense satellites (ASATs), which can attack Soviet
warning and communications satellites, imply a threat of preemption.
Likewise for their Soviet counterparts. Unless both sides can equip
warning and communication satellites against attack from the other
side's BMD and ASAT weapons, one or the other must fear preemption
once very capable space-based weapons are deployed.

Depending on how they are used, defenses create the same dilemmas as offenses. They can be used for slow and deliberate responses
after we have had every opportunity to assess the damage and consequences of an attack. Or they can be used quickly to maximize the
number of important targets destroyed on the other side. This choice
between rapid and highly automated, versus slower and more deliberate,

response will be important for the software developers of the U.S. missile defense system. The computer programs upon which boost-phase intercept will be dependent will have to instruct the battle management satellites to tell the missile defense satellites when to fire, at what targets, and at what threshold to accept a kill as decisive. Human managers will have to write these programs so that they optimize between the desire for rapid interception of as many Soviet delivery vehicles and reentry vehicles as possible and the desire for maintaining political control over the unfolding battle.

As a crude illustration, under normal peacetime conditions, the system might be turned off so that intercept is not automatically activated. As levels of alert rise, more restraints against automated response are progressively removed. At the highest level of alert, the system is programmed to fire automatically. There can be as many gradations of alert as there are capabilities in the computer program to include them and creations in the minds of programmers to write them in. What cannot be automated, however, is the political decision about our postattack objectives. Deterrence having failed, what do we want to accomplish with our defenses or our retaliation or both?

We argued earlier that without defenses it made sense not to retaliate, at least not immediately. A weakness in that strategy seemed to be a possible Soviet countercommand attack that weakened the U.S. command structure and possibly severed communications among warning sensors, force commanders, and forces. Whether the U.S. strategic command system is as drastically vulnerable as worst-case analysts have posited is a debated point. But it is certainly imperative that policy makers ascertain the weaknesses of the system so that command, control, and communications (C^3) vulnerability does not preclude our option of delayed or no retaliation. It is to the credit of the Reagan administration that it has placed high declared priorities upon C^3 funding and programs, as did its predecessor.[24]

A second weakness in the strategy of delayed or no retaliation is the possibility of ballistic missile defenses. Even defenses far less capable than those envisioned by SDI create additional temptations to rapid and grosser retaliatory strikes. The reasons for this greater temptation are several. First, the opponent's defenses must be attacked in addition to, and preferably before, his offenses can be struck. Second, if you do not strike back immediately you may give your opponent the chance to raise the level of preparedness of his defenses to blunt your retaliation. Third, if your defenses are much better than those of your adversary, you might be tempted to attack his vulnerable forces with your prompt counterforce weapons, counting on your superior defenses to absorb his retaliation.

We now come to the principal opportunity and risk for strategic

stability and the avoidance of nuclear war, in terms of our interest
in delayed retaliation and the implications of defenses for prompt
(compared with delayed) attacks. If both sides have deployed defenses
and war breaks out, the defenses must attack one another quickly.
Their degraded remnants will then be faced with the task of absorbing
offensive attacks that they can partially but not totally filter. Each
side will get the opportunity for a large but finite number of decisive
blows. Their military leaders will want to use those blows against
the most important targets as they perceive them to be. Those militarily determined most important targets will be the opponent's military forces and command centers and ours; we will neither await delayed postattack assessments nor exercise Occam's razor in our first
responses. Neither will the Soviets, expecting to encounter U.S. defenses of even modest capacity.

Defenses do not have to have only malign effects of this type, however. They could contribute to stability under certain conditions. For
one thing, space based defenses and their ancillary support capabilities
could make it possible for command and control improvements to take
advantage of the fourth medium of space. Direct satellite-to-satellite
communications data and voice relays could compensate for cumber-
some procedures now used to connect early warning satellites with
force commanders and attack assessment centers. Storage of space
satellites in "dark" or unacknowledged orbits could provide for recon-
stitution of communications and assessment after attack.

Space-based defenses could also contribute to stability through
delayed retaliation in another way. They could improve the chance
that U.S. or Soviet forces survived any first strike, no matter what
the opponent did. For defenses to have this effect, they would have to
meet certain demanding specifications. The superpowers would have
to have comparable systems at almost every phase of their deployment.
Neither side should have reason to fear a major breakthrough that
would change the qualitative balance of defensive capabilities. Offenses
would have to be limited by treaty or tacit agreement in size and character. Neither side could deploy ASAT weapons that were so capable
that they appeared to the other side as incipient BMD weapons.

If defenses could increase the protection of our retaliatory forces
while meeting the above conditions, they would contribute to stability.
This favorable outcome of their deployment is not precluded; neither
is it guaranteed. It will require the commitment of political leaders
in both Washington and Moscow to make defenses serve political purposes based on a shared understanding of those purposes. There are
military strategists who contend that the United States and the Soviet
Union can never have such shared understandings. But we are not discussing the wholesale adoption of one culture by another. Instead, we
are proposing that both sides reach common ground on a few basic

principles. We have discussed some of those principles and argued
that they lead to operational if not declared policies of delayed retaliation. Both offensive and defensive system modernization should be
pursued from this perspective.

But the policy may still be objectionable. We conceded earlier
that the objections have some merit. Thus further discussion of the
potential gains and risks for the United States is in order. (We cannot
prescribe for the Soviet Union, although we can hope.) As in discussion of any alternative to the status quo, it can be disputed from any
one of several familiar perspectives. The first is that the political
process cannot be moved very far from the status quo. The second
is that the Soviets will never buy it. The third is that the public will
never understand it.

All of these points are conceded in part because they are not decisive. First, history shows that new ideas can be adopted as part of
the policy mainstream; they are slowly swallowed and subject to
amendment, but change does occur. Second, we cannot dictate to the
Soviets their policy choices, but we can influence the extent to which
certain decisions by them are logical or illogical responses to our
decisions. Third, the public often understands general ideas and concepts better (and sees their flaws more quickly) than experts do, although its knowledge of details is understandably limited.

NOTES

1. See Matthew Bunn and Kosta Tsipis, "The Uncertainties of
Preemptive Nuclear Attack," Scientific American 249 (November
1983): 38-47.

2. Paul Nitze, "Assuring Strategic Stability in an Era of Détente,"
Foreign Affairs 54 (1976): 207-33; and T. K. Jones and W. Scott
Thompson, "Central War and Civil Defense," Orbis 22 (Fall 1978):
681-713.

3. John M. Collins, U.S.-Soviet Military Balance, 1980-85 (New
York: Pergamon-Brassey's, 1985), 54.

4. On the issue of command vulnerability, see Bruce G. Blair,
Strategic Command and Control: Redefining the Nuclear Threat (Wash-
ington: Brookings Institution, 1985); Paul Bracken, The Command
and Control of Nuclear Forces (New Haven, Conn.: Yale University
Press, 1983); and Desmond Ball, Can Nuclear War Be Controlled?
Adelphi Papers no. 169 (London: International Institute for Strategic
Studies, Autumn 1981).

5. James G. March and Herbert A. Simon, Organizations (New
York: Wiley, 1958), pp. 140-41.

6. See U.S. Arms Control and Disarmament Agency, An Analysis
of Civil Defense in Nuclear War (Washington: ACDA, December 1978).

7. President's Comission on U.S. Strategic Forces (Scowcroft Commission), Report, (Washington: GPO, April 1983).

8. This is the problem of insistence upon "dual phenomenology" before U.S. leaders assume they are actually under attack.

9. Blair, Strategic Command and Control, and Bracken, Command and Control.

10. The U.S. Triad of land-based missiles, sea-based missiles, and airborne missiles and bombs was never close to overall vulnerability. This is acknowledged by the Scowcroft Commission. See also Congressional Budget Office, Modernizing U.S. Strategic Offensive Forces: The Administration's Program and Alternatives (Washington: GPO, 1983). For very current estimates, see William Martel, "An Exchange Calculus of Nuclear War," in Stephen J. Cimbala, ed., Strategic War Termination (New York: Praeger, 1986), chap. 1.

11. Stephen M. Meyer, Soviet Theatre Nuclear Forces: Part II: Capabilities and Implications, Adelphi Papers no. 188 (London: International Institute for Strategic Studies, Winter 1983/84).

12. This bewilderment for Soviet attackers could be assuaged if their SLBM decapitated U.S. National Command Authorities and severed their connections with the commanders in chief of U.S. nuclear forces (CINCs). However, this would not guarantee any decisive victory to the Soviet Union and might enhance their destruction. A decapitated U.S. command structure could be impermeable to any proposed terms for concluding the war, even on terms judged favorable by the Soviet Union. On this topic see Bracken, Command and Control.

13. William Daugherty, Barbara Levi, and Frank Von Hippel, "The Consequences of 'Limited' Nuclear Attacks on the United States," International Security 10 (Spring 1986): 35.

14. Nitze, "Assuring Strategic Stability."

15. Albert Wohlstetter, "The Delicate Balance of Terror," Foreign Affairs 37 (January 1959): 209-34.

16. Caspar W. Weinberger, Annual Report to the Congress: Fiscal Year 1986 (Washington: GPO, February 4, 1985), 209.

17. Small Missile Independent Advisory Group (Schriever Commission), Report (Washington: Scientific Advisory Board, U.S. Air Force: September 1983).

18. Congressional Budget Office, Modernizing U.S. Strategic Offensive Forces.

19. The Soviet command apparatus may be more resistant to selective targeting than U.S. planners imagine. See Harriet Fast Scott and William F. Scott, The Soviet Control Structure: Capabilities for Wartime Survival (New York: Crane, Russak, 1983).

20. Robert J. Art, "Between Assured Destruction and Nuclear Victory: The Case for the MAD-plus Posture," Ethics 95 (April 1985): 497-516, esp. 509.

21. See Freeman Dyson, Weapons and Hope (New York: Harper and Row, 1984) for an argument on behalf of this position.

22. See James C. Fletcher, "The Technologies for Ballistic Missile Defense," Issues in Science and Technology 1 (Fall 1984): 15-29.

23. For BMD measures-countermeasures competition, see Union of Concerned Scientists, The Fallacy of Star Wars (New York: Random House/Vintage Books, 1984). Comments by Glenn Kent on the possibility of vulnerable space-based defenses inviting attack on themselves appear in Ashton B. Carter and David N. Schwartz, eds., Ballistic Missile Defense (Washington: Brookings Institution, 1984), 418.

24. According to Blair, Strategic Command and Control, however, the proportion of the Department of Defense strategic budget devoted to C^3I will not rise appreciably in the next five years.

Bibliography

Beres, Louis René, ed. Security or Armageddon: Israel's Nuclear Strategy. Lexington, Mass.: Heath/Lexington Books, 1985.

Betts, Richard K. Surprise Attack. Washington, D.C.: Brookings Institution, 1982.

Blair, Bruce G. Strategic Command and Control: Redefining the Nuclear Threat. Washington, D.C.: Brookings Institution, 1985.

Bracken, Paul. The Command and Control of Nuclear Forces. New Haven, Conn.: Yale University Press, 1983.

Brodie, Bernard M. Strategy in the Missile Age. Princeton, N.J.: Princeton University Press, 1959.

Bueno de Mesquita, Bruce. The War Trap. 2d ed. New Haven, Conn.: Yale University Press, 1971.

Carroll, John. Secrets of Electronic Espionage. New York: Dutton, 1966.

Carter, Ashton B., and David N. Schwartz, eds. Ballistic Missile Defense. Washington, D.C.: Brookings Institution, 1984.

Dalgleish, D. Douglas, and Larry Schweikart. Trident. Carbondale: Southern Illinois University Press, 1984.

Dismukes, Bradford, and James McConnell, eds. Soviet Naval Diplomacy. New York: Pergamon Press, 1979.

Douglass, Joseph D., Jr., and Amoretta M. Hoeber. Conventional War and Escalation: The Soviet View. New York: Crane Russak, 1981.

Dyson, Freeman. Weapons and Hope. New York: Harper and Row, 1984.

Feldman, Shai. Israeli Nuclear Deterrence: A Strategy for the 1980s. New York: Columbia University Press, 1982.

George, Alexander, and Richard Smoke. Deterrence in American Foreign Policy: Theory and Practice. New York: Columbia University Press, 1974.

Greene, Fred. Stresses in U.S.-Japanese Security Relations. Washington, D.C.: Brookings Institution, 1975.

Hermann, Charles F., ed. International Crises. New York: Free
     Press, 1972.
Huntington, Samuel P., ed. The Strategic Imperative. Cambridge,
     Mass.: Ballinger, 1982.
International Institute for Strategic Studies. The Military Balance,
     1985-86. London: 1985.
Intriligator, M. D. Mathematical Optimization and Economic Theory.
     Englewood Cliffs, N.J.: Prentice-Hall, 1971.
Janis, Irving L. Groupthink. Boston: Houghton Mifflin, 1982.
Janowitz, Morris. Military Conflict. Beverly Hills, Calif.: Sage,
     1975.
_____. The Professional Soldier. New York: Free Press, 1960.
Jervis, Robert. The Illogic of American Nuclear Strategy. Ithaca,
     N.Y.: Cornell University Press, 1984.
Kissinger, Henry A. Years of Upheaval. Boston: Little, Brown, 1982.
Klass, Philip. Secret Sentries in Space. New York: Random House,
     1971.
Knorr, Klaus, and Patrick Morgan. Strategic Military Surprise. New
     Brunswick, N.J.: Transaction Books, 1983.
Lebow, Richard Ned. Between Peace and War. Baltimore: Johns
     Hopkins University Press, 1981.
Morgan, Patrick. Deterrence: A Conceptual Analysis. Beverly Hills,
     Calif.: Sage, 1983. Second Edition.
Moskos, Charles C. Peace Soldiers. Chicago: University of Chicago
     Press, 1976.
U.S. Congress. Office of Technology Assessment. MX Missile Basing.
     Washington, D.C.: GPO, 1981.
President's Commission on U.S. Strategic Forces (Scowcroft Com-
     mission). Report. Washington, D.C.: GPO, April 1983.
Proceedings of the U.S. Naval Institute. The Maritime Strategy.
     Annapolis, M.D.: January 1986.
Richardson, L. F. Arms and Insecurity. Pittsburgh: Boxwood Press,
     1960.
Segal, David R., and Wallace Sinaiko, eds. Life in the Rank and File.
     New York: Pergamon Press, 1986.
Steinbruner, John D. The Cybernetic Theory of Decision. Princeton,
     N.J.: Princeton University Press, 1974.
von Clausewitz, Carl. On War. Edited by Anatol Rapoport. Baltimore:
     Penguin Books, 1968.
von Neumann, J., and O. Morgenstern. Theory of Games and Eco-
     nomic Behavior. 2nd ed. Princeton, N.J.: Princeton University
     Press, 1947.

Index

About the Contributors

LOUIS RENÉ BERES is Professor of Political Science at Purdue University. Beres has contributed to the academic literature in international relations, world order studies, and nuclear deterrence for many years. His publications on nuclear deterrence and strategy include Apocalypse: Nuclear Catastrophe in World Politics (University of Chicago: 1980).

DAGOBERT L. BRITO is Peterkin Professor of Political Economy at Rice University and was formerly Director of the Murphy Institute, Tulane University, and Professor of Economics and Political Science, Ohio State University. His recent research with Michael Intriligator has emphasized dynamic models of the arms race and conflict and redistribution. He is a member of the Econometric Society, the International Institute for Strategic Studies, London, and the American Economic Association.

STEPHEN J. CIMBALA is Professor of Political Science at Pennsylvania State University (Delaware County). He is the author of previously published works on U.S. nuclear deterrence policy, military strategy, and U.S.-Soviet strategic policies. He recently edited and contributed to The Reagan Defense Program: An Interim Assessment (Scholarly Resources: 1986), Artificial Intelligence and National Security (Lexington Books: 1987), and Strategic War Termination (Praeger Publishers: 1986).

D. DOUGLAS DALGLEISH teaches political science at Arizona State University. A Columbia University and University of Colorado graduate, as well as a Fulbright scholar, he served in U.S. Army intelligence in West Germany. He has published articles on national security and the West German government.

STEPHEN P. GIBERT is Professor of Government and Director of
the National Security Studies Program at Georgetown University.
Gibert specializes in international security affairs and U.S. defense
and foreign policy. He also emphasizes East Asian security and foreign policy issues in his work, which benefits from his having lived
in and traveled extensively throughout the region. Gibert is a member
of the editorial board of Asian Perspective. Among his many publications on East Asian-American relations is his monograph Northeast
Asia in U.S. Foreign Policy.

ROBERT E. HARKAVY is Professor of Political Science at Pennsylvania State University and the author of numerous works in the field of
international security studies, foreign policy, defense, and national
security issues. He was Foreign Affairs Officer with the U.S. Arms
Control and Disarmament Agency from 1975 to 1977 and an Alexander
von Humboldt Fellow at the Christian Albrechts University, Kiel,
Germany. His many books and monographs include Arms Transfers
and the International System and Great Power Competition for Overseas Bases.

JESSE J. HARRIS, D.S.W., is a colonel in the Medical Service Corps
and has spent six months in the Sinai with the first U.S. contingent
assigned to the Multinational Force and Observers. He is currently
Social Work Consultant to the Surgeon General of the Army and Chief
of the Social Work Service at Walter Reed Army Hospital.

CHARLES F. HERMANN is Director of the Mershon Center at Ohio
State University, a faculty research and education "think tank" devoted
to the study of national security and public policy. He is Professor of
Political Science at Ohio State University and has published numerous
contributions to the study of foreign policy decision making, international relations, and national security studies. Hermann has for many
years been one of the most highly regarded international authorities
on the nature and causes of international crisis. Before joining the
Ohio State faculty, Hermann worked on the National Security Council
staff of Henry A. Kissinger and taught at Princeton University.

MICHAEL D. INTRILIGATOR is Professor of Economics and Political
Science and Director of the Center for International and Strategic
Affairs (CISA) at the University of California, Los Angeles. Under
his direction, CISA has conducted a number of innovative studies into
the nature of arms control, including "Rethinking Arms Control" and
"Alternative Approaches to Arms Control." Intriligator has contributed
to the literature of international relations and rational decision analysis for many years, and his current work with Dagobert Brito focuses
on arms races and deterrence.

KEVIN N. LEWIS is a senior analyst with the RAND Corporation in Santa Monica, California, and has contributed to the field of national security and defense studies for many years. His publications and reports include studies of U.S. strategic and theater nuclear forces, conventional war in Europe, military preparedness, low-intensity conflict, and other issues. His recent work has focused on, among other things, the improvement of U.S. capabilities to provide reinforcement for NATO Europe.

CARNES LORD is Director of International Studies at the National Institute for Public Policy in Fairfax, Virginia. He served on the staff of the National Security Council from 1981 to 1984. His studies and publications include contributions on the topics of strategic command and control, U.S. nuclear strategy, arms control, and the evolution of strategic weapons technology.

DAVID H. MARLOWE, Ph.D., an anthropologist, is Chief of the Department of Military Psychiatry at Walter Reed Army Institute of Research. Much of his recent research deals with unit cohesion and with the stress of combat.

JONATHAN E. MEDALIA is Specialist in National Defense in the Foreign Affairs and National Defense Division of the Congressional Research Service (CRS) and was formerly an analyst in the same division. He was a Fellow at the Brookings Institution from 1972 to 1974 and a Postdoctoral Fellow at Massachusetts Institute of Technology from 1974 to 1975. Medalia has authored or coauthored numerous reports for CRS that are frequently cited as standard reference documents on the topics of strategic weapons, arms control, effects of nuclear war, strategic force projections, and other issues. His recent work focuses on Midgetman, force projections and SALT compliance.

PATRICK M. MORGAN is a Professor of Political Science at Washington State University. He has been a fellow at the Woodrow Wilson International Center for Scholars in Washington, D.C.; an American Council on Education fellow at the University of California, Berkeley; a visiting Professor at the University of Washington; and a Fulbright fellow at Katholeike Universiteit in Belgium. Morgan is the author of many works on strategy and international politics, including Deterrence: A Conceptual Analysis (Sage: 1983, 2nd edition) and Strategic Military Surprise (Transaction Books: 1983) with Klaus Knorr.

GEORGE H. QUESTER is Chairman of the Department of Government and Politics at the University of Maryland and has published for many years authoritative studies on nuclear deterrence, arms control, and

U. S. defense and foreign policy. He is the author of Nuclear Diplomacy (Dunellen Book Company: 1970) and the recently published The Future of Nuclear Deterrence (Lexington Books: 1986). His research interests include U. S. deterrence commitments to Europe, nuclear winter, and the relationship between strategic offense and defense.

JEFFREY RECORD is Senior Research Fellow at the Hudson Institute, and a prominent defense analyst and consultant whose works have been noted in academic and policy-making circles for many years. He was formerly legislative assistant for military affairs to Senator Sam Nunn. Record has written extensively about U. S. defense and alliance commitments, the relationship between strategy and force structure, and the geopolitical dimensions of U. S. defense responsibilities. His recent works include Revising U. S. Military Strategy: Tailoring Ends to Means (Pergamon-Brassey's: 1984) and Strategic Bombers: How Many Are Enough? for the Institute for Foreign Policy Analysis.

JOSEPH M. ROTHBERG, Ph. D., is a research mathematician in the Department of Military Psychiatry at the Walter Reed Army Institute of Research, where he has conducted studies of the health of army personnel on a peacekeeping deployment. He is currently doing research on suicide in the army at the Uniformed Services University of the Health Sciences.

LARRY SCHWEIKART is Assistant Professor of History at the University of Dayton. He writes extensively on business and financial history, including the economics of the defense industry. His most recent works include a history of the Trident submarine program, coauthored with D. Douglas Dalgleish, and articles in Naval War College Review and the U. S. Naval Institute Proceedings.

DAVID R. SEGAL is Professor of Sociology and of Government and Politics at the University of Maryland, where he directs the graduate program in military sociology. He is also a Guest Scientist in the Department of Military Psychiatry at the Walter Reed Army Institute of Research. He is Associate Chairman of the Inter-University Seminar on Armed Forces and Society and the editor of Armed Forces and Society.

JOHN ALLEN WILLIAMS is Associate Professor of Political Science at Loyola University of Chicago, where he teaches courses in U. S. foreign and defense policy. He has taught at the U. S. Naval Academy and the University of Pennsylvania. Williams is a Fellow and Executive Director of the Inter-University Seminar on Armed Forces and Society and a member of the Governing Council of the Section on Military

Studies, International Studies Association. He has published on U.S. and Soviet naval forces and missions, strategic nuclear policy, defense organization, and current defense policies. Williams is a Commander in the U.S. Naval Reserve, is a designated strategic plans officer, and has performed active duty in the office of the Chief of Naval Operations.